ChrisWith
Leves 15/9/2016

GW00703258

THE FATHERS
OF THE CHURCH

A NEW TRANSLATION

VOLUME 116

THE FATHERS
OF THE CHURCH

A NEW TRANSLATION

ST. CYRIL OF ALEXANDRIA

COMMENTARY ON THE TWELVE PROPHETS VOLUME 2

Translated by

†ROBERT C. HILL

THE CATHOLIC UNIVERSITY OF AMERICA PRESS
Washington, D.C.

The paper used in this publication meets the minimum requirements of
the American National Standards for Information Science—Permanence
of Paper for Printed Library Materials, ANSI z39.48–1984.

LIBRARY OF CONGRESS CATALOGING-IN-PUBLICATION DATA
Cyril, Saint, Patriarch of Alexandria, ca. 370-444.
Commentary on the Twelve Prophets / Cyril of Alexandria ;
translated with an introduction by Robert C. Hill.
p. cm. — (The Fathers of the church ; v. 116)
Includes bibliographical references and indexes.
ISBN 978-0-8132-0116-0 (cloth : alk. paper)
1. Bible. O.T. Prophets—Commentaries.   I. Hill, Robert C.
(Robert Charles), 1931–   II. Title.   III. Series.
BS1505.53.C9713 2007
224´.907—dc22

2007016972

CONTENTS

INDICES

The indices to this volume are combined with the indices to volume 1.

ABBREVIATIONS

AnBib   Analecta Biblica, Pontificio Istituto Biblico, Rome.

Aug   *Augustinianum.*

BAC   Bible in Ancient Christianity, Leiden and Boston: Brill, 2004–.

Bib   *Biblica.*

CCG   Corpus Christianorum series Graeca, Turnhout: Brepols.

CCL   Corpus Christianorum series Latina, Turnhout: Brepols.

DBS   *Dictionnaire de la Bible. Supplément,* IV, Paris: Librairie Letouzey et Ané, 1949.

FOTC   The Fathers of the Church, Washington, DC: The Catholic University of America Press.

GO   Göttinger Orientforschungen, Wiesbaden: Otto Harrassowitz.

HeyJ   *The Heythrop Journal.*

JECS   *Journal of Early Christian Studies.*

LXX   Septuagint.

NS   New Series.

OTL   Old Testament Library.

PG   Patrologia Graeca, ed. J.-P. Migne, Paris, 1857–66.

SC   Sources Chrétiennes, Paris: Du Cerf.

StudP   *Studia Patristica.*

TRE   *Theologische Realenzyclopädie,* Berlin: Walter de Gruyter, 1976–.

SELECT BIBLIOGRAPHY

Boulnois, M.-O. "The mystery of the Trinity according to Cyril of Alexandria: The Deployment of the Triad and its Recapitulation into the Unity of Divinity." In T. G. Weinandy and D. A. Keating, eds. *The Theology of St Cyril of Alexandria. A Critical Appreciation.* London and New York: T&T Clark, 2003. Pp. 75–111.

Daley, B. E. "Apocalypticism in Early Christian Theology." In B. McGinn, ed. *The Encyclopedia of Apocalypticism* 2. New York and London: Continuum, 2002. Pp. 3–47.

Doutreleau, L., ed. *Didyme L'Aveugle. Sur Zacharie.* SC 83, 84, 85. Paris: Du Cerf, 1962.

Fernández Marcos, N. *The Septuagint in Context: Introduction to the Greek Versions of the Bible.* Translated by Wilfred G. E. Watson. Boston and Leiden: Brill, 2001.

Harvey, E. R. "Cyrillus von Alexandria." *TRE* 8:254–60.

Hill, R. C. "The Mystery of Christ: Clue to Paul's Thinking on Wisdom." *HeyJ* 25 (1984): 475–83.

———. "Psalm 45: A *locus classicus* for Patristic Thinking on Biblical Inspiration." *StudP* 25 (1993): 95–100.

———. *Theodoret of Cyrus. Commentary on the Psalms.* FOTC 101, 102. Washington, DC: The Catholic University of America Press, 2000.

———. "Jonah in Antioch." *Pacifica* 14 (2001): 245–61.

———. "Theodore of Mopsuestia, Interpreter of the Prophets." *Sacris Erudiri* 40 (2001): 107–29.

———. *Theodore of Mopsuestia. Commentary on the Twelve Prophets.* FOTC 108. Washington, DC: The Catholic University of America Press, 2004.

———. *Reading the Old Testament in Antioch.* BAC 5. Leiden and Boston: Brill, 2005.

———. *Didymus the Blind. Commentary on Zechariah.* FOTC 111. Washington, DC: The Catholic University of America Press, 2005.

———. *Theodoret of Cyrus. Commentary on the Twelve Prophets.* Commentaries on the Prophets 3. Brookline, MA: Holy Cross Orthodox Press, 2005.

———. "Zechariah in Alexandria and Antioch." *Aug* 46 (2006).

Jouassard, Georges. "L'activité littéraire de saint Cyrille d'Alexandrie jusqu'à 428: Essai de chronologie et de synthèse." In *Mélanges E. Podechard: Études de sciences religieuses offertes pour son éméritat.* Lyon: Facultés Catholiques, 1954. Pp. 159–74.

Kelly, J. N. D. *Jerome. His Life, Writings and Controversies.* London: Duckworth, 1975.

Kerrigan, A. *St. Cyril of Alexandria, Interpreter of the Old Testament.* AnBib 2. Rome: Pontificio Istituto Biblico, 1952.

Olivier, J.-M., ed. *Diodori Tarsensis commentarii in Psalmos.* I. *Commentarii in Psalmos I-L.* CCG 6. Turnhout: Brepols, 1980.

Petersen, D. L. *Zechariah 9–14 & Malachi.* OTL. London: SCM, 1995.

Pusey, P. E., ed. *Sancti patris nostri Cyrilli archiepiscopi Alexandrini in XII prophetas.* Oxford: Clarendon Press, 1868.

Redditt, P. L. *Haggai, Zechariah, Malachi.* New Century Bible Commentary. Grand Rapids: Eerdmans, 1995.

Russell, N. *Cyril of Alexandria.* The Early Christian Fathers. London and New York: Routledge, 2000.

Schäublin, C. *Untersuchungen zu Methode und Herkunft der antiochenischen Exegese.* Theophaneia: Beiträge zur Religions- und Kirchengeschichte des Altertums 23. Cologne and Bonn: Peter Hanstein, 1974.

Smith, R. L. *Micah–Malachi.* Word Biblical Commentary 32. Waco, TX: Word Books, 1984.

Sprenger, H. N., ed. *Theodori Mopsuesteni commentarius in XII prophetas.* GO. Biblica et Patristica 1. Wiesbaden: Otto Harrassowitz, 1977.

Wilken, R. L. "Cyril of Alexandria as Interpreter of the Old Testament." In T. G. Weinandy and D. A. Keating, eds. *The Theology of St Cyril of Alexandria. A Critical Appreciation.* London and New York: T&T Clark, 2003. Pp. 1–21.

———."Cyril of Alexandria." In C. Kannengiesser. *Handbook of Patristic Exegesis* 2. BAC 1. Leiden and Boston: Brill, 2005. Pp. 840–69.

Zeigler, J. *Duodecim Prophetae.* Septuaginta 13. Göttingen: Vandenhoeck & Ruprecht, 1943.

COMMENTARY ON THE TWELVE PROPHETS

COMMENTARY ON THE PROPHET AMOS

PREFACE TO THE
COMMENTARY ON AMOS

MOS WAS A GOATHERD, raised in the ways and norms of shepherds. He passed his life in the wilderness to the south of the country of the Jews, which stretched from the shores of the Indian sea to the land of the Persians, and where countless barbarian nations grazed their stock. It was much suited to feeding flocks of sheep, being fertile, spacious, and offering a variety of fodder. Amos was from the town of Tekoa, at the very edge of the wilderness. Since he was a good man, practiced in complete simplicity, he was given the rich grace of the spirit of prophecy, prophesying not in Jerusalem but among the actual flocks, initially with attention to those with similar concerns to his own, and then (367)[1] going as far as Bethel. Tekoa, in fact, was subject to the kingdom not of Judah, but of Ephraim.[2]

Now, the fact that our statement of this is true you will easily gather and confirm from his own words; he prophesied in Bethel, as I said, saying that the altars of laughter would be abolished and the rites of Israel left desolate. He further said, "And I shall rise against the house of Jeroboam with a sword." The priest of Bethel, Amaziah, tried to pull the teeth of the prophet; he "then sent to Jeroboam king of Israel, saying, Amos has conspired against you in the midst of the house of Israel; the land is not able to bear all his words. For Amos says this: Jeroboam will die by the sword, and Israel will be deported as a captive from its land. And Amaziah said to Amos, On your way, O seer. Off with

---

1. Page numbers of the Pusey edition are included in the text for ease of reference.
2. Tekoa, in fact, is a town in the hill country of Judah just south of the border with Israel. Cyril is following Jerome closely here in matters topographical and linguistic, as well as in the lengthy citation from Am 7.

you to the land of Judah; live there and prophesy there. Continue prophesying no further in Bethel, because it is a king's sanctuary, and it is a king's temple. Amos replied to Amaziah, I was neither a prophet nor the son of a prophet; instead, I was a goatherd, a cutter of mulberries. The Lord took me from the sheep, and the Lord said to me, Go, prophesy to my people Israel."[3] So he was taken from the flocks, and prophesied in Bethel, where Jeroboam son of Nebat first set up a golden heifer.

Now, I think that also the fact is relevant that the father of Isaiah was a different Amos.[4] What (368) his words were *in toto*, and in reference to which matters, we shall clarify by addressing the text in hand.

3. Am 7.9–15.
4. Cyril derives this "relevant" item from Jerome, who proceeds to show its linguistic basis, that in Heb. (but not in the LXX) there is a considerable difference in the two names (that of Isaiah's father Amoz being an otherwise unattested form of Amaziah, in fact).

COMMENTARY ON AMOS,
CHAPTER ONE

The words of Amos, which came in Akkarim from Tekoa, which he saw on Jerusalem (v.1).

E IS SAYING THAT these are the words of prophecy of Amos from Tekoa, which came *in Akkarim.* Now, it should be realized that the Hebrew has no knowledge at all of this reading, *in Akkarim,* saying only, "The words of Amos from Tekoa." For their part the other translators put "cattlemen" for *in Akkarim.* So he is saying that these are the words of Amos from Tekoa, which came at the time when there was still grazing, and in the actual sheep pens.[1] The words *on Jerusalem* he says he did not so much hear as *see;* God made the events obvious to the holy prophets together with revelations as though they were actually taking place, the result being that *the words* even seemed visible in a way, the vision of the future perhaps being concurrent with what God said.

That item is worth questioning, however, of the possibility of anyone's believing *the words came on Jerusalem* only, despite God's accusing Judah and Israel in the statement of the same prophet. He said, remember, "Thus says the Lord: For three (369) transgressions of Judah and for four I shall not turn my back on them, because they have repudiated the Law of the Lord and have not observed his commandments. They have deceived themselves with the futile things they have done, which their fathers adopted. I shall send fire on Judah, and it will consume the foundations of Jerusalem." He went on, "Thus says the Lord: For three transgressions and for four I shall not turn away from him." He criticized the forms of sin and threatened dire punishment and

---

1. Again Jerome supplies the data, which Cyril compresses to suggest that all three translators offered the one alternative to the misreading by the LXX.

stated that the message involved the most severe retribution for both. So how are the words to be understood as then directed at *Jerusalem*, despite God's saying, "I shall send fire on Judah, and it will consume the foundations of Jerusalem"?[2] The form the explanation will take, therefore, come now, let us examine. We claim, then, that it is customary with the holy prophets at one time to refer without distinction to the two tribes in Jerusalem, Judah and Benjamin, as Israel, and at another to call the ten tribes in Samaria Israel, or Ephraim. Frequently, however, they make no such distinction: since they are all of the line of Israel, this is the name they give to the twelve tribes. If, on the other hand, they wanted to suggest to us perhaps the whole community of the Jews, we would find them no longer using the name Jerusalem to distinguish them.

The words of the prophecy of Amos, therefore, were delivered on the whole populace of the Jews, both in Jerusalem and in Samaria;[3] but there is need to explain how it would be *on* them. (370) Accordingly the explanation is twofold: on the one hand, he first introduced the God of all outlining the sins of the community of the Jews, then forecasting what would happen to them, and, on the other hand, he proceeded to mention the kindly manifestations of his clemency and the fact that in due course there would be generous pardon of them and restoration to their original condition. Amos himself in turn said as much, in fact, on the part of God: "Except that I shall finally not remove the house of Jacob, says the Lord. Because, lo, I shall give the command, and I shall scatter the house of Israel among all the nations in the way grain is scattered with a winnowing fan, and no fragment will fall to the ground."[4]

Of necessity, however, he also foretells the future redemption through Christ, and the fact that they would move to a restoration and enjoy the benevolence of a compassionate God. He spoke further in these terms: "On that day I shall raise up the tent of David that has fallen, rebuild its breaches, raise up its

2. 2.4–6.

3. Cyril parts company with Jerome, and with the Antiochenes and modern commentators, who see in the reference to Jerusalem an error of the LXX for Israel; and he develops and supports his interpretation at length.

4. 9.8–9.

ruins, and rebuild it as in the days of old."[5] The words, therefore, are *on Jerusalem*. And in another sense they could be understood to be *on* it: Syria, the kings of Damascus, and not a few of the neighboring nations caused damage to the country of the Jews, different ones at different times invading and devastating it, driving the people hither and yon, committing crimes of implacable wrath to the point of reducing it to extreme hardship. The prophet therefore has introduced God threatening all these people with desolation, and said they would be called to account for their sacrilegious exploits. So (371) the words of Amos are *on Jerusalem*, or on the whole community of the Jews; we shall grasp this clearly as we traverse the times of the prophecy. It proceeds as follows, in fact.

In the days of Uzziah king of Judah and in the days of Jeroboam king of Israel two years before the earthquake (v.1). I think someone will ask, however, what benefit it is to the readers to investigate in detail the dates of the reign of those just cited, namely, Uzziah and also Jeroboam.[6] In response we claim that it is necessary, containing as it does, so to speak, the whole of the circumstances of the prophecy; he threatens destruction, invasions, and incineration to Syria, Damascus, and the barbarous neighbors of Judea, and the divine oracles have begun at that point. It is therefore necessary to learn the reasons for inserting the dates of the kingdom, what and how great were the achievements in each case, how they lived, and what was worth hearing in both cases. After deviating into apostasy, therefore, *Israel* and *Judah* were chastised in various ways; when the leaders of Damascus and Syria overran them and mounted a siege, they devastated the country; and when the Moabites and Idumeans, Girgashites and Elamites, and inhabitants of Ashdod and Ekron did damage to Samaria and as well the kingdom of Judah, venting unchecked anger and implacable hostility, they went to the extremes of rage like wild bulls.

We shall find them guilty of this in various ways, for (372) ex-

---

5. 9.11.

6. While the biblical Word comes by oral/aural transmission, the commentary is read by readers. Cyril finds it necessary to defend an (admitttedly lengthy) unfolding of the historical background to the prophet's ministry; not all his fellows, it seems, thought it was required.

ample, when Ahab reigned over Samaria and Israel. It is recorded this way in the first book of Kings: "Ben-hadad gathered all
his forces, and went up and besieged Samaria; thirty-two kings
were with him, along with horses and chariots. They went up
and besieged Samaria and waged war on it."[7] Consider, therefore, how the king of Damascus—namely, Hadad—enlisted as
allies against Israel thirty-two other leaders of neighboring nations, and thus made war on the land. In the time of Jehoash
king of Judah, Hazael the Syrian made war on Jerusalem. It is
recorded likewise in the second book of Kings, "At that time
Hazael king of Syria went up and made war on Gath, and took
it. Hazael set his face to go up to Jerusalem. Jehoash king of Judah took all the holy things dedicated by Jehoshaphat, Jehoram,
and Ahaziah, his ancestors, kings of Judah, his holy things, and
all the gold found in the treasuries of the house of the Lord and
the house of the king, and sent it to Hazael king of Syria, and he
withdrew from Syria."[8] They did such things, in fact, in defiance
of divine wrath, when Israel had offended as a result of their severe decline and baleful involvement in worship of the idols.

In being victorious, however, the foreigners undermined the
glory of God; the wretches believed (373) that the hand aiding
them had grown limp, and they presumed to infringe the glory
of God. The Syrians, for instance, were weak, since Hadad was
besieging Samaria, and they made it an occasion for slander,
saying, "The God of Israel is a God of the mountains, not a God
of the valleys,"[9] believing that the people of Israel were victorious because God was able to save them only on the mountains
and on the hills. We were beaten, they said, therefore, because
the God of Israel is a God of the mountains; but if we engaged
them in battle on the level countryside, we would doubtless prevail over them, since the God of Israel is powerless in valleys.
Now, these were the crimes of pagan persiflage, the vile babbling of people who have no knowledge of the one who is God
in truth and by nature. The God who has power over all, there-

---

7. 1 Kgs 20.1.

8. 2 Kgs 12.17–18. The PG ed. generally abbreviates or omits the lengthy
citations of the biblical text.

9. 1 Kgs 20.23.

fore, was angry with the foreigners, and very rightly so, because in conquering Israel they made thanksgiving offerings to their own gods, and in their folly they thought they had prevailed also over its God.

With the passage of time, after the reign of Ahab and some others in the meantime, there emerged as king over Israel in Samaria a certain Jeroboam different from the first, the son of Nebat, but sharing with him his name, attitude, and impiety. In the years of his reign, however, the compassionate God then had mercy on Israel in its depths of adversity, and freed it from hardship by the hand of Jeroboam, despite his being wicked and unfaithful. He so worsted the foreigners, in fact, as to recover even cities snatched by them in the time of kings in the past, to subject them to his own (374) rule, and to bring numerous troubles on those who were formerly victorious. It is written of him in the second book of Kings, remember, "In the fifteenth year of King Amaziah son of Joash of Judah, Jeroboam son of Jehoash began his reign of forty-one years over Israel in Samaria. He did what was evil in the sight of the Lord; he did not depart from all the sins of Jeroboam son of Nebat, who caused Israel to sin. He it was, in fact, who established the border of Israel from the entrance of Hamath as far as the Sea of Arabah, according to the word of the Lord God of Israel, which he spoke through his servant Jonah son of Amittai, who was from Gath-hepher. Because the Lord saw the very bitter distress of Israel, with very few survivors remaining, and no one to help Israel. The Lord had not said he would blot out the offspring of Israel from under heaven; and he saved them by the hand of Jeroboam son of Jehoash. The rest of the acts of Jeroboam and all that he did, his might, all his battles, and his recovery for Israel of Damascus and Hamath from Judah, lo, is it not all written in the book of the annals of the kings of Israel?"[10]

See, he clearly says that the people of Israel suffered tribulation, with no one to save them, and that the survivors were few, though saved through Jeroboam. He said "through" in the sense of "by"; he was not one to crush Israel, instead fighting

10. 2 Kgs 14.23–28.

for it as its protector, recovering Damascus, extending the borders of Israel, and performing many mighty deeds. (375) During Jeroboam's reign Azariah, or Uzziah, was anointed king of Judah in Jerusalem; he was no less troublesome to the nations, and was vigorously opposed to those ravaging Judea. While he was a pious and godly man, and prevailed over the foe with divine permission to conquer, he suffered from arrogance; of his own volition he attempted to perform priestly functions, even presuming to ascend the divine altar itself and offer incense. Immediately, however, God rebuked him: he was struck with leprosy, a dire and incurable disease, the purpose being for him to be expelled from Jerusalem by Law as one unclean, and to cease acting as a priest for God, since priestly functions were unlawfully undertaken by him, and cease defiling the divine Temple. The sacred text speaks this way of him in the second book of Kings: "In the twenty-seventh year of Jeroboam king of Israel, Azariah son of Amaziah king of Judah came to the throne. He was sixteen years old when he began to reign, and he reigned fifty-two years in Jerusalem. His mother's name was Jecoliah of Jerusalem. He did what was right in the sight of the Lord, just as Amaziah his father had done. Yet the high places were not taken away, for the people kept sacrificing and offering incense on the high places. The Lord struck the king, and he was leprous to the day of his death."[11]

Now, while this is the account in Kings, in the second book of Chronicles (376) there occurs a more succinct version of it, as follows: "The people of the land took Uzziah, who was sixteen years old, and made him king to succeed his father Amaziah. It was he who rebuilt Eloth and restored it to Judah after the king slept with his ancestors. Uzziah was sixteen years old when he began to reign, and he reigned fifty-two years in Jerusalem; his mother's name was Jecoliah of Jerusalem. He did what was right in the sight of the Lord, just as his father Amaziah had done. He was a searcher after the Lord in the days of Zechariah, who was wise in the fear of the Lord; in his days he sought the Lord, and the Lord made him prosper. He went out and made war on

11. 2 Kgs 15.1–5.

the Philistines, and broke down the walls of Gath, the walls of Jabneh, and the walls of Ashdod; he built cities in Ashdod, and the Lord gave him strength among the Philistines, against the Philistines, against the Arabs dwelling on the rock, and against the Meunites. The Meunites paid tribute to Uzziah, and his fame spread even to the entrance to Egypt, for he became very strong."[12]

Then it went on about him, "He offended against the Lord his God, entering the Temple of the Lord to make an offering on the altar of incense. The priest Azariah went in after him, and with him eighty priests of the Lord who were men of valor. They withstood King Uzziah and said to him, It is not for you, Uzziah, (377) to make offerings to the Lord, but for the priests, the descendants of Aaron, who are consecrated to make an offering. Go out of the sanctuary, for you have been unfaithful to the Lord; it will bring you no honor from the Lord God. Uzziah grew angry; in his hand was the censer to make an offering in the Temple. When he grew angry with the priests, leprosy broke out on his forehead in the sight of the priests in the house of the Lord by the altar of incense. The chief priest and the priests looked at him and, lo, he was leprous on his forehead; they hurried him out of there, and he himself hurried to get out, because the Lord had rebuked him."[13]

So much for Uzziah's becoming leprous, therefore. The fact of his being a mighty warrior, on the other hand, invading the country of the Philistines, and reaching such a degree of might as even to build cities in their midst, impose taxes, and subdue them to his regime despite their being conceited, the sacred text conveyed adequately. Since the prophetic verse introduced at the outset the devastation affecting the Philistines, therefore, it was necessary to mention the reign of both Uzziah and Jeroboam, for it was by them that they were conquered, as we began by saying. So we are aware that Damascus was put to the torch at the hand of the Assyrians, and the Philistines were also no less devastated. But since one happened before the other, we shall necessarily address what happened to the Philistines in

12. 2 Chr 26.1–8, with the odd detail in error.
13. 2 Chr 26.16–20.

the time of both Jeroboam and Uzziah,[14] and no less to the actual leaders of the Assyrians. Since the prophet added the further detail *two years before the earthquake,* (378) we should make mention also of Uzziah's becoming leprous; when in defiance of Law he presumed to act as a priest, Jerusalem was hit by an earthquake, God clearly showing his wrath through this to the people of the time.[15]

He said, The Lord gave utterance from Zion, and released his word from Jerusalem; the pastures of the shepherds withered, and the crest of Carmel dried up (v.2). By this the whole thrust of the prophecy is highlighted for us; since the fulfillment, as it were, and discernment of the entire oracle are clouded in considerable obscurity, the force of the text at hand should be properly understood. The verse proceeds, in fact, by both simile and metaphor, referring to what is growing on the well-covered crests of the mountains, or even in the countryside that is sometimes denuded. Although mountains are bedecked with forests and trees, and the countryside is likewise covered in widespread and thick fodder, they can unexpectedly dry up when some chance pest or other contagion in the air affects them. Human affairs, too, likewise suffer a reverse when sometimes harsh and intolerable misfortunes befall cities and countries, which affect and destroy small and great; after all, who has been spared the sword of enemies or pestilence, tell me, which completely strikes down both the man conspicuous for wealth, reputation, and influence, and the man who is unknown and abject? A verse couched in terms familiar to him, therefore, was appropriate for the prophet in this case; (379) he was a goatherd, remember, and developed imagery from the frequent destruction of the *pastures* of his herd.[16]

What is the correct sense, then, of the statement? *The Lord gave utterance from Zion,* as from his own place, and *from Jerusa-*

14. The PG text mentions only Jeroboam here. Although that text does not reproduce the large slabs of biblical text from Kings and Chronicles appearing in the Pusey text, nevertheless Cyril has gone to an exorbitant length to make his point that v.1 of Amos should refer to the reign of the two kings.

15. Cyril would know also from Zec 14.5 that an earthquake occurred in Uzziah's reign; Jerome and Theodore encouraged him to see it as punishment for the king's effrontery, despite no biblical support.

16. It is Jerome who encourages Cyril to comment on the appropriate use of imagery by the prophet.

lem, as from a place attributed to him, the incorporeal not occupying a place. Since that celebrated Temple was in Jerusalem, the place seemed to be his own in the understanding of the ancients, who still had elementary ideas of God. Instead of *gave utterance,* the Hebrew has "bellowed" or "roared," as lions do. When it happened, *the pastures of the flocks withered,* by *the pastures of the flocks* meaning the foreign races, as though prostrate under their own leaders, who forced the people under them to comply with everything they wished. They *withered,* then; that is, they fell victim to every sorrow and trouble, grief occurring in the case of the dead. The cause of their misfortunes was God's roaring and, as it were, threatening ruin; the text says, remember, "A lion will roar, and who will not be afraid?"[17] It was not only that *the pastures of the flocks withered*; as well *the crest of Carmel dried up.* Now, Jerusalem is *the crest of Carmel,* he says, Carmel being a mountain in the country of the Jews, where Elijah the Tishbite dwelt. Often the whole land of the Jews is indicated by the name Carmel; there is a similar statement by God to the children of Israel in another prophet: "I led you to Carmel to eat (380) its good things and its crops, and you entered and defiled my land, and made my inheritance an abomination."[18] Since Jerusalem was more illustrious than the other cities of Judea and known by name, therefore, he calls it *crest of Carmel* in the sense of "raised to prominence," "pre-eminent," "more conspicuous" than the others in having the divine Temple and at times the kings of the tribe of Judah. Now, it is customary with the holy prophets deliberately to lend an obscure meaning to words on account of listeners' undisciplined reactions; they could not bear to listen to them when they spoke openly, taken aback at their frankness, and they warned the holy prophets in the words, "Instead, speak to us and tell us something different and deceptive."[19]

The Lord said, For three transgressions of Damascus and for four I

17. 3.8.
18. Jer 2.7, where the word is used not as a proper name but in the sense of a garden.
19. Is 30.10. By this citation, is Cyril suggesting that Carmel in the sense of a privileged site was in the case of the Jews a misleading reference? Chrysostom had (probably before this) listed this reason—that is, avoiding the risk of the messenger being shot—for the obscurity of Old Testament works, in his homilies on the subject.

shall not turn my back on them for cutting asunder with iron saws the pregnant women of Gilead. I shall send fire on the house of Hazael, and it will consume the foundations of the son Ader. I shall smash the bars of Damascus, and shall destroy inhabitants from the countryside of Ôn and cut down a tribe from men of Haran, and a distinguished people of Syria will be captured, says the Lord (vv.3–5). The divinely inspired Moses was amazed at God's goodness and patience, and rightly so; when Israel made a calf in the desert, and stupidly said, "These are your gods, Israel, who led you out of the land of (381) Egypt," it consequently gave offense. Yet although God had threatened once and for all to destroy them, Moses then prostrated himself and earnestly entreated the Creator and persuaded him to forgive the guilty. He offered songs of thanksgiving: "The Lord God is compassionate and merciful, long-suffering, rich in mercy and truthful, keeping steadfast love to the thousandth generation, forgiving iniquities, wrongs, and sins, not clearing the guilty, visiting the iniquities of the parents on the children and the children's children to the third and fourth generation."[20]

The Jewish populace did not correctly understand this, thinking that God was so harsh, inexorable, and persistent in his wrath as to impose the crimes of parents on their children's children. They said as much, for instance, in claiming, "The parents ate sour grapes, and the children's teeth were set on edge." Consequently, God said to the prophet Ezekiel, "Son of man, what do you mean by repeating this proverb in Israel, The parents ate sour grapes, and the children's teeth were set on edge? As I live, says the Lord, let this proverb no more be recited in Israel, because all lives are mine; the life of the parent as well as the life of the child are mine. Someone who is righteous shall not die; the child will not take on his parent's sin, nor (382) a parent take on his child's sin."[21] After all, how could the Lord of all still be long-suffering, rich in mercy, and truthful if he did not forgive sins and clear the guilty, but extended his anger to the third and fourth generation? What is the reasoning, then? While he is

---

20. Ex 32.4 and 34.6–7.
21. Ezek 18.1–4, 20. Again there is lengthy scriptural documentation for this time of God's long-suffering—which arises from the LXX's version, not Amos's point, and dwells on a subtext rather than on the lemma.

patient, as I said, and incomparably good, and does not immediately inflict punishment on sinners, he postpones it even to the second generation in the hope that perhaps some repentance may intervene and terminate the wrath. If this does not happen, however, and the third generation after the first and the fourth do likewise, or they are caught up in still worse evils, and are found to imitate their forbears' impiety, then and only then does he impose punishment after having already shown the family sufficient patience for past sins. This is the meaning of inflicting sins of parents on the third and fourth generations.

Surely, then, he asks, after having shown long-suffering often to Damascus, would I not fail to be angry, and rightly so, with the *third* and *fourth* sins? What sins did they commit? Many and varied.[22] They will pay the penalty for extreme cruelty: *I shall not turn my back on them for cutting asunder with iron saws the pregnant women of Gilead.* Gilead is a small town of Judea situated on the boundary of Palestine. The Syrians previously occupied it and reduced it to ruins, *cutting asunder with iron saws the pregnant women*, and along with the babies annihilating women's immature foetuses. By *iron saws* he refers to the (383) wheels of wagons with which the Syrians normally crushed the grain. God says somewhere in Isaiah, for example, to the community of the Jews, "Lo, I made you like wheels of a wagon, sharp, new, like saws."[23] So it is as if he were saying to Damascus, I shall sentence you for threshing and crushing those in Gilead in such a way as to show no mercy even on pregnant women, to whom mercy is due and shown by everyone.

Now, the fact that some of those from Damascus treated the people of Israel cruelly and savagely you could easily learn from attending to the words of the prophet Elisha. He arrived in Damascus, remember, and, when he met Hazael while Ben-hadad was ill, "the man of God wept. Hazael asked, Why does my lord weep? He replied, Because I know all the evil you will do to the

---

22. Cyril might have drawn on Theodore to make a note about the semitic usage employed by the author of numerical synonymous parallelism—though a modern commentator like Stuart can only remark, "It cannot be taken literally to indicate a precise number of crimes, but it does connote multiplicity."

23. Is 41.15.

people of Israel: you will set their fortresses on fire, kill their finest with the sword, dash in pieces their infants, and rip open their pregnant women."[24] When Damascus did this to Gilead, or rather to the whole country of the Jews, he threatened to set on fire *the house of Hazael, and smash the bars of Damascus.* This was done by Uzziah and Jeroboam individually and at different times (it was they who took Syria and conquered them by force), and with the passage of time also by the king of Assyria.

He next says, *I shall destroy inhabitants from the countryside of Ôn.* By *Ôn* the prophets refer to Bethel, where the accursed Jeroboam erected the golden heifer; at that time they normally called the whole country by that name because on that account it was all idolatrous (384)—hence the *inhabitants from the* land and *countryside of Ôn*, or the "futile things"—that is, idols—the version of the other interpreters.[25] I shall wipe out and *destroy*, he says, and *cut down a tribe from men of Haran*, a little town quite close to Damascus occupied by very warlike inhabitants. He also says the *distinguished people of Syria will be captured*, by *distinguished* meaning either "very celebrated" or "mercenary and allied to them," since they paid the neighboring Philistines, as I said, in campaigning against the country of the Jews. Or *distinguished* could mean "called" or "alien"; it should be realized that for *people of Syria* the Hebrew has Cyrene, Cyrene being a colony of Syria. We mentioned that, in the text of the second book of Kings, Ahaz began to reign in Jerusalem when Pekah and Rezin, kings of Syria and Damascus, attacked Jerusalem and devastated the cities subject to Judah. Since Ahaz, who was reigning over Judah, experienced unbearable fear, he bribed Tiglath-pileser the Assyrian to give aid. "The Assyrian king listened to him, and the Assyrian king went up to Damascus and took it, deported its people, and put Rezin to death."[26]

24. 2 Kgs 8.11–12, quoted by Jerome.
25. Jerome had, in fact, listed individual versions, only Aquila offering this one; with Jerome's help Cyril had canvassed the issue at Hos 5.8. As Haran does not appear in the Heb. or in Jerome's text, Cyril is left to his own devices in locating it.
26. 2 Kgs 16.1, 9. Cyril has been alerted by Jerome that the LXX has not done justice to the Heb. in arriving at "distinguished," the latter saying that the Heb. term for "Cyrene" has been thus misrepresented, and quoting 2 Kgs 16.9

Thus says the Lord: For three acts of godlessness of Gaza and for four I shall not shun them, because (385) *they took off into captivity the captivity of Solomon to confine it in Idumea. I shall send fire on the walls of Gaza, and it will consume its foundations. I shall destroy the inhabitants of Ashdod, and the tribe from Ashkelon will be eliminated. I shall put my hand on Ekron, and the remnant of the Philistines will perish, says the Lord* (vv.6–8). I think it is necessary before all else to say that neither the Hebrew nor the other versions make mention of *Solomon*; the Hebrew says, "Because they took captivity captive," while the other translators inserted for *Solomon* "complete" or "entire." We for our part, however, shall necessarily follow the text of the Seventy.[27] Gaza is rebuked, then—a Philistine city, which is now Palestinian—for *taking off into captivity the captivity of Solomon to confine it in Idumea.* Even if we take it in the way the other translators render it, they were not responsible for a casual sacking of Judea; instead, they took a large number *captive* and gave them into the hands of the *Idumeans.* Now, the Idumeans were of the line of Esau, always hostile to the people of Israel, and with them were associated and allied the people of Gath, Ashdod, and Ashkelon, as well as the people of the so-called Ekron and the other Philistines; they all tried to take the cities of Judea by force.

If according to the Septuagint, on the other hand, we were to read it, *taking off into captivity the captivity of Solomon,* (386) we would need to interpret it this way. Solomon was a vigorous and strong king, remember, and he so dominated the neighboring nations as even to build many cities among them and settle Israelites in them with the connivance of Hiram. The account is given in the second book of Chronicles in these terms: "At the end of twenty years, at the end of which Solomon had built the house of the Lord and his own house, Solomon rebuilt the

---

to show that Assyrians deported citizens of Damascus to Cyrene. Cyril misreads Jerome, and in likewise quoting 2 Kings he omits the term "Cyrene," which (even if wrong on Jerome's part) was the reason for referring to it.

27. Cyril, though benefiting from Jerome's linguistic skills here, asserts his commitment to the LXX. Jerome has told him that the alternative versions avoid the error of the LXX in reading Heb. *shalma* as Solomon instead of "entire," a lead he follows despite his regard for the LXX. This does not prevent his then trying to rescue the solecism involving Solomon, and again at great length.

cities that Hiram had given him, and settled the people of Israel there. Solomon went to Hamath-zobah and captured it. He
built Tadmor in the wilderness, and he built all the fortified cities in Hamath." And a little later, "Whatever Solomon desired to
build in Jerusalem, in Lebanon, and in all his kingdom. All the
people who were left of the Hittites, the Amorites, the Perizzites, the Hivites, and the Jebusites, who were not of Israel, from
their descendants who were left in the land after them—these
Solomon conscripted for forced labor, as is still the case today."[28]
So the people from Gath and Ashdod and the rest, allied with
those from Idumea, overthrew these cities, which were named
after Solomon, the result being that they no longer fell under
the kingdom of Judah, but were allotted, as it were, to the unholy leaders of the Moabites. Consequently, he says, Gaza would be
consumed by fire along with the others, (387) and the people
of Ashdod and the tribe of Ashkelon would be destroyed, and
fall under the punishing hand of Ekron, and *the remnant of the
Philistines would* completely *perish* along with them. Some of the
neighboring barbarians, in fact, probably served as mercenaries
and were called to lend assistance.

There is therefore difficulty and extreme danger clearly involved for those loved by God in wanting to be connected and
allied with wicked people and to persecute the saints. I mean, if
sometimes we were to suffer for our faults and be corrected by
God, he would still not completely scorn those consecrated to
him; after giving them useful correction, he would invest with
the instruments of his wrath those, that is, who vented their
spleen on them. This would be in keeping with that fine statement to Babylon in reference to the children of Israel, "Though
I gave them into your hands, you did not show them mercy."[29]
In other words, God is severely outraged and angry with violent
treatment at the hands of those bidden to take action.

*Thus says the Lord: for three godless acts of Tyre and for four I shall
not shun it for confining the captivity of Solomon to Idumea and not
remembering the covenant of brethren. I shall send fire upon the walls
of Tyre, and it will consume its foundations* (vv.9–10). The Tyrians

---

28. 2 Chr 8.1–2, 6–8, appearing textually also in the PG ed.
29. Is 47.6.

likewise together with those from Damascus, Ashdod, Gath, and Ashkelon, as well as those from Ekron, had exceeded the patience proper to God, and in a fashion surpassed the excesses of impiety. (388) They would therefore be subjected to wrath, according to the drift of the oracle, and suffer the most extreme punishment of all. Their crime was *confining the captivity of Solomon to Idumea* and not recalling *the covenant of brethren.* While the text has shown us sufficiently what *the captivity of Solomon* was, then, there is need to explain how it was *confined to Idumea* by the Tyrians. After enslaving a countless horde of the people of Judah and Israel, in fact, they sold them to the Idumeans. Having recently, by dint of fighting, given freedom to their *brethren,* they subjected them to the harsh yoke of slavery and forced them to live by pagan norms, as though the wretches were railing violently against the glory of God, implying that he neither preserved the freedom they received from their ancestors nor was capable of ensuring their enjoyment of a fine state of prosperity. The God of all says through another prophet, for instance, by way of severe accusation of those who *confined the captivity of Solomon to Idumea,* "What are you to me, Tyre and Sidon, and the whole of Galilee of foreigners? Surely you are not visiting retribution on me, or nourishing a grievance against me? Swiftly and promptly I shall return your retribution at your heads for your taking my silver and my gold, for introducing my choice things of beauty into your temples, for selling the children of Judah and the children of Israel to the children of the pagans so as to remove them from (389) their borders."[30] Now, the border, as it were, of the people of Israel was in a physical sense Judea, but in a spiritual sense the Law, from which they were removed by being wrongly sold to the pagans. This is what was done by the Tyrians along with the others when unmindful of the very *covenant of their brethren.*

Now, this could be understood in a threefold way; come now, let us explain who were *the brethren* and what was *the covenant,* guided by Holy Writ to an understanding of this text. Hiram, Tyre's king at the time, was a particular friend of the divinely

---

30. Jl 3.4–6.

inspired David, and then after him he was loved by Solomon
to the extent of making agreements of fellow-feeling with him,
doing everything in concert with him, and giving him appropriate attention when he was completing the divine Temple. While
he presented him with a great number of gifts, he himself also
gained a greater and more lavish advantage.[31] Or his meaning is
that the Tyrians made war on Israel, *not remembering the covenant
of* love for *brethren* in which they were linked to such a degree
of benevolence and affection as to seem even to be related by
blood. Or it means that the Idumeans, while being descended
from Esau and being brethren to the people of Israel, made war
on them, scorning the *covenant of brethren.* Esau, remember, was
hostile to Jacob and treated him like an enemy, offended over
the birthright in the beginning; but when in due course he left
the house of Laban and wanted to return home with his wife and
children, he met him as a brother. They embraced and clung
to one another, spoke in a way appropriate to friends, (390)
put behind them their former differences, and made covenants
of harmony and peace.[32] While that was the case with them,
however, the Tyrians by contrast *did not remember the covenant of
brethren,* set the families against one another, and persuaded the
Idumeans to take their fellows and brothers as slaves, thus rendering them by their complicity much stronger than those who
had prevailed. You might, on the other hand, make the claim
also of the Moabites themselves, who were descendants of Lot,
that the Tyrians transgressed a *covenant of brethren,* namely, that
between Abraham and Lot; when the shepherds quarreled with
each other, the text says, "Let there be no quarrel between me
and you, and between my shepherds and your shepherds, for
we are kindred." Consequently, the text was right to say [Tyre]
would be set on fire and overthrown from the very foundations;
the saying, "You shall not follow a majority in wrongdoing,"[33] is
universally valid.

31. 1 Kgs 5.1, 12, and 9.10–14. Cyril, despite being informed by Jerome of
the incorrect appearance of Solomon in the lemma, prefers to find an historical
reference to him or to some other incident in the Bible.
32. Gn 33.
33. Gn 13.8; Ex 23.2.

Thus says the Lord: For three godless acts of Idumea and for four I shall not shun it for pursuing its brother with a sword (v.11). The text now moves to Idumea itself, that is to say, the descendants of Esau, saying that they were very properly subjected to the effects of wrath. They had, you see, made war on (391) Israel, though he was their brother, and they had no qualms about drawing a bold and cruel sword against those who were related even by blood, thinking not in accord with the law of nature, not in accord with humanity; instead, being accustomed to conquer foreigners and bitter enemies with hostility directed at brothers, their thinking in this case as well was perhaps conceited. So let them hear from us, "Why does the mighty one boast of wickedness?" It could rightly be said of them, "Their glory is in their shame." In other words, since by a malicious decision they show respect for what it would be better to remove as far as possible from them, they will likewise hear, "Woe to you who call evil good and good evil, who put darkness for light and light for darkness, who say bitterness is sweet and sweetness bitter."[34]

It violated a womb on the ground (v.11). He helpfully lists the crimes of the Jews, referring to Esau in person, and presenting as ignoble those sprung from an unholy father, so that we may understand what is suggested indirectly in the saying of Isaiah, "From the seed of serpents will come forth offspring of asps."[35] He recounts, therefore, that Esau, who was their ancestor, *violated,* as it were, the good things accruing to him from the *womb* and his origins, and threw on the ground the privilege of being firstborn, according it extremely little value by comparison with bodily nourishment, which he took in exchange for the gift of nature. "For this reason," Scripture says, "he was called Edom," that is, "earthy,"[36] (392) whence I think his descendants also were then called Idumeans. He therefore says *it violated* the privilege that came from his birth and *the womb on the ground,* and exchanged it for an earthly thing.

34. Ps 52.1 (modern numbering for Psalms); Phil 3.19; Is 5.20.
35. Is 14.9. The LXX comes up with "womb" by misreading a similar Heb. form.
36. Gn 25.30. Cyril is astray in his etymology here (and elsewhere, misleading Theodoret as well, as on Is 63.1 and Song 5.10), confusing Heb. *'dama* and Edom.

Now, those who prefer enjoyment of fleshly things to spiritual would be caught up in similar crimes, giving preference to temporary things over eternal, and to impermanent over stable, despising glory from God and ill-advisedly giving higher esteem to what attracts attention from human beings and escapes the grasp of its possessors like shadows. It was very useful for the divinely inspired Paul also to cry aloud, "See to it that no one becomes like Esau, an immoral and loathsome person, who sold his birthright for a single meal."[37]

It snatched its horror in evidence against him (v.11). He proceeds to mention something else, blaming, as it were, the Idumean for being always mischievous and evil, malicious and hostile, especially to his relatives. Accordingly, it is written in Numbers, "Moses sent messengers from Kadesh to the king of Edom, saying, Thus says your brother Israel, You know all the trouble that has beset us, how our ancestors went down into Egypt, and we lived in Egypt a long time. The Egyptians oppressed us and our ancestors, and we cried aloud to the Lord, and the Lord heard our voice, sent an angel and brought us out of Egypt. Now we are in Kadesh, a city on the edge of your territory; we shall pass by your land, we shall not pass through fields or vineyards, (393) nor drink water from your well. We shall travel the king's highway, not turning aside to right or left until we have passed by your territory. Edom said to him, You are not to pass by me; otherwise, I shall come out to do battle with you as you come. The people of Israel said, We shall pass by the border; if we drink your water, I and my livestock, I shall pay you for it, but it is a matter of no significance—we shall pass by your border. But he replied, You are not to pass through me; and Edom came out against them with a large force heavily armed. Edom refused to allow Israel to pass by its borders, and Israel turned away from them."[38]

Consider likewise in this how dire and quite unreasonable the crimes of lack of affection: Although Israel was not looking for water from Edom without paying, the latter took up arms and deployed forces, resenting even their bypassing, and was

37. Heb 12.16.
38. Nm 20.14–21.

brought to such a degree of knavery as not to stop at bloodshed unless Israel turned away. Accordingly, *It snatched its horror in evidence against him*: whereas for fear of doing battle they declined and withdrew in order to avoid giving the impression of spurning love for their brethren, the other took the withdrawal or the dread prompting it (suggested by the term *horror*) as the occasion of inflexible testimony against them.[39] In fact, he openly threatened that unless they agreed to avoid the borders of the territory belonging to him, he would come out against them and then make war. Edom therefore lacked brotherly love, and was to no slight degree guilty of the crimes of hatred for brethren, and consequently abhorrent to God; "God is love," after all, as (394) John says, "and the one who abides in love abides in God."[40] So the person who opts to live without love is not in God, instead lying outside of a relationship with God.

It maintained its attack as a victory. I shall send fire on Teman, and it will consume the foundations of its walls (vv.11–12). This is the third fault of the descendants of Esau; *it maintained its attack*—clearly hostile and utterly godless—*as a victory*, that is, to the point of conquest and for all time. In fact, they in no way desisted from their godless exploits, despite Esau's abandoning that ancient godlessness, as I mentioned before. As well as not being murderous towards Jacob, he underwent a change to clemency and brotherly love; he tearfully embraced him as he left Laban's home, and was always given to shedding tears of benevolence. His descendants, on the other hand, were hardhearted, exceeding in their knavery even the depravity of their ancestor. It is true that without a doubt "the ways of the malicious lead to death";[41] hence his saying, *I shall send fire on Teman* (which is the capital of Edom) *and consume the foundations of its walls*. Teman, in fact, was burnt down when the enemy were in control, and was destroyed along with the others. (395)

It will therefore meet its end in fire and flames for hating its brethren and opposing its family, those linked in unity and fel-

---

39. The obscurity prompting such a lengthy citation and "clarification" is aggravated by the LXX's seeing "evidence" in a similar Heb. form.
40. 1 Jn 4.16.
41. Prv 12.27 LXX.

low-feeling by a spiritual relationship. Loving behavior, on the other hand, is immune from such troubles.

Thus says the Lord: For three godless acts of the people of Ammon and for four I shall not shun them for cutting open the pregnant women of Gilead in order to extend their boundaries. I shall set fire to the walls of Rabbah, and consume its foundations with a shout on the day of war, and it will be shaken on the day of its consummation. Their kings will go off in captivity, its priests and its rulers likewise, says the Lord (vv.14–15). The ferocity of Damascus is documented also from the Ammonites; they, too, personally killed *the pregnant women of Gilead,* not to give aid to some others nor to support the wrath of foreigners, but on their own behalf to ensure a wider sphere of influence and *extend the borders* of the kingdom further by the devastation of the whole land of the Jews and the complete upheaval of the people of Israel, as if God were a victim of impotence and real weakness despite his promise to save them, rendered vulnerable to those bent on waging war. After taking the cities, therefore, (396) they presumed to mock God their protector, and offered to the false gods thanksgiving and triumphal songs. Consequently he says that Rabbah will be *set on fire,* the capital of the country of the Ammonites; and he says that it will be destroyed *with a shout* when the Babylonians exult over it by the norms of war, taking it by force when Nebuchadnezzar invades it. They will go off *in captivity,* he says, subjects along with rulers, and those appointed to serve their own gods, gaining no help from them. After all, what could they do, or who could benefit from a deaf image?

The initiators of heresies also resemble those who *cut open the pregnant women in order to extend their boundaries.* In order to appear to be leaders of many, you see, they do violence to miserable souls, and by their deceptive words they cause the crude and immature faith, as it were, to abort by communicating to them twisted notions and spouting the thoughts "of their own heart and not from the mouth of the Lord." After all, no one says, "Jesus is Lord, except by the Holy Spirit, or Let Jesus be cursed," except by Beelzebul.[42]

---

42. Jer 23.16; 1 Cor 12.3. At this stage of his career Cyril does not go into detail about "initiators of heresies."

COMMENTARY ON AMOS,
CHAPTER TWO

The Lord says this: For three godless acts of Moab and for four I shall not shun
it for burning to ashes the bones of the king of Idumea. I shall send (397) *fire*
on Moab, and it will consume the foundation of its cities; Moab will die from
impotence, with noise and with sound of a trumpet. From its midst I shall de-
stroy a judge, and kill all its leaders with it, says the Lord (vv.1–3).

 HE MOABITES LIKEWISE were guilty of such extreme
impiety as to exceed even the inherent clemency and
patience of the God of all. Their crime was a sin against
a corpse, namely, *burning the bones of the king of Idumea*, and burning them in such a way as to reduce them to dust and *ashes*. What,
then, was the crime? Hatred, inhumanity, and unrestrained ferocity against the people of Israel. Burning the bones of the afore-
mentioned king would seem to be done for no other reason than
that it was against the people of Israel alone.

I shall in brief give a clear explanation of the facts. In the second book of Kings it says, "After the death of Ahab, the king of
Moab rebelled against the king of Israel. King Jehoram issued
forth from Samaria at that time and mustered Israel; he advanced and sent word to Jehoshaphat king of Judah, The king
of Moab has rebelled against me: will you go with me to battle
against Moab? He replied, I shall go up with you; my people
(398) are your people; my horses are your horses. He asked, By
which way shall we march? He answered, By the way of the wilderness of Edom. So the king of Israel, the king of Judah, and
the king of Edom set out, and made a roundabout march of
seven days. There was no water for the army or for the animals
that were with them."[1] Consider, then, how the king of Edom,
that is, of Idumea, joined forces with the kings; but since there

1. 2 Kgs 3.5–9.

was a shortage of water, they sent for the blessed prophet Elisha and asked for what they wanted to be given by God. When that happened, the Moabites were captured.

Further on, the text says, "Israel rose up and attacked Moab, who fled before them; they entered and struck Moab, destroyed the cities, and on every good piece of land everyone threw a stone and covered it, blocked every spring of water, and felled every tree to the point of leaving the stones of the wall destroyed."[2] The people of Moab were accordingly furious that the people of Israel had in due course been victorious with the help and connivance of the king of Edom; and since they could in no other way do harm to the dead, they sinned against his remains, consuming them by fire, and sparing not even the bones; as though the people of Israel were destroyed, they added to them the one who had proved at the time to be their ally. He therefore says that their cities would be burnt, and they would perish *from impotence*, not exhausted by disease or wasted by ordinary debility, but *with noise and with sound of a* (399) *trumpet*, that is, by war and fighting, as it were. He threatens that *judges* and *rulers* and all its leaders would perish along with the subjects; after all, they were responsible for counsel and initiative, and introduced the others to all the impiety.

Thus says the Lord: For three transgressions of Judah and for four I shall not shun them, because they have repudiated the Law of the Lord and have not observed his commandments, and have deceived themselves with the futile things they have done, which their fathers adopted. I shall send fire on Judah, and it will consume the foundations of Jerusalem (vv.4–5). To the lawless nations there has been attached the one guided by the Law, namely, Judah, the Judge being no respecter of persons. The fact that he is always tolerant of a sinner and shows long-suffering is indicated by his being moved

2. 2 Kgs 3.24–25. Cyril offers two explanations of Moab's sin of burning the bones of the king of Idumea. He first quotes at great length 2 Kgs 3.5–9, 24–25 (omitted by the PG ed.), the story of Israel and Idumea defeating Moab (not supported by archaeology), but stopping short of the part where the king of Moab burns his firstborn on the walls of the city. Then he takes a lead from Jerome to switch to the non-biblical story of the subsequent revenge of the Moabites against the bones of the king of Idumea. Cyril thus strives to provide an historical basis for his text.

only by the third or even the fourth sin. While it was necessary in all probability that he would accord more generous clemency to the other nations in so far as they did not have the divine Law, and be more generous in the extent of his pardon, he had to call Israel to account for its indifference in so far as it had been raised on the divine commandments and was not ignorant of the way to its own benefit. Yet he was tolerant of those who knew the Law as he was of those who did not know it.

When he observed, however, that they had descended to the excess of depravity and malicious thinking, then it was that he said that *fire* would take hold also of Jerusalem itself, (400) and the splendid and celebrated city would be consumed to its very foundations. While the crimes of the people of Israel were very numerous, it was especially for following the errors of their ancestors that God accused them; some accorded reverence to a calf after being victims of the oppression of the Egyptians and reared in their ways and laws, while others, despite escaping that burdensome slavery and being guided in many ways by the divine commandments to the clear knowledge of God's will, suffered a relapse, being swept up in their fathers' deception, though dreading the ugly fate of encountering the same troubles through worshiping the golden heifers themselves. Now, what was responsible for such impiety in their case was their *repudiating the Law of the Lord and not* choosing to keep *his commandments.*

How long, therefore, have we been keepers of the Law and lovers of God, zealous in observing his commands, wise and enthusiastic, practiced in every virtue, and what will not be the rich reward we shall be found to enjoy for this behavior? If, on the other hand, we had been inclined to indifference and spurned the divine laws, we would be carried along by every breeze, deprived of a noble way of thinking, and would even be "a prey for jackals," with the unclean spirits driving us hither and yon. Rightly and wisely, therefore, to be sure, the divinely inspired David also sings of every righteous person, "The law of God is in their hearts, and their steps will not slip."[3]

3. Pss 63.10 and 37.31.

Thus says the Lord: For three transgressions of Israel and for (401) *four I shall not shun them, for selling the righteous person for silver and the needy for sandals, while they trample them in the dust of the earth* (vv.6–7). He did not allow Israel, that is, the tribes in Samaria, to go unpunished; instead, he submitted them to punishment. Now, the fact that they had also sinned heedlessly, consuming, as it were, the serenity due from God to the weak, would be demonstrated by his shunning them for the *third* and *fourth* sins, to which they had to be subjected by suffering a dire fate and being in trouble of every kind. Accordingly, the divinely inspired David was also afraid of this, knowing it to be the source of ruin, and he makes this appeal: "Do not avert your face from me, or turn from your servant in anger."[4] Without doubt, wrath follows and, as it were, attends on his shunning us.

Now, he clearly declares what the crimes of the people of Israel were. They sold, he says, *the righteous person for silver and the needy for sandals;* that is, they could not bring themselves to say what was right and just, or deliver a sentence in accordance with the Law for each of those being judged. Instead, in the case of a man who was *righteous,* self-controlled and guileless, measured and unpretentious—*righteous* being understood in this way, and *needy* as poor in spirit—and was brought to court by one of the more influential, the latter would sell him to the enemy, despite the Law's clear declaration, "You shall not be partial in judgment," and again, "You shall not put to death the innocent and righteous."[5] After all, the person entrusted with judgment definitely sits in the place of God, to whom alone belongs the right to judge; (402) "there is one lawgiver and judge," in the statement of the holy one. So the one who twists the meaning of *righteous* and shows partiality insults the divine office without question, and offends God, who says, "Deliver fair judgments, and show mercy and compassion, each of you to your neighbor."[6]

Accordingly, he charges them with selling to the enemy both the *righteous* and the *needy,* and with normally doing this for some slight profit which would hardly be sufficient even for buying *sandals.* It would instead be far better for them to show respect

4. Ps 37.9.
5. Lv 19.15; Ex 23.7.
6. Jas 4.12; Zec 7.9.

for uprightness and God's will and to be, as it were, inebriated with the honors coming from him, as well as to enjoy the riches of a good reputation; Scripture says, "A good name is to be chosen rather than great riches." Now, it should be understood that he also says as much in Isaiah to the mother of the Jews, that is, Jerusalem: "Your silver has become dross; your innkeepers mix water with the wine; your princes are rebels, associates of thieves, loving bribes and looking for gifts, not defending orphans or rendering judgment for widows." And likewise in Jeremiah: "Its leaders gave judgments for gifts."[7] Giving judgments that are not upright and above board is therefore universally accursed, in some way hateful and impugned for its inequity. (403)

They slapped the faces of the poor (v.7). He clearly censures and blames them for oppression and injustice, for being ungodly and uncaring; those to whom they should have given care and respect and been prepared to apply loving assistance they normally by contrast treated unjustly, abusing them with intolerably harsh indignities, despite their being burdened with poverty. Our Lord Jesus Christ, on the other hand, takes what is done to them as directed at his own person, saying, "Whatever you did to the least of these, you did to me." We therefore seriously offend God in oppressing the weak and "striking the lowly with our fists," as Scripture says, aggravating the condition of those caught up in poverty by our hostility when we are obliged instead to extend to them brotherly love. "Indigence humbles a man," remember, "whereas the hands of the brave enrich him." The disciple of Christ also writes somewhere, "Religion pure and undefiled with the God and Father is this: to care for orphans and widows in their lowliness, and to keep oneself unstained by the world."[8]

7. Prv 22.1; Is 1.22–23 (abbreviated in the PG ed.); Mi (not Jer) 3.11. Cyril, we know, is inclined to speak interchangeably of Israel and Judah, and again with Amos he is not precise about the northern ministry of a prophet. But in this case he is awry in seeing Jerusalem in focus when the text speaks of Israel after having (possibly in a later insertion) already addressed Judah.

8. Mt 25.40; Is 58.4; Prv 10.4 LXX; Jas 1.17 (Cyril perhaps unfamiliar with the author's name). Cyril does not moralize; but when a text allows for moral elaboration (as many prophetic texts do), he can be found accepting the opportunity.

And they avoided the way of the lowly (v.7). You can take this two ways. Either he is saying that they were conceited and reached such a degree of the arrogance that is hateful to God as to avoid even their brethren unless they were flush with riches (404) and were conspicuous for affluence, while being unwilling to travel the same way as those not addicted to avarice, being *lowly*, disengaged from the normal uncertainties of life. Or he means that, being rulers and leaders of peoples, they direct the way of weaker people, or *the lowly*, namely, those who of themselves do not have a precise knowledge of what is for their good, and are dependent rather on the directions of their guides. Most people are in that situation: certain people live simple and untroubled lives, relying on the advice and guidance of teachers, and prefer a way they can easily learn. While some of those appointed to lead are wise and godly, and point out the straight and narrow, by which they plan and live a life pleasing to God, others set little store by the divine law, and direct *the way of the lowly* by making it depart from what is truly right and proper. Jeroboam did that kind of thing, persuading them to worship the handmade heifers, having shunned the straight and narrow, namely, that which leads to the one who is by nature in truth God and Lord.

Those people *avoid the way of the lowly* who are not averse to saying to people of immature thinking, "Come with us, have a taste of unlawful blood."[9] They also *avoid the way of the lowly* who twist the probity of church teachings to their own inclinations, and persuade the mind of simple people to follow the twists and turns of their path; (405) with them nothing is straightforward, and there are only twisted and ugly verbiage and conundrums full of impiety and ignorance.

A son and his father went into the same girl, profaning the name of their God (v.7). He further accuses them of fevered and punishable indulgence, revealing them to be guilty in this one sin of scorning all decency. It would, in fact, have been better to subdue their passions, control sinful indulgence, and excise loathsome lusts by the habit of checking the movements of the flesh

9. Prv 1.11.

and by persuading the flagrant tendencies in our limbs to be at rest. Instead, those people had lost sight of such eminent virtue, and were perhaps overcome by their fleshly passions. Further, how would it not be wise to opt for the better, at least in vile pursuits, and to reflect that among the really sinful actions is a *son's* invading his father's marriage bed, and a *father's* wanting in unholy manner to defile the very couch of his son, which nature knows is a vile action even apart from the Law of Moses, and deserving of condemnation by the impulse of wrath? Reuben, for instance, committed a grave offense by trespassing on his father's marriage bed; the divinely inspired Paul was also very angry with some people for a similar crime—Corinthians they were—and he said in writing to them, "It is actually reported that there is sexual immorality among you, (406) and of a kind that is not found even among the gentiles, for someone to live with his father's wife." This was not the extent of his anger, however: he handed the culprit over "to Satan for the destruction of the flesh."[10] Those guilty of such crimes, therefore, *profane the name of their God.* We do not say that they inflicted defilement and profanity on the divine nature. How so? Rather, they caused the God of all to be blasphemed as the ruler of profane people. He said somewhere to the Jews, "Because of you my name is everywhere blasphemed among the nations";[11] in other words, just as those living an upright life are said to cause God to be hallowed, so those who lead an impure and inglorious way of life would be considered to profane him.

Binding their garments with ropes, they laid hangings near the altar, and drank the wine of calumnies in the house of their God (v.8). Our Lord Jesus Christ taught that divine temples should be built for no other reason than to glorify the God of all in them and render worship appropriate to him. So he once upbraided the Jewish merchants who had introduced into the Temple sheep, cattle, and doves, actually "making a whip of cords and expelling them all from the Temple" with the words, (407), Scripture says, "My house will be called a house of prayer." The sacred text in-

10. Gn 49.4; 1 Cor 5.1, 5.
11. Is 52.5.

dicated that "the disciples remembered that it was written, Zeal for your house will consume me." The divinely inspired Paul also rebuked some people for being in the habit of committing such abuses, writing in these terms: "Surely you are not without homes to eat and drink in? Or do you show contempt for the church of God and humiliate those who have nothing?"[12]

It is therefore a distressing sight to have the divine houses everywhere treated as though profane and available to everyone in general. I mean, in what way is the reverence due to God maintained if we minister to the pleasures of the flesh in his sight? And how are we conspicuous for the reverence expected of us if we are ridiculed for descending to disgusting behavior and choosing to do what is not proper? He does not let people guilty of this go without blame, and rightly so; instead of ridding *the altar* of drapes, they fell under them and presumed to become intoxicated and involved in acts of pleasure, so as to be clearly told by God, "I am witnessing it, says the Lord." Yet from what inappropriate behavior would a drunken man refrain in his derangement and readiness to commit any evil? The God of all, remember, surveys even "what is in darkness," as Scripture says, and nothing at all escapes him. Now, it seems that what happens in churches in particular is done by us as though he were present and observing; and if getting drunk is truly vile (408) and bears the ultimate condemnation by the Law, how is it not inconceivable from the point of view of depravity for such people to be seen behaving this way in the very churches? And, what is even worse, if money is collected for such excesses from the proceeds of wrongdoing and vice? Those guilty of this will hear the Lord saying clearly, "Surely my house is not a den of thieves?"[13]

The crimes of others will therefore be of benefit to us, and we shall become better from sins committed by others if we avoid theirs. People of self-control would properly be more prudent if they chose to live by the Law, if they did not elect to imitate the wicked.

---

12. Jn 2.15, 17; 1 Cor 11.22.
13. Jer 29.23; Dn 2.22; Jer 7.11.

If, on the other hand, there were reference to Judah, or the two tribes in Jerusalem, in the verse, *Binding their garments with ropes, they laid hangings near the altar,* the interpretation just now given by us would be appropriate. But if the sin pertains to Israel, I would claim that it was not *in the house of the* one who is by nature and in truth God, nor close to *the altar,* that the tents were woven of drapes or the drunkenness occurred, but in the house of their own god—Baal, that is—or some other figure made on the model of an idol by human imagination. How then could it be attributed to Israel as a sin to get drunk on wine or weave tents in the house of an idol or near the loathsome object itself?[14] Because they honored such things, and turned the temples of their so-called gods into premises, as it were, for drunkenness and every vile pleasure, (409) despite being obliged to long rather for pure and holy worship of God, to enter into a truly holy house and treat the altar as venerable. Some were even anxious to treat as of no importance the objects that were so venerable and praiseworthy, paying honor to utterly vile things, presuming to behave drunkenly before their own gods, consistently trampling on the divine dignity, and heedlessly infringing the glory due to the one who alone is God by nature by applying it to the false gods and refraining from according him any importance.

I removed the Amorite from before them, whose height was like the height of a cedar, and who was as strong as an oak; I removed his fruit above and his root below (v.9). Do you observe how he now presents them as sacrilegiously insolent and bent on spurning him, choosing insanely and ill-advisedly to offend the one whom they should rather have gladdened with thanksgiving songs and responsiveness to every demand, as a result of consigning to oblivion all their benefits because of their extreme perversity? He says, in fact, *I removed the Amorite from before them;* that is, I destroyed the barbarian races (suggested perhaps by a single

---

14. Cyril is admitting to some difficulty in applying this verse to Israel, and understandably so. He is getting little help from Jerome to realize that the "ropes" and "calumnies" of the LXX (reading somewhat different forms) do not quite convey the inequity intended by the Heb. "pledges" and "fines." It is not a question of irreverence.

Amorite as someone tough and strong), I was responsible for the defeat of the one who was so arrogant and bold as to give the impression of the removal of a *cedar in height* and resemble a very strong *oak* for its might. There was in fact no one but I, he says, to wither him and strike him to the *roots* as if even desiccating his (410) *fruit.* You see, since he had spoken of him as a tree, it made sense for the treatment to continue in a figurative vein, saying that the damage reached the *roots,* and his *fruit* thus disappeared; a tree in the forest would die in no other way than this. After all, no one would be unaware that Amorites and Hivites, Girgashites and Jebusites perished when the people of Israel fought them—that is, with God fighting for them.

It would therefore be an act of malice to show scorn for Christ, who empowers us "to walk on snakes and scorpions and on all the might of the foe" that overthrows the weak and subjects the strong. "For our struggle is not against flesh and blood, but against the rulers, against the authorities, against the cosmic powers of this present darkness, against the spiritual forces of evil in the heavenly places."[15] All of these as well were vanquished by Christ. If by lapsing into indifference we were likely to offend our Savior and Redeemer, we would, to be sure, forfeit any chance and opportunity of being rescued from punishment and fire.

I brought you up from the land of Egypt, and conducted you through the wilderness for forty years to inherit the land of the Amorites (v.10). His clear comment is as I said, and the verse looks back, as it were, indicating briefly the movement from beginning to end: (411) I rescued you from slavery, he says, and freed you from the oppression of the Egyptians; I fed you in the wilderness by sending down manna for you from on high, letting springs of water flow as only God could do, and regaling you with gushing streams from the split rock. Far from being pointless, the hardship that their travel involved was for them *to inherit the land of the Amorites,* the land promised to their ancestors. But some descended to such a degree of perversity as perhaps even to be unaware of my love and kindness towards them.

15. Lk 10.19; Eph 6.12—readings abbreviated in the PG ed.

It is therefore necessary for us who are in Christ through faith to remember that we were freed from slavery and, as it were, transferred from Egypt to the wilderness—that is, to an evangelical way of life that is broad and truly pure, unmixed with evil. We have been enriched with bread from heaven that gives life to the world; we are strengthened in Christ, and in the writings of the holy apostles we have enjoyed springs of uncontaminated water, the prophet Isaiah referring to them this way: "With joy you drew water from the springs of salvation."[16] Some springs of salvation would definitely be those that flow with the saving and life-giving word, bringing the good news of the mystery of Christ and initiating the world under heaven.

I took some of your children to be prophets, and some of your young people for consecration. Is not this so, children of Israel? says the Lord. You made the consecrated ones drink wine, and you gave the prophets this instruction: Do not prophesy (vv.11–12). A severe reproach (412) and accusation of every wickedness is that of ingratitude to God, as it were, who regales us with everything necessary for reputation and life. Of all the nations throughout the world, in fact, he made Israel alone his chosen one; God then called and brought it to such a degree of fame as to dignify with the office of prophecy some who loved an upright and law-abiding life, and also took from their midst their *young people for consecration*, namely, those with strength of character and a healthy outlook. There were some called Nazarites, remember, who were consecrated by Law, who grew their hair for the Lord, abstained from *wine* and what came from it (vinegar, grapes, and raisins), and kept away from corpses; there is plenty of documentation on them.[17] God showed them honor, and promoted some of them to be *prophets* as examples and by *consecration*. Some people, on the other hand, were wrongfully anxious to impair their prominence and good reputation; they *made the consecrated ones* (those who had taken a vow of consecration) *drink wine*. In other words, they convinced them even to lose respect for their consecration, claiming dogmatically that the Law of God was of no value, and

16. Jn 6.33; Is 12.3.
17. Nm 6.1–8.

that it made no sense to people to want to be consecrated and fulfill the requirements for it.

In fact, even if the Law was at the level of shadows, it was still not completely devoid of teachings of truth; in the types the outline of piety beams forth.[18] On the other hand, to upbraid even the holy prophets themselves is the action of those completely undermining the word of God, (413) unwilling to be instructed by them, and unaware that they are honored, especially if, as a member of that group, they are called to have a share in the word with God, as it were. He continued in the middle of the verse to pose the question, *Is not this so, children of Israel? says the Lord.* Surely, he says, you are not denying such blatant behavior? Surely God will not require witnesses to convict you of being so guilty of such obvious calumny?

There is thus need to be consecrated and to attend on God of set purpose without giving admittance to evil attitudes. Scripture says, remember, "Bad company corrupts good morals," and the sentiments of pleasure-lovers spoil sanctification and every good disposition. In our case, therefore, we shall adhere to the statements of those who speak well of God, which the Savior himself confirms in saying, "It is not you who speak, but the Spirit of your Father speaking through you."[19]

For this reason, lo, I shall roll over you in the way a cart full of hay is rolled (v.13). It was the custom of the ancients to transport by carts the crops of the fields and all that filled the threshing floor, and the practice is still preserved by people east and west. The wheels *roll* jointly with the axles, the timbers emitting a loud and unpleasant creaking, complaining, as it were, of the load imposed on them. For my part, therefore, he is saying, I the Lord of all shall be like the thing that rolls under the cart, namely, the axle; as I said, it rotates the wheels jointly with itself, since they are fixed and attached to it. I shall cry aloud, as it were, about the wrongdoers, (414) no longer able to bear the oppression of their sins. In fact, "they have repudiated the Law of the Lord and have not observed his commandments, and have deceived themselves with the futile things they have done,

18. That is, the Old Testament, despite its limitations, has its value.
19. 1 Cor 15.33; Mt 10.20.

which their fathers adopted"; they have forgotten me, though I was the one who "brought them up from the land of Egypt," "removed the Amorite from before them," and took their sons "to be prophets" and their "young people for consecration." But while I showed them honor, they were guilty of such imprudence as to "bind their garments with ropes, lay hangings near the altar, drink the wine of calumnies in the house of their God," "make the consecrated ones drink wine, and give the prophets this instruction: Do not prophesy."[20] As though weighed down with your awful acts of impiety, therefore, like an axle under a cart that is full of hay and sheaves, I shall emit the loudest possible cry. The harm that will ensue from this, and the sufferings to befall them in turn, he immediately clarifies in what follows.

It is necessary to say that it is a really dreadful thing to provoke God, and then to descend to such a degree of depravity that our sin proves unbearable to him, despite his being by nature extremely good, kind, and lenient. There is therefore need, on the one hand, to avoid as far as possible the habit of offending him, and, on the other, if some human weakness occurs, not to be seen to delay repenting or to allow our lapses to grow in number, but instead by the use of holy vigilance to keep them in check (415) and strive to bring our ailing thoughts to a better condition. In this way, in fact, God will show long-suffering, and respond with his mercy, kind as he is.

The runner will be deprived of flight, the strong man will not exercise his strength, the warrior will not save his life, the archer will not stand firm, the swift man will not be saved by his feet, the rider will not save his life, and will find courage among the mighty. The naked will be pursued on that day, says the Lord (vv.14–16). Nothing will save offenders in the days of wrath, he is saying: fleetness of foot will not deliver the fastest runner from troubles, nor good health the strong, nor warlike skills the tactician renowned for fine archery and admired for it. Instead, the speed of horses will be of no use to those employing it, nor even familiarity with cavalry warfare. Each of these people *will find courage among the mighty*, he says—that is, when oppressed by disasters and conceding vic-

---

20. Am 2.4, 8–12, above.

tory without a blow to those bent on devastation. Then, in fact, there will be a terrible fate for the people of Israel, and such dominance by the Babylonians that they will even be able to pursue *the naked*, that is, to prevail over armed men, even should any of the Babylonians not be armor-clad, and the man without armor or weapons will be able to *pursue* those fully equipped.

When God reduces to impotence those choosing to do evil, therefore, (416) nothing would be of any avail. I think this is the meaning of what is said to us by the psalmist: "His delight is not in the power of horses, nor his pleasure in the speed of a runner," and again, "Unreliable is a horse for salvation; there is no safety in its great might"; such things are of no help at all unless God fights on our side. It is he, after all, who is the Lord of hosts, the one who gives strength to the weak and heartens the distressed; with his help "one man will rout thousands, and two will put tens of thousands to flight,"[21] whereas a mighty throng will be laid low when two or three oppose them unless God assists them. (417)

21. Pss 146.10 and 33.17; Dt 32.30. Cyril's first tome on Amos concludes at this point.

COMMENTARY ON AMOS,
CHAPTER THREE

Hear this word that the Lord spoke to you, house of Israel, and against every tribe that I brought up from the land of Egypt, saying, Only you have I known from all the tribes of the earth; hence I shall take vengeance on you for all your sins (vv.1–2).

HE VERSE COULD BE TAKEN as addressed to the whole of Israel, not citing Judah and Ephraim separately, but as though addressing a unit comprising every tribe, since *every tribe* of Israel was led out of *the land of Egypt*. With no one excluded, then, they are bidden to listen to what comes from God.[1] What was it? While the cities and towns throughout the world under heaven were beyond counting, he says, I made a choice *from all* of *only you*, the people of Israel, clearly making you mine by many marvels, rescuing you from harsh and unbearable slavery, rendering you zealous and thrice-blessed, guiding you by the Law to what pleases me, fortifying you with aid, and introducing you even into the land promised to the ancestors. But since, (418) despite being the only ones out of them all to be accorded such a splendid favor, you did not cease offending and transgressing in manifold ways, consequently I shall now exact an account of your folly, and show no patience for your continuing to sin and indulging a tendency to it with impunity.

Despising God, therefore, and spurning the Lord's wishes were at that time productive of ruin for those who acknowledged him or who also experienced from him at least a form of spiritual relationship. Paul in his wisdom, for instance, writes

---

1. Cyril is unable without help from Jerome, which was not forthcoming, to see in the oracle against Judah in the previous chapter a possible insertion into a work from a prophet to the north; thus he continues to think both kingdoms are in focus.

to those who had been called from the nations through faith and then suffered some debility and were inclined to relapse, in these words: "Now that you have come to know God, however, or rather to be known by God, how can you turn back to the weak and beggarly elements of the universe, and want to be enslaved to them again?"[2] The Creator knew them even before faith, in fact, since he is in no way ignorant of what exists; but in this passage, as I said, knowledge would quite likely suggest spiritual relationship.

Will two walk together unless they make each other's acquaintance? (v.3) The figure is profound, and the statement obscure; but we shall give an explanation as far as possible. Israel was accused, then, of "giving the prophets this instruction: Do not prophesy."[3] The reason why they incautiously forbade utterances by the holy ones it is necessary to declare. You see, since they announced the disasters that would result from wrath, and the events that would probably lead the guilty to reform out of fear of fulfillment of the prophecies, there was an effort to rebut and oppose them (419) on the part of those who were in the habit of distracting the will of their flock to what was improper, and who deceived their subjects. While they upbraided the prophets, in fact, they commended those they had deceived, saying that they were following the correct path; hence God says in Isaiah, "My people, those who compliment you are deceiving you and confusing the path for your feet." Amaziah the priest of Bethel also upbraided Amos the prophet in the words, "On your way, O seer, off with you to the land of Judah; live there and prophesy there. Continue prophesying no further in Bethel." Now, those who opposed the prophets as a result of utter knavery and dire disaffection misrepresented their opposition as seemly, and claimed, "The Lord has not sent you."[4]

Accordingly, he accuses them of denying that the prophets sent by him were from on high and brought messages from

2. Gal 4.9.

3. 2.12. The verse begins a sustained series of images, bearing on divine providence, that was notorious, not only for being "profound" and "obscure," but (we know from Chrysostom's homily on Is 45.6–7) for being commonly cited irresponsibly to justify lack of moral accountability.

4. Is 3.12; Am 7.12; Jer 43.2.

God; they believed instead that they uttered their own views and spoke what was at variance with the will of the Lord of all. Consequently he means, O stupid and mindless people, surely some of you will not become friends and take the same path in life without getting to know one another, that is, without perceiving that the other shares the same behavior and attitudes? Scripture says, remember, "Every creature loves its like, and people stick close to those like themselves."[5] If this is true, how would I admit the prophets to friendship and love, as it were, holy as I am, unless they, too, were holy? So why do you persecute the holy ones, to whom I have also confided my words, and whom I accepted as good on the grounds that they tread the same way as I wish? In fact, what I would wish (420) is what they also desire. To upbraid the prophets, therefore, is nothing other now than mounting criticism of me.

The Savior also said as much to the holy disciples: "Whoever receives you receives me; and whoever receives me receives the one who sent me." He bade them, when driven out, to shake the dust from their feet, in the words, "It will be more tolerable for the land of Sodom on the day of judgment than for that city." It is therefore necessary to welcome those who act as God's delegates and convey to us his will, such as the divinely inspired Paul, who writes in these words: "We are therefore ambassadors for Christ, since God is making his appeal through us, and we entreat you on behalf of Christ, be reconciled to God."[6]

Will a lion roar from the forest if it has no prey? Will a cub utter any kind of sound from its den if it has not caught something? (v.4) Those who investigate the habits of wild animals say that, when in need, the lion aggressively prowls around mountains, glens, and forests, casting its eye hither and yon in search of something grazing among the trees. When it espies something suitable for food, and then gets close, it makes its attack with a fearsome and awful roar. If, on the other hand, it brings something as food to the cubs, and gets close to its *den*, (421) they leap up and with a cry seize it and tear it apart. Why, then, blame God for delivering his threat before the onset of disaster? Why also

5. Sir 13.15–16.
6. Mt 10.40, 15; 2 Cor 5.20.

grind your teeth at the prophets for protesting at your impiety? I am like a *lion*, he says, that normally cries out before catching its *prey* as if to give warning in advance of its attack, while the prophets are like *cubs* in imitating my behavior, protesting at those given to impious behavior, as I said. Just as with animals in the mountains, however, the savage creature's warning is not without benefit in that it prompts them to flee before perhaps being taken, so, too, with sinners the threat and prediction before the disaster is most helpful, moving them to repentance and avoidance of their exploits. God therefore compares himself to a lion that does not attack and inflict on some people the effects of wrath before threatening in advance, his purpose being for them to repent and be saved by taking the prediction of the future before the onset of disaster as a saving remedy.

Will a bird fall to the ground if there is no hunter? Will a trap be sprung if there is nothing to catch? (v.5) In this case, too, the verse is presented figuratively on the basis of similarity. Hunters, you see, pull down some of the sparrows skillfully nesting in bushes, and some of them then strike the one caught in the *trap*. In this case the verse probably refers by sparrows (422) to people given to conceit, with arrogant and self-important ideas, who cannot bear to accommodate themselves to the lowly; they are lovers of earthly things caught in *snares*, seeking only what is fleshly and opulent. God this time compares himself to a *hunter* and a *snare*, bringing down to earth the haughty, and striking, as it were, and catching for punishment those whose minds are fixed solely on the earth. Now, the people of Israel were arrogant, despising God, rejecting prophets, and showing no respect for the Law. They were no less greedy for things of this world, interested only in earthly concerns, for which they were the victim of improper desires, not attending to the word of God, but offering opposition to those who called them to virtue; to the holy prophets they said, "Instead, tell us and announce to us something else that is deceitful."[7] If I am the one, he says, therefore, who, in the manner of a *hunter*, brings down the haughty, and, like someone in the role of a *snare*, is accustomed to strike the

---

7. Is 30.10.

one who like a fox or a mouse is greedy for the things of this world, why do you persecute to no purpose the holy ones for transmitting only my words to you, when I am discharging the effects of wrath directed at the impious?

Will a trumpet sound in a city if there are no people to be alarmed? Is there evil in a city if the Lord is not responsible for it? (v.6) While I inflict the effects of wrath, he is saying, the prophets also are helpful mediators only of my words, (423) transmitting to you whatever I command them through the Spirit. But you perhaps ignore or severely resent receiving only the words that sometimes come from them. What on earth, tell me, do you gain by this? What fear grips you? Or what change for the better do you experience? After all, if *a trumpet sounds in a city* announcing the outbreak of war waged by the foe, who would be so unresponsive as in no way to be struck by fear of the approaching troubles? Now, my *trumpets* are not remiss in giving prior warning of the future. But instead of gaining any benefit, on learning that you are to be wasted by the foe, you are so diverted at the extent of the threats as even perhaps to ridicule the prediction as something idle and to raise that well-worn and hackneyed cry of the foolish, "The vision that he sees is for many years ahead, and his prophecy is for distant times."[8] So why do you treat as a nuisance the trumpeters, as it were, if you treat the words as worthless? Perhaps your reply is that the outcome of the events distresses you considerably. Surely, then, *there is no evil in a city if the Lord is not responsible for it?* It would be like saying, Surely there is no human being capable of causing trouble to a city by disease, siege, spoiling crops, or anything of the sort?

Now, if no human being would do such things, and it depends rather on the decision and power of God, why shoot the messenger? Actually, there is an obligation to repent, and by efforts in that direction to appease the one who is offended and is able to bring trouble on the (424) guilty. By *evil* in the text that is caused by God in cities, therefore, we shall understand not depravity—perish the thought!—but rather harassment, or any wrathful response that he would make to sinners with the inten-

8. Ezek 12.27.

tion of converting them to what is more seemly. Scripture says, after all, "Keep their jaws under muzzle and tight rein if they do not come near you." Since he is kind, remember, and "wants everyone to be saved and come to the knowledge of truth,"[9] in a way he exercises pressure towards the better through the effects of wrath, and sometimes forcefully changes by means of terrors and threats those who are not persuaded by words and the guidance of what is for their good.

For the Lord God will do nothing without revealing his correction through his servants the prophets. A lion will roar, and who will not be afraid? The Lord God has spoken, and who will not prophesy? (vv.7–8) Do not the prophets, he asks, inflict the effects of wrath? How so? While they, too, are human in nature like you, they have been given the privilege by God of knowing whatever he wants to carry out, inflicting on cities and countries either good things or what is calculated to distress. Perhaps your response to this would be, Let them learn if that is decided, let them receive the gift from you of knowledge of the future, let all mysteries be revealed to them, but let them say nothing to anybody nor drum any of it into the ears of those who rebuff them.

What is God's response to this, then? (425) *A lion will roar, and who will not be afraid?* In other words, he is saying, if by the roaring of the lion, the strongest of wild beasts, a person would not be so unfeeling and insolent as not to feel the impact of terror, how could it be that when God speaks in his great might and bids them proclaim what they have been told, they would not be in fear of the bidder? Unlike us, you see, they are not contemptuous and perverse, setting at naught the will of the Lord of all. Accordingly, he protects the holy ones, and defends the prophets against the harm coming from those bent on abusing them. Now, this was nothing else than the gift of appropriate care; how would removal of physicians from our midst be anything other than depriving the infirm of assistance? He foretells as much also in the statement of the blessed David, "Lay no

9. Ps 32.9; 1 Tm 2.4. Chrysostom in his homily on Is 45.6–7 cited Am 3.6 as a text that people commonly cited to justify moral irresponsibility. Theodoret, too, saw the paradox involved, and to offset the improper application of the verse, like Cyril he took *kakia*, "evil," in the sense of *kaka*, "troubles" (Cyril's *kakôsis*, justified "harassment").

hand on my anointed, nor abuse my prophets," and to them he says somewhere, "The one touching you is like the one touching the apple of his eye."[10] In other words, the person who gnashes his teeth at the heads of the saints, assails them sacrilegiously, and does not even desist from maltreating them, does considerable harm to their own soul.

Proclaim to districts in Assyria and to the districts of Egypt, and say, Gather on Mount Samaria, and see many wonders in its midst and oppression (426) *in it. It did not know what would happen in its sight, says the Lord; those storing up iniquity and hardship in their districts [did not know]. Hence the Lord God says this: Tyre and your land round about will be devastated; it will rob you of your strength, and your districts will be plundered* (vv.9–11). He threatens once more to inflict on them what would be the likely suffering and fate of those who had reached such a degree of depravity as even to upbraid God, to censure prophets, and to ignore completely the oracles given through Moses. Now, it should be realized that in this passage as well there are different readings in the Hebrew and the text of the Seventy: the Hebrew reads, "Proclaim to districts in Ashdod and to the districts of Egypt," while the Seventy reads, *Proclaim to districts in Assyria and to the districts of Egypt.* Ashdod is a close neighbor of the country of the Jews, whereas the district of the Assyrians—that is, the Persians and Medes—is situated at their eastern border, as it were. Our view, then, is that there is no difficulty in the reference being to either Ashdod or Assyria; the text of the divinely inspired Scripture will be true in both cases, as we shall demonstrate in clarifying the contents of the passage.[11]

What is suggested recalls the facts in the second book of Kings and in the second book of Chronicles; I shall give a very brief précis to avoid the impression of being verbose.[12] There

---

10. Ps 105.15; Zec 2.8.

11. While Cyril owes to Jerome the detection of the discrepancy, and the latter admits he can see no reason for the departure by the LXX, Cyril is again committed to upholding its validity. It is also typical of him to sanction indiscriminate use of Assyrians, Persians, and Medes.

12. Cyril is sensitive to charges of *makrēgorein*, but launches into extensive documentation (appearing this time also in the PG ed.) that seems attributable only to his desire to uphold the version of the LXX referring to Assyria and to Tyre (instead of the Heb. "adversary").

came to the throne in Jerusalem at a certain time Manasseh, who was son of Hezekiah but utterly different in his ways from (427) his father's piety; he was an evil man, very disposed to any form of wrongdoing, profane and idolatrous, and deeply devoted to the deceits of the demons. He erected altars and shrines to Baal, worshiped all the host of heaven, made his children pass through fire, and organized soothsayers and those interested in false prophecy, who thought they had vital knowledge but in fact knew nothing, speaking rather from their own hearts. There was perhaps no form of extreme depravity that was not followed at his whim. During his reign God said somewhere through the prophets about Jerusalem and all the country of the Jews, "Lo, I am bringing such troubles on this people that the ears of everyone hearing of them will ring." When Manasseh died, his son Amon succeeded to the throne, who fell in no way short of his father's depravity, cultivating all that his father had; but he lived only two years.[13]

Then after him, however, his son Josiah was anointed king, a wise and shrewd man, and particularly godly. The man of God on coming to Bethel gave advance notice of him when Jeroboam was standing at the altar and inaugurating the festival of the heifers; he said, "O altar, altar, thus says the Lord: Lo, a son is born to the house of David, Josiah by name, and he will sacrifice on you the priests of the high places sacrificing on you, and he will burn people's bones on you." On becoming king, in fact, Josiah destroyed the shrines of the idols, overturned (428) the altars, demolished the groves, burnt the chariot of the sun, slaughtered the priests of the high places in Bethel, incinerated people's bones on the altar of the heifers, drove out the seers—false prophets, I mean, visionaries and ventriloquists—and gave orders for the oracles of the wise Moses to be observed and in force in Israel; in his time they sacrificed the lamb and celebrated Passover in Jerusalem.[14]

Now, since he was a good man and sincere in his dealings with God, he sent to the prophetess Hulda in his desire to find out if the Lord of all would desist from his wrath, if Israel would

---

13. 2 Kgs 21.1–6, 19–20; Jer 19.3.
14. 2 Kgs 22.2; 1 Kgs 13.1–2; 2 Kgs 23.

enjoy a high level of prosperity, and if what had been prophesied against it through the prophets would now not apply. She replied to them, however, "Thus says the Lord, the God of Israel: Tell the man who sent you to me, Thus says the Lord: Lo, I am sending troubles on this place and on its inhabitants—all the words of the book that the king of Judah has read. Because they have abandoned me and sacrificed to other gods, so that they have provoked me to anger with the works of their hands, my wrath will be enkindled in this place and not be quenched. But as to the king of Judah who sent you to inquire of the Lord, you shall say to him, Thus says the Lord, the God of Israel: Regarding my words that you have heard, because your heart was penitent and you humbled yourself before the Lord when you heard what I said against this place and against its inhabitants, that they should become a desolation and a curse, and because you have torn your garments and wept before me, I also have heard you, says the Lord. It will not be like this; lo, I shall gather you to your ancestors, (429) and you will be gathered to your grave in peace; your eyes will not see all the troubles that I am inflicting on this place and on its inhabitants."[15]

The promise was fulfilled: the Lord of all postponed his wrath in the period of his kingship, which lasted thirty-one years. At the end of this period, however, Pharaoh Neco, leader of the Egyptians, campaigned against the Babylonians, and left his own country with all his forces. Since Josiah suspected that he was coming to devastate Judea, he equipped himself for war and was bent on opposing him. The other bade him to withdraw, claiming he was heading for the river Euphrates and proceeding against the land of the Assyrians. When his ensuing opposition proved fruitless, he was struck down in battle; at his death he was brought home to Jerusalem by his own people. His son Jehoahaz was anointed king; he had lasted only three months when Pharaoh Neco removed him from the throne, bound him, and had him kept in Egypt. At the cost of a heavy tribute he finally allowed Eliakim, or Jehoiakim, who was also Josiah's son, to reign in Jerusalem. He brought such pressure to bear on Israel (by which I mean both those in Samaria and those in

15. 2 Kgs 22.15–20.

Jerusalem) that they imposed tribute on everyone throughout the land and exacted taxes from everyone.[16]

In this situation, when Jehoiakim was conducting his reign, Nebuchadnezzar attacked, gaining such power over Jerusalem (430) as to take Jehoiakim captive, force him to pay tribute, and, in short, devastate the whole city. Far from confining to this the disaster visited upon the perpetrators of sacrilegious deeds, God proceeded to add some further and more onerous burden; bands of brigands from all the neighboring lands and countries—namely, Syria, Tyre, Ashdod, Idumea, and Moab— invaded the land of the Jews, place by place, and ravaged it. The description is as follows in Chronicles: "At that time the land began to pay tribute to Pharaoh, each one being obliged by the king of the land to pay silver and gold according to his ability to Pharaoh Neco. Jehoiakim was twenty-five when he began to reign, and he reigned eleven years in Jerusalem; his mother's name was Zebidah daughter of Pedaiah of Rumah. He did what was evil in the sight of the Lord as his fathers had done in every-thing. It was in his time that Nebuchadnezzar king of Babylon came to the land, and he was enslaved to him for three years, when he rebelled against him. The Lord sent against him the Chaldeans, robber bands of Syrians, robber bands of Moabites, and people of Ammon and Samaria."[17] This fate completely be-fell Israel for its insolence against the glory of God and its sac-rilegious corruption in the direction of choosing to adore "the works of their hands," as Scripture says.[18] (431)

Now that the facts have been sufficiently exposed to you, therefore, come now, let us touch lightly on the verse and say what has to be said. *Proclaim to districts in Assyria and to districts in Egypt, and say, Gather on Mount Samaria, and see many wonders in its midst and oppression in it,* as if to say, Let someone quickly tell the Egyptians and Assyrians when people in force are in-vading the *mountains of Samaria,* or the land itself, which they say is mountainous. Now, when they come, they will *see many*

16. 2 Kgs 23.29–35. Cyril continues to be unclear about the fall of the north-ern kingdom and deportation of its people a century before.

17. A conflation of 2 Chr 36.4–6 and 2 Kgs 23.36–24.2.

18. Jer 1.16.

wonders in its midst and unexpected *oppression*; the former victors will be pitiable and enslaved, he is saying, looking askance at all the nations, so to speak, and will be desperate and in abject submission to the enemy, suffering such awful oppression as to consider it a boon to survive, live in slavery, and pay tribute to the conquerors. But Samaria *did not know what would happen in its sight,* that is, what would befall it. Next, where now are *those storing up iniquity and hardship in their districts?* In other words, what use is greed and their accumulation of sins through their lack of desire to know what is due to God? Surely, then, the fate awaiting the offenders will not be deferred until the attack of the Assyrians and Egyptians? *Hence the Lord God says this: Tyre and your land round about will be devastated; it will rob you of your strength, and your districts will be plundered.* Now, you should take the phrase *Tyre and* [land] *round about* this way: the countryside of Tyre and your environs will be devastated (432) when the rampaging robber bands invade it, as I said. Then it is, in fact, that *they will rob you of your strength;* that is, all your might will be crushed as if sapped and exhausted.

If by chance the Hebrew text should read, "Tell the country in Ashdod," and if the Septuagint has *in Assyria,* the meaning in both cases is true; it was not only the Assyrians that pillaged, but also people advancing in numbers from Syria and Ashdod to do harm to Israel in the manner of brigands.[19]

The Lord says this: In the way a shepherd pulls from the mouth of the lion two legs or an ear lobe, so will the children of Israel be rescued who live in Samaria opposite a tribe and in Damascus (v.12). Be ever on the alert, and you will be full of admiration for the close observation of the prophecy. I mean, since Israel did not completely perish, a "remnant" surviving, as Isaiah says,[20] in case truth should be proven false, he contributes to the prophecies of calamities a merciful act of clemency. So he is saying, just as a lion is sated after savaging a straggler, with barely a couple of remnants left, perhaps *two legs or* part of *an ear,* and in tears the herdsmen collect them, so will it be for the *children of Israel in Sa-*

---

19. Theodoret will avoid this massive excursus aimed at justifying a patent misreading by the LXX.

20. Is 10.22.

maria who live opposite a tribe, that is, those ever hostile (433) in attitude and opposed to the tribe of Judah. The inhabitants of Samaria, in fact, were taken by force, ravaged by foes, and with war consuming everyone, as it were, only very few were saved. The survivors remained in the country, or in another sense they were *pulled from the mouth of the lion*; they were deported to Assyria, and though eventually released from captivity, very few of those deported survived. Now, the fact that the Assyrian Tiglathpileser once took Damascus and deported it to his own country is quite clear, in my view; in the second book of Kings he was called on by Uzziah king of Judah to lend assistance when Pekah son of Remaliah and also Rezin king of Syria were waging war on him. On his arrival he killed Rezin and took Damascus itself.[21]

If, on the other hand, you prefer to apply the sense of the verse to all human beings, you would not miss its thrust; you would be right in thinking that Satan seized and wasted people on earth like an animal that is taken. But "the good shepherd who lays down his life for the sheep" came on the scene and cried aloud; he *pulled* us free when we were survivors among living beings and as good as dead. As the blessed psalmist says, in fact, "The Lord smashed the lions' teeth," (434) and as Paul says, "He died and lived again, so that he might be Lord of both the dead and the living."[22]

O priests, hear and testify to the house of Israel, says the Lord God almighty, that on the day when I shall take vengeance on Israel for its impiety and take vengeance on the altars of Bethel, the horns of the altar will be overturned and fall to the ground. I shall smash and strike the winged house on the summer house; the ivory houses will perish, and many other houses will be done away with, says the Lord (vv.13–15). Once again he returns to giving a clear account of the fate of the impious, clarifying the same message as he often does for the benefit of the listeners. In his realization that such a procedure is not without use, in my view, the divinely inspired Paul also says in writing to certain people, "To write the same things

---

21. 2 Kgs 16.5–9, Ahaz (not Uzziah) the king of Judah at the time. Cyril outdoes the Antiochenes in giving the verse a precise historical referent.

22. Jn 10.11; Ps 58.6; Rom 14.9.

to you is not troublesome to me, and for you it is a safeguard."[23] By raising his own voice, therefore, he bids the sacred ministers, as it were, to adjure Israel to foretell clearly all of the things due to befall them.

And who are we to understand or claim to be the ones bidden to utter a piercing cry—the priests of the heifers, or those of the idols in another shrine? This is unconvincing, however, in my view: they were not the ones to protest the deception that they and the others had committed. So who were the *priests* bidden at that time to do so? Those of the bloodline of Levi; not all (435) had been involved with the people deceived in Samaria, or brought themselves to serve the idols; instead, they consequently abandoned the religion of the Samaritans and returned to Jerusalem. There is reference to them in the second book of Chronicles; while the account deals with Jeroboam,[24] therefore, it then describes the power attaching to him: "He held Judah and Benjamin. The Levites and the priests who were in all Israel presented themselves to him from all the territories. The Levites had left the dwellings on their holdings, and had come to Judah and Jerusalem, because Jeroboam and his sons had expelled them from service of the Lord. He appointed his own priests for the high places, the idols, futile objects, and heifers made by Jeroboam. He expelled those from the tribes of Israel who had set their hearts on seeking the Lord the God of Israel, and they came to Jerusalem to sacrifice to the Lord the God of their ancestors. They strengthened the kingdom of Judah."

Since those referred to in the passage were in fact very badly treated, driven out from kindred, property, and even priestly service when Jeroboam expelled them, consequently it is they whom he bids proclaim the sacking of their idols and Samaria's, to console them, as it were, and to inform them that by choos-

23. Phil 3.1.
24. The following verses, 2 Chr 11.12–17, begin in fact with reference to Rehoboam. The mention of "priests" in v.13 of the Amos text rightly poses a question for Cyril; it has evidently occurred as a result of a transliteration, at the end of v.12, of the unusual Heb. word for "couch," *heres*, as *hieres*, which was then copied as *hiereis*. Perhaps as a result of his commitment to upholding the LXX text, Cyril has ignored Jerome's clear recognition of the faulty reading, and so launches into another of his lengthy textual citations.

ing God's way of thinking and by loving the Lord of all, they would not perish along with the others, but would escape the divine wrath. In other words, he is saying, when I assault (436) the people of Israel for their sins, then *I shall take vengeance on the altars of Bethel; the horns of the altar will be overturned and fall to the ground.* Surely, then, the sacking of Samaria will not extend to them, or be confined only to destroying the shrines by those ordered to ravage them and overturn altars? Not at all: *I shall smash and strike the winged house on the summer house.* What that means is something like this: the people of Samaria were very fond of luxury and very affluent, making summer and winter houses for themselves. The winter house they called *winged*, as if to imply that they were surrounded on all sides by wings or walls so as to be inaccessible to the onset of winter, as it were, whereas the *summer* one was flimsy and exposed to the wind currents. He therefore says, *I shall smash* the altars overturned and at the same time *strike the* winter and *summer* houses. And *the ivory houses will perish*; we recall that when Ahab was king, he made that kind of house in Samaria.[25] *Many other houses will be done away with*, the text says, that is, those belonging to inferior and less prominent people, or the vulgar masses. At any rate, the whole of Samaria at that time perished as one, with every house collapsing.

What, then, shall we once more learn from this if we opt for sound thinking? That for people of worldly splendor there will be no benefit from wealth, importance, or anything else that contributes to luxury if the love of God is lacking and if righteousness is in no way respected by them. Scripture says, remember, "Treasures will not benefit the lawless, (437) whereas righteousness rescues from death."[26] It would therefore be better to have a deep love for righteousness, store up treasure in heaven, desire what is on high, and come to rely on hope in God. Things of this world, in fact, are insignificant and temporary, and are no stable guarantee of security, whereas those latter things abide forever without perishing, and are equal in permanence to the unending ages.

25. 1 Kgs 22.39, to which Jerome has referred Cyril, as he had also suggested the meaning of "winged" houses.
26. Prv 10.2.

COMMENTARY ON AMOS,
CHAPTER FOUR

Listen to this word, cows of Bashan, who are on Mount Samaria, oppressing the poor, trampling on the needy, saying to their masters, Give us something to drink. The Lord swears by his holy ones that, lo, days are coming upon you, and they will take you with weapons, and burning pestilences will cast those with you into heated kettles. You will be led out naked, husbands and wives in the sight of each other, and you will be cast out to Mount Harmon, says the Lord (vv.1–3).

 HE PEOPLE OF SAMARIA WERE conspicuous for extreme arrogance and luxury, surpassing all others for the abundance of their wealth; as I said, they built themselves fine and lavish houses suited to the seasons—I mean winter and summer—which the oracle announced in advance would completely and utterly perish. (438) It is therefore to these people who owned their own houses and were devoted to spoiling themselves with fading luxury he refers as *cows of Bashan.* Now, the country of Bashan was wooded and leafy, very suited to being able to provide abundant fodder to whatever grazed there. God therefore compares to *cows of Bashan* prosperous and well-nourished people concerned for fine living. He accuses them of *oppressing the poor* and, as it were, with their own feet trampling on *the needy;* as Scripture says, "The poor are feeding grounds for the rich." He proceeds to say, *They say to their masters, Give us something to drink,* showing that they are lacking in submission and unwilling to yield to those in charge of them in respect of royal power; instead, in extreme arrogance they then allot the role of servant to their own masters, since the presumption of saying to one's superiors and overlords *Give us something to drink* is a mark rather of those anxious "to be served" than "to serve."[1]

1. Sir 13.19; Mk 10.45.

What, then, will happen to those who have now reached such a degree of folly? *The Lord swears by his holy ones*, it says (or by what is sanctified, or the mysteries, meaning himself, since he has nothing greater to swear by), that times and *days* will come when, despite your luxurious living and habits of riotous behavior, the fear of suffering will cause you to be involved in the hardships of war and to take up arms. Nevertheless, despite your being armed this way, *they will take you*, he says, along with wives, loved ones, and retinue, who were always in your company flattering you with incessant compliments and calling you (439) thrice-blessed, since tribes of flatterers always acclaim those who feed them. Nevertheless, whereas they will be *burning*, for they are *pestilences* and in receipt of nothing more, admiring the vile and sinful, you by contrast will be stripped of importance, removed from all enjoyment, deprived of that former prosperity, now deported as slaves and captives, and *cast out to Mount Harmon*. It is in Armenia, situated at the extreme frontiers of the land of the Persians, the countries being neighboring and adjacent.[2]

Accordingly, it is possible to see from this that the desires of the lovers of luxury will come to a bitter end, in keeping with the Savior's statement, "Blessed are those who mourn, for they will be comforted." In other words, while luxurious living will finish in tears, the end of hardship is respite, as is confirmed by someone's statement, "The fruit of good labors is renowned."[3]

It is not implausible to take *cows of Bashan* as the women in Samaria, who were given to luxury, delicacies, and cosmetics, and to titivating their bodily charms, and who oppressed the *poor and trampled on the needy*, inciting, as it were, to wrongful pleasures the weak and those in spiritual need, who lack the wealth of strength from on high and whose heart is enervated by the onset of the passions. So it is the *cows* who *say to their masters, Give us something to drink;* women are ever on the lookout for partners, and, as it were, tease with their excessive blandishments those in their clutches. (440) Even if they had them as *masters*, they would be seen to be victims of enjoyment, and they easily

2. This datum Cyril gains from Jerome.
3. Mt 5.4; Wis 3.15.

persuade them to do their bidding in every way. But you, *O cows*, he says, *they will take you with weapons;* that is to say, they will not be in the role of lovers when they flatter, beguile, and spoil you as a result of being in the grip of lust after you. Instead, cruelly, savagely, and by the norms of war they will set fire to those very lovers who lived in luxury with you; stripped of those wrongful adornments, *you will be cast out to Mount Harmon.*

You went into Bethel and committed sin, into Gilgal and extended your godless behavior (v.4). He immediately parallels the sins with the penalties, and helpfully gives a clear proof of their sacrilegious behavior in association with the accounts of the disasters, in case anyone should mock or blame God for being obliged to impose a harsh punishment on the people of Israel. Such-and-such will befall you, he says; and in response to their claiming that it will come in the meantime, he cries out, *You went into Bethel and committed sin*, the place where the profane Jeroboam set up the golden heifer; you were caught there committing dire and heinous sins. He had legislated, remember, through the wise Moses, "You shall not make gold and silver gods for yourself," and (441) "You shall worship the Lord your God, and serve him alone." But in mockery of my Law, he says, you worshiped the works of your hands; and on seeing a golden heifer made of lifeless materials, you had no objections when the originator of the deception said, "These are your gods, Israel, who led you out of the land of Egypt."[4] You committed the worst possible impiety *in Gilgal*, a city across the river Jordan, deeply involved in the apostasy. The God of all says of it, for example, "All their wickedness began in Gilgal, because it was there I hated them for their evil pursuits." Hence the author of Proverbs says, "A man's ways are under the eyes of God, and he examines all their paths";[5] while he accepts those intent on following the right way, he rejects the one who strays from the straight and narrow, and who is bent on traveling where he should not.

You offered your sacrifices in the morning, and your tithes every three days. They read out a law in public, and invoked an agreement. Proclaim that the children of Israel loved these things, says the Lord God

4. Ex 20.23; Dt 6.13–14; 1 Kgs 12.28.
5. Hos 9.15; Prv 5.21.

(vv.4–5). It is a truly dreadful and extraordinarily impious act to presume to counterfeit God's glory, which is due to him and only to him, and to apply it to the honor of the idols. Those in the habit of doing so, in fact, as far as they can manage, dislodge the divine and heavenly nature from the throne that belongs to it and only to it, and dismiss it from the sacred seat, installing on it, as it were, the unclean demons. It is these so frightening crimes, then, that we shall see Israel guilty of in its madness. The God of all, in fact, issued a decree through Moses that they had to sacrifice two lambs each day in the holy tabernacle, one *in the morning*, and the other in the afternoon, thus suggesting obscurely and in type the church's constant and unfailing fragrance—of a spiritual kind, that is. He proceeded to require as well, "Three times a year every male shall appear before me." At these three separate occasions by Law, they offered *tithes*, first-fruits of the fields, sacrifices, and thanksgiving offerings; as Scripture says, "They shall not appear before me empty-handed."[6]

What was thus duly prescribed by the wise Moses, however, they transferred to the glory of idols by offering in their shrines *sacrifices in the morning*, and bringing as well their *tithes every three days*. By *every three days* he means the three days a year when, as I said, every male had to appear before God. Far from this being the limit of the impiety of the people of Israel, however, *they read out a law in public;* that is, they showed respect for the law of foreigners, according scarcely any regard to the one from God. They made the offerings in the (443) shrines of the idols at set times, in fact, and observed as precisely as possible the customary festivals for them. Hence his saying, They applied my Law to the idols, offering them sacrifices *in the morning* and devoting to them *tithes every three days. They invoked an agreement,* by *invoked* meaning "prayed over," that is, "promised," and *agreements* meaning "votive offerings by Law," what someone would offer God voluntarily.

He next tells the priests to *proclaim* and testify *that the children of Israel loved these things,* that is, that they did not commit it only once, but even *loved* it—that is, hating God. They were obliged

6. Ex 29.39 and 23.17, 15.

to be exclusive, in fact, and, striving to proceed on one foot or the other, aroused strong disapproval from God; the Savior himself confirms this in saying, "No one can serve two masters: either he will hate one and love the other, or be devoted to one and despise the other."[7] It is an awful offense to direct to another what is meant for the glory of God, and to accord others the honor due to him; what is peculiar and special to him is not properly given to someone else—only to him alone.

I shall give you grinding of teeth in all your cities, and lack of bread in all your places, and you did not turn back to me, says the Lord. I withheld rain from you for three months before vintage; I shall send rain on one city, and no rain on another city; on one part there will be rain, and another on which there will be no rain will dry up. Two or three cities will gather at one city to drink water and will not be filled, and you did not turn back to me, says the Lord (vv.6–8). The passage once again responds to those in the habit of finding fault and, on the basis of extreme folly, of ill-advisedly disparaging the calmness inherent in God.[8] You see, some people may possibly ask, Why does he inflict on the people of Israel such an immoderate and intolerable punishment while as God he is by nature kindly? So in this he mounts a kind of defense, and then presents them as in the grip of relentless wrath. By this he brings out that he strikes sinners more mildly in the beginning, not exacting a penalty but in his natural loving-kindness converting them to himself and, as it were, bringing them by "both scourge and hardship"[9] to opt for the better. Since they were guilty of what I mentioned, and their offenses were no longer bearable, he instructed them with *grinding of teeth* and even *lack of bread*, that is, by hunger. *You did not turn back to me, says the Lord. I withheld rain from you for three months before vintage*, or, as the Hebrew put it more appropriately, for "three months before harvest," when there is particular need for watering of the crops, which is vital for (445) a good yield.[10]

---

7. Mt 6.24.

8. In place of "calmness" another manuscript speaks of God's "goodness."

9. Jer 6.7 LXX.

10. For the textual note Cyril is indebted to Jerome, who notes that if the months of May to July are indicated, rain is unlikely in those parts in any case, as he knows from personal experience.

Now, there was such shortage of water, he says, that by the judgment and verdict of God, who knows everything, there is rain *on one city* but lack of it *on another;* again, *two or three cities will gather at one city,* and even so will still thirst. *And you did not turn back to me, says the Lord.* Now, such a fate befell the people of Israel in actual fact and also in a spiritual sense; as the Savior's disciple said, "Elijah was a human being like us, and he prayed fervently that it might not rain on the earth, and it did not rain for three years and six months." Such a severe famine occurred in Samaria that the head of an ass was sold for many denarii.[11] In the time of the prophecy of Jeremiah as well, the God of all withheld rain; for example, he made the following statement about the lack of rain: "Judea mourned and her gates were empty; they were in darkness on the ground; the cry of Jerusalem arose. Their nobles sent their young ones for water; they came to the wells, found no water, and returned with their vessels empty. Working the land was fruitless because there was no rain; the farmers were ashamed; they uncovered their heads. Hinds gave birth to young in the fields and abandoned them because there was no grass. Wild asses stood in the glens, panting for air; their eyes failed because there was no hay as a result of the people's iniquity."[12]

Since the people of Israel acted with extreme impiety, therefore, God *withheld rain* and gave them *grinding of teeth and lack of bread in all its cities.* (446) As I said just now, however, we shall find them suffering the same fate in a spiritual sense:[13] while earthly bodies require food and drink, the produce of the land and water for the senses, a person's soul is nourished on divine and heavenly words. It needs the spiritual draught, a spring that brings it spiritual water that is the divinely inspired Scripture speaking of the mystery of Christ. Just as in the case of *teeth* that suffer *grinding,* however, of which only the strongest would be able to masticate and chew food, so too a human spirit that is reduced to infirmity and undergoing the ailment of torpor would

---

11. Jas 5.17; 2 Kgs 6.25. Again a statement of Cyril's bifocal hermeneutic: *historikôs* and *pneumatikôs.*

12. Jer 14.2–7.

13. "In a spiritual sense": the hermeneutical term here is *noêtôs.*

be unable to achieve spiritual knowledge or succeed in concocting anything on the basis of dull insights. Israel's heart was thus deadened, with no understanding of the mystery of Christ; consequently, they had a *lack of* spiritual *bread* and a shortage of water, since they did not have the Word that came down from heaven and gives life to the world to nourish them by irrigating souls with the grace of the Spirit, the living spring, the Son of the God and Father, the comfort of Law and Prophets. As the prophet Isaiah in fact says, "He directed the clouds not to rain on him."[14]

I struck you with mildew and blight. You multiplied your gardens, your vineyards, your fig trees, and your olive trees, which the locust consumed, yet even so you did not turn back to me, says the Lord. I sent death upon you in the way of Egypt, (447) *and I killed with the sword your young men with the capture of your horses. In my wrath I put your camps to the torch, yet even so you did not turn back to me, says the Lord* (vv.9–10). There would be no way of arousing those impervious to the effects of wrath befalling them, supine victims of such indifference as never to entertain even the idea of repentance; instead, they outdo one another in proceeding to a worse state of distress. Since correction by the lack of food and drink scarcely moved the people of Israel to reform, therefore, some worse form of suffering than that was inflicted, bodily weakness, as happens *with mildew and blight*. We shall find this stated also in Jeremiah: "Thus says the Lord: Lo, I am imposing weakness on this people, and fathers together with sons will be weak from it, their neighbor and familiar will perish."[15] Since they were guilty also of base gain, greatly attached to bribery, and consequently *multiplying gardens, vineyards, fig trees, and olive trees,* God touched as well what was a probable cause of their severe indifference toward returning to a sound mind and opting for benefit instead of harm, (448) his intention being to heap troubles on them with a view to their being saved by being struck from all sides.

Because this was of little help, however, he proceeded to apply something worse. Since you showed no respect for my hand,

14. Is 5.6.
15. Jer 6.21.

he says, in fact, classing as weak, as it were, the God who can do all things, you followed the *way* to Egypt, preferring the "flesh of horses" to care from me, giving pride of place to the "Egyptian man."[16] Then it was that your most warlike class was consumed by the sword of the Babylonians. All of your cavalry was captured when God unnerved even those with the skill to prove themselves, to whom victory in battle was not unfamiliar. You can, however, take the verse *I sent death upon you in the way of Egypt* in another fashion. When Josiah was king of Judah, Pharaoh Neco ruler of Egypt campaigned against Babylon. As he had need to pass through the land of the Jews, however, Josiah thought the trip to Babylon only an excuse and that Egypt was armed against him, and rashly opposed him; Israel was beaten.[17] So he says, *I sent death upon you in the way of Egypt,* that is, as in the Egyptians' bypassing you; then it was that *I put your camps to the torch,* meaning, I utterly overthrew your walled and fortified cities. Now, he said as much also in the beginning: "Israel went to Assyrians, and Judah made fortified cities. I shall send fire on his cities, and it will consume their foundations."[18] So he is saying, I threw down your fortified camps to their very foundations, *yet even so you did not turn back to me, says the Lord.* (449)

I overthrew you as God overthrew Sodom and Gomorrah, and you became like a brand snatched from a fire, yet even so you did not turn back to me, says the Lord (v.11). Perceiving no reform occurring in them, he is saying, I augmented the afflictions with others worse than these, and rendered my anger with them more ardent: *I overthrew you like Sodom and Gomorrah, and you did not turn back to me.* In this he was probably suggesting to us the eventual sacking that happened in the time of Jeremiah by the hand of Nebuchadnezzar, who took the whole of Judea, set fire even to Jerusalem itself and its neighboring cities and towns, pulled down the divine Temple, took captive the survivors from the fighting, and as a glorious conqueror went back home with the captives, who

16. Is 31.3.
17. 2 Kgs 23.29.
18. Hos 5.13 and 8.14. Cyril now sees The Twelve as one work—in Theodoret's phrase, "the book of The Twelve"—though initially treating Hosea as a distinct book; see FOTC 115, 27 n. 1.

finally returned to Judea at the completion of the period of seventy years. It was in fact Cyrus, as I said, who took Babylon and released the captives who were left as survivors from the people of Israel. For this reason, he says, *you became like a brand snatched from a fire*, like a burning brand left among the few remnants.

When God corrects us, therefore, it is pure malice to be unresponsive; but what will be the cause of still more oppressive troubles in the case of the indifferent is to continue on an uninterrupted course of doing and thinking what is forbidden. In other words, it is like those struck down with bodily ailments, who (450) have the skill to be able to cure them, cleanse the wounds of offensive matter by means of hot and sharp treatment, diminish the intensity of the infection lodged in them, and induce them to yield to the medical procedures. In similar fashion, too, the God who knows everything afflicts those who are unresponsive to minor prompting with still more severe correction, the onset of which someone of wisdom and sense would properly avoid before actual experience.

For this reason I shall treat you this way, Israel (v.12). Despite my doing the former, he says, proceeding to the latter, and, as it were, applying every form of affliction and hardship, I observed and learned from experience that you are unmoved. Consequently *I shall treat you this way* as well. In what way? Since initial measures did not suffice, I proceeded to an overthrow similar to the Sodomites'; this was the kind of thing, as I said, that was inflicted on them by divine wrath.

But because I shall treat you this way, prepare to call on your God, Israel (v.12). If you want, however, he says, to discover the reason why *I shall treat you this way*, you will definitely learn when you are punished and I cry out and say to you, *Prepare to call on your God, Israel.* By *prepare* he means "hasten," that is, to be enthusiastic and ardent in *calling on* no (451) foreign or false god but *your God, Israel*, that is, the one whom you know through actual experience to be God by nature and in truth, not devised by some people's artifice, like those made from sticks and stones.

Hence, lo, I am the one who establishes thunder, creates wind, and announces to people his anointed, making dawn and dark, and mounting lofty places of the earth; Lord God almighty is his name (v.13). By comparison with what is eminent, it is easy to establish what is presumed to be inferior. With the intention, therefore, of highlighting the impotence of the idols for those who believe on the basis of extreme stupidity that they are gods and deserve to be adored, the God of all makes himself very clear to us and introduces the Maker and Creator of all things, possessing authority over our situation, and a kind of governor of human affairs, superior to all height and eminence, and controller, as it were, of the whole of creation. God's nature, in fact, surpasses everything, not by local altitude but by the pre-eminence of glory, and excels by his incomparable power the measure of everything that is brought into being.

Accordingly, he says, *Call on your God, Israel,* in the knowledge of his authority and the degree of his pre-eminence. I and no other, he says, *am the one who establishes thunder,* that is, who conceals the sky in cloud, sends down rain, (452) *creates wind,* who is likewise Maker of winds. *Announces to people his anointed,* as if to say, "Through me kings reign, and through me tyrants rule the earth." Here, you see, *anointed* does not mean Emmanuel, but the one anointed as king, and likewise *wind* not the divine and holy Spirit—even if some of those bent on distorting correct doctrines are deranged—but what is part of the cosmos and in the sky, to which the Savior himself also refers: "The wind blows where it chooses, and you hear the sound of it, but you do not know where it comes from or where it goes; so it is with everyone who is born of the Spirit." He is saying, therefore, I am the one who assembles clouds and *establishes thunder,* and "draws winds from their storehouses,"[19] who gives prominence to the one whom I choose to adorn with the kingly throne. Therefore, as King of kings and Lord of lords, by nature God, I am the one who makes the *dawn,* that is, day or daylight; I am the one who makes *dark,* that is, darkness or night; I am the one *who mounts lofty places of the earth,* who is superior and above everything lifted up and elevated, with a *name* fitting and very appropriate to his glory, that of *Lord almighty.*

---

19. Prv 8.15–16; Jn 3.8; Ps 135.7. We cannot be sure whether Cyril noted Jerome's reference to the faulty version of the Heb. in "thunder" and "anointed," and still upheld the reading of the LXX.

Observe, therefore, the great clemency and loving-kindness the God of all shows us; after delivering threats, and announcing what has already occurred and what is still to be, he calls us to knowledge, guides the one who is called, and brings to understanding the one caught up in ignorance. To those who do not know the one who is by nature and in truth Lord on the basis of his ability to achieve everything and (453) rule over all, he clearly reveals himself. This is the mark of the one who brings people to their senses "by hardship and scourging,"[20] bringing them, as it were, against their will to conversion by correction, and helpfully applying the means by which they would be likely to learn a better frame of mind.

20. Jer 6.7 LXX.

COMMENTARY ON AMOS,
CHAPTER FIVE

Hear this word of the Lord that I adopt in lamentation over you: the house of Israel has fallen; it will no longer rise. The virgin of Israel has been cast down on her land; there is no one to raise her up (vv.1–2).

N LEARNING IN ADVANCE OF THE troubles befalling some people, the blessed prophets were filled with terror at the prospect and grieved bitterly for them as brethren; sometimes they delivered their reproof ardently, as if moved by love to weeping, and prompting them to alertness by prediction of all that had yet to occur. This is the process the prophet follows in this case, too, speaking as if on his own part, not, however, from his own understanding, but on the basis of divine oracles. Consequently he says, *Hear this word of the Lord that I adopt in lamentation over you*: it is the God of all who has spoken in me, and my lamentation has been composed over you for forsaking him. What in fact is the lamentable song? What the lament? What is my weeping for? The dire and unimaginable disaster: *the house of Israel has fallen*. While God was honored and loved, in fact, it stood firm, but now it has fallen (454) when he was provoked by the folly of the deceived.

Next, who is there to raise up the one fallen by divine decree? *The virgin has been cast down*; that is, she has lost her virginity. Who is she? Definitely Israel once more, or the assembly of the Jews, to whom it was said by God, "Did you not refer to me as house, father, master of your virginity?"[1] So the one who was given God as master of her virginity *has been cast down on her land*, that is, she has inexcusably lost her virginity; she lost it in one case in Egypt, but she was not in her own land, being subject to the laws of those in power, perhaps unwillingly forced

1. Jer 3.4.

to observe their ways, with ancestral piety necessarily forsaken. Now, on the contrary, there is no wantonness brought to bear; she is in her own land where she has the Law as guide, leading her to the one who is by nature and in truth God, and the way to every good pursuit is completely unfettered, free, and blameless. What form of excuse would be available to her in this case, then? In fact, she was unfaithful without being forced. How so? She acted voluntarily. Consequently, she *has been cast down; there is no one to raise her up.*

Let it therefore be clearly said by us as well to God, who is able to do all things, "You are fearsome: who will resist you in your wrath?"[2] The mass of the Jews has fallen in another way as well, driven to ruin through their frenzy against Christ, and now left with no one to help them, awaiting only the further grace of the compassionate one—I mean Christ. (455) Even they, in fact, will be called to knowledge through faith in the last days of this age.

Thus says the Lord: The city whence a thousand issued forth, a hundred will be left, and whence a hundred issued forth, ten will be left in the house of Israel (v.3). In this he makes very clear the way it will fall: the cities will remain depopulated when war consumes those in them, and their wretchedness reaches such a degree that scarcely a tenth part remains in them. You see, since they provoked God by offering to the unclean demons tithes every three days, scarcely a tenth part of them would be left, as if God were taking compensation for the sin and exacting a penalty commensurate with their impious behavior. It is therefore surely a fearsome thing to be corrected by anger; consequently, the prophet also implores God in the words, "Correct us, O Lord, but with justice, and not in anger, lest you reduce us to a few."[3]

Hence the Lord says this to the house of Israel: Seek me out, and you will live. Do not seek out Bethel, do not go off to Gilgal, and do not go up to the well of the oath, because Gilgal will surely be captured, and Bethel will be nonexistent. Seek the Lord and live, (456) *lest the house of Joseph light up like fire, and it will devour it, and there will be no one*

2. Ps 76.7.
3. 4.4; Jer 10.24.

to extinguish it for the house of Israel (vv.4–6). Once again he does
not allow the sinners to get caught up in despair, despite being involved in dire and intolerable sins. He also conveys God's
promises so as to land them as a catch for repentance. He also
presented him here as necessarily promising to forgive their sins
and free them from both the penalty and the terrors associated
with it. The Creator, after all, is kind, "long-suffering and rich
in mercy, and repenting of the troubles," as it is written, and as
he himself says in Ezekiel, "He does not wish the death of the
dying so much as to convert him from his wicked path and have
him live."[4] If, therefore, you set great store by being alive, which
seems desirable for you to be, desist from deception, abandon
such longstanding ignorance, and *seek me out*, he is saying—that
is, serve me, the one who is by nature God, the Life-giver, the
one able to save, rescuing from every trouble those who reverence me. It is necessary, however, he says, to cleanse yourselves
in advance, removing the stain of apostasy from your soul, utterly canceling the stain of being deceived, and then cleaving to
God in his goodness.

Now, what those needed to do who opted for repentance he
makes clear in the words, *Do not seek out Bethel, do not go off to
Gilgal, and do not go up to the well of the oath.* By *the well of the oath*
(457) he means Gerar, a city of the Philistines, or Palestinians;
when Abraham and Abimelech swore an oath to one another,
and made a covenant of peace at the well, the city then changed
its name to *well of the oath.*[5] *Gilgal* and *Bethel*, then, and also Gerar
were cities much involved in the distortion of impiety, transmitting the manifold error to those deceived. He consequently ordered them to desert them, combining his words with a threat
so as to force them in every way towards their own good; Bethel
and the others will disappear, he says, one falling as a captive to
the enemy, the other being incinerated so as to give the impression of being *nonexistent.* Let God therefore be sought, so that

4. Jl 2.13; Ezek 18.23 (where other mss read "death of the sinner").
5. Cyril is directed by Jerome to the pact between Abraham and Abimelech
in Gn 21.22–32, where the etiology of Beer-sheba is being investigated, a name
which could refer to a well "of the oath" or "of seven (sheep for sacrifice)," some
miles from Gerar. Only partially following his mentor, Cyril picks up a reference
to Gerar (which he then gratuitously declares apostate), but not Beer-sheba.

you may live, before *the house of Joseph lights up, and it will devour it, and there will be no one to extinguish.* By *light up* he means "catch fire," therefore, and by *house of Joseph* he refers to Ephraim, or the people in Samaria, Ephraim and Manasseh being sons of Joseph. So just as when he calls them Israel, we understand that they are called after their father, so if he says *Joseph*, you will understand it similarly.

Repentance, therefore, is a fine thing, eliminating retribution as it does, anticipating the effects of wrath, placing its practitioners beyond the Lord's chastisement, and freeing us from all misfortune.[6]

It is the Lord who exercises judgment on high and placed righteousness on earth, (458) *the one who made everything and transforms it, who turns the shadow into morning and darkens day into night, who calls forth the water of the sea and pours it on the face of the earth; Lord God almighty is his name, who separates injury from strength, and brings hardship upon a stronghold* (vv.7–9). The passage introduces us to mysteries, and is particularly suited to those called to knowledge of God and enthusiastic for the entrance of the light of truth. It is the prophet's task, in fact, to inform the deceived, first, that power belongs to the God of all, that everything is guided by his decisions, that the most blessed company of angels submits to the law of righteousness, and that without any doubt people living on earth are subsequently and of necessity subject to the norms of the righteousness stemming from him. After all, if it is better for them to serve God, and that holy company submits itself in fear to the directions given on high, how or in what way could it be that something that is inferior in nature and splendor—I mean the human being, that comes from dust and returns to dust—could without rebuke kick against the goad?

Accordingly he says, *It is the Lord who exercises judgment on high,* as if to say, the one who by his decrees on high and below imposes the ways of righteousness suited to them, by *judgment* meaning righteousness. He also imposed *righteousness on earth*; that is, he determined norms also for those on earth by which they should

6. The moral comment after the lengthy process of "clarification" is brief and perfunctory.

live if by reason proper existence and life for them are imposed, as well as a share in clemency and loving-kindness from him. Now, the fact that as God he is *almighty* and all-powerful, that nothing at all is beyond him, (459) that the very nature of the elements yields to him, and that what exists responds to his will, he brings out by taking as an example his *turning the shadow into morning and darkening day into night*, and in addition to this the fact that with ineffable power he also calls water from the sea to high and low, and releases a sweet liquid to those on earth when it has changed to what is beyond nature by the wishes of the one in charge. He says *the shadow*—that is, night—*is turned into morning*, or darkness into day. Just as blessed Moses writes, remember, "In the beginning darkness was over the abyss," that is, *shadow*, but "God spoke, and there was light,"[7] so we say *the shadow*, that is, darkness, was changed *into morning*, that is, day; and in turn night takes over when day is finished, the meaning of *darkening day into night*. For this reason, in fact, and rightly so, he says the *name* befitting him is *Lord God almighty*.

The prophet does a service to those who are deceived, therefore, by presenting the one who is by nature and in truth God not as lifeless matter, or of equal status with golden heifers, or like any of the gods devised by human ingenuity, but as King and Lawgiver even of the spirits on high, and likewise of those on earth, Lord also of the elements, who brings the nature of what exists to accord with his will. For this reason, in fact, and rightly so, he says the name befitting him is *Lord God almighty*. Now, since this is what he is by nature and in truth, *he separates injury from strength, and brings hardship upon a stronghold*; he lays hold of the conceited, (460) and apportions injury to those who resist his yoke. Even if some in their stupidity perhaps think they are high and mighty, *he brings hardship upon* such people. This was part of his clever insinuation that if they should choose to be slothful, to persist in the crime of arrogance, and to entertain a high opinion of themselves, they would encounter extreme hardship under the holy impact of the hand that controls all things. Scripture says, remember, "The Lord resists the ar-

---

7. Gn 1.2–3.

rogant," and takes as his enemy the haughty, disobedient, and unresponsive, his gaze being "on the lowly and tranquil person who trembles at his words,"[8] which is a fine example, truly worthy of imitation by those choosing to live an excellent life.

They hated the one reproving at the gates, and loathed a holy word (v.10). Once again the verse observes due sequence; since the divinely inspired prophet had referred to God as *almighty* and all-powerful, and proceeded to say "he separates injury from strength, and brings hardship upon a stronghold" (v.9), consequently and now of necessity to prevent anyone from forming the idle opinion that he inflicts his wrath on those whose offenses are slight, he lists the crimes and focuses on the reasons why he apportions to some people *injury* and *hardship.* He says, in fact, that *they hated* people of sobriety, set at naught those delivering *reproof* and in the habit of directing people to what pleases God, and considered *loathsome* every *holy word*, that is, the word inviting and urging people to holiness and sanctification. By *at the gates* you will understand a manner that is open, forthright, and confident, thus seeming to refer to their derangement and hostility toward Prophets and Law.[9] (461) You see, the prophets used to deliver *reproof*, openly accosting them; and the Law was a *holy word* that said that God is a governor of righteousness, a guide to piety and a revealer of the one who is by nature and in truth God. Hence blessed Paul also spoke of the commandment given through Moses as "holy, righteous, and good." It is therefore the worst of ailments, and a kind of root and source of the passions in the soul, to resist advice, *hate reproof,* and give the impression of not even acknowledging God's Law. The person reduced to such a degree of depravity, therefore, will definitely be like a ship without a pilot, having no captain, tossed about by every breeze, borne hither and yon indiscriminately like a drunkard, and thus seeming to be at the mercy of the waves. David in his wisdom declares to us, on the contrary, his blessing

8. Prv 3.34; Is 66.2.

9. Perhaps because Jerome does not suggest it, Cyril ignores Theodore's judgment here that reference is being made to the practice of holding meetings at the city gates as recorded in Ru 4 and Dt 25.7 (though Theodore prefers to cite the Psalms).

of that righteous person in the words, "The Law of his God is in his heart, and his footsteps will not falter,"[10] since the Law gives directions to pleasing God.

Hence in return for your buffeting the heads of the poor, and taking from them chosen gifts, you built houses of polished stone and will not dwell in them; you planted desirable vineyards and will not drink their wine (v.11). There is absolutely no doubt that abstaining from good things gives rise to depravity, and turning from what is useful and naturally beneficial to what is not so (462) necessarily causes us to stumble; just as when light is excluded, darkness immediately ensues, so relinquishing virtue brings the consequent onset of depravity. Accordingly, since *they hated the one reproving at the gates, and loathed a holy word,* they were drawn into sin of many kinds, turning to avarice and practicing the oppression that is particularly hateful to God, striking "the lowly with fists"[11] and *buffeting the heads of the poor,* though affluent and surpassing other people in reputation and wealth; specifically, they solicited gifts, taking from them against their will their more precious possessions.

He further shows to our benefit that, for people in the habit of doing such things and being partial to base gain, this foolish avarice ends in grief and finally brings an accounting; if they will not enjoy houses erected in haste and ambition, if their work in the fields is in vain, and their possession of what they love has an unexpected outcome on account of their avarice and their love of money, how would their grasping habits not seem to some people vain and idle? It is therefore wise to take the view that the author of Proverbs expresses: "Better to have slim possessions with righteousness than a large income with injustice." Paul also refers to avarice as idolatry, and rightly so; it is a godless vice, and people who trample on love for their brethren, which is the fulfillment of the Law, are on a par with those who do not know the one who is God by nature. Now, not to know the Law is to deny the Lawgiver. (463) Christ himself makes us more restrained and superior to the wrongful love of

10. Rom 7.12; Ps 37.31.
11. Is 58.4.

possessions when he says, "What good will it be for a person to gain the whole world and suffer the loss of his soul? Or what will a person give in exchange for his soul?" "Treasure will be of no good to the lawless," Scripture says, "whereas righteousness will rescue from death."[12]

Because I know your many acts of impiety, and your sins are grave, trampling on justice, taking bribes, and pushing aside the needy at the gates. For this reason the sensible person will keep silent at that time because the time is evil (vv.12–13). He tries to teach us that, far from avenging the minor or accidental faults of offenders, God instead is long-suffering in the case of moderate lapses and only inflicts the impulse of his wrath on unrestrained tendencies to depravity. He says, note, that the people of Samaria will be deprived of their homes and also their vineyards and, in my view, of everything conducive to gladness and satisfaction. Their sins had therefore proved to be serious, grave, and no longer supportable; they oppressed the righteous, or any man at all, their eyes only on godlessness, and placed no importance on upright and righteous verdicts, which is a form of oppression and avarice without respect for the intentions of the Law. In fact, they took *bribes*—that is, payments and gifts for unjust judgments; and, in addition to this, *pushed aside the needy at the gates.* What does that mean? (464) He means either that they repelled those in favor of moderation and forthrightly recommending it, or that they presumed to twist verdicts against the needy quite openly. In what way? Without even disguising their impiety, but, as it were, *at the gates,* that is, blatantly and in the sight of many people, evincing no shame at all nor showing any respect for the divine Law. They had in fact descended to such a degree of depravity and wickedness as to make even the wise and those capable of understanding the scheme of things think better of reproving any further or correcting those who had opted for impious behavior, probably because the reproved were like people without ears, barked like dogs at those intending to reform them, and cast in the role of enemies those introducing them to better ways. In fact, they upbraided the holy prophets and

12. Prv 16.8; Col 3.5; Rom 13.10; Mt 16.26; Prv 10.2.

caused them to suffer trials, sometimes when they were exposing them and conveying to them messages from on high. When
on one occasion Jeremiah was reporting a message from God,
for instance, Zedekiah imprisoned him, and on another occasion he also lowered him into a pit, meaning to drown him in
the water.[13]

There is therefore need to repent when faults are still slight,
and not to provoke God, as it were, against his will by further
sins of greater seriousness. After all, if *the sins* are *grave* and
very numerous, then he will definitely respond by emitting the
flames of his indignation. Now, by calling the sins *grave* we mean
serious and insupportable, because "not every sin is mortal," in
John's wise statement, even if no sin can overcome the loving-
kindness of God, to whom be the glory forever. Amen.[14] (465)

Seek good and not evil so that you may live, and the Lord God al-
mighty will be with you just as you said: We hated evil and loved good;
restore justice at the gates so that the Lord God almighty may have mercy
on the remnant of Joseph (vv.14–15). I have previously said on many
occasions that there was not just one captivity but different individual ones at different times. Pul the Assyrian, remember, was
the first to attack the two tribes in Samaria across the Jordan,[15]
and after overthrowing the cities there he left; after him Shalmaneser captured not the whole of Samaria but only a part, and
he took it off to his own country along with the captives. Now,
God did this as part of his plan, to chastise Israel "with hardship
and scourge"[16] for its lapse to bring it to better behavior and
more fitting ways of thinking and acting. It therefore happened
that those who were able to survive the wars just mentioned by
us were conscious of their limitations, repented of their deception, and acknowledged and confessed that the effects of divine
wrath had then been inflicted on them for committing many
intolerable sins. They next promised God, as it were, to reform

13. Jer 37.15–16; 45.6.
14. 1 Jn 5.17. The final concessive clause does not appear in the PG ed. At
this point the second tome on Amos concludes.
15. 1 Chr 4.26 refers to the deportation by Tiglath-pileser of "Reubenites,
Gadites, and the half-tribe of Manasseh."
16. Jer 6.7 LXX, a favorite phrase of Cyril's, though in this case it is Jerusalem that is in focus.

their ways, saying, *We hated evil and loved good.* You therefore mentioned the way, he says: *Seek good and not evil,* so that in living and being saved you may attain a proper life, and the Lord God, who has power over everything, may *be with you.* Also, *restore justice at the gates;* that is, be just judges, not delivering unfair verdicts against the weak, not undermining the force of justice, not *buffeting the heads of the poor,* nor twisting the way of the lowly, so that then God *may have mercy on the remnant of Joseph* who survived being captives.[17] Once again he refers to Ephraim, or the ten tribes; as I said before, since Ephraim was a son of Joseph, he consequently refers to him also by his father's name.

It is really necessary, therefore, to have sound attitudes and direct our own thinking to attitudes that are pleasing to God, to living virtuously, to adhering to the ways of righteousness and being wise devotees of uprightness. This, in fact, is the way we shall have the God of all to accompany and protect us.

Hence the Lord God almighty says this: In all the streets wailing and on all the roads lamentation will be raised. (467) *The farmer will be summoned to grieving and to wailing, and to those versed in lamentation, and on all the roads there will be wailing, for I shall pass through the midst of you, said the Lord* (vv.16–17). Having tasted the troubles stemming from war, he is saying, and considerably distressed at what happened, you promised to *hate evil and love good.* But in a short time, when hardly released from the terrible things involved, you lapsed into indifference, and were seen to be caught up no less in your former troubles. Consequently, the cities are now full of weeping and wailing, there is grieving and weeping everywhere, and there will be a search for *those versed in lamentation.* And when you are not content with city dwellers for this, even a *farmer* will be enlisted so that a rustic melody may ring out and the misfortunes of the fall may be lamented in bucolic tunes. *I shall pass through the midst of you,* in fact, he says, surveying the sins and still not keeping my distance from those whose impious behavior is insupportable. As long as God does not yet chastise, you see, he seems in some way not to be pres-

17. Despite his expansive treatment of the text generally, Cyril does not elaborate at length on the social justice themes of Amos in this chapter. Neither had Jerome or Theodore.

ent, whereas by inflicting the effects of his wrath he is present, as it were, and imposing punishment. This is also the way angels visited Sodom, by incinerating those guilty of impiety,[18] so that by not punishing them they kept their distance. Hence by the phrase *I shall pass through the midst of you* he refers to oversight and the moment of impending punishment.

Woe to those who long for the day of the Lord! What good to you is this day of the Lord? It is darkness and not light. Just as if someone fled from a lion and (468) *chanced upon a bear, and burst into a house and rested his hand on the wall, and a snake bit him. Is not the day of the Lord darkness and not light? And darkness with no brightness in it?* (vv.18–20) When the holy prophets predicted the future for them and the fact that they would fall foul of harsh and ineluctable calamities since they inclined incessantly to the practice of error, they mocked them and were carried away. Sometimes they claimed that what was prophesied would be long delayed; sometimes they completely despaired and presumed to say, in the terms of Jeremiah, "Where is the word of the Lord? Bring it on," their belief being that the prophets uttered falsehood and filled them with idle fears—or if some war was really heading their way, they would prevail over their hand, opposing them with a strength and enthusiasm that was harsh and irresistible. There is truth in fact in the scriptural statement, "When an impious person descends to the depths of trouble, he despises it."[19] People who have this attitude, however, like wounds beyond hope, cry aloud, as it were, that they need burning and cutting, and long for such things; in a way they thirst for punishment, even if not putting it in so many words.

Woe, then, he says, to *those who long for* and welcome nothing other than *the day* of punishment, which he calls the day *of the Lord*, brought on as it is by God. *What*, then, he asks, (469) is it but *darkness and not light* on account surely of being filled with extreme misfortune? There would in fact be no escaping it, he says, nor would anyone survive the trouble; instead, should anyone flee one, he would be taken by another, and the second would encounter those eluding the first (the meaning of escap-

18. Gn 19.15.
19. Jer 17.15; Prv 18.3.

ing the mouth of *a lion* but *chancing upon a bear*). But even if one thought, he says, perhaps to be safe, and entered *his house*, he would fall foul of death there, unexpectedly becoming the victim of snake bites; after all, if God drives one to ruin and hardship, who could rescue us? Who could help and free us from retribution? Or what way would there be of eluding it and being free from trouble? None at all: as Scripture says, "Who will divert the hand lifted up?" and "If he shuts someone in, who will open up?"[20]

I hate, I reject your festivals, and I take no delight in your festal assemblies. Hence if you bring me your holocausts and offerings, I shall not accept them, nor have regard for your saving presence (vv.21–22). The verse would apply particularly to the people of Judah and Benjamin. You see, whereas the tribes in Samaria were totally devoted to the worship of the idols, and were proven to be extremely lax and very neglectful of the laws of Moses, the people in Jerusalem, though sacrificing (470) in the high places to Baal and pouring libations to the host of heaven, in addition made a pretense of paying respect to the Law and of being anxious to perform sacrifices and *festivals*. The fact that the Lord hated this he made clear also in Isaiah: "Hear the word of the Lord, you rulers of Sodom; pay heed to the Law of God, people of Gomorrah: what value to me is the multitude of your sacrifices? says the Lord. I have had enough of burnt offerings of rams, I have no wish for the fat of lambs and the blood of bulls and goats, not even if you come to appear before me. After all, who looked for this from your hands? Do not continue trampling my court. It is futile for you to offer flour; incense is an abomination to me; I cannot bear your new moons, sabbaths, and great day; my soul hates your fasting, rest, and festivals; in my view you have gone to excess."[21] In our view, the text has the following sense: *I hate, I reject your festivals*, he says, and I would find nothing to commend in your *sacrifices*, nor would I ever reckon as an odor of sweetness your *holocausts* and offerings for your *salvation*.

Now, these were forms of sacrifices that differed at times and in particular ways: *holocausts*, one kind; *sacrifice* and *saving pres-*

20. Is 14.27; Jb 12.14.
21. Is 1.10–14.

ence, another—that is, coming before God and bringing offerings for salvation. What we have just mentioned, however, would rightly have been appropriate for Jews particularly devoted (471) to impiety. What God very readily accepts and admits are sacrifices offered in faith, spiritual holocausts, and presence at festivals; it is not we who lend ourselves a pleasing fragrance, but what is in us through the Spirit, namely, Christ. Unacceptable as a sacrifice, on the other hand, and rightly so, would be what is offered by unholy heretics and those who cannot say, like the genuine faithful, "We are the sweet odor of Christ to God," whereas their smell is from Beelzebul, if it is true that "no one says, Jesus is cursed" except by Beelzebul.[22] The wretches brazenly blaspheme and infringe the glory of the Only-begotten, not with a spiritual fragrance—rather, they have a mentality intoxicated with mire.

Take away from me the sound of your songs; I shall not listen to the melody of your instruments. Justice will roll on like water, and righteousness like an impassable torrent (vv.23–24). God dismisses the praise given on *instruments,* disqualifying lifeless matter from offering praise, and transferring participation in such splendid commendation instead to those who give expression with pure minds, since such fine hymns of praise are pleasing to the Lord of all. He rightly refers to the praises devised goodness-knows-how by the Jews—obviously on *instruments,* as I said—as *sound of your songs,* as if to imply some superfluous and idle sound that emits an undistinguished and inept (472) song. Now, the fact that these also were inventions deriving from Jewish misjudgment he indicated by speaking of a *melody of your instruments,* as if to say, Not mine, since it is beyond the Law, and Moses made no mention of them.[23] So he says, I shall not be appeased, nor will he cancel their crimes on account of pleasant sounds from *instruments.* Rather, *justice will roll on like water, and* the *righteousness* coming from me—namely, the righteous verdict against you—will be *like an impassable torrent,* that is, dragging away what

22. 2 Cor 2.15; 1 Cor 12.3. Again Cyril does not elaborate on Amos's celebrated moral theme of the priority of social justice over insincere cultic observances.

23. Can we draw from these remarks the impression that Cyril and his church (like eastern churches generally) were not in favor of instrumental music in the liturgy?

falls into it and sparing nothing, since torrents descend from the mountains with a rush. This is also the way with the divine verdict: if it is delivered against some people, it will be nothing other than invincible *water* and an irresistible *torrent*.

Repentance, therefore, emerges as in every case useful and necessary, like appeasing divine wrath by recourse to better things, uttering to God a cry that is not completely useless or unclear but giving vent from a sincere mind to a song that is truly wise and rhythmic. "Offer a sacrifice of praise," Scripture says, remember, "and render your prayers to the Most High; call on me in a day of tribulation; I shall rescue you, and you will glorify me."[24]

You did not offer me victims and offerings in the forty years in the wilderness, house of Israel, says the Lord. You adopted the tent of Moloch and the star of your god Raiphan, the images you made for yourselves. I shall deport you beyond Damascus, says the Lord God, almighty is his name (vv.25–27). In what was commented on just now, it was God who was saying to (473) those of the line of Israel, "I hate, I reject your festivals, and I take no delight in your festal assemblies. Hence even if you bring me your holocausts and offerings, I shall not accept them, nor have regard for your saving presence" (vv.21–22). In other words, in order that it might emerge that he was the one who in his characteristic clemency saved Israel, and in memory of the ancestors showed mercy to the children, not doing so by way of compensation and, as it were, remuneration for sacrifices, he is obliged to say that they had spent quite a few years in the wilderness. They had manna for food, a cloud to cover them by day as they walked, and a pillar of fire at night; the ark was considered as a type of God, going ahead and spying out a place of rest for them, and they suffered lack of no necessities, since water sprang up unexpectedly and enemies fell. With all this happening, they received the laws about sacrifices, on the one hand, and, on the other, they heard at every point and at each stage the oracles that said, "If the Lord your God leads you into the land he swore to your fathers to give you,"[25] you will do such-and-such, and also offer sacrifices.

24. Ps 50.14–15.
25. Ex 13.5.

In the forty-year period they were in the wilderness, therefore, they willingly kept offering sacrifices, with no one exert-
ing pressure on them. But the practice was delayed until they
entered the land promised to their ancestors. Consequently he
says, *Surely you did not offer me victims and offerings in the forty years
in the wilderness, house of Israel? says the Lord.* At that time they
were saved (474) even without sacrifices, and as he says likewise in another prophet, "You have not bought incense for me
with money, nor sheep for me with your produce, nor have I
burdened you with incense."[26] They in turn had no grounds for
their apostasy, but at that time were fickle, dishonoring the one
who is by nature and in truth God and *adopting the tent of Moloch
and the star of your god Raiphan.* We need to consider what this
means.

Whereas the divinely inspired Moses, therefore, went up the
mountain and received the Law, the people of Israel rebelled
against Aaron in the words, "Make us gods who will go before
us; as for this Moses, the one who brought us out of the land of
Egypt, we do not know what has happened to him."[27] So they
made a calf in the wilderness; while it was obvious, and the calf
was, as it were, an idol for everyone, they did many other things
individually. In fact, once they reverted to their former error,
and forsook piety towards God, each one made an image at his
own whim and shaped one for himself according to their custom previously in Egypt—or, rather, they were addicted to the
worship of the stars. You will perhaps ask, How did this happen
and what form did it take? For those interested there is no great
difficulty unearthing it; we shall learn it from the sacred Scriptures themselves.

The divinely inspired Moses, remember, was upset and re-
monstrated with Aaron, then fell before God, saying, "I beg you,
Lord; this people has committed a grave sin: they made themselves gods of gold";[28] although what was made was a calf, (475)
he was not unaware that others had fashioned statues. Blessed
Stephen, when accused at one time by the leaders of the Jews

26. Is 43.24, 23.
27. Ex 32.1.
28. Ex 32.31.

of reviling God and Moses, refuted the calumny with an appropriate defense, proceeding to prove that they had committed serious impiety, and by their frenzy against Christ they were imitating the depravity and hard-heartedness of their own ancestors. He made clear reference to the making of the calf in the wilderness, and said of the wise Moses, "He is the one who was in the congregation in the wilderness with the angel who spoke to him on Mount Sinai and with our ancestors, and he received living oracles to give to us. Our ancestors were unwilling to obey him; instead, they pushed him aside, and in their hearts they turned back to Egypt, saying to Aaron, Make gods for us who will go before us; as for this Moses who led us out of the land of Egypt, we do not know what has happened to him. They made a calf at that time, offered a sacrifice to the idol, and reveled in the works of their hands. But God turned away from them and handed them over to worship the host of heaven, as it is written in the book of the prophets, You did not offer me victims and offerings in the forty years in the wilderness, house of Israel, says the Lord. You adopted the tent of Moloch and the star of your god Raiphan, the images you made for yourselves. I shall deport you beyond Babylon."[29]

Note, therefore, that even the divinely inspired Stephen, a man full of the Holy Spirit, confirmed that they had made a calf and also took to worshiping the host of heaven, and (476) cited also the passage from the prophet. From this you can understand that in addition to the calf *they adopted the tent of Moloch*, making a tent and installing an idol, which they called Moloch or Molchom, an idol of the Moabites, with shining precious stones on top of its forehead as a type of the morning star. *Moloch* means "their king," the translation given by Aquila and Theodotion, the artefact being an effigy of the morning star. So he says *you adopted the tent of Moloch*, that is, your king. Of what kind was this king? *The star of your god Raiphan.* Now, *Raiphan* means "darkening" or "blinding"; they worshiped the morning star as a harbinger of the flashing of the sun, introducing the beginning of day to people on earth, whereas to his worshipers

29. Acts 7.38–43.

he proved to be *Raiphan*, that is, darkening or blinding—not that it brought about blinding of the star in them, but that reverence for it was responsible for their being darkened. Since you imitated the madness of Moab and its neighbor Damascus, he is saying, consequently you will be deported *beyond Damascus* and to places still more remote, namely, Babylon. What, then, are we to say to this? Blessed Stephen cited the Hebrew text, which wanted to refer to what was *beyond Damascus*, namely, Babylon; perhaps (477) the country and land of Babylon immediately bordered Damascus, or the kingdom of the Syrians as far as the cities to the east.[30]

30. Cyril transmits (in altered fashion) Jerome's comments on Moloch and Raiphan (Kaiwan or Kaiphan in modern versions, perhaps an Akkadian name for Saturn); the rare citation of the alternative versions is also courtesy of Jerome. He also misunderstands Jerome's accounting for Stephen's (Luke's) replacement of Damascus with Babylon, viz., that the NT authors feel a freedom to alter texts to bring out the sense.

Woe to those who scorn Zion and trust in Mount Samaria! (v.1)

NCE AGAIN THE VERSE deplores not only the people from Ephraim, or the two tribes in Samaria, but also those from Judah and Benjamin. He had previously demonstrated that even those before them were always unstable and fickle in mind, having made a calf and *adopted the tent of Moloch.* He now accuses them of imitating their ancestors and following in their footsteps by way of impiety in bringing the ire of the Lord of all upon themselves. He says that those from Judah and Benjamin *scorned Zion*; though they abode in Jerusalem and had the divine Temple, they set no store by reverence and love for God. Instead, as the sacred text says, "They kept sacrificing on the high places under oak, poplar, and shady tree"; they also worshiped the host of heaven. The God of all, for instance, said to Jeremiah with considerable resentment, "As for you, do not pray for this people, do not ask for mercy to be shown them, and do not intercede with me for them in petition and prayer, because I shall not hearken to you." He then adduces the reason for their apostasy in the words, "Do you not see what they are doing in the cities of Judah and the streets of Jerusalem? (478) Their children gather wood, their fathers kindle fire, and their women knead dough to make cakes for the host of heaven, and they poured out libations to other gods to provoke me."[1]

So the people in Jerusalem had *scorned Zion*; accordingly, it was appropriate that *woes* should be brought upon them. Now, such a statement would be applicable also to those who *trust in Mount Samaria*, that is, those who dwell in Samaria and *trust* in

1. Hos 4.13; Jer 7.16–18.

it. After all, they thought that they would prevail over the enemy even without God and enjoy the benefits of prosperity, and that every pleasurable desire of theirs would be satisfied permanently.

To be caught up in such a degree of folly is therefore surely a bitter and truly abominable fate, to presume to set at naught love for God, to be involved in wrongdoing and to commit what is unlawful, to offend him and to conclude that good things will come to us without his giving them. In fact, "every generous act of giving and every perfect gift are from above, coming down from the Father of lights";[2] it is good to cleave to him, and to regard him as our hope and support. On the other hand, they *scorn Zion,* that is, the church, who promote unholy doctrines, trust in their own eloquence, and are in the habit of taking pride in the unholy inventions of their reasoning and in worldly wisdom. To them, even before the others, *woes* would be appropriate.

They harvested the governments of nations, and it was they who entered. House of (479) *Israel, cross over, all of you, pass from there to Hamath Raba, and go down to Gath of the Philistines, the strongest of all these kingdoms, and see whether their territories are greater than your territories* (vv. 1–2). He presents them as ungrateful and unwilling to remember his beneficence, despite their constant obligation to confess his most generous grace and offer songs of thanksgiving not only for rescuing them against the odds from the grip of unbearable slavery but also for bringing them into the land sworn to their ancestors. Now, he brought them in by laying low in battle many nations that were difficult opponents unaccustomed to being vanquished; blessed David also said to God somewhere in reference to the people of Israel, "You brought a vine out of Egypt; you drove out the nations and planted it."[3] They were therefore reproached, and rightly so, for being very ungrateful by offending the benefactor by their recourse to every kind of wrongdoing; *they harvested the governments of nations,* he says, making their country their own inheritance when God made their foes tremble in their weakness, and with his inef-

2. Jas 1.17.
3. Ps 80.8.

fable power undid the strength of the adversaries. He instructs them, however, to learn by scrutinizing the *governments* or kingdoms of places near and far, that they had inherited a rich and fertile land abounding in every good thing, better and more extensive. Go, he says, *to Hamath Raba and to Gath of the Philistines*, (480) which enjoy a higher reputation than the other kingdoms, and seek there *whether their territories are greater than your territories.*

While the kingdoms of the nations—Moabites, Idumeans, people of Ammon—were individually numerous, therefore, there was nothing notable about them. Damascus and Palestine were more splendid than the others; subject to Damascus were two cities situated to the east called Hamath, one bigger and more extensive, the other less (*Raba* meaning "bigger" or "more extensive"). So travel *to Hamath Raba*, that is, to the larger and more extensive Hamath; it had the same name as the other one, as I said, but was bigger. Now, they claim that this town is now Antioch, whereas the smaller and less extensive one nearby is Epiphaneia; Antiochus, called Epiphanes, gave his name to Antioch, and conferred the title Epiphaneia on the other one in his honor. Gath was a city of Palestine that was more splendid than it is now; its residents were Anakim and those called Philistines, since the people of Israel had not annihilated them at that time. Consequently, he calls it *Gath of the Philistines*, and therefore says, Go to *Hamath Raba and to Gath of the Philistines*, and take careful note as to whether you yourselves are not living in a more extensive country that is larger and more eminent than all the others. Now, we should be aware that the Hebrew text (481) mentions Calneh first; he says, Go into Calneh, Hamath, and Gath, Calneh being subject to the kingdom of the Persians and now called Lysippon. Since the Hebrew text mentioned also the kingdom of the Persians, consequently in our view blessed Stephen said "I shall deport you beyond Babylon" instead of "beyond Damascus."[4]

---

4. Cyril may have noticed from Theodore that the Antiochene (and thus the Heb.) text included Calneh in the list of cities. Jerome had not said so, but he did help Cyril identify Hamath the greater (but not Hamath the less). We mentioned above the unlikelihood of Cyril's guess about Stephen's changing Damascus for Babylon in Acts 7.43; see p. 82, n. 30.

The charge against the people of Israel, then, was ingratitude in not according thanks to God for their inheriting a land so rich, extensive, and level, and instead *scorning Zion* in one case, and in another *trusting in Mount Samaria,* but giving no priority to respect for him. Now, the verse, Go *to Hamath Raba and to Gath of the Philistines, and see whether their territories are greater than your territories,* would obviously be useful for those who after coming to faith marvel at the wisdom of pagans to the extent of considering their views better than ours, and who are inclined to seek to adhere to people who distort the truth and undermine the correctness of church teachings. The inspired Scripture, you see, is more extensive than the quibbles of the pagans, spreading the light of truth, contributing the knowledge of beneficial teachings, and bringing the mind of believers to everything commendable.

The message about the truth is likewise more extensive than the narrowness of heretics; some of them fight against it and, as it were, drown while swimming in their frigid and obscure reasoning, while others are locked in debate with the teachings of true religion, give careful consideration to the splendid beauty of truth, (482) and find their way to the spreading ocean of understanding, "taking every thought captive to obey Christ," rushing hither and yon, and drawing from the divinely inspired Scripture what contributes to true knowledge. The divinely inspired Paul, for example, in writing to Corinthians who had chosen to forsake "the holy commandment transmitted to them" and who were in the habit of unwisely giving contrary teaching to their adherents, said, "We have spoken frankly to you, Corinthians; our heart is wide open to you; there is no narrowing in us, but there is narrowing in your affections. In return—I speak as to children—open wide your hearts also. Do not be mismatched with unbelievers."[5]

Woe to you who are coming to an evil day, who approach and apply yourselves to false sabbaths (v.3). He had said, "Woe to those who scorn Zion and trust in Mount Samaria" (v.1); and since he had mentioned two groups, namely, those scorning Zion and

5. 2 Cor 10.5; 2 Pt 2.21; 2 Cor 6.11–14.

those trusting in Mount Samaria, in a necessary investigation into the thrust of their thinking we attributed the blame for scorning Zion to the people of Judah and Benjamin, and the trusting in Mount Samaria to the people of Ephraim. The verse is therefore retrospective, once again listing the crimes of both and applying *Woe* to them. Now, it is customary with the divine Scripture to use the word *Woe* in direct speech, as for example, "Woe to you who long for the Day of the Lord," and again, "Woe to you who rise early (483) in search of strong drink."[6] Hence his saying, *Woe to you who are coming to an evil day,* that is, those in Jerusalem; reluctance to repent and refusal to admit fear of the impending fate prophesied are, as it were, a longing to fall foul of a day of ruin. It is as if someone were saying in regard to one of the sinners, He longs to die, even though the person had no wish for such a fate. Why say so? He goes as far as wanting to commit, even incessantly, what is at variance with the laws, as if fond of the punishment and retribution due to sinners.

Those who are reluctant to repent, therefore, and desirous of falling foul of *an evil day* and of being caught up in the calamities previously foretold are those *who approach and apply themselves to false sabbaths.* The Temple and the altars in it were still standing, in fact; while they offered to God sacrifices by Law and observed the sabbath rest, they were not completely diligent, but instead were quite careless and very indifferent. Through the prophets, for instance, he blamed them for not observing the sabbath;[7] so he says *Woe* to those pretending to *approach* God by pretending still to respect the Mosaic laws and dabbling in *false sabbaths.* Do you see how he has represented them as not keeping the rest appropriate to sabbath observance rightly and carefully?

In another sense—I think there is need to say something more urgent on this passage—*false sabbaths* are what is done by the Jews, especially since the Law is a shadow, and what was given through Moses is a type of the reality. The type is not the reality; (484) rather, it provides an outline of the reality. Accordingly, the divinely inspired Paul in writing to the Hebrews

6. 5.19; Is 5.11.
7. Cf. Ezek 20.13, 16, 21, 24.

says of the former things, "Sabbath surely still remains for the people of God"; Joshua had not given them rest, nor have they entered into God's rest. Rather, it is we who in a spiritual sense practice sabbath in Christ by undoing and forsaking sins, on the one hand, and, on the other, by putting an end to every corruptible and earthly practice. Blessed Paul writes, remember, "Those who enter his rest cease from all their labors as God did from his."[8]

Those who recline on ivory beds and behave wantonly on their couches, who eat kids from flocks and sucking calves from the midst of a herd, who clap their hands to the tune of instruments and think things are permanent and not ephemeral, who drink strained wine and anoint themselves with the best oils, and were not affected by the oppression of Joseph (vv.4–6). The usual woes once again for those *who recline on ivory beds,* in the habit of doing this-and-that. He severely accuses the more prominent people in Samaria, who took pride in wealth greater than that of others, of being under the influence, as it were, of great prosperity and so distracted by the extent of the luxury as to have no suspicion at all of (485) the disasters, or not to think that the God of all was ever provoked by people with this attitude and would inflict punishment on those given to sin. He describes with precision their laxity and dissolute tendency to high living: *reclining on ivory,* he says, lavish and delicate beds, the choicest lambs, nursing *calves* their food, songs and tunes, all the sounds of *instruments* accompanying the high living, carousing and clapping—and, what is worse, the fact that they *think such things are permanent and not ephemeral,* whereas in fact such things are evanescent, and worldly deceit has no firm foundation. It disappears like shadows, you see, and "the present form of this world is passing away," as Scripture says;[9] luxurious living comes to a complete end for the dead.

Now, in the case of the people in Samaria, the sense of the words could be taken also in another way: since they were destined before long to be captured, he calls the things idly de-

8. Heb 4.8–10. For Cyril, the Old is but *skia* and *typos* of the *alêtheia.* Theodoret learns this from him. As it happens, the LXX of this verse departs considerably from (our) Heb.

9. 1 Cor 7.31.

vised for their enjoyment *ephemeral and not permanent* because they were soon to disappear. So *they clap their hands to the tune of instruments, drinking wine* that was perhaps scented and very carefully strained; *they anoint themselves with oils,* applying the choicest ones, and give no importance at all to *the oppression of Joseph.* As I said just now, though aware in advance of the calamity soon to eventuate, [namely], the capture of Samaria and the *oppression* that would happen to those of the line of *Joseph,* they did not neglect their customary high living.

It is therefore a truly dreadful thing for (486) those appointed to govern countries or cities or peoples to succumb to bodily luxury. Since there is, in fact, the obligation for them rather to adopt carefully the usual vigilance and pay attention to what is beneficial, give direction to people unduly carried away, and in every way appease God, who has been offended, how would it not be quite unconscionable to be caught up in high living and consider nothing better than loathsome delights of the flesh? It is perhaps in reference to such things that he says through the statement of the holy ones, "O the shepherds who scatter and destroy the sheep of my pasture"; the fact that the obedient are endangered by the indifference of shepherds would be clear from another distinct statement of God: "Because the shepherds were stupid and did not seek out the Lord; hence the whole flock did not understand, and were scattered."[10]

Hence they will now become captives of the leadership of the mighty, and neighing of horses will be removed from Ephraim (v.7). They lived luxuriously, forsook love for God, trusted in Mount Samaria—that is, the residents of Samaria—and developed a sense of their own importance in the belief that they governed an immeasurable multitude and had a fighting class beyond number. Consequently, he says, the time of captivity for all will definitely come, and with great ferocity, beginning with the more powerful. In sacking a city, after all, enemies always make their way to the houses of more prominent people, pillaging everything in them. Now, since it was the custom for the prominent people in Samaria to like to ride special horses, which probably (487) pa-

10. Jer 23.1 and 10.21.

raded through the streets neighing in a comprehending, wise, and, as it were, knowledgeable way (for the animal is willing to put on a good appearance and to learn what is appropriate for it, strange to say), this, too, will cease, he is saying; *neighing of horses will be removed from Ephraim,* he says. It is as if he were to say, The exceeding insolence of people in Samaria will come to an end, and despite them they will be deprived of the publicity of their processions from the neighing of the horses, which are distinguished by their splendid patches, are perhaps familiar with their rider, and, as it were, are very proud to be carrying a noble and august personage.

You would learn from this the security that comes from vigilant leaders, and the harm from their preferring slumber; on them even before others will fall the effects of wrath. They will be deprived of all renown, and they themselves will fall together with the others, receiving a harsh and bitter judgment, and will render an account not only for their own destruction but for being responsible also for that of others through their own lawlessness.

Because the Lord swore an oath by himself, I loathe all Jacob's insolence and hate his places (v.8). He brings out the immutability of his wrath by presenting God as swearing an oath that he would *hate Jacob's insolence.* It is not at all our view that the divine word to us delivers a curse on our forefather Jacob; it would be very silly to accept this interpretation, since God loved Jacob from the womb and chose him even when unborn. By *Jacob,* however, he means those of the line of (488) Jacob, whose accursed arrogance he says he *hated* (the divine Scripture normally referring to haughtiness as *insolence*). After all, would it not be haughtiness after that to spurn reverence for God, to accord to idols the glory most appropriate to him in particular, and, further, not to want to hear the things he chose to convey through the holy prophets, but rather to treat his threats as a joke, and by trusting in the vast number of allies to ignore completely his mercy and assistance? Further, how is there any doubt of this?

Accordingly, it says, *the Lord of all swore an oath by himself—by himself* because "he had no one greater by whom to swear."[11]

11. Heb 6.13.

What did he swear? *I loathe all Jacob's insolence*, or Jacob's haughtiness, *and hate his places*; there was no one in them to fulfill the divine wishes, no one to accord him reverence, or conspicuous for the ornaments of righteousness. God would not have turned away, in fact, if there had been some among them, even if easily counted, who were concerned for what pleased him. He said through Jeremiah, for instance, "Run about through the streets of Jerusalem, look around and take note on its streets if you find a man, if there is anyone who acts justly and loves faith, and I shall be merciful to it, says the Lord."[12] Since, however, *Jacob's places* were lacking any good man or godly man, consequently they have been given over to desolation, and the cities have perished along with the inhabitants. There is therefore great need of holy people; they save cities, and by the probity of their life rid places of impending disaster by quelling the anger aroused by indifference (489) and by diverting, as it were, the movements of divine wrath befalling some people.

And I shall remove the city along with its inhabitants. If ten men are left in one house, they will die, and the survivors will remain. Their kin will lay hold of them and make efforts to carry their bones out of the house, and he will say to those in charge of the house, Is there anyone still left with you? He will reply, No more, and he will say, Be careful about mentioning the name of the Lord (vv.8–10). Since he hated their places, after all, and abominated all Jacob's insolence, or their arrogance, he says that consequently the cities along with their inhabitants will be destroyed. He describes in detail in each case how the fate will befall the sinners: *I shall remove* whatever *city* I wish, and take from its midst *its inhabitants* as well. If it happens that there are ten of them from one house fleeing the enemies' sword, and they take refuge in the recesses and interior of the house, they will die, perhaps afraid of peeping out a little from the inside. Accordingly, he says, hunger will follow upon the hand of the striker, and kill those hidden. With the departure of the foe, some of their kith and kin will emerge, and *make efforts to carry out their bones.* Whom will they force to collect the (490) remains? Themselves, clearly: it was a truly burdensome and difficult task to touch bodies that were rotting and decay-

12. Jer 5.1.

ing, and I would think it was necessary for those performing it to block their noses, for nothing could be worse than such a stench. They will therefore oblige themselves, out of sympathy for the departed and the victims of hunger, by according them funeral and burial. Those engaged in this, he says, will inquire of anyone familiar with the house as to whether there is anyone else after them, either still alive and escaping notice inside, or already dead and emitting a stench. They reply in the words, *No more*. Now, this is nothing other than clear proof of utter devastation.

If, on the other hand, it were *those in charge of the house* who said this, let them hear from the one giving a reply, *Be careful about mentioning the name of the Lord*. There is need to see what is the meaning of this. Some commentators believe and claim that when *those in charge of the house* are about to swear, the respondents caution them against swearing in *the name of the Lord*. They proceed to say that the mind of the people of Ephraim had reached such a stage of ungodliness that they could not tolerate anyone choosing to *name* the God of all. In my view, on the contrary, such a view is quite silly and unappealing.[13] Admittedly, no one would doubt that the people of Ephraim had abandoned the love of God; but after suffering punishment and scourging, they had probably instead come to experience a little fear and arrive at a better frame of mind, and not express (491) such fierce opposition to piety towards God. Furthermore—to add something in addition to what has been said—what need would there have been for *those in charge of the house*, when asked whether there was still someone alive there, or dead but still unnoticed, to reply also with an oath that there was no one among them?

So what is the meaning of *Be careful about mentioning the name of the Lord?* Our view is that it was customary with those of the bloodline of Israel to call it a curse and blasphemy against God on the basis of the commandments of the Law. It is recorded in Leviticus, remember, that two men were fighting together in the assembly when one of the combatants blasphemed, the son of an Egyptian woman, and he met his death by stoning.

13. The view he classes "quite silly" is in fact Jerome's.

God immediately gave a law on this matter in these words: "Anyone who curses God shall bear the sin, and anyone who names the Lord's name shall be put to death."[14] So *naming the name of the Lord* is blasphemy, and is expressed in the sacred text in euphemistic terms. Since, however, many people have the custom if they are in distress to let loose sometimes derogatory words against God, therefore the one *in charge of the house*, he says, in reporting that there is no one with him and what he suffered from the intolerable calamity, will stop himself from *naming the name of the Lord*, that is, from using derogatory words against God. Now, it is not without purpose for him to highlight the scourge befalling them, and not idle for him to punish them; rather, it is useful and necessary. You see, it is possible, and very easily so, to see from what had happened that the punishment of the sufferers encouraged reverence (492) in those still alive and surviving, and caused them to dread further offending God, even distressing him by mere words, despite their former habit of doing so incautiously, and proceeding to add insult to injury. It is therefore far better for those who are truly good and self-controlled to move to the pursuit of what is beneficial before punishment and scourging, to anticipate the experience of the effects of wrath by abandoning depravity, and to opt to perform what is in truth pleasing to the all-holy God.

Because, lo, the Lord will command, and will strike the great house with ruin and the small house with cracks (v.11). He clearly threatens the capture, or rather the ruin, of cities along with their inhabitants. Now, the fact that the event is from God and will not be an accidental happening is clearly suggested by his *commanding* those able to do damage, on the one hand, and, on the other, by their easily performing whatever the divine anger determines. By *small and great homes* he perhaps refers to Ephraim and Judah; Ephraim was very numerous, comprising ten tribes, whereas Judah was smaller, comprising two, confined to Jerusalem and the tribe of Benjamin. Now, it is logical to take the view that while the *ruined* house suffered complete collapse, the *cracked* one could rightly be taken as suffering that fate partially.

---

14. Lv 14.10–16 (where it is the blasphemer's father who was Egyptian).

The house of (493) Ephraim, or Israel, in fact, experienced total capture and the irreversible misfortune of war, whereas Judah did so partially, suffering limited *cracks*. The Judge is therefore righteous and no respecter of persons; clearly, he makes the punishment of cities and countries commensurate with the crimes, and inflicts on each one proportionally the punishment that is capable of bringing benefit. Let us not scorn God in our knowledge of the strength of the supreme hand; understanding this is a great virtue.

Will horses chase on rocks? Will they keep silent among mares? Because you twisted judgment into anger, and the fruit of righteousness into bitterness (v.12). Of the fact that it is he once again who gives the command to "strike the great house with ruin and the small house with cracks" (v.11), even if it is done through the hand of the Assyrians, he convinces us by saying, *Will horses chase on rocks?* It would be like saying clearly, While the horse is a proud animal and one of the swiftest when the place is suited to racing, it is not so if it is rocky and very uneven—only if it is smooth and level. Then how have the Assyrians run over you, despite the people's being rough and, as it were, rocky in former times, and never trampled down by any of the enemy? God was dishonored, however, and what was rugged and inaccessible he made accessible to horses. Just as *horses* would not cease being excited, he is saying, (494) spurred on by natural stimulation at the presence of *mares* and very frisky, so the foe would not rest from making fevered and implacable charges against the enemy. What is the occasion of this? You, and no one else: you turned my just judgment regarding you *into anger*, and instead of bearing *the fruit of righteousness*, you forced the source of all your prosperity to wrath by committing offenses deserving of *bitterness*. The God of all, you see, had mercy on Israel in its hardship, as in Egypt, but they did not cease provoking him—the meaning, in my view, of *you twisted judgment into anger.*

It was therefore a dreadful crime of ingratitude; it was punished, and rightly so: the one they should rather have continued to pacify by praise and gladdened by words of thanksgiving, how will it not be a source of every trouble for them to provoke him in their stupidity?

You who rejoice in no good word, who say, Do we not by our own strength possess horns? Because, lo, I am raising up a nation against you, house of Israel, and they will oppress you so as to prevent your entering Hamath and as far as the torrent of the west (vv.13–14). Accordingly, he says, *you twisted judgment into anger, and the fruit of righteousness into bitterness,* taking pride in yourselves and acting conceitedly against God, exulting in a silly and foolish *word.* You claimed, in fact, that I was not the source of the strength in you and your being able to oppose the enemy; instead, you attributed the achievements to your own powers, (495) and presumed to say, *Do we not by our own strength possess horns?*[15] That would be like their then thinking of capture and stupidly saying, It is we who have the power and it is we who shall prevail over the foe; even if God does not choose to protect us, we are victorious and should take credit for such splendid achievements, attributing nothing at all to God. Such senseless thinking and speaking was therefore arrogance and insolence against God. The divinely inspired David was particularly wise to give glory to God, who has power over all, in saying, "You are the boast of their power," and again, "Through you we shall prevail over our foes, and by your name we shall annihilate our adversaries; it is not in my bow that I trust, nor will my sword save me." That is to say, all my strength is from him, and there would be nothing remarkable from us if he did not accompany and protect us; "the Lord will crush enemies," Scripture says.[16]

Now, since you have now fallen victim to such a degree of brazen arrogance, he is saying, *I am raising up a nation against you*—that of the Assyrians, clearly—*and they will oppress you so as to prevent your entering Hamath and as far as the torrent of the west.* Hamath, then, is one of the cities of that name, located to the east and at that time subject to the reign of Damascus; it is now called Epiphaneia, as I said, after Antiochus. By *torrent of the west* he refers to the river of the Egyptians, since Egypt lies to the west of the land of the Jews. Now, since it was the custom of the

---

15. Jerome did not alert Cyril to the possibility that in the LXX's reading "no good word" and "horns," it is missing the Heb. place names Lo-debar and Kannaim that appear in our modern versions.

16. Pss 89.17 and 44.5–6; Ex 15.3 LXX.

people of Israel, when war was about to break out upon them, at one time to seek help from Damascus and Syria and at another to make for the land of the Egyptians, consequently he inflicted *tribulation* on them with the result that they were unable then to *enter Hamath or as far as the torrent of the west*—that is, to call for help from Damascus or the might of the Egyptians. As Scripture says, remember, "If God shuts them out, who will open to them?"[17] What will be the chance of survival when the one with power over all drives them to ruin?

17. Jb 12.14.

COMMENTARY ON AMOS,
CHAPTER SEVEN

This is what the Lord showed me: a plague of locusts coming early, and one young locust King Gog. They will finish eating the grass of the land. I said, Lord, Lord, be merciful: who will raise up Jacob, for he is tiny? Relent, Lord, in this matter. This will not happen, says the Lord (vv.1–3).

OD REVEALS TO THE PROPHET WHAT nation will be brought upon the people of Israel, or what harm will befall them; on the other hand, he follows his custom of informing him of what will be done through things of which he has a precise knowledge. The *locust* and the *young locust* always strike shepherds as being frightful, and really are; when fodder is, as it were, sheared off by them, the flocks then necessarily perish. God therefore indicates the calamities of war to the prophet as to a shepherd. (497) He indicates the Assyrian under the guise of a *locust*, eating and consuming, as it were, the land by its unlimited numbers; and he calls it *early* as though falling like dew and poured out on the land in the manner of snowflakes. There was, however, he says, *one young locust;* it was *King Gog.* Then God says, *They will finish eating the grass of the land,* that is, when they finish eating the numerous herd that is in Samaria, obviously, and in the cities of Judea. Then, when he is on the point of adding something else, the prophet intervenes, asking him to cease his wrath: *Lord, be merciful: who will raise up Jacob, for he is tiny?* That is, if you intend, as I see you do, to surrender Israel to the enemy as food, it will be quite *tiny.* In reply, *This will not happen, says the Lord*; I would not grow weary or give up, for I would never cease from chastising offenders.

There being need to investigate who *Gog* is, our view is that the blessed prophet Ezekiel also uses him in writing a lament at God's direction. In our opinion he is Sennacherib; when the Rabshakeh mocked God, "an angel of the Lord issued forth and in a single night slew a hundred and eighty-five thousand Assyrians from the camp."[1] Now, we shall quote what is recorded of him in the account of Ezekiel, which goes as follows: "Thus says Lord the Lord to Gog: Are you the one of whom I spoke (498) in former days by my servants the prophets of Israel in those days and years that I would bring you against them?" Do you hear how he says it was he and no one else who threatened through holy prophets to attack the people of Israel? The fact that he was called to account for his brazen language, and when expecting to dominate he was unexpectedly done away with and fell in the land of Israel, he goes on straightway to indicate by saying, "And you, son of man, prophesy against Gog, prince of Meshech and Tubal: I shall assemble you, guide you, and lead you to the remotest parts of the north, and bring you to the mountains of Israel. I shall strike your bow from your left hand and your arrows from your right hand. I shall bring you down on the mountains of Israel, and you will fall along with those about you, and the nations about you will be given to a large flock of birds. I have given you to every bird and to all the wild beasts of the plain to be eaten; you will fall on the open plain, for I have spoken, says Lord the Lord." And later again, "On that day I shall give to Gog a place for burial in Israel, the cemetery of those traveling to the sea. They will block the mouth of the valley and bury there Gog and all his multitude, and it will then be called cemetery of Gog. The house of Israel will bury them so as to be purified in seven months, and all the people of the land will bury them, (499) and it will bring them honor on that day, says Lord the Lord."[2] When, in fact, the Assyrians fell, who are referred to as *Gog*, perhaps the population of Israel buried the dead to prevent cities and countries being harmed by the unbearable nature of such a terrible stench.

This is what the Lord showed me: the Lord called for judgment in fire, and it devoured the great abyss and devoured a part. I said, Lord, Lord, cease: who will raise up Jacob, because he is tiny? Relent, Lord, in this.

---

1. 2 Kgs 19.35.

2. Ezek 39.1–5, 11–13. While the Antiochene commentators are content to take the Gog of Ezek 38–39 as an historical character in his own right, Cyril prefers to see him as a figure for Sennacherib. None of these commentators sees the genre of apocalyptic being adopted by the biblical author.

This will not happen, says the Lord (vv.4–6). He envisions Gog, or the Assyrian, as *locust* and *young locust*, and refers to him as *judgment* by *fire;* the Babylonians were not content with consuming Ephraim by the sword, but as far as possible set fire to the cities in Samaria. So the *judgment*, he is saying—that is, vengeance by *fire*—consumed *the great abyss*, that is, Ephraim, referred to as *abyss* for its great and immeasurable numbers. It consumed no less, however, the smaller *part*, that is, Judah and Benjamin; after burning the numberless cities of Judea, the arrogant Rabshakeh went on then to besiege Jerusalem as well. When in turn the prophet, on the other hand, tries to win over and persuade the God of all to *relent*, or change his mind, the God of all says it would not happen. What, then, shall we in turn learn from this? That sins beyond telling (500) provoke God terribly, accustomed though he is to being very tolerant, and render the prayers of the saints, as it were, inefficacious. He said, for instance, to the prophet Jeremiah regarding the people of Israel, "As for you, do not pray for this people, do not ask for them to be shown mercy, and do not approach me on their behalf, for I shall not hearken to you."[3]

This is what the Lord showed me: a man standing on a wall of adamant, and in his hand adamant. The Lord said to me, What are you looking at, Amos? I replied, Adamant. The Lord said to me, Lo, I am placing adamant in the midst of my people Israel; I shall never again pass them by. Altars of laughter will be destroyed, and the initiations of Israel will be left desolate, and I shall rise up against the house of Jeroboam with a sword (vv.7–9). Having presented to the prophet the Assyrian, or Gog, as *locust* and *young locust*, and as *judgment in fire*, God now shows himself *standing on a wall of adamant*, so that in this he may be understood to be mounted, as it were, on unbroken power and in possession of unshakable security for his good things; his strength is divine, after all, and has a solid base, unable to fall, immune to change, and ever reliable, as I said, in its good things.

He appears, then, *standing on a wall of adamant.* Adamant is unbreakable and resistant to stone, unlikely to yield to what is tough and inclined to resist, nor (501) does it surrender to oth-

3. Jer 7.16.

er materials its innate power to be able to offer opposition, and is perhaps inclined to scorn even the strength of fire. Now, since the one *standing on a wall* was carrying *adamant in his hand*, he asked the prophet a question: *What are you looking at, Amos?* He understood and told him what it was, *Adamant,* and was clearly obliged to *place adamant in the midst* of Israel. Now, by *adamant* you should understand either the Assyrian for being inflexible and bold and assigned to this by God, for the Lord of the powers empowers whomever he chooses, or the unbreakable and strong Word of God, which "cannot return empty" or be rendered inefficacious, since whatever God utters follows its course to the end with no one to oppose it, This is what our Lord Jesus Christ also said: "Heaven and earth will pass away, but my words will not pass away."[4] He said that he would not *pass by* Israel; that is, he would call them to account for their unholy offenses against him, and instead of showing further long-suffering, he would then surrender them to those called against them, along with shrines, altars, and the idols: *Altars of laughter will be destroyed.* The making of every idol is a matter of *laughter,* therefore; it would in my view be appropriate to think in particular and specifically of Baal of Peor as *laughter,* especially because of the actual ugliness of its appearance; but he ridicules all idolatry by reference to this individual example of depravity.[5] He therefore says that *the altars* will be pulled down, *and the initiations of Israel* abolished, that is, the diversions of idolatry and its profane and loathsome mysteries. He makes clear mention of the fact that (502) Jeroboam, bedecked with the trappings of kingship, will proceed to ruin along with his own gods. We need to remember, however, that the king referred to here is a different one from the former one, who was son of Nebat; this one is son of Jehoash.

While this would bear to some extent on the factual account, he will present Christ, the Lord of the powers, as the true *adamant,* with unyielding and irresistible strength, vanquishing enemies, conquering adversaries, and broken by nothing. He is set as a chosen stone in the midst of the people; Scripture says,

4. Is 55.11; Mt 24.35.
5. Jerome did not help Cyril to see that the LXX has not recognized in "laughter" the roots of the name Isaac as found in Gn 21.6.

"he appeared on earth and lived among human beings." Accordingly, he is also called in the angel's statement "Emmanuel, which means God with us,"[6] in fact being with us when he became like us. So he was *placed among us* by the God and Father as *adamant*, he brought down the devil's unlawful rule, and truly he abolished *the altars of laughter*. As soon as Emmanuel shone forth and spread the light of true knowledge to people throughout the earth under heaven, he gave us a glimpse of himself as image and likeness of the Father. Then it was that he dissipated the darkness of the former error, the loathsome and ungodly idolatry took its leave, and the very patron of error also fell—Satan, that is.

Amaziah, the priest of Bethel, sent to King Jeroboam of Israel, saying, Amos is conspiring against you in the midst of the house of Israel, and the land cannot bear all (503) *his words. For Amos says this: Jeroboam will fall to the sword, and the people will be taken off in captivity from its land* (vv.10–11). Falsehood is always unsupported by itself, and the feet of error rest on shaky ground. Accordingly, it is mocked, incapable of being sustained without support. The situation of the idolatry of Israel was like that; the diversions devised by them, golden heifers, came from drunken people, "objects molded by a craftsman," as Scripture says,[7] products of human hands, the invention of unholy industry. The blessed prophets, on the other hand, call on those in the grip of error to be on the alert, whereas the devotees of the idols, as though their whole fabric is collapsing, are very indignant, start alarms, and lament the revival of the deceived, knowing that the profanity of their worship is easily visible to a sharp and alert mind. The vile Amaziah, therefore, was afraid that the people who had been persuaded to worship the golden heifers would be brought by the prophet's words to a sound understanding, that he would be expelled from the priesthood, and the shrines and their contents would be destroyed. Accordingly, he tried to stir up Jeroboam, claiming that Amos was rebelling against his kingship, as it were, and was presuming to deliver dire and intoler-

6. Is 38.16; Bar 3.37; Mt 1.23.
7. Jer 10.3.

able speeches to the effect that he would die *by the sword* and Israel would depart *in captivity.*

This is the kind of thing that the wretched Jews also did in concocting calumny against Christ; when he astonished Judea by his miracles and called everyone to himself, (504) the scoundrels admitted the flames of envy to their mind, presented him to Pilate, and even cried, "If you do not kill him, you are no friend of Caesar."[8] The crimes against the saints through similar exploits on the part of all those who constantly oppose the true religion are therefore of the same kind, since falsehood is everywhere the victim of weakness.

Amaziah said to Amos, On your way, seer; off with you to the land of Judah; live there and prophesy there, but continue prophesying no further in Bethel, because it is a king's sanctuary and a temple of a kingdom (vv.12–13). He was now clearly shameless, and pitted his own envy against the divine words. They used to call the prophets *seers,* in fact; but instead of deigning to dignify him with the term for prophecy, he misrepresented him, as it were, as one of the false prophets, with the order, *off with you to the land of Judah.* And he proceeded to say, *Live there,* in this sense: If it is mere profit you are after, and by charming some people in word you seek to earn the necessities of life, leave Samaria and speak to those of the tribe of Judah, and *continue prophesying no further in Bethel, because it is a king's sanctuary.* By *sanctuary* he meant "offering," or "place of offering," for it was there that the former Jeroboam offered the golden heifer; and to present it as a crime on the prophet's part, and to give honor to the ruler, he said, *it is a temple of a kingdom.* You are upsetting royal privilege; you are stirring up trouble (505) by recklessly opposing the rulers' wishes. Take careful note, therefore, how this statement of God to Israel is true: "You made the consecrated ones drink wine, and you gave the prophets this instruction: Do not prophesy."[9]

Amos said in reply to Amaziah, I was not a prophet nor son of a prophet; instead, I was a goatherd, a picker of mulberries. The Lord took me from the sheep, and the Lord said to me, Go, prophesy to the

8. Jn 19.12.
9. 2.12.

people of Israel. Now hear the word of the Lord: You say, Do not prophesy against the people of Israel, and do not preach against the house of Jacob. Hence the Lord says this: Your wife will be a prostitute in the city, and your sons and your daughters will fall to the sword; your land will be measured by line, and you will die in an unclean land, and Israel will be taken away in captivity from its land (vv.14–17). When the practitioners of depravity inflict insults on honest people, they accuse them of their own behavior, and by censuring them for the ugliness of their own faults they think they are in the grip of a drunken rage. They deceive themselves, however, painting, as it were, a picture of themselves, and revealing what they are like to others. In this case we shall find Amaziah in his folly having just this experience; as a false prophet, and attending on the altars of the idols, he gathered up the parts and (506) leftovers of slain animals, and was an inveterate addict of base gain. Yet he mocked Amos, and told him he should leave Samaria and go to Judah, if he wanted, and live there; it is there, he said, you will have no difficulty speaking falsehood, defrauding many, collecting contributions for your living and, more so, finding the necessities of life. The phrase *Live there*, in fact, reflects such an attitude, as I said before.

Such was not the prophet's purpose, however, nor was he interested in easy money; instead, he served the Lord's wishes, and consequently he filled the role befitting a prophet. He tried to bring that out very modestly by saying, *I was not a prophet nor son of a prophet*—that is, by upbringing or inspiration, like Elisha the son of Elijah. Instead, he was a *goatherd*, living a simple rural life without malice, with quite little for sustenance, content with the produce of the fields that no one would even buy, namely, *mulberries*. When those in charge of flocks are at leisure, they make for the shade of the trees and pass the time, as it were, with the temptations of idleness by picking the fruit and satisfying the need of their stomachs as it arises. When I was one such, he says, God made me a prophet according to his will, and bade me inform the people of Israel of their impending fate that would shortly come to pass. You, on the other hand, who pit your will against that from on high, tell me to keep quiet. Now, consequently, *the Lord says this: Your wife* (507) *will be a prostitute in the city,* obviously a victim of enemy outrage, subject of necessity to the unbridled lewdness of her captors. Your children also will be done away with, falling to the sword. In addition, *your land will be measured by line,* that is, it will be subject to tribute, and will pay taxes to its overlord. Furthermore, you who now believe you are dwelling in Bethel and occupy a king's sanctuary will go off into captivity and die in misfortune, never to return; after all, how could you return, when you abide as a corpse in foreign parts and the *unclean land* of the enemy? *Israel itself will be taken away in captivity* after having chosen you as prophet and patron of the holy ones.

It is therefore a serious fault to oppose the divine decisions and proceed incautiously to take it upon oneself on occasion even to punish the holy ones who interpret God's will; it has even been said to them by him, "The one who touches you will be like the one touching the apple of his eye."[10] Now, observe how the holy ones have a single, praiseworthy purpose, namely, to minister without flinching to God's words and set no store by human considerations, even if some people afflict them with war and tribulation. Blessed Amos, note, paid no heed to the knavery of Amaziah; instead of keeping quiet, he vigorously delivered a curse on him. The divinely inspired disciples, when at one time bidden by the scribes and Pharisees to keep quiet, openly declared, "As to whether it is right in God's sight to listen to you rather than to God, you must judge; as for us, we cannot keep from speaking about what we have seen and heard."[11]

10. Zec 2.8.
11. Acts 4.19–20.

COMMENTARY ON AMOS,
CHAPTER EIGHT

This is what the Lord showed me: a fowler's basket. He said, What do you see, Amos? I replied, A fowler's basket. The Lord said to me, The end has come for my people Israel: I shall never again pass their way. The ceilings of the Temple will lament on that day, says the Lord; the fallen will be numerous in every place, and I shall cast silence (vv.1–3).

HE PROPHET'S DISCOURSE continues on its way; the matters that have been touched on received adequate treatment, and the order of the visions is adjusted to the purpose proper to it. So he saw the vast numbers of the Assyrians like an early plague of locusts, and with them Gog, or Sennacherib, described under the form of a young locust on account of the creature's vigorous leaping on the ground; the arrogant person is something like this, ever leaping on high, declining to live the life of lowly people. He also saw judgment referred to as fire, and adamant placed in the midst of Israel standing on the wall of adamant.

What next? *A fowler's basket.* I repeat what I said initially, that, to the prophet raised as a rustic, God reveals mysteries through what happens particularly in the countryside. *Fowlers*, you see, and what is caught by them—birds, I mean—would be suited not to city folk but to those whose interests and lifestyle were the countryside and what is in it. Now, (509) the fact that the chosen race of those in Samaria—I mean the arrogant and the high flyers like birds—would along with the masses without any doubt be caught for slaughter, as though by the hand of fowlers, the force of the visions suggested in obscure fashion, the vision being *a fowler's basket.* The God of all is thus saying, *The end has come for my people Israel*, and that he *would never again pass* over their crimes; he mentioned that even the Temple itself would be burnt down, housing as it did the golden heifer

105

in Bethel, when he said, *The ceilings of the Temple will lament on that day.* Now, *ceilings* normally referred to the roof, or the part around it, cleverly made of varied materials by the artifice of the builders according to the verse in the Song of Songs, "Our beams are of cedar, our ceilings of cypress."[1] He says *the ceilings will lament,* uttering not an articulate sound, but rather one that comes from the creaking and groaning of collapse. Since *the fallen will be numerous in every place,* he says, *I shall cast silence;* because the whole place will be given over to desolation, with no inhabitants, the *silence,* or tranquillity, will be deafening, as in deserts and untrackable wastes.

The God of all, therefore, is by no means at a loss if he chooses to chastise sinners; rather, many and varied are the chastisements available to him, and nothing will stand in the way of his imposing penalties on the offender. On the other hand, the one who averts wrath by repentance will escape, by winning over to clemency the Lord, who is kindly and compassionate.[2] (510)

Hear this, you who oppress the needy in the morning and withdraw the rights of the poor to the land, who say, When will the moon pass and we shall engage in commerce? When will the sabbath come and we shall open the stores so as to set the measure short, increase the weight, make the balance unfair so as to get ownership of the poor with silver and of the lowly for a pair of sandals, and to trade by every kind of sale? (vv.4–6) One of the Pharisees once asked our Lord Jesus Christ what is the first and greatest commandment in the Law, and was told that the first commandment is this: "You shall love the Lord your God with all your heart and all your strength, and the second is like it, You shall love your neighbor as yourself." You would see (511) the divinely inspired Paul himself also relating every form of virtue to love, as it were, confidently calling it greater than both faith and hope,[3] and clearly taking it for granted that the person lacking it would be nothing, even if giving his possessions to those who ask, even if giving his body to persecutors to be burnt. Everything great and remarkable in

---

1. Song 1.17.
2. It is a suitable moment for Cyril to close his third tome on Amos, who now begins a fresh appeal for social justice.
3. Cf. Mt 22.36–39; 1 Cor 13.13.

us, therefore, is completely the result of love for God and the brethren. If, on the other hand, you were at variance with the laws of love, and were seen not to share in its blooms, you would be completely useless and would rightly be considered to be involved in every form of depravity, since wherever good is left untried, there sin truly blossoms.

Note, therefore, the overall plan of the text. He initially accused Ephraim, or Israel, of godlessness, remember, and exposed them adoring heifers and having no love for the one God, who is divine by nature, doubtless because of their attachment to the works of their own hands. He now presents also their truly unholy treatment even of their brethren and their complete lack of love for the neighbor. He mounts his charge in general, very clearly and in brief, yet lists the crimes; consequently, he says, *Hear this, you who oppress the needy in the morning and withdraw the rights of the poor to the land.* It is as if he were to say, The statement is addressed to you in your great zeal to wrest the land from the weak and withdraw the rights of the needy in the morning. While some people, you see, are lovers of the moderation that is pleasing to God, offer thanksgiving to God for the dawning of the day, worship him, pray to him, and devote attention to him for every praiseworthy happening, others have an eye only to dominating people, think nothing is comparable to oppressing them, and make it their endeavor from the very moment of leaping out of bed at the break of day to proceed to their customary depravity and oppression of whomever they can. It is as if they blame night for interrupting them and not giving them the opportunity for oppression sufficient for their needs. These are the ones who say, *When will the moon pass and we shall engage in commerce?* This is the wish of moneylenders and misers, mean and sordid people, who are always anxious for the end of the month so that by amassing money bit by bit they may make their own gain more substantial, and by piling interest upon interest they grind down weaker people in defiance of the Law's clear statement, "If you lend money to your neighbor, you shall not be insistent with him, you shall not exact interest from him."[4]

4. Ex 22.25.

But while some ask, *When will the moon pass and we shall engage in commerce?* others, who are affected with an equal or even worse ailment, in thrall to base gain, ask in turn, *When will the sabbath come and we shall open the stores so as to set the measure short, increase the weight, and make the balance unfair?* There is need to explain what this means: the sabbath they wanted to pass so that they might *open the stores so as to set the measure short and increase the weight.* The text of Deuteronomy says, "Every seventh year you shall grant a remission of debts. This is the manner of the remission: you shall remit every debt your neighbor owes you, and (513) you shall not require it of your brother, because remission has been proclaimed by the Lord your God. Of a foreigner you shall exact what is owed you by him; you shall remit your claim on your brother." And likewise further on, "If there is among you anyone in need from your brethren in one of your cities in the land that the Lord your God is giving you, you shall not be hard-hearted or tight-fisted toward your needy brother. You shall open your hand to him, willingly lending him whatever is required to meet the need." It gives an exhortation in the words, "Be careful to avoid keeping an unspoken thought hidden in your heart, The seventh year is approaching, the year of remission, and your eye will look with malice on your needy brother, and you do not give him anything. He will cry against you to the Lord, and it will be a serious sin for you."[5]

The Law therefore ordered cancellation of debts in sabbath years, as it were, commanding it be done every seventh year. There was then a reminder to be not malicious but openhanded to those in need, even if the year of remission was not far off. People with large and abundant stores were tight-fisted, and anxiously awaited the seventh year, which was already at their doors; they then lent money in such a way as to avoid the debt being imposed in the times of remission. These are the ones who asked, *When will the sabbath come*—that is, the sabbath of years—*and we shall open the stores?* The offense did not stop at that; instead, they took advantage of the misfortunes of the poor, (514) giving portions with *short measures* and taking with

5. Dt 15.1–3, 7–9.

weights that were not equal but even heavier and much weightier than the original, despite God's saying through the wise Moses, "There shall not be in your bag a large weight and a small weight; there shall not be in your house a large measure and a small measure. You shall have a fair and just weight, and you shall have a fair and just measure, so that your days may be long in the land that the Lord your God is giving you as an inheritance, because everyone who does this, everyone who commits injustice, is an abomination to the Lord your God."[6]

They placed no importance on righteousness, however; instead, with an eye to profit they oppressed the needy, getting the better, as it were, of the miserable, and using them like *sandals.* "The poor are the pastures of the rich," Scripture says. The author of Proverbs brings us no little benefit in saying, "Let a man's heart ponder justice so that his steps may be guided by God. For a man's ways are before God's eyes, and he surveys all his paths." Since God observes, then, and carefully scrutinizes all our affairs, truly good and prudent people should follow straight paths and consider nothing to be as important as love for God and brethren. Love for God involves a faith that is genuine and lasting, and love for the brethren is linked to the achievements of righteousness, for the statement is true, "Love does no wrong to a neighbor."[7]

Now, in my view, people who wish to be well thought of and lead a lawful (515) life should "clothe themselves in compassion," carefully avoid accursed avarice, and make available their goods to the needy. By observing in this way the law of love, in fact, they will be illustrious and held worthy of imitation by God and man. Scripture says, remember, "He distributed his goods and gave to the needy; his righteousness abides forever."[8]

The Lord swears by the arrogance of Jacob: All your deeds will ultimately not be forgotten, and the land will not be alarmed for this; all of its inhabitants will grieve, and the end will rise up like a river, and

---

6. Dt 25.13–16.

7. Sir 13.19; Prv 15.29, 5.21, and 4.26 LXX; Rom 13.10.

8. Col 3.12; Ps 112.9. This time Cyril has warmed to Amos's strictures against social injustice (by his usual means of lengthy scriptural quotation rather than his own parenesis). Neither Jerome nor Antioch prompted this, Theodoret not even quoting the text of Amos.

subside like a river of Egypt (vv.7–8). God charges the descendants
of Jacob with a crime of pride, scorning the divine laws, completely spurning the Lord's wishes, and trampling even on love
for brethren. So he *swears by the arrogance of Jacob.* Not that we
claim that the God of all takes some people's pride as an oath;
he *swears by it* in the sense of determining an appropriate penalty for it. Now, what does he actually *swear?* Not to bypass the
crimes and show them tolerance forever—the sense of *ultimately,* in my view, being "forever," "reaching a conclusion." He next
says that with the removal of forgetfulness regarding their unholy exploits, how would *the land* not be filled with panic once
the foe strike it, and instead they will *grieve* for their endurance
of a harsh and ineluctable (516) calamity? What, in turn, is this
calamity? There will rise up on them *the end,* he says, *like a river of
Egypt,* submerging everything, and drowning the whole land of
Samaria with its numerous floods that cannot be resisted; and
in similar fashion it will *subside,* dragging down everything that
falls and sparing nothing at all.[9] Sennacherib, remember, came
up with his countless hordes, covering the land *like a river,* and
subjecting everything to himself; and he went back to his own
country, drawing a vast and innumerable people into captivity.

When we scorn God, therefore, we shall find the powers
within us rebelling, the result being that we experience tumult
and grief, falling under their power, as it were, and of necessity reduced to service befitting a slave. They will, in fact, oppose us like irresistible water dragging us to ruin and causing
us to perish by drowning. "Rivers will not close us in," Scripture
says, nor "will the depths submerge or the tempest overwhelm"
those bent on pleasing God. Then it is, in fact, then it is that by
vigorously casting off the demons' oppression and taking very
little notice of their knavery we shall rejoice to say, "If the Lord
had not been with us, let Israel say, if the Lord had not been
with us when people rose up against us, they would surely have
swallowed us alive"; and again, "Our soul crossed over the tor-

---

9. The LXX has difficulty rendering v.8, where our Heb. mentions "the
Nile." Various forms of the LXX differ also as to whether an interrogative is involved (Pusey's lemma not in accord, it seems, with Cyril's commentary). Theodore, unusually, declines to cite the text, and Jerome is of no help to Cyril.

rent, surely our soul crossed over the rising water."[10] In other words, if the water of the devil's insults—that is, the onrush of passions—rises up and cannot be resisted by our minds, (517) through Christ we shall succeed; we shall cross over the onset of his malice like some torrent.

On that day, says the Lord God, the sun will set at midday, and the light on the earth will be darkened in daytime. I shall turn your feasts into mourning, and all your songs into lamentation. I shall bring sackcloth on all loins, and baldness on every head. I shall make Jacob like mourning for a beloved, and those with him like a day of sorrow (vv.9–10). This gives rise to a double interpretation. It is generally the custom for the holy prophets, you see, especially at the end of their discourse, to mention Christ and give an explanation of the mystery concerning him, even if still shrouded in obscurity. So come now, considering both meanings, let us state what is likely. We shall first detail the sequence of the passage, and then proceed to apply the sense of the words to the interpretation about Christ. *On that day*, then, when the *end* comes upon all of Samaria like *a river of Egypt*, a terrible and profound *darkness* will descend on all its inhabitants, so to speak, like sunset, though it is *midday*. We do not claim that the light of the sun really set; rather, it was the disaster of war that came upon the inhabitants of Samaria like darkness; an overwhelming grief disturbs the mind (518) when it disappears, the heart is darkened by a fate beyond hope and expectation, and the severity of the calamities produces a kind of mist and gloom in the hearts of those affected.[11]

They will therefore see darkness, he says, even if *the sun* is still *at midday*. Those in former times, on the other hand, who celebrated feasts in splendid style, always making use of strings, lyres, and the most melodious songs, will desist from such diversions and instead mock them, turning their *songs into lamentations*, adopting the weeds of mourning, namely, *sackcloth and*

10. Is 43.2; Pss 69.15 and 124.1–5.
11. The apocalyptic description has Cyril (and his Antiochene counterparts) struggling to give adequate comment; he settles for an historical substrate relayed in figurative fashion, though promising also a christological elaboration—"customary," he says, when a prophet nears his conclusion, though still "shrouded in obscurity."

baldness. Now, it was a shameful thing to go baldheaded; the divinely inspired Job, for instance, cut his hair when his children perished.[12] The text says, *I shall make Jacob like mourning for a beloved*; that is to say, those who see him in this condition will grieve over him as a mother or father over the loss of an only child who is beloved. *And those with him like a day of sorrow*: those from neighboring Judah and Benjamin who worshiped idols along with Ephraim and were *with him* in this respect, will be found to have *a day of sorrow* and suffer pangs, as it were, singing songs of troubles, grief, and hardship. Sennacherib had ravaged Samaria, remember, and taken all their cities; then he sent the Rabshakeh from Lachish to Jerusalem, where he threatened a dire fate to those on the wall. He so shattered the indifference of the residents of Jerusalem that they immediately expected to perish along with the Samaritans. Then it was that King Hezekiah in deep depression sent someone to the prophet Isaiah with the words, "Today is a day of tribulation, reproach, reproof, and (519) wrath, because the pregnant woman is suffering birth pangs and has no strength to give birth."[13] He therefore speaks of a *day of sorrow* as though of the pangs and depression of childbirth. They were thus in a *day of sorrow*, the residents of Jerusalem who expected to perish, following Ephraim in the practice of idolatry.

While this is relevant and applicable, as I said, to those at that time who provoked the Lord of all against themselves, you could also apply it no less to those who offended Emmanuel himself at the time of the Incarnation. They were the ones, in fact, who *oppress the needy in the morning*, that is, those who were reluctant to choose to live a lawful life, who had no other concern than to undermine justice, and presumed to set at naught what had been clearly determined by the divine commandments and to oppress consistently any weaker people they chose. They were the ones who would ask, "When will the moon pass and we shall engage in commerce? When will the sabbath come and we shall open the stores so as to set the measure short, increase the weight, make the balance unfair?" (v.5) The fact that the scribes

12. Jb 1.20.
13. 2 Kgs 18.28–35; Is 37.3.

and Pharisees were very greedy and miserly we would learn in many ways by concentrating on the sense of the Gospel compositions. On the one hand, Christ recommended the lovers of the goodness that is pleasing to God to be seen to be above base gain and freed from all avarice, while on the other he urged them to go still further and provide and distribute one's goods to the needy. What did the evangelist say? "The scribes and the Pharisees, who were lovers of money, heard this and ridiculed him."[14] It would therefore be rightfully said of them, "The Lord swears by the arrogance of Jacob: Your deeds will ultimately not be forgotten." It was truly pride for them to set at naught divine laws and, what is still worse than this, then to rage against Christ himself. Consequently, their sins will not now pass into oblivion; the "end has risen up" once more against them, as it were, and the Roman war like an overflowing "river" (vv.7–8).

Now, when they consigned the Lord of all to crucifixion, *the sun* set on them, and *the light was darkened*; there was "darkness from noon till three in the afternoon." This was the clear sign to the Jews of the spiritual darkening of the souls of those who had crucified him. "A hardening has come upon part of Israel," remember, as the divinely inspired Paul writes, and "to this very day whenever Moses is read, a veil lies over their mind." Blessed David also cursed them, saying out of love for God, "Let their eyes be darkened so that they do not see, and forever bend their back." Now, the fact that they have also been mourning, turning their *feasts* to gloom, would be clear also from Christ's words to the women weeping over him as he was being led out to the cross: "Daughters of Jerusalem, weep not for me, but weep for yourselves and for your children."[15] They have in fact been mourning as they perished along with the city and the divine Temple itself as Romans incinerated everything.

Accordingly, he says, *I shall make him* (Emmanuel, that is) *like mourning for a beloved*, (521) *and those with him like a day of sorrow:* the believers mourned Jesus crucified, and in their grief the

---

14. Lk 16.14. In place of recognition of the apocalyptic character of the verses, Cyril is launching into quite fevered polemic against leaders of the Jews of NT times. Theodoret will learn this tendency from him.

15. Mt 27.45; Rom 11.25; 2 Cor 3.15; Ps 69.24; Lk 23.28.

women stood at a distance, Mary Magdalene and likewise Mary the mother of James and some others with them. Creation itself also mourned its Lord: the sun was darkened, rocks were split, the Temple itself took on the appearance of mourners when the veil was rent "from top to bottom." God suggested as much to us in the statement of Isaiah, "I shall clothe heaven with darkness, and make sackcloth its clothing." So the *mourning for him* was *as for a beloved*; and *those with him*, the disciples, are made *like a day of sorrow*. After all, who could doubt that they also were mourning? In fact, it was to people grieving that the women reported the resurrection of Christ; then it was that, after briefly refusing to accept it, they ran to the tomb. Perhaps it was to these women as they brought the good news of the resurrection that the prophet Isaiah said in spirit, "Hurry, you women coming from a spectacle; this is a people without understanding (the people of the Jews, obviously); therefore, he who made them will not have compassion on them, and the one who formed them will not have mercy."[16]

Lo, the days are coming, says the Lord, and I shall send hunger on the land—not a hunger for bread or a thirst for water, but a hunger for hearing the word of the Lord. The waters will be shaken as far as the sea, (522) *and from north to east they will run about in search of the word of the Lord, and will not find it* (vv.11–12). Scripture says, "Lord, in distress we remembered you, your correcting us by slight distress." In his knowledge that distress is excellent and truly beneficial, the divinely inspired David also said at one time, "In distress I called on the Lord," and likewise at another, "It was good that you humbled me so that I should come to learn your ordinances."[17] Distress brings us to our senses, you see, and withdraws us from the toils of indifference by inducing us to love the practice of goodness and by submitting the inflexible and rebellious person to the yoke of holiness and obedience out of necessity and fear.

When Samaria had been laid waste, therefore, and the Babylonian had burnt its cities, even if at that time some people wanted to learn what was God's will, and what to do and say to

16. Mk 15.40; Mt 27.51; Is 50.3 and 27.11.
17. Is 26.16; Pss 118.5 and 119.71.

gain mercy from him so as to be delivered from his wrath, there would be no one to tell them, he says. In fact, I shall give rise in them to a *hunger* for the words of God such that no prophet at all would be found, even if they should travel from west to east, from south to north. This resembles what was said by God to blessed Ezekiel: "I shall bind up your tongue; you shall be speechless and not be a man reproving them, because they are a rebellious house";[18] that is to say, once they had spurned the word from God, they would have no rightful claim to receive it even if willing to. Now, by *waters being shaken* he refers to the immeasurable mass of the Jews being affected by panic (523) and then resembling the waves of the sea that are tossed in all directions by the gusts of wind.

A different interpretation: when Christ was crucified, the wretched Jews had a *hunger* for words from God; there was no longer any prophet in their midst, no teacher with precise knowledge of the way to render digestible the density of the Mosaic narrative and to clarify the mysteries buried in the text. They had not given credence to Christ's words: "I am the bread of life come down from heaven to give life to the world." Consequently, they heard him also speaking of old through Isaiah: "Lo, my servants will eat, but you will go hungry; my servants will drink, but you will go thirsty." It is true, in fact, that "the Lord will never let the righteous go hungry, but he will thwart the life of the impious" by not sending down to them the word that nourishes their mind to have a longing for virtue. As the Savior himself said, remember, "Not by bread alone will a person live, but by every word that issues from the mouth of God."[19]

On that day the beautiful young women and the young men will faint for thirst, and those who swear by the propitiation of Samaria, and will say, As your god lives, Dan will fall, and as your god lives, Beer-sheba will fall, never to rise again (vv.13–14). The passage highlights the seizure by the enemy of their sons and daughters, the sense of *the beautiful young women and the young men,* for we shall find that people of this age in particular (524) were normally taken off into captivity. On the other hand, the passage probably conveys

18. Ezek 3.26.
19. Jn 6.48, 32–33; Is 65.13; Prv 10.3; Mt 4.4; Dt 8.3.

something else as well of the hidden meaning. There were some *young women* living in the shrines of the idols, and with them youngsters or adolescent boys, through whom the dabblers in magic thought something could be learned from the demons; by calling on them as though on uncontaminated bodies, they tried to get a response in unspoken whispers. It is said that some who were willing to be involved in the sacrilege prophesied in a similar manner. Accordingly, the fact that there will be a failure in Israel, not only of the word from God through holy prophets that was both useful and necessary for reform, but also of the one from the false seers or demons that came to some through girls and boys, he suggests by saying, *On that day the beautiful young women will faint*, as if to say, your beautiful young women will perish along with the others.

The passage also makes ironic reference to the *swearing by the propitiation of Samaria* on the part of young men along with the maidens.[20] It was their custom, you see, to take oaths by the gods in Samaria, or the heifers, and perhaps by way of mockery of God they applied to the statues the words, *As your god lives, Dan, and as your god lives, Beer-sheba.* These were cities of Judea, situated at the very extremities of the country, setting the limits, as it were, of the land from the south to the sea. So it would be like saying, As the god of the land of the Jews lives—that is, the calf; the interior is included in mention of the extremities, and there is reference to the whole.[21] He says, *the young women and the young men will faint for thirst*, no longer supplied with the false prophecies of the demons on account of (525) their being subject to the foreigners, or victims of the sword, or experiencing infamous and intolerable captivity.

When Christ was crucified, along with the sun throughout the world and its visible light, spiritual shining and enlightenment through the Spirit also set on the Jews; they were deprived of the divine word and consolation from on high. So the *maid-*

20. The Heb. reads "shame," not "propitiation," as Jerome observed.
21. This is a somewhat different explanation of the mention of these cities from before; Amos had mentioned Beer-sheba at 5.5 as a place of illicit pilgrimage for northerners (cf. 2 Kgs 23.8), as Dan had been the site of one of Jeroboam's golden calves (1 Kgs 12.30).

ens together with the *young men* among them *failed*—that is, the fine and estimable souls; their being uncontaminated is suggested by mention of their *maidenhood*, and their strength and vigor by mention of their *youth*. After all, who was holy among them, since the Law could make nothing perfect,[22] nor did it suffice for righteousness for them? Whence would come their spiritual health and vigor of mind when they were unacquainted with the conspicuous achievements of the Gospel way of life? Would they not all be torpid, in sin, and slothful in thinking? How could there be any doubt of this? They were *fainting for thirst*, therefore, and it is not to them that the statement is made, "Draw water with joy from the springs of salvation"; instead, "I commanded the clouds to rain no rain on them" because they were disobedient to Christ himself when he cried aloud in the words, "If any thirst, let them come to me and drink." They abandoned him, despite his being "a fountain of life, and they dug broken cisterns unable to hold water," giving heed to human teachings and commandments,[23] which are unable to give water for life, or to bring those using them to salvation.

22. Heb 7.19.
23. Is 12.3 and 5.6; Jn 7.37; Jer 2.13; Is 29.13; Mt 15.9.

COMMENTARY ON AMOS,
CHAPTER NINE

I saw the Lord standing at the altar. He said, Strike the altar, and the gates will be shaken; break it on everyone's heads, and their survivors I shall kill with the sword (v.1).

ITH THE EYE OF THEIR MIND enlightened by the torch of the Spirit, the blessed prophets were not only beneficiaries of knowledge of the future, but also at times had a vision of the events themselves as though they were painted on a tablet. While themselves aghast, they strove to make the listeners similarly affected in their earnest efforts to clarify the force of the visions. Blessed Amos had thus said, "The Lord said to me, The end has come for my people Israel: I shall never again pass their way. The ceilings of the Temple will lament on that day, says the Lord; the fallen will be numerous in every place, and I shall cast silence."[1] And, lo, he sees what had been foretold taking effect in actual events in keeping with the prophecy; he says that he had a vision of *the Lord standing at the altar* as if beginning the overthrow and bidding it to happen. Now, God was *standing at the altar*, not to pay it honor—a silly interpretation; it would be most absurd to think and claim that God was paying respect and honor to the altars of idols: how could he honor the altar of the heifers? Rather, he stood there for the purpose of destroying and bringing it to the (527) ground.

Consequently, as if on the point of beginning the overthrow, he gave the prophet instructions in these words: *Strike the altar;* and he said, Let *the gates* shake and then the temple totter as though on the point of immediate collapse. And *break it on everyone's heads,* that is, begin with the more prominent among

1. 8.2–3.

them, and strike the leaders, who act as *head* of the others. *The survivors will perish along with them* and share the fate of the leaders, falling to the sword themselves. It is like what was said in Ezekiel to the six men who began from the gate facing north, carrying axes and following the man clad in the frock; it was said to them by God, "Pass through the city behind him and kill; show no pity or mercy. Slay old and young, women and children without exception, beginning with my sanctuary."[2] Do you observe how he made the leaders the first spoils of the wrath, or those who gave the impression of being venerable and holy as a result perhaps of enjoying also the glory of priesthood, or distinguished by other honors? As such, you see, they were *heads* of the others.

Now, this happened also to those who vented their frenzy on our Lord Jesus Christ. The wretches set little store by Law and Prophets, remember, and did not accept Christ, the fulfillment of Law and Prophets; instead, though clearly aware that he was the heir, (528) they cast him out of the vineyard and eventually crucified him. So they were given over to devastation by the Roman generals, that celebrated Temple was burnt down, the *altar* in it was thrown down, *the gates* shaken, and the leaders perished along with the masses, for war spared none of their number.

Each of the faithful, too, if they are a temple of God by having him dwelling within, or are considered an altar by offering their own life to God, but then provoke God by setting their gaze on indifference, will be reduced to nothing and suffer dreadful overthrow. The Lord is no respecter of persons, after all, and "the righteousness of the righteous will not save them on the day they are led astray," as Scripture says.[3]

No fugitive of their number will escape, and no survivor of their number will be saved. If they dig into Hades, from there will my hand snatch them; if they climb to heaven, from there I shall bring them down. If they hide on the top of Carmel, from there I shall search out and take them; if they hide from my sight at the bottom of the sea, there I shall

---

2. Ezek 9.5–6.
3. Ezek 33.12. Cyril reverts to the hermeneutical process he prefers, moving from the historical substrate to a New Testament fulfillment and then to a spiritual application.

command the sea serpent, and it will bite them. If they go in captivity in front of their enemies, there I shall command the sword, and it will kill them. I shall fix my eyes on them for trouble and not for good (vv.1–4). It will then perhaps in good time be said to those of their number who hear the hymn to God of blessed David, (529) "Where am I to go from your Spirit? And where am I to flee from your face? If I ascend to heaven, you are there; if I descend to Hades, you are present. If I were to take my wings at dawn and dwell at the farthest limits of the sea, even there your hand would guide me and your right hand hold me." The Divinity is all-seeing, in fact, and as well is all-powerful; you could not escape the notice of the unsleeping eye; he said, remember, "I am a God who is nearby, not a God who is far off; surely nothing will be hidden from me?" No one would escape the calamity befalling them by divine decree; Scripture says, "Who will avert the uplifted hand?"[4] In other words, what stratagem would be of any good to us? What kind of assistance would be of assistance to us if God determines we should suffer?

Accordingly, the fact that planning and scheming and every form of deliberation are completely useless for the victims of divine wrath he makes clear by saying, No one would *escape*, even if they were to hide in *Hades*—a hyperbolic expression—even if climbing to *heaven* and passing to the *top of Carmel*; wherever they went, they would be seized. Even if they went into the *sea*, they would fall foul of the *sea serpent*, or according to the Hebrew text they would be handed over to the huge fish; even if they were among *enemies* and then *in captivity*, miserably subjected to the yoke of slavery, even so, he says, it would not suffice as a penalty for them, for the terror of the *sword* would beset them. (530) The God of all would not cease *fixing his eyes on them*, an index of anger and threat; we, too, sometimes fasten our eye on offenders, regarding them with a fierce and unsmiling look. Since God surveys also good and righteous people, however, he distinguishes between the different glances by saying *for trouble and not for good*; he regards them, he is saying, not to grant them anything good, but so that they may receive a penalty and ret-

---

4. Ps 139.7–10; Jer 23.23 and 32.27; Is 14.27.

ribution determined by him that is unchanging and, as it were, fixed.

The Lord, the Lord God almighty, he who touches the earth and moves it; and all its inhabitants will mourn; its end will rise up like a river, and fall like a river of Egypt (v.5). Out of love the prophet does not allow the listeners to disbelieve his words as unlikely to take effect. This was the mark of a man recommending that they learn to choose the better part and, out of respect, to do what is to their advantage so that God, for his part, might put an end to the effects of wrath, hold the disaster in check, and (531) accept their repentance, as he always has compassion on those willing to be converted. He therefore mentions that God is powerful, and is quite capable of bringing to pass what he said: *The Lord*, he says, *the Lord God almighty, he who touches the earth and moves it.* It is as if to say, Do not think of someone offended in your terms; the Lord is no human being. Instead, he is the Lord of hosts, who with his own hand *touches the earth*—Samaria, I mean—*and moves it*, not causing it to experience a normal earthquake, but shaking it all with war and insufferable calamities and making it totter. Consequently, he says, *all its inhabitants will mourn; its end will rise up like a river of Egypt*, overflowing and flooding everything; in this way it will recede in turn, dragging and carrying down everything in similar fashion. Now, we remarked that he compares Sennacherib, the vast numbers of the Assyrians, and the war waged by them against Samaria to the waves of the rivers.

While flight will be pointless for those offending and distressing God, the hand of retribution will be utterly strong and ineluctable, nor would there be any assistance or consolation for those in its grasp. "If he closes the door on you," Scripture says, remember, "who will open it?" It would instead be far better to avert the wrath by recourse to what is pleasing and acceptable to him. Now, this would happen in proper fashion if we were to forget the past,[5] disown shameful practices, and gain luster for ourselves by increase in virtue; then it is that we shall escape the effects of his anger, and easily bring the Creator, who is kindly by

---

5. Jb 12.14; Phil 3.14.

nature, (532) to accord us oversight that is loving and merciful.

He who builds his ascension into heaven and his promise on the foundations of the earth, who summons the water of the sea and pours it out on the face of the earth, the Lord God almighty is his name (v.6). He continues with a multitude of words to alarm those who abandon God and force them into a change for the better by skillfully outlining the pre-eminence and might of the divine nature. He endeavors to prove that without question he implements his promises, with no one to impede him; "he who touches the earth and moves it" (v.5), he said, in the metaphors just now explained by us. He is the same one *who builds his ascension into heaven,* as if to say, He possesses complete authority to mount the heavens themselves and to gain such power over all things as to hold in subjection to himself creation below and also those in heaven, that is, the blessed multitude of the holy angels. It should be realized that the divinely inspired Jacob also witnessed this in an obscure fashion; there was a ladder reaching from earth to heaven, and "the Lord stood above it,"[6] and he saw the angels ascending and descending—the meaning, (533) in my view, of *building his ascension into heaven.*

Whatever was *promised* to those *on earth,* he is saying, is quite immovable, permanent, and, as it were, laid *on foundations;* the Lord of hosts will in no way fail in vigor, nor would any word of his prove ineffectual. The Savior confirms this for us in saying, "Heaven and earth will pass away, but my words will not pass away."[7] It is he who is the one who also draws up *the water of the sea* by ineffable powers, and sends it as rain *on the earth;* in other words, once again it is he who manages human affairs with such strength as even without difficulty to transform the nature of what is made to whatever he wishes, his name being *Lord God* and in addition to this *almighty.* The name is not an idle one, as in the case of a human being; instead, it is correctly devised on the basis of actual reality. He is given that name, in fact, by us and by the holy angels on the basis of his being Lord by his essence and his enjoying control of everything. The prophet's purpose, therefore, is, as far as possible and to the extent of his

6. Gn 28.12–13.
7. Mt 24.35.

ability, to terrify those who are deceived, and firmly to persuade them to reverse their steps with determination, consider righteousness a splendid thing, and likewise regard reverence for God as preferable to the terrors of the future as a strong deterrent against an inclination to shameful behavior. This in my view is the proper meaning of the statement of David to the Lord of all, "Keep their jaws under tight muzzle and rein if they do not come near you."[8] (534)

Now, the statement *He who builds his ascension into heaven* could be a reference also to Christ, and rightly so; it is he who came from on high and from heaven, being born by nature God from God. Accordingly, he also said, "I am from above"; and John in his wisdom said of him, "The one who comes from above is above all." It is of his essence that he has *ascension into heaven*; it is applied to him as God, as I said. He made it accessible to people on earth, ascending to the Father as "a forerunner on our behalf"—and as the divinely inspired Paul writes, "he opened for us a new and living way"—and appearing as man "on our behalf in the presence of the God" and Father, who also "along with him raised us and seated us in the heavenly places."[9] You see, when Christ ascended, *he built* his own *ascension* also for us if what blessed Paul says is true: "For this we declare to you by the word of the Lord, that we who are alive, who are left until the coming of the Lord, will by no means precede those who have died. For the Lord himself with a cry of command, with the archangel's call, and with the sound of God's trumpet, will descend from heaven, and the dead in Christ will rise first. Then we who are alive, who are left, will be caught up in the clouds together with them to meet the Lord in the air, and so we shall be with the Lord forever."[10] He therefore ascended as man, his purpose being that the ascension befitting him and only him, being God and from God, he might make accessible also to us who believe.

He it was who also set *his promise* (535) *on the foundations of the earth*; far from proving false, he puts into effect whatever he

<hr />

8. Ps 32.9.
9. Jn 8.23; 3.31; Heb 6.20, 10.20, and 9.24; Eph 2.6.
10. 1 Thes 4.15–17.

promised to achieve for us. He said, remember, "It is to your advantage that I go away, for if I do not go away, the Paraclete will
not come to you; but if I go, I shall send him to you." Accordingly, he also bade the holy apostles "not to leave Jerusalem, but
to wait for the promise of the Father" that they had heard from
him. He poured out grace generously on them; hence they also
became "witnesses of his glory in Jerusalem and in Judea" and
in all the earth. We shall also find a different sense in the *found-
ing of his promise;* we have believed that he will raise us from the
dead, make us proof against corruption, "transform the body of
our lowliness that is to be conformed to the body of his glory,"[11]
and make us sharers in his kingdom.

He it is *who summons the water of the sea and pours it out on the
face of the earth;* that is, he transforms what is bitter, unacceptable,
and unsuited for us into what is beneficial. "The letter of the
Law kills,"[12] remember, according to Paul in his wisdom, and in
itself it is a useless shadow, but it has become for us who understand it most beneficial for an understanding of Christ, and has
emerged as a kind of spiritual shower irrigating in some fashion
the earth under heaven. It is true that the Law, which formerly
was harsh and unbearable for the ancients, has become for us
a guide to the mystery of Christ so that even through it we may
succeed in bearing fruit by reducing the density of the shadow
(536) to the reality. We shall therefore take the statement as an
example, adducing as a proof also the water of Marah that had
been bitter but was sweetened when God showed the wood to
blessed Moses and bade him put it in the water.[13] The wood was
an image and type of the precious cross, through which the Law
became sweet and, as it were, potable, despite in the past being
bitter; "the letter kills," as I said—or, rather, as Paul wrote in his
wisdom.

*Are you not to me like the people of Ethiopia, people of Israel? says the
Lord. Did I not bring Israel up from the land of Egypt, the Philistines
from Cappadocia, and the Syrians from Bothros? Lo, the eyes of the Lord*

11. Jn 16.7; Acts 1.4, 8; Phil 3.21.

12. 2 Cor 3.6. A key hermeneutical principle of Cyril's is that the Old Testament, superficially of little value, has a role in explicating the mystery of Christ
for those who have true faith and understand it in the light of the crucifixion.

13. Ex 15.23–25.

God are upon the kingdom of sinners, and I shall remove it from the face of the earth (vv.7–8). The people of Israel were forever conceited, parading hither and yon their ancestors' nobility and giving their tongue free rein to claim, "We have Abraham as our ancestor." But they were given a reply by Christ in these terms: "If you were children of Abraham, you would do the works of Abraham." In fact, "not all Israelites truly belong to Israel, and not all Abraham's children are his true descendants."[14] It is rather the similarity of works that rightly confers the ability to make open boasts of ancestors' nobility. By contrast, they disparaged all the other nations by claiming that of all the nations God treated them as special, rescuing them *from the land of Egypt* and bringing (537) them into the land of promise. While the claim was true, and they in particular should with due recompense have brought joy to the one who showed them esteem, they wrongfully insulted him with complete apostasy and sank into all sorts of depravity. The wretches then reached such a degree of derangement as to think that for them descent from Abraham was sufficient grounds for prosperity and good reputation, and for their being brought from Egypt to the land of promise.

So that they might realize, therefore, that such boasting brought them no benefit when they lapsed into indifference and were unprepared to be pious, he consequently says, Even if you perhaps enjoy nobility from your ancestors, shall I not think of you in the same way as the people of *Ethiopia*, who are not descended from Abraham? The Divinity, after all, is no respecter of persons or biased, and does not recognize nobility of the flesh that is deprived of good deeds. It accords complete respect to spiritual nobility, which is accompanied by the adornment of splendid achievements. Being transferred from Egypt to another country, however, also seems to you to be something extraordinary and special: why so, and what good did it do you? Others also can claim to have received this from me; I brought *Philistines*—that is, Palestinians in the Hebrew text—and I brought from *Bothros the Syrians*, that is, all those who were at that time subject to the kingdom of Damascus. (537)

Now, it should be realized that for *Bothros* the Hebrew has

14. Mt 3.9; Jn 8.39; Rom 9.7.

Cyrene; so while the Palestinians were settlers from *Cappadocia*, the Syrians were from Cyrene. He called Cyrene *Bothros*, although quite elevated and situated on high, on account of its being situated in a deep hollow; the whole land of Libya, so to speak, has hollows that are coastal and exposed.[15] My purpose as I gaze on all equally, therefore, he is saying, is to clear the land of *every kingdom of sinners.* Hence hereditary fame would be of no use to those who possess it; good behavior and a strong disposition to a longing for virtue is judged by God as nobility, along with a readiness to match the piety of one's ancestors.

Except that I shall finally not remove the house of Jacob, says the Lord. Because, lo, I shall give the command, and I shall scatter the house of Israel among all the nations in the way grain is scattered with a winnowing fan, and no fragment will fall to the ground. All the sinners of my people will die by the sword, those who say, Troubles will not approach or come upon us (vv.8–10). The remnant will once again be preserved for the house of Israel "on account of the ancestors";[16] they will not undergo complete destruction, he is saying, nor will the whole race of *Jacob* disappear. Instead, he says, as though tossed about by a *winnowing fan* they will be scattered to *all the nations*, yet *no fragment will fall to the ground*, that is, the race of Jacob will not fall to such a degree that it will be completely fragmented, but will be (539) saved in the part that is the object of mercy—in other words, at that time some were brought back from captivity. There was also salvation through Christ; not a few of the Jews have believed, and at the end-time the remnant also will be saved when the mass of the nations is invited to enter.

Next, as though someone asks, If Jacob in turn is saved, who is the object of the threats? he gives a helpful explanation, that the anger is not directed indiscriminately at everyone, nor will

15. Cyril had seen in both Jerome and Theodore a debate about the place names, the latter not realizing that *bothros* might be simply the common noun "ditch," and dismissing the discussion as unnecessary precision, *akribologia*. Cyril agrees with this to the point of claiming that Amos is wanting only to undermine Israel's false claim to singularity, which is not the same as universalism, as some would see Amos's theme. Modern commentators also note the break in continuity at this point, and question the chapter's integrity.

16. Rom 11.28.

the effects of wrath fall on all without distinction. Instead, it will affect those whose sins were unbearable—the meaning of *All the sinners of my people will die by the sword, those who say, Troubles will not approach or come upon us.* Some of them reached such a stage of derangement, in fact, as to think that the holy prophets lied, and they actually claimed that no prediction would take effect. Jeremiah in his wisdom also confirms this in saying to God, "Lo, these people say to me, Where is the word of the Lord? Bring it on."[17] The sin of people so disposed is therefore twofold: they were guilty of provocation in many ways, and they thought reality was a fairy story.

Now, we shall find also at the time of his coming the leaders of the Jews not paying heed to the words of our Savior. Accordingly, they were also told, "Woe to you, scribes and Pharisees, hypocrites, for taking away the key of knowledge, not entering yourselves nor allowing those entering to enter"; and again, "Woe to you, scribes and Pharisees, hypocrites, for crossing sea and dry land to make a single convert, and when it happens, (540) making him twice as much a child of hell as yourselves."[18] Accordingly, instead of rightly being reputed to be children, they forfeited their ancestors' nobility and were reckoned as sons of Ethiopians; they have been consumed by the sword, and paid the judge a penalty commensurate with their folly.

On that day I shall raise up the tent of David that has fallen, rebuild its breaches, raise up its ruins, and rebuild it as the days of the age, in order that the remnant of the human race and all the nations called by my name may seek out the Lord, says the Lord, who does all this (vv.11–12). He kept making the promise that the race of Jacob would not finally meet with destruction, even if tossed about in some fashion with a winnowing fan; they would be refugees and exiles, expelled from fatherland and home, inhabiting a rough and foreign country, but would not be completely wiped out or meet with utter destruction. Consequently, he says that he will *raise up the tent of David that has fallen* and revive its remnants *as the days of the age,* that is, for length of days. He says that this will be a proof and confirmation for the other nations, near

17. Jer 17.15.
18. Lk 11.52; Mt 23.15.

and far, of the need to turn to God and (541) opt to seek him, marveling in every way at the magnitude of God's clemency and strength. You would therefore say that *the tent of David* refers to the race of the Jews, or the house of Jacob. Now, it should be understood that when Cyrus released them from captivity, they then returned to Judea and rebuilt the Temple; they fortified the devastated cities, built houses in them, and dwelt in security, undergoing wars waged by some enemies, like Antiochus and Hadrian, but no longer in captivity or suffering devastation, as they were while under the Babylonians.

While such is the factual reference in the passage, therefore, the deeper meaning closer to reality would be in Christ. You see, when the God and Father raised his *tent* that had *fallen* into death—that is, raised the flesh from the ground—and he came back to life, then it was that he restored all human things to their former condition, and imparted a fresh appearance to everything of ours that had been cast down. "Anyone who is in Christ is a new creation," Scripture says,[19] remember; we have been raised with him. Death *ruined the tents* of all, but the God and Father rebuilt them in Christ. It will not be for a limited time that we enjoy this, but for *the days of the age;* the good that is incorruption is not to be lost by us, and death will no longer have control over those who have been saved in Christ. Then is the time when *the remnant of the human race* acknowledges the one who is by nature and in truth God after the believers from Israel, abandoning that loathsome error of the past; it is not possible (542) that Christ was lying when he said, "Unless a grain of wheat falls into the ground and dies, it remains just a single grain; but if it dies, it bears much fruit"; and again, "When I am lifted up from the earth, I shall draw all people to myself." *On that day*, therefore, when I raise *the remnant* and *the fallen tent of David, all the nations* will be called, and it will be *my name* that

19. 2 Cor 5.17. With typical balance, Cyril first endeavors to find an historical substrate to the passage and then moves to a christological interpretation, the rebuilding of the "tent of David" being a key element. This phrase led Theodore to see Zerubbabel in focus initially, though constrained to adopt also a longer perspective by its citation at the council of Jerusalem in regard to the mission to the gentiles (Acts 15.16–17, strangely not cited by Cyril). Theodoret will firmly dismiss Zerubbabel's claims.

they will have. The fact that the predictions will completely and utterly take effect he confirms by adding, *says the Lord, who does all this;* if God is truly Lord, he will do this completely and utterly, being in no way limited, performing "marvelous and inscrutable things, glorious and wonderful beyond number."[20]

Lo, the days are coming, says the Lord, when the threshing will overtake the harvest and the grape will ripen in the sowing, the mountains will drip sweetness and all the hills will grow together with them. I shall turn back the captivity of my people Israel, and they will rebuild deserted cities and inhabit them; they will plant vineyards and drink their wine; they will plant gardens and eat their fruit. I shall plant them in their land, and they will never be plucked up from their land that I gave them, says the Lord God almighty (vv.13–15). He gave the same clear interpretation as I did. (543) If you chose to give a superficial, factual explanation, you would say again that he clearly promises the return of those who endured the captivity, and the fact that they will occupy their land, rebuilding cities and homes, and then enjoying a high level of prosperity. They will have an abundant harvest from the fields and involve themselves in farming with good cheer, so that their work of harvesting the most enjoyable crops proves unremitting as the yield from the threshing floor accompanies *the harvest.* The harvest is likewise extended to the period of *sowing,* so that the farmer moves from winevat, sickle, and grapes themselves to the ploughing of the fields, then clears the dust from the threshing floor and gives his attention to the winevats.

If, on the other hand, we opted to supply something more subtle and spiritual in interpreting the text, it would be quite appropriate to take the following meaning. When Christ returned to life, as I said, thanks to the Father's raising up the *tent of David* and rebuilding its ruins, there was an abundant and generous supply of spiritual goods for all people, both Greeks and Jews; "God is one, and he will justify the circumcised on the basis of faith and the uncircumcised through faith."[21] There is therefore as great a provision as possible of spiritual fruits to the believers, which is suggested very nicely by earthly fruits; grain

---

20. Jn 12.24, 32; Jb 5.9.
21. Rom 3.30.

and wine are in abundance, he says. We shall in this life receive grain for strength—namely, spiritual strength: Scripture says, "Bread strengthens the human heart," (544) bread that is wholly spiritual, divine, and from above—and *wine* for joy, Scripture likewise saying, "Wine gladdens the human heart," and, according to the statement of blessed Paul, we rejoice "in hope."[22]

As well, *the mountains drip sweetness.* By *mountains* here, therefore, he probably refers to the churches of Christ on account of the sublimity of the teachings in them and the excellence of piety towards God, and the fact that while the *mountains* appear covered in various plants, the churches of Christ have as their heads countless saints, like tall cedars and trees set close to the channels of spiritual water. Just as on mountains covered in trees vast numbers of bees hover about and produce honey that is sweet and valuable, so, too, in the churches likewise those who are more eminent than the others and better endowed with virtue and understanding collect the sweet honey of teaching on Christ and, as it were, distill it into the hearts of others. So it is in this sense, in my view, that *the mountains will drip sweetness.* He also said *the hills grow together* with them, the hills being second and of lower ranking in virtue compared with those more conspicuous for it; there are measures of holiness and righteousness in churches, and as Paul says, "according to the grace given to each one" by God,[23] who distributes such things. They will *grow together,* then, he says, luxuriant and fruitful, with a mind richly bedecked with the correctness of divine teachings.

Now, there is no doubting that the God of all also *turned back* our *captivity;* Christ proclaimed "release to captives," and from the devil's oppression he rescued (545) the earth under heaven. Then it was that, like farmers, we became completely attentive to spiritual fruitfulness, *planted gardens and vineyards, and will eat their fruit;* we shall receive the reward of our labors, and harvest the fruit of goodness. The fact that we have in God an immovable abode, and that, once the inheritance is given by him, no one shall dismiss those in it, he clarifies by saying, *I shall plant*

22. Ps 104.15; Rom 12.12.
23. Rom 12.6.

them in their land that I gave them, says the Lord God. "The gifts and the calling from God are irrevocable," remember,[24] and we shall have a stable hold on every good, with Christ himself as guide and festal leader. To him, together with the God and Father along with the Holy Spirit, be glory and honor for ages of ages. Amen. (546)

24. Lk 4.18; Rom 11.29.

COMMENTARY ON THE PROPHET OBADIAH

PREFACE TO THE
COMMENTARY ON OBADIAH

T IS LIKELY THAT OBADIAH LIKEWISE prophesied at the same time as Joel, and was, as it were, accorded the same vision and shared the explanation. While the divinely inspired Joel, remember, at the very end of his prophecy says, "Egypt will become a wasteland, and Idumea a desolate countryside for the wrongs done to the children of Judah, in return for the innocent blood they have poured out in their land,"[1] the other in due course explains in detail the manner and style of the destruction of Idumea. Since it is useful for the readers of the historical account in the book to learn precisely, even before other matters, about Idumea, its fate, and the reason for its being subjected to the disastrous effects of divine wrath, come now, let us give an explanation to the extent of our ability by clearly going into detail about such matters for eager students.

Idumeans, then, are called after Esau, from whom they are descended. Since he was called Edom—that is, "earthy"—surely on account of selling his (547) birthright, spurning the distinction due to him from it and preferring instead the offer of a single meal, paltry though it was, consequently they also called his descendants Idumeans. Now, the country of the Idumeans is also called Seir and Teman: Seir because of the report that its inhabitants were hairy, Esau also being hairy—in fact, covered in hair—and Ser meaning "hirsute" or "growth of hair"; and Teman likewise on account of being far to the south, Teman in Hebrew meaning "south."[2] Some commentators, on the other

---

1. Jl 3.19. Cyril is encouraged by the mention of Edom's fate by Joel (whose ministry he had placed prior to the invasion of Assyrians, or at least Babylonians) to see the two prophets as contemporaries. He thus implicitly rejects a date for Obadiah after the fall of Edom to the Nabateans in the fifth century.

2. The etymology of Seir and Teman Cyril derives from Jerome. He is mis-

hand, think it was called Teman for a different reason, claiming that in due course Esau had a son Eliphaz, whose son was Teman, and it was after him that the country was called Teman.[3]

While that suffices for Idumea and the people in it, their destruction was due to the following. When Jerusalem was under siege by Nebuchadnezzar, remember, and was at its last gasp, countless numbers falling to the swords of the nations, some few were saved and were deported to the countries of the neighboring nations. The majority of the people of Israel went down to Idumea, a neighbor of theirs, thinking that they would share their grief with them as brethren, recall their blood relationship, and accord assistance to those in distress. The latter, on the contrary, though obliged to have compassion on them as brethren, received them into their land but proceeded to slaughter them,[4] patrolling the exits in the manner of brigands and robbing them in their terror and panic. They were so cruel as to surpass even the ferocity of the Babylonians; they attacked them in their desperate condition, as I said, mocking them (548) and making the misfortunes of their kith and kin a cause for celebration.

The Jews of the time, therefore, departed for the country of the Persians and Medes. When at the expiration of seventy years God had pity on them, however, and they returned to Judea, they were zealous in rebuilding the city itself and in turn restoring the Temple in it. Again, however, the Idumeans, their brethren and neighbors, were goaded by envy and wanted to obstruct such endeavors, stirring up barbarians nearby of a similar mind, and actually going to war. But they fell and perished in the valley of Jehoshaphat when God protected the people of Israel. Since the Idumeans were more troublesome than the foreigners, however, the people of Israel made assaults on their country, killed some on the spot and hunted down others in rocky hideaways, caves, and hollows of the land, killing those they found.

---

reading Gn 25 (as Theodoret also will) to see the meaning "earthy" in the name Edom; the Genesis text suggests rather "reddish," a popular etymology.

3. Gn 36.10–11.

4. The PG text shows the Idumeans "not" admitting the Jews. Is Cyril confusing this (unsubstantiated) account with the incident of the Edomites' refusal of entry to Moses and the people in Nm 20.14–20, which he has cited before?

COMMENTARY ON OBADIAH

Vision of Obadiah. The Lord God says this to Idumea: I heard a report from the Lord, and he dispatched a confinement to the nations. Up, rise to battle against it (v.1).

 N THIS VERSE HE EXPLAINS to us the overall purpose of his prophecy, or vision, and specifies his focus; he tries to confirm that his vision deals with what is going to happen to Idumea. He confirms the listeners in the belief that what is said will completely come to pass, and endeavors to persuade them by saying that, far from being his, the words are rather from God. Hence his saying, *I heard a report from the Lord against Idumea.* How it should be understood he personally clarified straightway by going on, *he dispatched a confinement to the nations.* Which nations? Those of (549) Idumea; he said that the *confinement,* or siege, had been sent against them, since the divine judgment necessarily obliged them to suffer desolation.

Or in another sense as well: he ordered the *confinement,* or siege, to be imposed by the nations around Idumea.[1] Instead of ordering them quite openly, however, he, as it were, rouses them as God, and stirs them up against them, saying that the nations also were persuaded by the divine edict and cried out speedily to one another, *Up, rise to battle against it.* In other words, the neighboring nations were involved with the people of Israel in devastating Idumea.

Lo, I have made you insignificant among the nations; you are very much despised. The arrogance of your heart lifted you up, though you inhabit the crevices of rocks. Elevating its dwelling, it says in its heart, Who will bring me down to the ground? If you are exalted like an eagle, and set your nest among the stars, I shall bring you down from there,

---

1. Jerome simply offers his translation of the Heb. term "messenger, ambassador," which the LXX has evidently misread as "confinement." Cyril does not note the discrepancy, something Theodoret will learn from Symmachus.

says the Lord (vv.2–4). He says it occupies an *insignificant* and *despised* position *among the nations* on account of its small numbers when compared with the vast numbers of the attackers, since those ranged against it were very numerous, as I said. Or he means that they were few because war consumed their race and reduced it to very small numbers. Now, the prophetic word presents the Idumean as the victim of inane conceit as a result of extreme stupidity; (550) he thought he would be invulnerable to the foe, not on account of innate strength and skill in warfare, but because the rough and inaccessible nature of the country was likely to guarantee them salvation. There were hills everywhere, you see, sheer rocky ridges instilling terror, rough hilly terrain, and high mountains. Why, then, he asks, did you idly boast against the hand of the attackers? Even if you dwelt in a country endowed with inaccessibility, lofty and elevated, even if you became a kind of eagle, with a nest in the air, as it were— again the expression is hyperbolic—nevertheless you would be plucked from there when God dislodged you; for nothing at all is impossible to him.

If thieves went into you, or brigands by night, where would you be cast out? Would they not steal your possessions? If harvesters went into you, would not gleanings be left? How has Esau been examined and his hidden things been taken? (vv.5–6) We previously said that the people of other nations who assisted and conspired with the Israelites searched clefts in the mountains, caves, and crevices in rocks as well as woods in slaughtering the Idumeans, the result being that very few or practically no one succeeded in escaping. The passage therefore mocks them, adopting, as it were, an ironic style in saying, If you experienced a break-in by brigands, and bands of robbers visited you, would they not be content to take what was sufficient for them? And if some people made a collection from, say, a vine, would not *gleanings* escape the eye of those who normally do the collecting, despite the careful search? (551) This is inevitable in their case, however, even against their will, because fear prompts flight and undetected departure in the case of *thieves*; if they steal something that is readily available, in their view it is enough to satisfy them. Luxuriant foliage is always an obstacle to the search of those collecting grapes, hiding what can escape detection. But in your case, *Esau*—that is, Idumea, descended from Esau—a worse fate has befallen you, he is saying: *your hidden things have been taken;* no one has escaped; flight is pointless, despite the inaccessible countryside.[2]

They dispatched you to the borders; all the men of your confederation rebelled against you; your men of peace prevailed against you; your dining companions hatched a plot against you; there is no understanding in them. On that day, says the Lord, I shall wipe out sages from Idumea and understanding from Mount Esau. Your warriors from Teman will be dumbfounded at everyone's being removed from Mount Esau on account of the slaughter and the offense to your brother Jacob. It will cover you in shame, and you will be carried off forever; from the day you rebelled, on the day foreigners took possession of his might and strangers entered his gates and cast lots for Jerusalem, you also were as one of them (vv.7–11). When they wanted to prevent the people of Israel from rebuilding the Temple and refortifying the holy city, the descendants of Esau made pacts of fellow-feeling with the neighboring nations, (552) as we already remarked. But when the people of Israel launched a campaign and their country was taken, then it was that their former friends, conspirators, and fellow warriors proved more troublesome than all the others by pillaging and fighting. So the war *dispatched you to the borders*, that is, made you invisible—the sense of *dispatched*—not invading part of your country but taking it all by force, and to its very borders reducing it to desolation. They *rebelled*, however, and made war on you, though they might have shared your grief according to your expectation and belief. Instead, *they hatched a plot against you* when you expected to be saved by them.

Now, the clause *there is no understanding in him* bears the following sense: they gave the name *wise* and *intelligent* to the false seers and hangers-on, imposters, augurs and astrologers, who in some cases reached such a degree of silliness as to make the idle claim to a knowledge of the future. People committed to

2. Despite his familiarity with Jeremiah and Jerome's making the point, Cyril makes no mention of the close resemblance of these verses to Jer 49.14–16, 9, which could give rise (at least in a modern commentator) to a discussion of the relationship between the two works in terms of dating and authorship.

the worship of the idols were much struck by this, and the Idumeans were likewise afflicted with the same ailment along with the others; with the impending war bruited abroad, they pondered the likely outcome. Assembling the *sages* in their midst, they bade them proclaim how the war would turn out for them. In all likelihood these people foretold a victory for them, but instead they were taken and killed, their skill failing them; the wretches were proven to be utterly without understanding in their false prophecy. The fact that while people *from Teman* were formerly audacious, the Idumeans in turn would be weak and needy (553) he indicated by adding, *Your warriors from Teman will be dumbfounded at everyone's being removed from Mount Esau,* that is, to the point where the last of the Idumeans perishes.

He makes clear, for instance, the cause of the impending disaster, *on account of the slaughter and the offense to your brother.* Since you did away with your kith and kin, he says, namely, Jacob, or the descendants of Jacob, you will be consumed by war and completely eliminated, full of shame and remorse. He also mentions that their fate would be ineluctable and they would suffer such dire calamities when he says, *You will be carried off forever.* By the phrase *From the day* he recalls the time when Babylon subjugated Israel, pillaged their possessions, and took for an inheritance what was collected from Jerusalem; then the Idumeans ensnared and slaughtered the fugitives, conspired, as it were, with foreigners, and took off into captivity the descendants of Jacob. They were thus guilty of exulting in the misfortunes of their brethren, and yielding little to the Babylonians in cruelty.

Do not despise the day of your brother on the day of foreigners, do not rejoice in the children of Judah on the day of their ruin, and do not gloat in the day of their distress. Do not enter the gates of peoples on the day of their hardships nor despise their assembly on the day of their overthrow. Do not join in attacking their might on the day of their ruin. Do not block their exits to annihilate their survivors nor cut off their fugitives on the day of distress (vv.12–14). Once more the crimes of the Idumeans are listed to show they are harsh and pitiless. The verse is expressed in such a way as if he were striking and scourging them, with God proclaiming and reproaching them for the different forms of sin. *Despise* means "mock" and "take satisfaction in brethren in distress," and "make the misfortunes of others a cause of glee," despite the divine Scripture's saying one should never mock those in distress. By the mention of *Do not rejoice* and the rest, the crimes of the Idumeans are likewise listed, showing them to be harsh and pitiless, even to brethren. Like the Assyrians, he says, you did not even hasten to stand inside the gates and offer a helping hand to them like brothers; instead, you ravaged them. *Do not despise their assembly* that has been miserably overthrown, nor add further troubles to the people already severely oppressed by you. Do not prove a snare to the fugitives, watching exits and laying nooses so that no victim of your pitilessness should be saved, even if escaping the sword of the adversaries.

At all points the passage criticises the Idumeans' inhumanity so that the divine judgment may be seen to be truly holy and blameless, with punishment inflicted on the people guilty of those sins.

Because the day of the Lord is nigh against all the nations. As you have done, so will it be to you: retribution will return on your own head. Because, as you drank on my holy mountain, all the nations will drink wine, they will drink and go down, and will be as though they do not exist. There will be salvation on Mount Zion, however, and it will be holy (vv.15–17). Again he foretells (555) the time of war (referred to as *day of the Lord*), when the neighboring nations that are assembled with the Idumeans in the valley of Jehoshaphat will pay a severe penalty; it was God who surrendered the unholy wrongdoers to the people of Israel. He confirms that they will be punished by a holy judgment in saying, *As you have done, so will it be to you*; the divine nature measures out each person's failings and imposes a penalty that is completely commensurate with whatever sins each is guilty of committing. Now, by the phrase *Because as you drank* he indicates the following: it is customary with those who prevail over their enemies to exult over the vanquished, hold celebrations and drinking bouts, give vent to triumphal cries, and indulge in drunken orgies. So he is saying, as you mocked and jeered at the people of Israel, drinking and dancing and making the misfortunes of your brethren the occasion of festivities, so *all the nations will drink* and dance over you; they will also *go down* against you, that is, overrun your country. You will be reckoned among those who *do not exist*, being so far eliminated as to seem already non-existent.

Now, the inspired Scripture refers by *Mount Zion* to the church: it is really lofty and a true lookout, and holy as well, especially since it is the house and city of the all-holy God.

The house of Jacob will take possession of those possessing them. The house of Jacob will be a fire, and the house of Joseph a flame, whereas the house of Esau will be like stubble; they shall be enkindled (556) *against them and consume them. There will be no firebearer for the house of Esau, because the Lord has spoken. Those in the Negeb will take possession of Mount Esau, and those in the Shephelah the Philistines; they shall possess the mountain of Ephraim, the plain of Samaria, Benjamin, and Gilead* (vv.17–19). Whereas the foolish Idumean expected to possess as an inheritance the *house of Jacob*, that is, the descendants of Jacob, and actually ravaged and divided up the land, they will instead suffer a reverse. They will in fact become a *possession* of the descendants of Jacob, and will be so consumed, as it were, like *stubble* in *flame;* in fact, *the house of Jacob will be a fire, and the house of Joseph* will not suffer by comparison with the power of *a flame.* They will be completely devoured, therefore, the result being that people would not be able to find a single *firebearer* in all the tribe or race. Now, the passage would seem logical in employing the figure of *firebearer*, having spoken of *the house of Jacob* as a *fire*, and *the house of Joseph* as a *flame.* By *house of Jacob* could properly be understood the people of Judah and Benjamin, and by *house of Joseph* the people in Samaria, that is, the ten tribes whose kings at one time were from the tribe of Ephraim, since Manasseh and Ephraim were sons of Joseph.[3]

Now, by the phrase, *Those in the Negeb will take possession*, the following is suggested. When the Babylonians left their country and advanced on Jerusalem, the whole land of the Jews was nec-

3. As had Theodore, Cyril is reading the *purophoros* that the LXX finds in the Heb. form for "survivor" as though derived from *pur*, "fire," instead of *puros*, "wheat," the derivation that leads to Jerome's *frumentarius*. Theodoret will avoid the double solecism by checking with the alternative versions. Cyril is still insisting, against the evidence, on putting Judah as well as Israel in focus.

essarily devastated, (557) and then brought to such a state of hardship as to be completely reduced to desolation and left bare of inhabitants. When God had pity, however, and released them from the snare of captivity, they returned once more to their own land; he says that they became so prosperous and grew into such a large population as to take over the lands of the nearby nations, since Judea was too small.[4] Now, this would be a very clear sign of blessing from God: *Those in the Negeb*—that is, to the south, Negeb meaning "south"—will take as their *possession Mount Esau*—that is, Idumea; as it is in the south, the inhabitants of the south of Judea will completely occupy it as a neighboring area. *Those in the Shephelah*, on the other hand—that is, those in the plain, since it is the part of the country of the Jews that is much further north—will *take possession of the Philistines*, referring to Philistines or Palestinians. They will nonetheless occupy *the mountain of Ephraim, Samaria, Benjamin, and Gilead*, allotments made at one time to the tribes of Israel when Joshua was in charge after Moses. Since they were devastated by the Assyrians under Kings Pul and Shalmaneser before the coming of Nebuchadnezzar, consequently he also says that they will be occupied and escape the desolation that formerly occurred.

The land of the Canaanites as far as Zarephath will be ruled by the transmigration of the people of Israel, and the transmigration of Jerusalem as far as Ephrathah; they will take possession of the cities of the Negeb. (558) *The men who have been saved will go up from Mount Zion to take vengeance on Mount Esau, and the kingdom will be the Lord's* (vv.20–21). By *transmigration* here he refers to the people of Jerusalem, or those who migrated from all of Judea to Babylon. He says that *they will rule it* in the sense of its being a possession under their control and authority, as if you were to refer in the case of a ruler to the *rule* of such-and-such a person. So he is saying that *the land of the Canaanites* will be the *rule* and possession of those who formerly transmigrated, referring to Arabia even *as far as Zarephath*, or Sidon, for you to take this to mean Phoenicia. He says it will be extended *as far as Ephrathah*, or the term given by the other translators, "as far as the Bosphorus,"

---

4. The PG text reads "Idumea" at this point.

that is, the southeast.[5] He says *the cities of the Negeb*, that is, of the south, will also fall under their control. Now, the text seems to suggest to us the Indian nations, since the Indians and their lands are furthest south; it would be like saying, Everything will be full of them—those to the south, those to the north, those to the east, and those to the west—in a word, they will possess every city and country.

Now, by the phrase *men will go up* he summarizes in a fashion the purpose of the prophecy: the inhabitants of Zion, *saved* by God and divesting themselves of the bonds of captivity, will in due course *go up* and *take vengeance on Mount Esau*. After all, as I said, they had made war on the Idumeans after the time of the captivity, and the God of all had become their king despite formerly being provoked and abandoning Judea on account of their apostasy; they had served idols and the golden heifers. But when (559) they returned, he welcomed them again and reigned over them;[6] the Lord is loving and benevolent, easily reconciled with those who offend him, provided we only give evidence of some slight conversion to him. To him be the glory forever. Amen. (560)

5. Jerome informs Cyril of the preferable version.
6. The PG text omits the remaining clauses.

COMMENTARY ON THE PROPHET JONAH

PREFACE TO THE
COMMENTARY ON JONAH

HE DIVINELY INSPIRED JONAH was the son of Amittai,
and came from Gath-hepher, a little city or town of the
land of the Jews, so the story goes. He probably delivered his prophecy at the same time as those before him, namely,
Hosea, Amos, Micah, and the rest.[1] You could find him uttering
a great number of oracles to the Jewish populace, transmitting
the words from God on high and clearly foretelling the future.
Though no other prophetic text from him is extant than this
one, therefore, the divinely inspired Scripture confirms that he
continued predicting to the Jewish masses what would happen
in future times. In the second book of Kings, remember, the
sacred text reports the discourse about Jeroboam—not the first
of that name in the beginning, the son of Nebat, who "caused
Israel to sin," as Scripture says,[2] namely, by persuading them to
worship the golden heifers—(561) but the other Jeroboam,
who came after many others.

Now, what blessed Jonah prophesied the text made clear:
"He restored the border of Israel from the entrance of Hamath
as far as the Sea of the Arabah, according to the word of the
Lord, the God of Israel, which he spoke by his servant Jonah
son of Amittai, the prophet, who was from Gath-hepher. For the
Lord saw that the distress of Israel was very bitter; there were
few survivors, suffering need and affliction, and there was no
one to help Israel. The Lord had not said that he would blot out

---

1. The mention in 2 Kgs 14.25 of a Jonah son of Amittai prophesying in
the reign of Jeroboam II is sufficient for Cyril to group him with other eighth-
century prophets. This time Cyril seems to be following the sequence of the LXX
in omitting Joel from the opening group, whereas Jerome (and Theodore's Antioch text) had led him to comment on him after Hosea in accordance with the
Heb. He does not begin by distinguishing between author and eponymous hero,
nor does he bother to locate Gath-hepher in Galilee.

2. 2 Kgs 13.11.

their offspring from under heaven; and he saved them by the hand of Jeroboam son of Jehoash."[3] The phrase "by the hand of" means "through"; Jeroboam, who was the son of Jehoash, as I said, made war on the Philistines, brought once more under his control the cities seized from the land of the Jews, and was of no little assistance to the people of Israel, thanks to God's protection and willingness to bring salvation, despite their being reduced to extreme hardship.

While other prophetic words came to blessed Jonah at various times as well, then, the account of him in this case has been recorded for our benefit and as part of the divine plan; it is in fact worth hearing, namely, his preaching to the Ninevites and his experiences in the meantime. It describes in shadows, as it were, the mystery of the Incarnation of our Savior as well; Christ himself, at any rate, said in addressing the Jews, "An evil and adulterous generation asks for a sign, and no sign will be given to it except the sign of the prophet Jonah: just as Jonah was in the belly of the sea monster for three days and three (562) nights, likewise the Son of Man also will be in the heart of the earth for three days and three nights."[4] The mystery of Christ, therefore, is foreshadowed and somehow represented to us in the story of the divinely inspired Jonah; I shall see it as my task to explain that to the readers.

When a text is developed at a spiritual level, and its central character is selected and adopted as a representation of Christ the Savior of us all, a person of wisdom and understanding should judge which details are irrelevant to the purpose in question, and which in turn are relevant and applicable, and likely to be of particular benefit to the listeners.[5] Take as an example blessed Moses: he represented Israel to God on Mount Sinai, becoming mediator between God and man. In fear, the people of

3. 2 Kgs 14.25–27.

4. Mt 12.39–40 (omitted in PG ed.); cf. Mk 8.12; Lk 11.29–32. Cyril and Theodoret take a leaf out of Theodore's book in seeing the story of Jonah as prefiguring the divine *oikonomia*, prompted by the familiar citations of the story in the synoptic gospels. Again the question arises (but is not acknowledged): is it Jonah as author or as central character that is significant?

5. Cyril sees the reader of texts like Jonah requiring skill to recognize the particular *theôria*. In commentary on Zechariah, Didymus had spoken in similar terms of the reader's being "a seer" in such cases.

Israel made supplication, remember, saying, "Speak to us yourself; do not let God speak to us lest we die." The fact that this incident foreshadowed the mediation of Christ, the God and Father himself conveyed by saying, "They are right in all they have said. I shall raise up for them a prophet like you from among their brethren," clearly someone to mediate and represent the human race to God and announce to everyone throughout the earth the unspeakable plan of the God and Father. "I shall put my words in his mouth, and he will say to them everything I command." The divinely inspired Moses, then, was adopted as a type of Christ. We shall not apply the whole story of Moses to him, however, in case we prove to be doing and saying something inappropriate; Moses admitted, remember, that he was slow of speech, slow of tongue, and ill-equipped for mission, saying, (563) "I am slow of speech and slow of tongue; I have never been eloquent, neither in the past nor even now that you have begun to speak to your servant." He begged him, "Lord, I beg you to appoint someone else to send who is more capable."[6]

Christ is not slow of speech, however, or slow of tongue like him; rather, he is the mighty trumpet, the blessed prophet Isaiah referring to him as such in the words, "On that day they will blow the mighty trumpet"; the Savior's message has been bruited abroad and heard by people throughout the earth. Blessed David was also aware of this in saying, "The Lord, God of gods, has spoken and summoned the earth from the rising of the sun to its setting."[7] While Moses mediates as a type of Christ, therefore, his role as a type is not demonstrated in his slowness of speech. Blessed Aaron, in turn, was adopted as a type of Emmanuel, bedecked as he was with the ornaments of a high priest, entering the holy of holies, and clad in that conspicuous and admirable attire. But in turn we do not apply everything about him to Christ: he was not completely above reproach, once being chastised along with Miriam for criticising Moses, and in another case as well not being guiltless when Israel made the calf in the wilderness.[8]

6. Ex 20.19; Dt 18.17–18; Ex 4.10, 13.
7. Is 27.13; Ps 50.1.
8. Nm 12; Ex 32.

Not everything in texts and types, therefore, is relevant to spiritual interpretations—only if a character is introduced who in himself prefigures Christ for us; then we properly pass over human elements and focus only on relevant details, in every case highlighting what is conducive to supporting the purpose of the text. This, in fact, is the process by which we shall understand the divinely inspired (564) Jonah as well, namely, the way he presents the mystery of Christ to us. Not everything that befell him, however, should be understood as relevant and applicable to this process. For example, he was sent to preach to the Ninevites, but tried to flee from the face of God, and proved reluctant about his mission; the Son also was sent by the God and Father to preach to the nations, but did not lack enthusiasm for his ministry, nor seek to flee from the face of the God and Father. The prophet exhorted the sailors, "Pick me up and throw me into the sea, and the sea will give you respite";[9] he was also swallowed by the sea monster, then after three days regurgitated; later he went to Nineveh and discharged his ministry, but felt no little disappointment when God had compassion on the people of Nineveh. Christ even underwent death willingly; he remained in the heart of the earth three days and three nights, came to life again, later went into Galilee, and gave orders for the beginning of the preaching to the nations; he instructed the disciples, remember, to "make disciples of all the nations, baptizing them in the name of the Father and of the Son and of the Holy Spirit."[10] On the other hand, he was not disappointed to see them saved for repentance, as of course blessed Jonah was.

If we do not apply the whole story to the purpose of spiritual interpretation, then, let no one find fault: just as bees in traversing meadows and flowers always gather what is useful for making honey, so the skillful commentator studies the holy and inspired Scripture, ever gathering and compiling what contributes to the clarification of the mysteries of Christ, (565) and will produce a mature and irreproachable treatment. It is therefore now time for us to begin the commentary.

---

9. Jon 1.12.

10. Mt 28.19. Cyril has produced a lengthy hermeneutical prologue to the Jonah text, as had Theodore and less so Jerome. Theodoret will continue the practice. See Hill, "Jonah in Antioch," *Pacifica* 14 (2001): 245–61.

COMMENTARY ON JONAH,
CHAPTER ONE

The word of the Lord came to Jonah son of Amittai, Rise up, go to the great city of Nineveh, and preach in it, because a clamor has ascended to me from their wickedness (vv. 1–2).

ITH AN UNDERSTANDING of the ministry and mission of Jonah's prophecy, you would be quite right to make the opportune remark in terms of the praise uttered by blessed Paul, "Is he the God of Jews only, and not of gentiles also? In fact, he is the God of gentiles also, since God is one, and he will justify the circumcised on the grounds of faith and the uncircumcised through that same faith." And having learned this through experience, the divinely inspired Peter himself also proclaims it to us in the words, "I truly understand that God shows no partiality; rather, in every nation anyone who fears him and does what is right is acceptable to him."[1] After all, it is he who created earth and heaven and everything in them, and made the human being in the beginning in his image and likeness to be devoted to virtue, to live a commendable life of holiness and blessedness, and to enjoy a rich share of his gifts. They were then led astray into sin, tricked by the devil's wiles; consequently, they were accursed and also subject to corruption. Christ was therefore preordained and foreknown before the foundation of the world to set everything right; the God and Father was pleased to "gather up (566) all things in him, things in heaven and things on earth."[2]

Some achievements of this kind were kept for the Only-begotten, who became like us and shed his light on the world in the flesh. But God also wished to confirm in practice the fact that even before the moment of his coming he showed a necessary

1. Rom 3.29–30; Acts 10.34–35.
2. Gn 1.26; Eph 1.10.

care for those who had been deceived, and bestowed his regard on those who had lapsed through ignorance. Consequently, he bade the blessed prophet to go *to Nineveh.* Now, Nineveh was a Persian city, situated in the east, celebrated and, as the prophet Jeremiah says, "a land of statues." A great number of cities bordering on the Jews, in fact, were given over to worship of the idols; "Tyre and Sidon, and the whole of Galilee of foreigners,"[3] remember, worshiped the works of their hands, and in their midst were temples, altars, and shrines of innumerable demons. So why, tell me, does he bypass the neighbors' cities and send the prophet *to Nineveh,* situated at a great distance, in which especially, as I remarked, there was an uncivilized multitude of people given over insatiably to sun and stars and fire? In fact, it was also a prey to unbounded religious quackery hostile to God; it is said of it in Jeremiah, "a beautiful and charming whore, mistress of potions."[4]

In my view, then, the God who knows everything had the beneficial intention of demonstrating even to the ancients that people who were quite alienated and caught in the toils of deception would also be attracted in due course to the knowledge of the truth, even if quite desperate, stubborn, and completely in the grip of obduracy. The word of God, you see, is quite capable even of succeeding in (567) forming attitudes and persuading people to learn the things that make a person wise. Listen to his saying to Jeremiah at one time, "Lo, I am now making my words in your mouth a fire, and this people wood, and it will consume them," and at another likewise, "Are not my words like a fiery flame, says the Lord, and like an axe that cuts rock?"[5] It was therefore not without purpose that the divinely inspired Jonah was sent to the Ninevites; rather, it was for him to be a kind of harbinger of God's inherent clemency, which is bestowed even on people led astray by ignorance. At the same time, however,

3. Jer 50.38; Jl 3.4. If it is true that only at a late stage of the Assyrian empire was Nineveh its capital, after Ashur and Calah, falling in 612 B.C.E. to a coalition of Medes and Babylonians, Cyril is astray in thinking of Nineveh as a Persian city at the time he sees Jonah exercising his ministry, viz., the eighth century.

4. The words rather of Na 3.4.

5. Jer 5.14 and 23.29.

what happened was by way of condemnation of Israel; they were convicted of being froward, unresponsive, paying little heed to the laws of God. After all, at a single prophet's preaching, the Ninevites were instantly brought around to a sense of obligation to repent, despite suffering from extreme deception, whereas those others set at naught Moses and prophets, and spurned Christ himself, the Savior of us all, despite his supporting his teachings with miracles, through which they should have been convinced quite easily that he was God by nature and became man to save the whole earth under heaven, and them before all others.

Now, the fact that the event had the effect of convicting the people of Israel, and rightly so, Christ himself makes clear in saying, "Men of Nineveh will rise up at the judgment with this generation and condemn it, because they repented at the preaching of Jonah and, lo, a greater than Jonah is here."[6] How is there something greater in Christ than Jonah? Whereas he threatened the Ninevites only with overthrow, our Lord (568) aroused wonderment by astonishing them with his ineffable wonderworking, and the miracle accompanying the message is always a means of conveying people to faith. It was therefore very much part of the divine plan that blessed Jonah was sent to preach to the Ninevites the message that *a clamor has ascended from their wickedness* to the God of all. He is, in fact, by no means ignorant of anything; but if he should be prompted to punishment of people's sins, then Scripture says that a cry ascends to him from their behavior. Scripture also says that the blood of Abel shed by Cain cried aloud, as did the extremity of depravity of the cities of Sodom.[7]

Jonah arose with the intention of fleeing from the face of the Lord to Tarshish. He went down to Joppa, and found a ship going to Tarshish; he paid his fare and went on board to sail with them to Tarshish from the face of the Lord (v.3). Joppa is a city of Palestine, then, on the coast, a port for cargo for people of Judea going to sea, especially for cities of the east. So the prophet went down, and then took a ship sailing for Tarshish; a journey there was probably

6. Mt 12.41.
7. Gn 4.10 and 18.21.

preferred by ship.[8] He paid his fare, and sailed in company with
the others. Now, by *Tarshish* he refers to what is now called Tarsi,
or Tarsus; some people believe that by this is meant the city of
Ethiopia or India, and it is agreed that by them it is called *Tarshish*; at any rate, all of the country of India is implied by *Tarshish*.
My opinion, on the other hand, is that at present (569) that
is not what the word means; it would be likely that for people
wanting to sail to the Indian nations the voyage would not be
from Joppa but by way of the Red Sea, unless you thought that
the prophet meant to make his flight via Persia and Assyria to
innermost Ethiopia. So by *Tarshish* he probably referred to what
is now Tarsi, a city of Cilicia, watered by the river Cydnos, and
lying at the very foothills of the Tauri, the high mountains of
Cilicia.[9]

   In any case, the prophet took his leave, the purpose of his
departure being to *flee from the face of the Lord*. In this instance
we should not proceed to seek out the reason, but rather the
manner of the flight; my view, then, is that his declining the
mission and his being reluctant, as it were, about the ministry
explain his *fleeing from the face of the Lord*. On the other hand,
I cannot understand why he left for Tarshish or what he had
in mind, unless you were to take the view that he, like others
of the older saints, had a poor opinion of God; some believed
that the power of the God of all was confined to the land of the
Jews, restricted to it, as it were, and excluding others. The divinely inspired Jacob, for instance, once left his ancestral home,
and went to Laban in Mesopotamia; he then camped in a certain place, putting a stone under his head and going to sleep as
usual. He then had a vision of a ladder reaching from earth to
heaven, with the angels of God ascending and descending by
it, and the Lord resting on it. (570) Waking up, he said, "God
is in this place, and I did not know it."[10] My view, therefore, is

   8. The PG text reads, "preferred to Nineveh."
   9. While Theodore soon dismisses the identification of Tarshish as "an irrelevant chase after detail," Jerome argues the toss, making the point that an
inland town like Tarsus (Cyril's choice) can hardly be a port. Theodoret opts for
Carthage, criticising those like Cyril who made the phonetic confusion between
Tarshish and Tarsus (found also in 2 Mac 3.5), while modern commentators
also look to the west as the likely alternative to Nineveh.
   10. Gn 28.16.

that the prophet had some such understanding, left Judea, and made for the Greek cities.

Now, the excuse of reluctance and lack of enthusiasm in choosing to discharge the ministry we will come to discover from his own words; though he later did go off and preach, yet he was very distressed when the contents of his prophecy did not take effect. He actually said, "O Lord, were these not my words when I was still in my own country? This was the reason I took the initiative of fleeing to Tarshish, knowing that you are merciful and compassionate, long-suffering and rich in mercy, ready to relent from imposing calamities. Now, Lord God, take my life from me, because it is better for me to die than to live."[11] As a prophet, he was not ignorant of the outcome of his ministry; he was afraid that the fate proclaimed by him might not take effect, and that the Ninevites, though unaware of the kindness of the compassionate God, might take advantage of it and do away with him as a charlatan, deceiver, and liar who had persuaded them to make needless efforts. Barbarians, you see, are ever disposed to anger and quite ready to act like a bull, even without any real basis for their frenzy.

The Lord stirred up a mighty wind on the sea; a mighty storm at sea developed, and the ship was in danger of breaking up. The sailors were afraid, and each prayed to his own god; they threw the ship's cargo into the sea to lighten it for them (vv.4–5). The storm fell upon the ship as a result of God's intervention and his subjecting the sea to fierce gusts of wind. (571) Terror gripped the seamen, and their talk was already about the end to it all, as the ship was probably creaking and threatening, as it were, to be on the point of breaking in pieces. The ship's company adopted the usual recourse of lightening the ship so that it might ride on the waves and thus have a smoother passage. Convincing proof of the stormy conditions was the impact of terror upon the sailors themselves and their ardent appeals for salvation to their own gods, having already despaired of rescue.

Jonah, by contrast, had gone down into the ship's hold, and was fast asleep snoring. The captain approached him and said to him, Why are you snoring? Get up and call on your god in the hope that the god

11. 4.2–3.

will save us, and we shall not perish (vv.5–6). Indifference about praying and a preference for sleeping are hardly appropriate to a prophet's alertness in the face of danger, when the occasion and the situation call one to action, and the proper response would rather be to appease the God of all. Hence we might presume that the sleeping was done before the storm, and that his going down to the actual hold of the ship was a mark of one accustomed to being on his own; after all, it is always a preference and a concern for the saints to avoid hubbub, absent themselves from crowds, and be on their own, as the divinely inspired Jeremiah also says, "It is a good for a man to bear the yoke of his youth; he will sit alone because he has taken it on himself." And likewise he cried aloud about the multitude of unbelievers, "Lord almighty, (572) I did not sit in their company when they jested; instead, I showed respect in the presence of your hand; I sat alone because I was filled with bitterness."[12] "Sitting alone," I think, means a life of solitude, being free from life's cares and concerns, and not mixing with others who prefer a life of pleasure and fleshly delights. The prophet therefore was dozing, not ignoring his duty, but, as I said, doing so before the onset of the storm. The captain roused him, at any rate, telling him instead there was need to *call on his god*; it is always distressing to those in danger that some people seem to be proof against fear and to indulge in idleness at the wrong time.

Each said to his neighbor, Come, let us cast lots and learn on whose account this calamity has come upon us. They cast lots, and the lot fell on Jonah (v.7). The mariners adopted a strange and unusually inquisitive ruse, anxious to discover by lot the person with whom God was displeased. It was part of the divine plan, however, and useful in bringing to light the one who thought he could flee from the presence of God; the lot fell on him, and he was seen to be subject to the accusation on the basis of the facts. He was probably afraid, in fact, that the accusation was made more obvious by his own reflection. The advice is recommended as wise,

---

12. Lam 3.27–28; Jer 15.17. Jonah's going below and falling asleep intrigue the commentators. Cyril chooses to take Theodore's line of acquitting Jonah of any blame by claiming (without textual support) that he had done so before the storm broke, whereas Jerome says he was depressed by remorse.

therefore, for those willing to observe it, "Do not be ashamed to confess your sin."[13]

They said to him, Tell us why this calamity has befallen us, what your occupation is, where you come from, where you are going, from what country and from which people you are. (573) *He replied to them, I am a servant of the Lord, and I worship the Lord God of heaven, who made the sea and the dry land. The men were struck with a great fear, and said to him, Why have you done this? For the men knew that he was fleeing from the face of the Lord because he had told them* (vv.8–10). It was useful for them to be curious, knowing as they already did by lot the one responsible, but not being able to gain a clear explanation of the kind of sin. Since they were idolaters, however, they bade him tell his occupation, his country, and city, and the people he was from, their aim being to learn, in my view, what god he had offended; each of the sailors, in fact, had his own god, and not the one God of all. They believed that by paying homage to the demon offended by him they would obviate the harm from the tempest. But when the prophet referred to himself as *servant* of the God who fashioned both earth and heaven,[14] and said he adored him, they immediately realized that he had fled from the face of God. How did they realize it? Because it was not permitted for Jews to leave the country allotted them, visit foreigners, or enter cities given over to idolatry, whereas among them such behavior was blameless and did not imply apostasy.

He seemed to be quite at variance with the Law, and liable to condemnation and punishment. Our Lord Jesus Christ, for example, clearly confirmed that they would be deprived of his salvation—namely, that which comes by faith—if they did not choose to seize the opportunity while he was still present and living in the world. He said, remember, "I am with you a little while longer, and I go to him who sent me. You will search for me, (574) and you will not find me; where I am you cannot come." In reply the Jews, who reproached the gentiles with apostasy, stupidly said, "Where does this man intend to go that

13. Sir 4.26.
14. The version comes from a misreading by the LXX of Heb. *'ibri*, "(I am) a Hebrew," as *'ibdi* (as Jerome points out).

we shall not find him? Surely he does not intend to go to the Dispersion among the Greeks, and teach the Greeks?"[15] In other words, it was such an unheard-of practice, deviant and quite unfamiliar to them, believing as they did that association with the Greek populace was blameworthy. Accordingly, they formed the impression that he had not remained within the boundaries of Judea but was sailing with them to Tarsi, and they guessed that he was perhaps repudiating life within the Law, and in order to give himself up to the nations of the Greeks he had set his mind on flight from the face of God.

They said to him, What are we to do with you so that the sea may lose its force against us? For the sea was rising, and further stirring up a storm. Jonah replied to them, Pick me up and throw me into the sea, and the sea will lose its force against you, because it is on account of me that a mighty storm has come upon you (v.12). While they were afraid that the sea was raging against them in irresistible fashion, it was no less the God of the Hebrews that they feared; they were not ignorant of his inherent power and glory, foreigners though they were. But since he had said he was a servant of God, they were then at a loss and in two minds: they were slow to commit murder, suspecting the wrath of the God who can do all things; on the other hand, with the sea rising against them no less than before, they were forced to be worried about themselves. Consequently, they appealed to him to say what they needed to do for the storm to abate, (575) the waves to subside, and themselves to escape the ultimate danger. So what does the prophet say? He confesses his sin, expresses shame for his offense, and is condemned on his own admission, saying, *Pick me up and throw me into the sea*, which was as good as saying that he deserved to be punished by them for reluctance in accepting his mission; he realized that the storm would spare the ship if it got what it was after, and the sea would cease its opposition once it received the offender.

The men exerted themselves to reach land, but were unsuccessful, because the sea rose and was all the more stirred up against them. They cried out to the Lord, Let us not perish on account of this person's life,

15. Jn 7.33–35.

and do not hold us guilty of innocent blood, because you, Lord, have done as you intended. They took Jonah and threw him into the sea, and the sea ceased from its raging (vv.13–15). The prophet for his part had condemned himself to death, and asked for them to be relieved of the fear of losing their own lives. For their part, the men were fearful and reluctant to take a life, and wanted to save the one who was God's servant and bring him alive to shore, thus appeasing his wrath. Consequently, they exerted themselves to beach the ship, but the purpose of their endeavors was thwarted as the wind made the swell irresistible for them, and the ship was sinking under the very savage onslaught. They consequently appeased him with prayer and begged God to pardon them, (576) unwilling as they were to take a life; but they yielded to his judgment, which was then forcing them to throw Jonah into the sea, and they gave in. On receiving him it was finally appeased; it let peace reign and gave the sailors hope of being saved. It everywhere responds to the divine wishes and eagerly serves the Lord's commands, as is clear from experience itself.

The men were fearful of the Lord with a deep fear; they sacrificed to the Lord and made vows (v.16). It was of considerable benefit to them to believe that there is one God who is divine by nature, even though they shared a range of wrongful errors and thought there were countless gods throughout the world. Accordingly, they offered sacrifice to the one who alone is God by nature and in truth, bypassing their own, though believing they benefited from those that were venerated out of deception and that laid claim to the glory due to God. They also made vows, despite being in the custom of doing this to the maritime demons. The pagans, you see, chose to attribute power over the sea to a certain Poseidon; their religion consisted completely of fairy tales, quackery, and awful stupidity. By contrast, we glorify the one who is God by nature, and are correct in saying to him, "You have control of the power of the sea, and you still the raging of its waves. The heavens are yours and the earth is yours; you laid the foundations of the world and all that is in it."[16]

16. Ps 89.9, 11.

The Lord ordered a huge sea monster to swallow Jonah, and (577) *Jonah was in the belly of the fish three days and three nights* (v.17). God *orders the sea monster* by willing it; his wanting something to take effect is both law and fulfillment, having the force of law. We do not claim, in fact, that the God of all gives orders to the *sea monster* as he does to us, or to the holy angels since he communicates to their minds what has to be done, and instills in their hearts the knowledge of whatever he wants. It would be silly and close to insanity, you see, to think seriously that the God of all deals with even monsters in this manner; if he were said to give a general command to brute beasts or the elements or a part of creation, we would refer to his will as a law and command. Everything, you see, yields to his wishes, and while the form of response is to us beyond words, he is fully aware of it. So he came to no harm in being swallowed by the sea monster, and was inside it *three days and three nights.*

Now, this fact would perhaps seem distasteful to some people, exceeding the bounds of what is proper; before all others those who do not know the one who is God by nature and in truth, being devoted to the deceits of the demons, would not believe it. They would say, How would he stay alive while inside the sea monster? How would he not be destroyed by being swallowed? How could he stand the heat generated? How could he live in so much moisture—in its gut, I mean—and not rather be digested and consumed like food? A thing of flesh, after all, is very weak and quite liable to corruption. Our explanation, therefore, is that the event would rightly be taken to be truly remarkable and surpassing rhyme or reason. If God were said to be responsible, however, who would still demur? (578) The Divinity is powerful, and easily changes the nature of living things to whatever he chooses, nothing standing in the way of his ineffable wishes; what is by nature corruptible would prove superior even to corruption if he willed it, and what is permanent and unchanging and resistant to the norms of corruption would easily fall victim to corruption, since the nature of what exists is in my view something decreed by the Creator.

This, too, should be understood, however: that in concocting fairy tales about themselves the pagans claim that Hercules, son of Alcmena and Zeus, was swallowed by a sea monster, and re-gurgitated as a result of the heat generated, with his hair singed and suffering the loss only of his hair. Lycophron records the story; one of the verses in it goes as follows: it refers to him as "a lion of three nights, whom once a savage dog chewed up with the jaws of Triton." Our faith in the Divinity, however, is not de-rived from the fairy tales they have; we mention them to con-vince unbelievers that even the stories they have do not present such accounts as unacceptable.[17] Since, however, I believe that there is need to accept the extraordinary event even on the ba-sis of what is still done according to God's will, come now, let us mention that even in the womb the foetus is immersed in natu-ral moisture, is buried, as it were, in the entrails of the preg-nant woman, and cannot breathe, and yet is still alive and well, being nourished remarkably by God's wishes. No explanation could be given of such things, however, nor would the things of God be easily apprehended by anyone; Scripture says, after all, "Who has known the mind of the Lord?"[18] (579) Or who has grasped the ways of extraordinary things? Or whose mind is not surpassed by what exceeds the power of reason? To fail to be-lieve, therefore, is risky, even if God performs something quite beyond reason; we, on the other hand, accept it as true,

Now, when we take the blessed prophet as a type of the min-istry understood in Christ, there is need to add that the whole world was at risk and the human race was affected by tempest, as if the waves of sin itself were raging; the dire and insufferable pleasures were overwhelming it, corruption impending in the form of a storm, fierce winds buffeting it—namely, the devil and the wicked powers subject to him and working with him. When we were in this situation, however, the Creator had pity, and the God and Father sent us the Son from heaven; he took on flesh,

17. Cyril quotes two of the iambic lines of the poem *Alexandra* (or *Cassan-dra*) of Lycophron of the third century B.C.E. in reference to the twelfth labor of Hercules, his three-day visit to the underworld to fetch the "savage dog" Cer-berus. Jerome had also acknowledged that the historicity of Jonah's stay in the belly of the sea monster could prove a problem for some readers, and had cited pagan classics—specifically, Ovid's *Metamorphoses*—in support. Cyril further up-holds historicity by citing the case of an unborn child in the womb.

18. Is 40.13; Rom 11.34.

arrived on earth when it was at risk of tempests, and willingly went to his death to make the storm abate, allow the sea to become calm, settle the waves, and put an end to the storm; by the death of Christ we were saved. The tempest abated, the rain passed, and waves settled down, the force of the winds diminished, deep peace then prevailed, and we enjoyed fair weather of a spiritual kind, since Christ has suffered for us.

You find something like this in the Gospel accounts. At one time, remember, the apostles' boat was plying the sea of Tiberias; then a strong wind fell on the water, and they were lashed intolerably with a tempest. In danger of perishing, they awoke Christ, who was with them asleep, crying out loudly, "Lord, save us, (580) we perish." Waking up, the text says, he rebuked the sea, saying with authority, "Peace, be still," and saved the disciples.[19] Now, the incident was a type of what happened to the human race: through him, as I said, we were freed from death, corruption, sin, and passions, and with the departure of the former tempest, our situation was transformed into peace.

19. Mt 8.25; Mk 4.39.

COMMENTARY ON JONAH,
CHAPTER TWO

Jonah prayed to the Lord his God from the belly of the sea monster, saying, I cried aloud in my distress to the Lord my God, and he hearkened to me; from the belly of Hades you heard the sound of my cry (vv.1–2).[1]

OMING TO NO HARM, using the sea monster as a home, thinking clearly, and suffering no kind of ill effects of body or mind, he sensed divine assistance, knowing God is benevolent. On the other hand, not unaware that what had happened was due to his reluctance for ministry, he turned to prayer, uttering sentiments of thanksgiving, at the same time confessing the glory of his Savior, admiring his power, and proclaiming his clemency. He said, in fact, that his prayer was accepted, in my view coming to this realization from a prophetic spirit. Now, by the phrase *from the belly of Hades,* by which he means the stomach of the sea monster, he nicely compares the beast to Hades and death in that it knew how to kill and savagely consume its prey.

You cast me into the depths of the sea's heart, and floods encircled me. All your billows and your waves passed over me. I said, I am being driven out of your sight (vv.3–4). He comments (581) in various ways on the happening, referring it to grace from on high, and attributing to divine decrees the ability to rescue easily from every trouble. He says, in fact, that he was in the very recesses of the sea and in the melée of surging waters, which were drowning him like flooding billows; he was caught up in such a degree of misfortune as to have a full realization at that point that he was suffering the aversion of the divine eyes, and to be brought to despair of rescue.

It is a terrible thing leading to ruin, namely, being removed

1. This is the numbering of modern versions. In the Heb., in the PG, and in Pusey's text the verses are numbered 2–3.

from God's eyes. Accordingly, the divinely inspired David also makes supplication in the words, "Do not avert your face from me, nor turn away from your servant in anger."[2] Suffering divine wrath follows as an inevitable consequence of such aversion—or, rather, the anger of aversion precedes and prepares for it.

Surely I shall never again gaze upon your holy temple? (v.4) On the one hand, he is aware that he has been preserved, thanks to God's power, has been accorded assistance, is alive and well—and this in the sea monster and in the animal's belly, something against the odds and beyond belief. He is probably uncertain as to whether he will be regurgitated and emerge into the light of day again. On the other hand, he also considers most desirable and truly an object of prayer his return to the divine Temple itself and offering praise to the God who saved him; he prays to attain this grace, attributing to God, as I said, the ability to achieve everything.[3]

Water flooded around me at the risk of my life; the deepest abyss enclosed me; (582) *my head sank into the mountain caverns. I descended onto land, whose everlasting bars held me tight. May my life rise up from corruption towards you, O Lord my God* (vv.5–6). Saved by God with ineffable power, he was intent on offering more splendid songs of thanksgiving. He describes completely what had happened, and conveys in detail the calamity he was caught up in, and again proclaims how he was saved. As a prophet he was not unaware, therefore, that he was in the sea, in a mighty *abyss* and in *mountain caverns,* where the sea monster probably lurked in rocks and in sea caves. He says that he arrived *onto land, whose everlasting bars held him tight,* that is, Hades—not that he was really there: we shall find that he was not dead; rather, the enormity of the danger and the gravity of the events did not prevent his thinking that he was dead and had arrived at Hades itself, whence no one emerges or in any way returns after once being entrapped. In my view, this is what is suggested by *everlasting*

2. Ps 27.9.

3. Not having located Jonah's hometown, Gath-hepher, in Galilee, nor identified him as an eighth-century prophet working in the northern kingdom, Cyril has no difficulty now with his expressed devotion to the Temple.

bars held him tight, meaning "unbreakable," never overcome or undone by anyone. Now, the fact that he was not dead, as I said, but was alive in the sea monster, and suffered nothing in it contributing to death or corruption, would easily be grasped from his having hopes of his being rescued. Consequently he says, *May my life rise up from corruption towards you, O Lord my God;* he prays to emerge into the light, and be delivered up from the sea monster's stomach as though from Hades. (583)

As my life was leaving me, I remembered the Lord; may my prayer come to you in your holy temple (v.7). Hardship is not without benefit to those prepared to be tested, nor would suffering tribulation be considered burdensome. Blessed David will confirm this by saying, "In tribulation I called upon the Lord"; and another of the holy authors, "Lord, in tribulation we remembered you." The divinely inspired Paul also chose to embrace and commend tribulation, clearly of the kind involved in virtuous living; he said, "Tribulation produces endurance; endurance, character; character, hope; and hope does not disappoint."[4] So when the prophet's *life* was exposed to danger and underwent hardship in the extreme, he likewise had recourse to something beneficial, not like some people giving way to depression and falling to cursing the divine decrees, but remembering the one who saves. He cried aloud to him, note, and longed for his assistance; aware as he was of his clemency and the abundance of his power, he addressed supplication to him, begging for his life to be rescued from death and corruption. It is therefore a wonderful and praiseworthy thing to avoid depression in hardship, and rather to appease the Lord with entreaty and supplication, and seek from him repeal of the trouble and relief from misfortune.

Those who respect vain and false things forsook their mercy. For my part, on the contrary, with words of praise and confession I shall sacrifice to you; the vows I have taken I shall render to you the Lord for my salvation (vv.8–9). For their part, he is saying, others are unaware of the Lord of all, the Creator, and are thus caught up in the toils of futility, (584) paying homage to the false gods, pursuing birds on the wing—that is, hope in them—and shepherd-

---

4. Ps 118.5; Is 26.16; Rom 5.3–5.

ing the wind.[5] So they do not beg mercy from you, nor do they enjoy hope of such a thing. For my part by contrast, I am not like them. How so? I know you to be a kind and compassionate ally. Accordingly, I shall *confess to you in word* and supplication, and offer songs like some kind of sweet-smelling incense; that is, I shall offer to you spiritual sacrifices of thanksgiving, of praise, of benediction. I shall fulfill with great enthusiasm my *vows for salvation*, that is, all those that brought about my being saved and were of benefit to my life. Now, this was in response to everything God wanted, a discharge of the prophetic ministry, now that all reluctance and pusillanimity had been removed.

It is therefore while in the sea monster that the prophet prays. While he is a human type, the true image of the event—namely, Christ—emerged before the precious crucifixion, with the passion, as it were, already impelling him, and said to the Father in heaven, "If it is possible, let this chalice pass from me,"[6] fearful as he was and, as it were, depressed. Now, whether on arriving in the nether regions, on the other hand, he had said something of a human character, he himself would know; it is risky for us to say. We shall find the divinely inspired Peter, however, attributing to him what was said by David: "For this reason you will not abandon my soul to Hades, nor let your holy one see corruption." His flesh, in fact, did not see corruption; in three days he came back to life, just as it was impossible for him, being life by nature, to be subject to the bonds of death.[7] (585)

He ordered the sea monster, and it expelled Jonah onto dry land (v.10). Again the sea monster is given orders by some divine and indescribable power of God to perform his will. It releases the prophet from its innards, who had profited from the ordeal—or, rather, was given heart by the experience and gained a clear knowledge that it is risky to resist the divine decrees.

5. Prv 9.12 LXX.
6. Mt 26.39.
7. Ps 16.10; Acts 2.27, 24.

COMMENTARY ON JONAH,
CHAPTER THREE

A word of the Lord came to Jonah a second time: Get up, go to Nineveh, the great city, and preach in it the message I told you before (vv.1–2).

AKING ADVANTAGE OF HIS MORE ardent enthusiasm, then, God bids him again go to Nineveh and adopt the same message communicated to him at the outset, the meaning of "a clamor has ascended to me from their wickedness." Although I previously stated what relates to Christ, therefore, I shall still repeat it, feeling no reluctance; Scripture says, remember, "To say the same things is not wearisome to me, and for you it is a safeguard."[1] So before the precious crucifixion we shall find Christ still somewhat hesitant—that is, as far as proposing the message of the Gospel oracles to the gentiles goes. For instance, he openly admits, "I was sent only to the lost sheep of the house of Israel," and he personally instructs the holy disciples, "Go nowhere among the gentiles, and do not enter a town of the Samaritans, but go instead to the lost sheep of the house of Israel."[2] He was "in the heart of the earth three days and three nights," and went "to the springs (586) of the sea, and walked in the recesses of the deep." He entered "mountain caverns," as it were, and descended to the earth, whose "eternal bars" were shut tight. He then plundered Hades, preached to the spirits there, opened the immovable doors, and came to life again; his life came back from corruption, and in this condition he appeared, before the others, to the women seeking him in the garden. After telling them to rejoice, he then bade them report to the holy disciples that he was going before them into Galilee.[3]

---

1. 1.2; Phil 3.1.   2. Mt 15.24 and 10.5–6.
3. Mt 12.40; Jb 38.16; Jb 2.6–7; 1 Pt 3.19; Mt 28.9–10.

Then it was that his message finally went also to the gentiles by means of the blessed apostles; then it was that *he preached the message told before.* It was not, you see, that before his death he provided guidance to Israel by one set of commandments, and afterwards to the gentiles by another; instead, it was the Gospel that was given to everyone. The knowledge of the divine disciples was definitely the same, there being no difference between that for the people of Israel and that for us, who are called from the gentiles to holiness through faith.

Jonah arose and went to Nineveh as the Lord had said. Now, Nineveh was, thanks to God, a very large city; it required a journey of three days, as it were. Jonah began to go into the city on a journey of about one day, so to speak, and he preached in these words: Three days more, and Nineveh will be overthrown (vv.3–4). The prophet is sent, and, endowed with irresistible enthusiasm, he sets about his task; with great vigor he enters the foreign city Nineveh in discharge of the divine decrees. Though it was a large city and extended to such huge dimensions as to require *a journey of three days,* if anyone chose to visit it, he crossed it in *one day*—or, as other commentators think, it was on completing a journey of *one day* in it that (587) he delivered the divine message.[4]

Now, the prophet aroused wonderment, a Hebrew man, coming from foreign parts, perhaps unknown to anyone there, walking through the middle of the town, and crying aloud in the words, *Three days more and Nineveh will be overthrown.* So what are we to say? That he was guilty of falsehood, speaking from his own heart instead of from the mouth of the Lord, as some commentators claim? This is not our view; rather, we claim that, while the prophets often suggest the manner of their mission, they do not altogether deliver to us all the words that came to them from God, nor the words from them to God.[5] The fact that the Lord said to him, remember, "Rise up, go to Nineveh, and preach in

4. The ambiguity is commented on also by Theodoret (thanks to Cyril) and by modern commentators.

5. The second half of this sentence does not appear in the PG ed. Despite Jerome's comments, Cyril does not advert to the occurrence of "*three* days more" in the LXX for the "forty" of the Heb. (and alternative versions, cited by Theodoret, who deferentially attributes the error rather to copyists), an error probably made under influence of the "three" in the previous verse.

it, because a clamor has ascended to me from their wickedness,"
we heard clearly at the very beginning of the prophecy; but what
he for his part said to God we do not know. We shall, however,
find him saying, "Were not these my words when I was still in my
country? This was the reason I took the step of fleeing to Tarshish, that I knew you are merciful and compassionate."[6] Do you
see that he did not state most things, including what was said
without our knowledge by God and to God, alike through the
Holy Spirit? It is therefore logical to attribute truth to the statements of the saints; they would hardly be guilty of falsehood, enriched as they were with the spirit of truth. (588)

*The men of Nineveh believed in God, proclaimed a fast, and donned
sackcloth, from the unimportant to the important among them* (v.5).
The verse is charged with meaning: *the people of Nineveh believed;*
that is, the people of a city that had been condemned for all its
inveterate wrongdoing, a city in which there was a vast prolifera-
tion of idols beyond counting as well as innumerable shrines,
and unspeakable practices were popular. Soothsaying and false
prophecy were shown respect by them, astrologers were considered wise, and anyone with a facility for any kind of vice enjoyed
great renown. Yet they *believed in God, from the unimportant to the
important,* that is, prominent and undistinguished, famous and
abject, both affluent people and those overcome with the burden of poverty—all felt the same zeal in acceding to the words
of the prophet. He was an object of great wonderment, attract-
ing considerable commendation from the believers; without
hesitation they responded to his call to reform, and subjected
to the divine proclamation their neck, which was accustomed to
luxury, despite his being a single foreigner, otherwise unknown,
who called them to repentance.

While this was the situation of the Ninevites, however, Israel
in its stupidity did not obey the Law, mocking the provisions of
Moses and setting no store by the statements of the prophets.
Why do I make this claim? They also turned killers of the Lord,

6. 1.1–2 and 4.2. Cyril's worry, as it was Theodore's and less so Theodoret's, is
the historical unlikelihood of conversion in response to a one-liner from a complete stranger. Jerome does not share this Antiochene (moral as well as hermeneutical) preoccupation, whereas Theodore even rewrites the text to offset it.

not even believing Christ himself, Savior of us all. The position of the Ninevites was therefore better; the truth of this was demonstrated by the God of all, who spoke to the blessed prophet Ezekiel in these terms: "Son of man, go in to the house of Israel, not to many people of foreign tongues and languages or those of obscure accents whose words you will not understand. If (589) I sent you to such people, they would hearken to you, whereas the house of Israel will refuse to listen to you because they do not want to hearken to me, for the whole house of Israel is contentious and hard of heart."[7] In other words, the people of foreign tongue, unintelligible and of obscure accents—namely, the Ninevites—respected the oracles and without delay moved to repent, whereas contentious Israel did not respect them, as I said, or the very Lord of Law and Prophets.

The news reached the king of Nineveh; he rose from his throne, divested himself of his robe, put on sackcloth, and sat in ashes. A proclamation was issued in Nineveh by the king and by his nobles, saying, No human being or animal, no oxen or sheep are to taste anything, feed, or drink water. People and animals were covered with sackcloth, and cried at length to God; they all turned from their evil ways and from the iniquity in their actions, saying, Who knows if God will relent and be appeased and turn away from the wrath of his anger, and we may not be lost? (vv.8–9). He develops at length his commendation of their responsiveness, and greatly admires the readiness of those called to repentance. When they heard the prophet's words, note, (590) even the very person appointed to reign and enjoying the highest reputation immediately left the throne of kingship, bade farewell to the clothing befitting him, put off the purple, and donned sackcloth, the vesture of mourning. Sitting among the ashes, he gave an example to the others as well to abstain from food and unceasingly in prayer to beseech and beg God for mercy.

Now, the Ninevites were very wise, devoting themselves to an abandonment of depravity by means of fasting, this being the single authentic and blameless form of repentance. Since Israel by contrast did not possess a facility for it, and sometimes gave

7. Ezek 3.4–7.

evidence of a fasting that was ill-considered and profane, God ordered the prophet to raise his voice and proclaim to them, "This is not the fasting that I wanted, says the Lord"; and he supplied the reason for his mentioning it: "On your fast days you serve your own interests and oppress all your workers; you fast to quarrel and to fight, and to strike the lowly with your fist. Why fast, I ask you, so that your voice may be heard today in a loud cry? This is not the fasting that I wanted, a day for people to humble themselves."[8] The Ninevites therefore did better by performing for God a pure and blameless fast, the sacred text confirming that *they all turned from their evil ways and from the iniquity in their actions*. What was done was reasonable and sensible; they believed that *God would relent and turn away the effects of his wrath.* Now, by *relent* he means "have second thoughts" on seeing them abandoning (591) depravity for goodness, when he for his part would adopt the benignity and love dear to him, being kindly by nature. On the other hand, he inflicts punishment on sinners and on those inexorably committed to obduracy, imposing the effects of his wrath like a kind of bridle to check them and bring them to compliance.

Now, consider how the Ninevites said, *Who knows if God will relent and be appeased and turn away from the wrath of his anger, and we may not be lost?* whereas Israel in its wisdom, though instructed by Law that the Lord is good and kind, could not bring themselves to take this view. Instead, remember, they exclaimed, "Our transgressions and our sins weigh upon us, and we waste away because of them: how then can we live?" despite their hearing God's clear statement, "Turn back, turn back from your evil way: why will you die, house of Israel?"[9] That was really what the Ninevites did, averting the wrath directed at them by a change for the better. They even ordered *people and animals* to join in mourning, to abstain from food and drink, and to be forced, as it were, to grieve—a case of hyperbole: it did not necessarily happen, God's requiring hardship on the part of the animals. Instead, the sacred text suggested it as well to bring out the extraordinary de-

8. Is 58.3–5.
9. Ezek 33.10–11.

gree of the Ninevites' repentance. I am aware, then, that some commentators are embarrassed at this, claiming that by *animals* we should understand the most brutish of human beings. Scripture is true, and it would be right at times for this view to be taken by some; but as far as the meaning of the present passage goes, the other interpretation could perhaps be applied, namely, the indication of the extraordinary degree of repentance, (592) by assigning the hardship also to the very animals.[10]

God saw their actions, that they turned from their wicked ways, and God repented of the evil he said he would bring upon them, and did not do it (v.10). The Lord is quick to show mercy and bring salvation to the repentant; he immediately relieves them of their former crimes if they desist from their sin, cancels his wrath, and thinks instead of kindly actions. When he sees them turning to good behavior, he makes a change to clemency, puts off their overthrow, and accords them pity. Scripture is in fact right to say, "Why will you die, house of Israel? For I have no pleasure in the death of anyone, says the Lord Adonai, my wish being for them to turn from their way and live." Now, when the text says *evil*, think not of depravity but of wrath that brings troubles; our God who loves virtue is not an agent of troubles.[11]

10. Unlike the Antiochenes, who have no trouble with animals being involved in penitential works, Cyril is aware that some of his school prefer to give such extraordinary features of the sacred text a metaphorical or spiritual meaning (as in the case of Hosea's marriage to a prostitute). Here he settles for staying with the literal sense understood as literature and involving figures such as hyperbole.

11. Ezek 18.31–32. Cyril makes the distinction he had made on Am 3.6 (as will Theodoret at both places, and as had Chrysostom elsewhere).

COMMENTARY ON JONAH,
CHAPTER FOUR

Jonah felt a great distress, and was troubled. He prayed to the Lord, saying, O Lord, were not these my words when I was still in my country? This was the reason I took the step of fleeing to Tarshish, that I knew you are merciful and compassionate, long-suffering, rich in mercy and relenting in the case of evils. Now Lord and Master, take my life from me, because it is better for me to die than to live (vv.1–3).

INCE GOD IS COMPASSIONATE (593) TO those who avert the effects of wrath by repentance, even when the time had passed for the decreed outcome, and what had been foretold was due to occur and yet none of the expectations had come to pass, the blessed Jonah was extremely distressed. It was not because the city had escaped destruction—the attitude of a wicked and envious man, unbecoming a saint—but because he gave the impression of being a liar and a braggard, idly alarming them, speaking his own mind and not at all what came from the mouth of the Lord, as Scripture says. Some other commentators think that the prophet was distressed for other ineffable reasons, claiming that since he knew that the call went out to the mass from the nations whereas Israel had completely forfeited hope in God, he was very dejected as the fulfillment drew near, and was gloomy, as it were, at the loss of his kith and kin.[1]

It is he himself, however, who abjures this position, admitting openly that he left for Tarshish (though apprehended after showing reluctance about his mission) on account of the clear realization that the Lord was kind and *compassionate, relenting in the case of evils.* Since this is what you are like, he says, in fact, why did you idly bid me proclaim overthrow to them? Human-

1. Jer 23.16.

ly speaking, he was mean-spirited, insisting that he used those words even in the land of the Jews, and he begged to meet an early death, raising no little protest, as it were, about God's way of doing things. His attitude was unstable, unworthy of a saintly mind; if no one in his right mind upbraids medical personnel for applying beneficial remedies to wounds, how would it be right for you (594) to criticise the God who knows everything and gives thought to healing for our minds that is fitting and truly useful? After all, he is a healer of spirits, who allays the ferocity of our passions, sometimes with hardship, sometimes with the good effects of his clemency.

The Lord replied to Jonah, Are you very distressed? Jonah left the city and sat down opposite the city; he made himself a tent there and sat under it until he saw what was going to happen to the city (vv.4–5). Far from allowing the prophet's mind to fall victim to depression, he lent vigor to him in his weakness, as it were, kindly but helpfully accusing him of being *distressed.* In my view, you see, he was suggesting nothing else by his inquiry, *Are you very distressed?* as if to chastise him both for being distressed and for failing to understand the purpose of the divine judgments. The days had already passed when the threats should have been realized, as I said, and furthermore divine wrath was still not taking effect; so he understands that God had shown mercy, and not everything had gone as he had hoped. He believed that because of their decision to repent they were given a postponement of the disaster, but that the effects of the wrath would occur if they did not display works of repentance commensurate with their sins. After all, why should three days' effort benefit people who were buried in every form of wrongdoing and guilty of such dreadful sins? It was probably with thoughts like this within him that he left the city, waiting to see (595) what would happen to them. He expected, in fact, that it would perhaps be shaken and collapse, or be burnt to the ground like Sodom. Instead, it was his house that was ruined, the shelter he had built himself.

The Lord God gave orders for a pumpkin vine, and it rose above Jonah's head to give shade over his head to shelter him from his troubles. Jonah was very happy with the pumpkin vine (v.6). God gave the further order for a *pumpkin vine,* as he also had for a sea monster, and clearly his wish was sufficient for it to be done. Immediately it grew up lovely and bushy, providing cover for the shelter at once, and by its excellent shade it promoted his sense of well-being, as it were. The prophet was very happy with it, and really exulted in it as a wonderful and commendable development. Notice in this as well his tendency to innate simplicity of mind: whereas he was extremely distressed that the outcome to his prophecy was not realized, in turn he *was very happy* with a vegetable and a plant. The unsophisticated mind is very easily disposed to both distress and satisfaction; you will see the accuracy of my comment if you observe the ways of infants, who often get upset at something of no consequence and weep loudly at nothing, while, on the other hand, finding enjoyment and undergoing a sudden change from distress to joy, sometimes under the influence again of a thing of no consequence. This happens, in fact, with human bodies: when not normally strong, they collapse easily at someone's touch, even if not done with vigor, (596) but, as it were, touched with a gentle hand. The mind that is not resilient is likewise easily disposed to an influence from whatever delights it or naturally distresses it.[2]

The Lord ordered a morning worm the next day, which attacked the pumpkin plant, and it withered. At sunrise the Lord God ordered a blast of burning heat, and the sun struck the head of Jonah; he became depressed, renounced his life, and said, It would be better for me to die than to live (vv.7–8). By *morning worm* he refers to the locust because of its taking the beginning of its existence from the dew that falls in the morning. God gave orders also for the *heat* in the sense of his giving orders both to the pumpkin plant and to the sea monster in the way we have explained. While its burning up was unexpected, the *heat* struck it severely, and imparted a warm blast to the distraught man when he was deprived of shade; hence his discontent was greatly aggravated. He was reduced to such a state of depression as even to consider death very desirable.

---

2. Unlike Theodore, Cyril acknowledges weaknesses in the prophet. He bypasses, incidentally, Jerome's lengthy justification of "ivy" as the correct name for the plant, a choice that led to Augustine's letter (71A) castigating his preferring the *Hebraica veritas* to the LXX and upsetting all those Christians unfamiliar with the term.

*The Lord said to Jonah, Should you be very distressed at the pump-
kin plant? He replied, I am distressed enough to die* (v.9). Notice
once more the God of all in his immeasurable loving-kindness
playing, as it were, with the innocent souls of the saints especially, and falling in no way short of the affection of parents.
(597) The pumpkin plant provided shade, remember, and the
prophet was very pleased with it; but in the scheme of things
the locust later undermined it, and the heat struck it, showing
that the shade was so useful and necessary for his well-being
that when deprived of the advantage he became upset instead.
In his great distress at a trifle—I mean the pumpkin plant—he
then no longer blamed the divine loving-kindness for deciding
to bestow pity and clemency on the cities' notables along with
an innumerable multitude of inhabitants. So he asked, *Should
you be very distressed* at a mere vegetable? This he admitted, thus
providing the loving God with the basis of an explanation.

*The Lord said, You showed concern for the pumpkin plant, for which
you did not labor and which you did not grow, which came into being by
night and perished by night. Should I, on the other hand, show no concern for Nineveh, the great city, in which there are more than a hundred
and twenty thousand persons who do not know their right hand from
their left, and many animals?* (vv.10–11) O what wonderful clemency that beggars comparison and understanding! What words
would suffice for us to sing its praises? Or how could we open
our mouths to offer songs of thanksgiving to one of such compassion and goodness? He puts far from us our iniquities, and
like a parent showing compassion to his children, the Lord has
compassion for those who fear him, for he knows how we were
made.[3] Notice, in fact, how he presents Jonah being distressed
not at an appropriate time nor when it was called for, despite
being obliged like a saint to applaud and praise the Lord for
his goodness. If you took it personally, he says, note, (598) or
rather were brought to the extremes of distress because your
pumpkin plant withered, which grew up in a single night and
perished likewise, how for my part should I not take account of
a populous city, *in which there are more than a hundred and twenty*

3. Cf. Ps 103.12–14.

thousand persons who on account of their age cannot discern what is their right and what their left? This is something beyond infants, and it is logical to accord them loving-kindness before all others, since they have not sinned; what sins could they be guilty of if still unfamiliar with their own hands?

Now, if he also refers to the *animals* and accords them pity, this too is kindly; after all, if "a righteous person has compassion on the souls of his animals,"[4] and this redounds to his credit, why is it surprising if the Lord of all himself also accords pity and compassion to them as well? This is the way Christ saved everyone, giving himself as a ransom for small and great, wise and foolish, rich and poor, Jew and Greek, of whom it could also rightly be said, "Lord, you will save human beings and animals alike, as you made your mercy abound, O God; all people will hope in the shadow of your wings."[5] To him be the glory and the power, together with the Father, who has no beginning, and the all-holy Spirit, who is good and gives life, for ages of ages. Amen. (599)

4. Prv 12.10 LXX. All our commentators adopt this interpretation of the number of people in Nineveh. Cyril does not follow Jerome (though perhaps aware of his interpretation), however, when he takes the cattle to mean foolish people.

5. Ps 36.6–7.

COMMENTARY ON *THE*
PROPHET *MICAH*

PREFACE TO THE
COMMENTARY ON MICAH

HE SINGLE PURPOSE OF all the holy prophets, dear also to God, was to persuade Israel to decide to part company resolutely with deception and instead to opt for serving God, living and true, and glorying in the ornaments of righteousness by removing as far as possible their involvement in wrongdoing. There was a long series of them as God in some fashion gave prior assurance and clearly predicted in a great number of statements that, unless they chose to live an upright life and to set great store by making a change for the better, they would bring punishment upon themselves, and after experiencing self-imposed destruction (600) they would find the reason for their suffering in their own free will. Now, if the discourses of the holy prophets should contain the same content, let no one find fault with them by making allegations of repetitiveness in their case. Instead, let them adopt the following clear line of reasoning: we should focus on no time when there was not anyone capable of reforming sinners. Just as no one in his right mind would quibble if at any one time physicians checked by suitable treatment the same effects of the ailments affecting us, it would in my view be similarly unreasonable to upbraid the prophets if they, too, appeared to proceed with the same actions and words. It is one Lord, after all, who spoke to everyone and brought to light for the deceived at every period those with the ability to return them to the straight and narrow. They all, in fact, foretold wars, captivities, desolation of the cities, hardship, grief, mourning the dead, trials of the neglected, cruelty of raiders; in short, you would find the contents broaching every form of severity with a view to what is required for the benefit of the deceived. Sometimes, you see, even the unbridled tendency to apostasy and sin is checked by terrifying stories.

Accordingly, the blessed Micah also prophesies at the time of the reigns of Jotham, Ahaz, and Hezekiah. Pekah son of Remaliah and Rezin king of Syria campaigned against Jerusalem during the reign of Jotham; he was succeeded at his death by Ahaz, who paid money to the Assyrian when the war was protracted, and begged him to lend assistance since he was unable to resist the attacking forces. At that time, when the kings in Samaria were Jeroboam son of Jehoash, after him Azariah, and thirdly Menahem, King Pul of Assyria advanced; he accepted a generous bribe to return to his own country. After Pul, Tiglath-pileser the Assyrian advanced on Judea and overthrew a great number of cities in Samaria, and in addition to them the whole of Galilee as far as Naphtali. While this was recounted in detail when we compiled our commentary on the blessed prophet Hosea, we felt the need to remind you of it here as well, with a view to settling the dates of Micah's prophecy; it was necessary, you see, it was necessary for the earnest scholar not to be ignorant of the reason why the kings of Jerusalem rated a mention—Jotham and Ahaz, that is.[1] Now, the period of the prophecy extends to the reign of Hezekiah as well, when Sennacherib also reigned as king of the Assyrians; he took Samaria by force, and ravaged also the cities of the Philistines, that is, Palestine. He then took Lachish, a city of the kingdom of Judah, (602) and from there sent Rabshakeh to besiege Jerusalem; he incurred punishment for arrogance and for cursing God, and in a single night a hundred and eighty-five thousand of the Assyrian army died.[2] Accordingly, the text says, the word of the Lord came to Micah of Moresheth.

---

1. Cyril feels that studious readers require at least factual details to appreciate Micah's message, and so he relays the contents of 2 Kgs 15–16, aware that he did so as well in introducing Hosea. Just as he did there, however, he arrives at the name Azariah for King Zechariah of Israel, unknown to the biblical text, and likewise fails to realize that Pul and Tiglath-pileser refer to the one Assyrian king.

2. 2 Kgs 19.35.

COMMENTARY ON MICAH,
CHAPTER ONE

The word of the Lord came to Micah of Morathi in the days of Jotham, Ahaz, and Hezekiah, kings of Judah (v.1).

GAIN IT SHOULD BE UNDERSTOOD that the Hebrew text has Moresheth in place of *Morathi*, the intention being to give the name not of the father but of his native place; they say *Morathi* was a town or little city of the country of the Jews. The other translators agree with this text as well; so *Morathi* would not be the prophet's father; instead, by mention of Moresheth, as I said, there is a reference to his native place.[1] We need now to study what the words were that came to him. *Which he saw concerning Samaria and Jerusalem;* that is, he sees future events in a vision, as it were, troubles that had not then come to pass or were at the very doors, which he received not only in his mind but as far as possible by sight (603)—a vision, that is—and of which he dreaded the outcome. So he necessarily delivers his prophecy *concerning Samaria and Jerusalem.*

Listen to the words, all you peoples, and let the earth and all its inhabitants give heed. The Lord God will give witness to you, the Lord from his holy house (v.2). He bids them be ready to respond, bending their ear, as it were, to grasp in detail the force of the divine sayings. Now, the fact that the account comes not from human will or intention but actually from God, who has control of all things, he confirms by adding, *The Lord will give witness to you.* In other words, he is saying, Even if it is I, Micah, who delivers the message, even if as a man I perhaps act as mediator, still it is the God of all in person who adjures you, lending his own voice to his lordly oracles. He will therefore be a *witness* to you, the one to whom you erected this celebrated and splendid Temple,

1. Cyril does not follow Jerome in proceeding to locate Moresheth.

to whom the divine altar was raised by you, to whom you have been instructed by Law to show reverence, who has ever spoken to the holy prophets from his own *house.* Before the others he spoke to blessed Moses, who erected that ancient tabernacle in the wilderness; he used to speak from above the mercy seat, and, as the sacred text says, "Moses would speak, and God would reply (604) to him in a mighty sound." He now adjures you, it says, *from his house;* so *listen, peoples, and let the earth give heed.* Similar to this is the statement in Isaiah, "Listen, heaven, and give heed, earth, for the Lord has spoken."[2] While the Most High does not dwell in handmade temples of stone, therefore, yet since we claim the holy houses are erected to the glory of God, consequently we believe it is not unworthy of the God of all to dwell in them, even though filling the heavens, the earth, and the nether regions.

Now, you would be justified in applying this also to Christ when he calls to salvation not only peoples who were descended from Abraham, but also the whole earth. He adjures them, in fact, by saying in the words of David, "Hear this, all nations; give ear, all you who dwell in the world."[3] There is no doubting the fact that the Word has come down from heaven to us, as it were, from his own *house,* which is very dear to him. It would not be wrong to speak of heaven as God's *house* when the inspired Scriptures speak of the earthly Zion, taken as a type of the church, as his house and city; the divinely inspired David somewhere sings, "Glorious things have been said of you, city of God."[4] So the church of Christ, who fills all things in his divine nature, would be, as it were, a city and house.

For, lo, the Lord is issuing forth from his place; he will walk upon (605) *the high places of the earth. Mountains will shake under him, and the valleys will melt like wax in the face of fire and like water falling in descent* (vv.3–4). Such a passage is very obscure and full of riddles; but we are obliged to make the claim that, while reference to God is communicated in words we use, the expert who is skilled in understanding "a proverb and obscure statement,

2. Ex 19.19; Is 1.2; Acts 7.48.   3. Ps 49.1.
4. Ps 87.3.

the words of the wise, and their riddles"[5] will appreciate them in detail and as far as possible in a manner befitting God's ineffable nature. His being seated, enthroned, and rising are, in fact, spoken of by the saints, as also travel and journeys, not to mention other human details. But as I just said, such items for our consideration would properly be understood in precise detail by good people of mature judgment; the descriptions are phrased in comparisons and metaphors in use by us.

So when you hear the prophet saying, *For, lo, the Lord is issuing forth from his place; he will walk upon the high places of the earth,* and proceeding to say, *Mountains will shake under him, and the valleys will melt,* then is the time for you to go beyond a material impression and rise to a more subtle understanding in your consideration. In this case, therefore, you will understand God's emergence happening, as it were, *from his* own *place* like a kind of movement from a state of rest to one of performance of (606) some tasks; it would be like saying, The one who was formerly long-suffering is now stirred to move, and he will cease his inaction against those who offend him, in a sense abandon his customary mildness, and now inflict punishment. In fact, *he will walk upon the high places of the earth*; that is, he will now tread on the elevated parts, by which we should understand the people reigning in both Samaria and Jerusalem. *Mountains will shake;* that is, those who outranked others and were greatly elevated in importance, quite comparable to mountains, will in turn be shifted from their positions of privilege. *The valleys will melt like wax;* that is, the lowly and abject, displaying the behavior of the masses, being very obdurate and reluctant to respond to the divine oracles, *will melt like wax* as though exposed to the *fire* of divine wrath; they will become *like water falling in descent,* that is, careering down a cliff in a rapid and headlong fall. You see, as I previously remarked, the kings of the Assyrians savagely plundered both Samaria itself and the kingdom of Judah, deported

5. Prv 1.6. Cyril goes to some length to warn against misinterpreting anthropomorphisms, as will Theodoret more concisely after him; it is the principle of scriptural considerateness, *synkatabasis* in Chrysostom's term. The prophet's double focus on northern and southern kingdoms, on the contrary, receives little attention.

some of the kings, and killed all the leaders, and in a kind of rapid course *like water* down a cliff they deported to their own country the mass of common people. This was *the water falling in descent* moving rapidly from Samaria to the country of the Persians and Medes.

Now, the Word of God *issues forth from his place;* though God by nature, he became man. (607) By this he seems somehow also to undergo movement, although not experiencing change but rather being by nature steady and as God enjoying stability. He also walked upon *the high places,* has *shaken mountains,* and made *valleys melt* and flow *like water falling in descent.* By *high places of the earth* are to be understood the spiritual powers raised up against everyone and the spiritual forces of wickedness, and by *mountains shaken* the demons relieved of control over us; they have been cast out, and we have now been called to submission to the one who is God by nature and in truth. *Valleys* in turn would be the vast mass of demons, lowly and abject, *melted like wax,* flowing also *like water* into the recesses of Hades. The wicked spirits, remember, made their approach to Christ and "begged him not to order them to go back into the abyss";[6] since others had previously been dispatched, the rest were horrified at the prospect.

If, on the other hand, you wanted to take *high places, mountains,* and *valleys* as the leaders of the Jews and the crowds subject to them, who on account of frenzy against Christ were also relieved of their control, you would not be wide of the proper purpose. They also *melted like wax* from the misfortunes of the war with the Romans as though exposed to flame, and "were set at naught like water running away, and they vanish like melted wax."[7] (608)

All this is the result of Jacob's impiety and the sin of the house of Israel (v.5). After saying that the God of all will walk on the high places of the earth, the mountains will be shaken by him, and the valleys will melt like wax and flow like water, he now continues, *All this is the result of Jacob's impiety.* Note, therefore, how he speaks of hidden mysteries, and does not arrive at the meaning of the

6. Lk 8.31.
7. Ps 58.7–8 LXX.

passage at a material level; instead, he arrives at it obliquely by describing calamities that would happen later in Samaria and Jerusalem. After all, what terror would be involved in the shaking of the mountains, or how would it bring distress to people in Samaria or the others? In what fashion would valleys melt or be in descent like rushing water? His habit instead is to convey in an adequate manner what would happen to the people of Israel. Consequently, he now applies punishment of necessity, not speaking to them as though they were ignorant, in my view, but as if to reprove them, and properly bring them round to opting for a positive and seemly way of thinking. Hence his saying, *All this is the result of Jacob's impiety and the sin of the house of Israel*, so that the race of Israel might be understood to have offended both God and men, by *impiety* probably referring to failings against God, and by *sin* those against kith and kin.

What is the impiety of Jacob? Is it not Samaria? And what is the sin of the house of Judah? Is it not Jerusalem? Referring by *Jacob* to the descendants of Jacob—that is, Ephraim, (609) dwelling in Samaria—he makes clear their crimes. He says *Samaria* is a form of *impiety*—not, of course, that he is blaming the country itself: it would be silly to take that view. Instead, by *Samaria* he means what happened in Samaria, like the calves, Chemosh, Baal, and what was done in it to some people through the oppression by those in power. Scripture said, remember, "They slapped the faces of the poor, and avoided the way of the lowly," and in addition said, "When will the moon pass, and we shall engage in commerce? When will the sabbath come, and we shall open the stores so as to set the measure short, increase the weight, make the balance unfair?"[8] He also says that *Jerusalem* is *the sin of Judah*. We would not be thinking right to blame the city itself in any way for this; rather, we would consider what was done in it to be a sin for Judah. Somewhere God accused the Jews of frenzy, and even said clearly, "For you have as many gods as you have towns, O Judah, and have devoted as many altars to sacrifice for Baal as you have thoroughfares. Why do you speak to me? You have all sinned, and have all offended me, says the Lord almighty." He

8. Am 2.7; 8.5.

upbraids them also in Isaiah, "How the faithful city of Zion has become a whore! She that was full of justice, where righteousness lodged, but now murderers. Your silver has become dross; your innkeepers mix wine with water; your rulers are rebels, accomplices of thieves, lovers of bribes, looking for kickbacks, not judging in favor of orphans, nor giving (610) judgment in favor of widows."[9] So the unholy deeds in *Jerusalem* proved *sin* for *Judah*, not the city itself.

It is therefore necessary to love God, and this with all one's soul and heart, to shake off one's lethargy in good works, to do no harm in any way to one's neighbors but rather win them over by kind treatment, to desist from evil behavior and be devoted instead to the practices of righteousness. By contrast, if we are negligent about such commendable pursuits and choose to spurn them, he will inflict the effects of wrath, melt us like wax by punishing us in fire, and scatter us like water, not continuing to accord us pity and love.

I shall turn Samaria into a fruit shed in a field and a vine plantation, and shall pull down its stones into an abyss and uncover its foundations. They will knock down all its images, and set on fire all its earnings, and all its idols I shall reduce to nothingness (vv.6–7). He outlines clearly what in turn will be the sufferings of those who have offended in this way. Samaria will in fact, he says, be like *a fruit shed in a field and a vine plantation.* Some people, you see, preserve what grows in a field by weaving shelters and sitting in them, thus warding off all harm from it; but when the fruit is gathered, the guards cease their labor and go off home after upturning their shelters. We shall find Samaria having this experience: since it sinned gravely, (611) or rather committed impiety even against the God of all, paying homage to its own works, it was overturned and fell when abandoned by those formerly ordered to preserve it, namely, holy powers and angels. The blessed prophet Isaiah also said something similar about it: "Daughter Zion will be abandoned like a shelter in a vineyard and like a fruit shed in a cucumber patch."[10] Now, why was it abandoned? The rational multitude of heavenly ranks that con-

9. Jer 2.28–29; Is 1.21–23.
10. Is 1.8.

stantly attended on it took their leave, as I said. It will therefore be like *a fruit shed in a field and a vine plantation.* It would be like saying, Bereft of cities and houses, and transformed into the appearance of fields.

You could also take it another way if you wanted. When the cultivators of the vineyards take possession of a site particularly suited to them, they plough it up, turning the soil this way and that. He threatens the land of the Samaritans with this fate, as if to say it will be land for ploughing, as I said, with cities and houses done away with. Hence, he says, *I shall pull down its stones into an abyss and uncover its foundations.* He also says that in addition to this it will be a laughing stock; what they expected to be their saviors as gods will in fact perish along with the people in the habit of adoring them; *all its earnings will be set on fire, and all its idols reduced to nothingness.* By *earnings* it indicates what was burnt in honor of the idols, perhaps by way of offerings; they brought some of their own wealth to the shrines to devote it to the glory of idols, despite their being of no help or avail to give assistance, (612) as if to make a thanksgiving payment or recompense for what they thought they received from them.

Now, we recall that also in Hosea he accused the assembly of the Jews in these words: "She did not know that it was I who gave her the grain, the wine, and the oil, and lavished silver on her; instead, she used silver and gold for the Baal" (as offerings, clearly). The fact that Israel in its derangement regarded prosperity as *earnings* and recompense for its zeal in being deceived you would understand no less from God's further words: "I shall do away with her vine and her fig trees, all the payment, she said, that my lovers gave me";[11] in other words, she believed that it was due to the decision of the idols that she was flush with wealth and luxury and enjoyed prosperity. The mind of those who are deceived is therefore blind; if it were not ignorant of the one who is God by nature, it would pay homage rather to him and not to some others; it would offer prayers of thanksgiving to him; it would confess him as the giver and manager of every good thing. If, on the other hand, it had chosen to be of this mind, it would not have

11. Hos 2.8, 12.

become *like a fruit shed in a field* or *like a vine plantation*; rather, it would continue to enjoy the blessings of unshaken prosperity and to be admired for being fortified by benevolence from on high and established in a high degree of satisfaction.

Because it assembled them from the earnings of prostitution and collected them from the earnings of prostitution (v.7). The passage continues the mockery, ridiculing the Jews' stupidity (613) with considerable skill; it makes clear the folly of their inherent silliness, and clearly highlights what lay within their mind and heart. To be sure, he is saying, it was right and just for Israel in its good sense, its gratitude and wisdom, to offer thanksgiving to stones; it was aware that they were the ones who honored it, supplied its prosperity, amassed wealth for it, and caused it to enjoy well-being. It believed, in fact, that it enjoyed prosperity as a payment for spiritual *prostitution*, and since it sacrificed to idols and worshiped sticks and stones, it would not be lacking what it prayed for. It *assembled*, he says, and became rich *from the earnings of prostitution, collected* and amassed them, and enjoyed unrelieved satisfaction. We shall therefore understand the force of the passage to be marked by artistry and irony intermingled with threats.

For this reason it will wail and mourn; it will go barefoot and naked; it will do its wailing like dragons and its grieving like daughters of sirens. Because its affliction has overwhelmed it, because it has reached Judah and got as far as the gate of my people, as far as Jerusalem (vv.8–9). Because it continued to live in error, he is saying, and in no way ceased distressing its Lord, offering to the images thanksgiving offerings in which they took satisfaction and enjoyment, and furthermore went to the extent of blasphemy, consequently *it will wail and mourn*. It will not be for other people or for foreigners that it will grieve, shedding tears of love, as it were; instead, it will bewail its own misfortunes. Now, its being *naked* (614) *and barefoot* suggests the condition of captives; the blessed prophet Isaiah likewise traversed Jerusalem "naked and barefoot" to suggest the captivity shortly to befall them when God gave orders for it to happen.[12] It will therefore imitate in its

12. Is 20.2. The instruction was given at the time of the fall of Ashdod to Sargon II in 711.

own sufferings the laments of *dragons* and the grieving of *sirens;* some commentators claim that if a *dragon* is hit, it is then likely to lament, indicating this by striking the ground with its tail and being in the habit of creating a loud noise. By *sirens* the Greeks and their followers refer to birds accustomed to sing, capable of charming the listeners with the tunes of their songs.[13]

The divinely inspired Scripture, on the other hand, refers by *sirens* to the most vocal of sparrows in the habit of uttering pleasant sounds, or even nightingales, which lay eggs in hollows by the sea and sing a sad tune when the nest is taken by the waves, mourning in some way the loss of their young. He said *Samaria will mourn* in similar fashion the destruction of its own children; *its affliction has overwhelmed it,* reaching as far as *Judah and the gates of Jerusalem.* Now, by this the passage seems to suggest to us the war waged by Sennacherib, who took the whole of Samaria, plundered Judea, surrounded Jerusalem, and, arriving at its *gates,* threatened to burn it; he actually was unable to do so, since God protected it in the time of the reign of Hezekiah.[14] When we abandon the one who by nature and in truth is Lord, therefore, and commit ourselves to adhering to the unclean demons, then we shall completely and utterly *mourn* for ourselves, lament our own folly, be deprived (615) of his grace and help, and live a shameful and repulsive life (the meaning of *barefoot*). We shall instead be subject to Satan, who strikes us, and there will be nothing to prevent our being caught up in every trouble.

You inhabitants of Gath, do not become conceited, and you inhabitants of Enakim, do not rebuild mockery from the house: sprinkle dust on your mockery (v.10). The language is obscure, and the sense of the passage and of what follows very hard to grasp; but I shall try to explain it as far as I can. When war overran the cities in Samaria, and others fell under the rule of Judah and Benjamin, Israel was mocked with great glee by the neighboring foreign-

---

13. Jerome is not much help in teasing out the import of these creatures, which Theodore dismisses as mythical.

14. Theodoret will see the more likely reference also to the fall of Samaria to Shalmaneser (and Sargon II) in 722, as well as Sennacherib's failed attempt to take Jerusalem in 701.

ers, all of nearby Judea, and nations in the vicinity for finding no help from God. They were in fact convinced that the hand of their Savior was suffering impotence and necessarily lacking strength in the face of attacks by the raiders. It would have been better for them to realize that through choosing to distress their Savior and offending God they were experiencing calamities and were given into the hands of the foe. Since it was one of their faults, however, to come to the conclusion that it was through the power of idols of their own making that they enjoyed a high degree of prosperity, and, on the other hand, that Israel met with death and destruction as a result of the weakness of their Savior, consequently God handed over to devastation by Sennacherib the very cities of their neighbors as well. The Rabshakeh, for example, in addressing the people of Jerusalem on the wall, mentioned these very ones in saying, "Where is the god of Hamath and Arpad? Where is the god of the city of Sepharvaim? Surely he has not rescued Samaria from my hand? Which among all the gods of those nations has rescued his country from my hand?"[15]

So *Gath* of the foreigners known as Philistines is the capital of Palestine, and *Enakim* similarly is a small city likewise situated on the borders of Judea, in the desert to the south, subject to the power of Judah, no longer concerned with Jewish affairs but attached to the neighboring nations—namely, Moabites and Idumeans.[16] Accordingly he is saying, *You inhabitants of Gath, you inhabitants of Enakim,* do not make the misfortunes of others an occasion of festivity; *do not become conceited* on that account, or because your neighbor's house—Israel, that is—has been devastated, and therefore gloat over them as though they have perished. *Do not build mockery from the house;* instead, as though you yourselves are destined to suffer a turn for the worse, *sprinkle* the future like a kind of *dust on your mockery,* and lament your own misfortunes. After all, the Babylonians will dance in triumph

15. Is 36.19–20.
16. The LXX does not resonate to the wordplay in the Heb. of vv.10–15 lamenting the fate of twelve cities, some obscure, and the result is a garbled version. Jerome is of limited help, and Theodore dismissive, while Cyril has recourse to some creative commentary in being definite about a city the LXX presents as Enakim but which modern versions read as Beth-leaphrah.

over you, and the foe will mock you in your piteous plight. It is therefore wise to remember the one who says, "If your enemy falls, do not rejoice over him, because the Lord will see it, and it will not please him, and he will turn away his anger from him."[17]

Now, those who do not know Christ are also guilty of this; when at times the churches are persecuted, and the saints in them are put to the test, then it is in particular that they are in admiration of their own gods. Their mockery ends in tears, however, as Christ alleviates the troubles, (617) stills the turmoil, assuages the distress, and communicates to the saints satisfaction and joy; fame and enjoyment are in fact the outcome of hardship. Blessed David seems to me to say something similar to the God of all: "We passed through fire and water, and you brought us out to refreshment."[18]

Comfortably occupying her cities, she who dwells in Zennaar did not come out to mourn a house next to her; she will suffer the onset of pain from you (v.11). While the Seventy render it *Zennaar,* Aquila put Zenan, and Symmachus "healthy," which is perhaps the sense of Zenan. If *Zennaar* is the acceptable version, however, we claim that it is a place of many cities and towns occupied by foreigners, though in the territory of Judea; but if Zenan is the correct version, there is reference to a fine and important city in Egypt. There is no doubt, on the other hand, that it is "healthy" in the sense of being lush with crops. So he means *Zennaar,* or Zenan, is *comfortably occupying her cities.* The message will be directed at their inhabitants; she did not weep over those nearby who perished piteously and miserably; *she did not come out to mourn a house next to her;* that is, she did not mourn inhabitants of neighboring towns. Now, *Zennaar* was near Judea, as I said, as was Zenan, that is, the city in Egypt. Far from lamenting the fall and plundering of Israel, she took satisfaction in it and even exulted, (618) like those from Gath and Enakim. What, then, Israel? Surely the mockery of the neighboring nations will not go unnoticed, nor will God tolerate their committing these crimes? Surely he will not allow his glory to be mocked by foes? Far from it, it says: *she*

17. Prv 24.17–18.
18. Ps 66.12.

will suffer the onset of pain from you, or on account of you; in other words, she will be plundered along with the others. *Zennaar* was also raided, like the Egyptian city, when Sennacherib invaded it.

There is therefore need for the one who stands firm to be careful not to fall, and to abstain utterly from mocking those who suffer. Instead, one should "weep with those who weep" and not be smug about others' misfortunes, but rather dread encountering a similar fate.[19]

Did anyone dwelling in pain take a turn for the better? Because troubles from the Lord descended on the gates of Jerusalem, the din of chariots and cavalry (vv. 12–13). O inhabitants of Gath, of Enakim, of Zennaar (or Zenan), you did not lament the misfortunes of your neighbors; the terrible and unbearable fall and destruction of Israel in the past proved for you an occasion for mockery. You concluded that even God their Savior had grown weak while the works of your hands had grown strong and enjoyed such strength as to be able suddenly to save your cities. Come now, therefore, let us examine from actual events who God is by nature and in truth, who the strong one is, assigning irresistible help to those he chooses. In fact, (619) the cities both of Israel and of yourselves have been ravaged, he says, and you suffered a common fate, as it were. So which city is in pain and in dread of ultimate destruction (the sense of *dwelling in pain*) and has unexpectedly taken a turn *for the better,* that is, to safety and prosperity? Surely not one of you? Not at all, he says, only my Jerusalem: *troubles from the Lord descended on it.* In other words, I had been offended and had administered correction, inflicting the Assyrian on them, and as a result of my wrath ill treatment of them occurred; but it has been allayed and relieved, thanks to my victorious hand, which has against the odds rescued those who show respect for my power.

Now, we know that the Rabshakeh reached Jerusalem with plenty of cavalry,[20] and, as it were, touched its very *gates,* but did not capture it; in fact, the Assyrian was laid waste in a single night. The people in Jerusalem, for their part, were in mourn-

19. 1 Cor 10.12; Rom 12.15.
20. Division of verses this way has obscured the wordplay on horses and Lachish in v. 13.

ing, as though about to die, and spent a sleepless night weeping. But at daybreak the unexpected became clear: numberless corpses lay on the ground, leading those who, thanks to God, had against the odds been victorious and were saved to exult and say, "Weeping will last till evening, and joy till morning."[21] Do you see, then, how it was the first and only one of all the cities to *take a turn for the better*, despite *dwelling in pain*? After all, God does not in any way overlook his own; instead, after administering some limited correction, he proceeds to save them and shows no little interest in the glory befitting him, even if we offend. He said somewhere, in fact, through one of the prophets, "It is not on your account that I act, says the Lord, but for the sake of my name."[22] (620)

Inhabiting Lachish, she is the leader in sin for daughter Zion, because in you were found the offenses of Israel (v.13). Lachish in turn is a city subject to the rule of Judah, a close neighbor of the Philistines, but wrongfully hostile and given to idolatry, unconcerned for piety towards God and respect for the Law, actively engaged in deception and bringing other cities to ruin. It was perhaps the first of the cities subject to Judah and Benjamin that Sennacherib captured, and from there he sent the Rabshakeh to Jerusalem. Lachish, therefore, at one time enjoying comfortable occupancy and a secure foundation, was *the leader in sin for daughter Zion*, or Jerusalem; in her *were found the offenses of Israel*, that is, handmade images and a considerable number of false gods.

So what does the verse mean? In some way he mounts a defense to the Philistine population and endeavors to persuade them to adopt the attitude in the future that the saving God has not lost his strength. Since the cities of Judah offended him, however, they were surrendered to the foe; Lachish was *leader in sin for daughter Zion*, and as the principal base of apostasy was given over to Sennacherib. So Israel perished, as it is possible to see from Lachish, not that God was lacking strength—far from it—but because it suffered from being deceived and foolishly attached to the worship of the idols. (621)

21. Ps 30.6.   22. Ezek 36.22.

For this reason you will give envoys to the inheritance of Gath, futile houses. It was rendered useless for the kings of Israel, until they lead the heirs. She who inhabits the inheritance of Lachish will come as far as Adullam (vv.14–15). When Israel fell victim to the impulse of divine wrath and paid the penalty for its sins against God, the people of Gath and Enakim presumed to ridicule the glory of God, concluding, as I said, that he did not save his own, as though overcome by the hand of the Assyrians. Then in response God wanted to persuade them, beginning with Lachish, that they were given over to the foe because of the discovery of many offenses of Israel in them, and because they proved "leader in sin for daughter Zion" (v.13), that is, Jerusalem. When God said this, the blessed prophet before the others understood clearly what was meant, accepted the message, and, as if to crown it with his own verdict in favor of its truth, immediately exclaimed, *For this reason you will give envoys to the inheritance of Gath, futile houses.* Yes, O Lord, he is saying, they will go to the foe, sent as *envoys* by you, leaving their own country and moving to the land of the Assyrians, not only those in Samaria but also those in Gath. They proved guilty, in fact, of apostasy and insult, and could not bring themselves to follow your oracles; instead, they mocked the abused, and turned what happened to a curse of your glory. It is he, therefore, who *gives envoys to the inheritance of Gath, futile houses,* (622) the *futile houses* being those of Ephraim and the people of Gath, doubtless on account of reluctance in honoring God and according worship to images, and for the reason that they were interested only in things of the flesh and attached to earthly things, giving no importance to virtue.[23]

He then inserts a kind of complaint, as if the blessed prophet were wringing his hands when considering what was done at a time in Samaria. He ponders the kings' arrogance and the fact that unholy acts of their depravity took place that Israel had committed under them; for instance, there were novel practices, the heifers, and the shrines of the various idols. They did not cease provoking the Creator in every way. In his irritation,

23. Cyril is trying to uphold the version of the LXX, where the wordplay on the names of the towns of Moresheth-gath (Micah's hometown, in fact), sounding much like the Heb. for "dowry, gift," and Achzib, "lie," is lost.

therefore, the prophet says, *It was rendered useless for the kings of Israel, until they lead the heirs*, which is like saying, The kings did not desist from exercises in futility until they reached such depths of misery as to become others' inheritance awarded them by God. Now, because the Assyrians were on the point of taking control of two cities lying at the extremities of the whole country, namely, Lachish and Adullam,[24] which Rehoboam had built, he goes on to say, *She who inhabits the inheritance of Lachish will come as far as Adullam.* That is to say, She will inherit (in the sense of "occupy") Lachish even though it is highly fortified, and will extend as far as Adullam.

If you chose to be wise and compliant and (623) to oppose the divine decrees, therefore, you would enjoy extended prosperity and occupy your own inheritance in peace; you would revel in sound hope and in due course share the splendor of the saints. But if you proved to be obdurate, disobedient, and resistant to the divine laws, you would completely forfeit the hope of the saints and lose the inheritance given by God, and would instead become an inheritance of your foes, according to the song in the Psalms about some people: "They will be prey for foxes,"[25] that is, prey for wicked powers, evildoers, and scoundrels.

Glory of daughter Zion, shave and shear your head for your spoiled children; extend your widowhood to be like an eagle, for they were taken off from you into captivity (vv.15–16). It would be like saying, O daughter of Zion once thrice-blessed, enjoying pre-eminent and conspicuous *glory*—Jerusalem or Samaria—*your spoiled children* depart, the formerly riotous mob, notorious and effeminate, "who recline on ivory beds and behave wantonly on their couches, who eat kids from flocks and sucking calves from the midst of a herd, who clap their hands to the tune of instruments and think things are permanent and not ephemeral, who drink strained wine and anoint themselves with the best oils." (624) O naked daughter Jerusalem, then, divested of your glory and shown to be stripped of that former prosperity, lamenting to an

---

24. At this point the PG text omits a lengthy section that includes the remainder of comment on chapter 1 and the opening of chapter 2.

25. Ps 63.10.

extraordinary degree and bidding fair to imitate the sullenness of *eagles*, mourn *your children*, for they will go off into captivity, and you will be childless and solitary. Now, experts who busy themselves with the nature of birds in particular as far as it is possible claim that the *eagle* is fond of its young, and is extremely upset if chicks fall from its nest or are stolen from it. That the bird would not be unrelated to habits of fondness for its young the divinely inspired Moses convinces us by saying of God and the descendants of Israel, "As an eagle hovers over its nest and is fond of its chicks, spreading its wings, taking them up, and carrying them on its back."[26] Do you see how he said that the eagle is fond of its chicks and shows its affection with its feathers to such an extent as to shelter the young out of great love? So he says, *Extend your widowhood to be like an eagle.*

Now, you would mention this as well with good reason not only to the former populace of the Jews, but also to those living at the time of the Savior's coming, when by handing him over to crucifixion they fell foul of terrible and ineluctable misfortunes. They were scattered to every quarter, undergoing the hardship of captivity in a different form, as it were. (625)

26. Am 6.4–6; Dt 32.11. Cyril alone of the commentators reads in his form of the LXX "widowhood" (χηρεία) for the "baldness" (ξύρησις) in the Heb. and in the form of the LXX known to Jerome and the Antiochenes, and sees the eagle as a model of attachment to its young. The others see a reference to its loss of plumage, which in the case of daughter Zion is a symbol of grief for a lost generation.

They turned to pondering hardships and devising troubles on their beds, and at break of day they put them into effect because they did not raise their hands to God. They set their heart on properties, robbed orphans, took possession of houses, cheated a man of his house, a man of his inheritance (vv.1–2).

HEN THE GOD OF ALL DELIVERS a long passage on the punishment of some people, he begins by citing their crimes and exposing the magnitude of their impiety to avoid being thought harsh and wrathful instead of as a just Judge properly weighing up each one's faults and treating the guilty according to their works. So he mentions the ways in which they are evil and then reach such a degree of knavery as to plan at night to make *hardships* the object of their attention—that is, to hatch plots against someone—and *devise troubles*—that is, scheme to conduct prosecutions and be in a position to disadvantage weaker people. Despite the need in that case for a change of heart and a turn for the better by giving no opportunity for their schemes, at the very *break of day* they put their decisions into effect, despite being obliged[1] rather to *raise their hands to God* by the offering of a morning sacrifice to God. The plans they had formed at night and the schemes in leisure time included coveting others' properties, appropriation of houses, avarice, and oppression, *cheating a man of his house*. Consequently, they were rightly dismissed (626) as "futile houses,"[2] people unaware of what was pleasing to God.

It would therefore be incomparably better to spurn such practices and shun all depravity, utterly rejecting avarice, not hankering after what is unnecessary, and being satisfied with food and

---

1. At this point in the PG ed. the commentary resumes.
2. 1.14.

clothing and what temperate people need to live. After all, "those who want to be rich fall into many senseless and harmful desires that plunge people into ruin and destruction."[3] In addition to this it is harmful also to waste time at night on sinful schemes; better to imitate the blessed psalmist in saying to the God of all, "At midnight I rise to praise you for your righteous ordinances," and again, "O God my God, for you I watch; my soul thirsted for you; how often my flesh longs for you," and again, "When I thought of you on my bed, I meditated on you at daybreak."[4]

For this reason the Lord says this: Lo, I am planning for this tribe troubles from which you will not extricate your necks, and you will not walk upright at once, because the time is evil (v.3). Since, on their part, they are *pondering hardships and devising troubles* for some people, and rejecting as futile and senseless the raising of one's hands to God, consequently I, for my part, he says, *shall plan troubles for this tribe;* that is, I shall consider in which (627) *troubles*, or unbearable misfortunes, they would find themselves. What is inflicted on them, he is saying, would be so intolerable and burdensome that the sufferers would be similar to people bent over, or somehow stooped, in their terrible and insupportable depression. It will in fact, he says, be *an evil time* when the effects of wrath will hang over them. This in my view is what is wisely referred to in song: "Because my iniquities have gone over my head, they have weighed upon me like a heavy weight." Our Lord Jesus Christ, however, invited those so depressed to a removal of what weighed them down: "Come to me, all you who labor and are heavily burdened, and I shall give you rest."[5] Some paid homage in faith to the one who called and shook off the weight; others, however, who offended by unbelief, rightly remained stooped and burdened—I mean scribes and Pharisees, and with them the rest of the multitude, who could not *walk upright.* Aware of this the divinely inspired David cried aloud to God, "Let their eyes be darkened so that they cannot see, and let their backs remain forever stooped,"[6] so that they may not look up or be able to raise the eye of their mind to the

---

3. 1 Tm 6.8–9.   4. Pss 119.62 and 63.1, 6.
5. Ps 38.4; Mt 11.28.   6. Ps 69.23.

hope of the saints and the beautiful city in heaven, thus seeing only what is on earth, as if stooped, directing their insolent and ungodly minds to what is evanescent and fleshly.

On that day a proverb will be recited against you, and (628) *a dirge sung that says in song, We were distressed with distress; my people's lot was measured with rope, and there was no one to prevent him turning away* (v.4). He says that two things will happen at the same time, a *proverb* and a *dirge*. The *proverb* probably suggests the phrase that was, as it were, in everyone's mouth regarding them or about them: the highlights of the problems are generally recalled; the report of such events reaches cities and towns and spreads to the very ends of the whole earth. The *dirge*, on the other hand, indicates the weeping and wailing about them perhaps done by others or that they themselves do in crying over their own sufferings. Consequently, he says, *We were distressed with distress.* The form this distress takes he clarifies by saying, *My people's lot was measured with rope, and there was no one to prevent him turning away.* The inheritance, he is saying, which was allotted to my people, whom I loved—namely, Israel—*was measured* by foes, that is, was subjected to taxes and tribute. Then, when this happened and exceeded expectations, *there was no one to prevent him.* Where, then, were the heifers, Chemosh, Dagon, the Baal of Peor, Baal, and the manifold works of their hands in the shrines of Samaria? They had nothing to say; they offered no resistance to the people parceling it out; they were of no help to their worshipers; they displayed no anger to those *measuring* the land. He says something of this kind also in Jeremiah about the people of Israel: "In the time of their trouble they will say, Come and save us! Where are your gods that you made (629) for yourself? Will they arise and save you in your time of trouble?"[7] How would they rescue others, however, if they easily fell victim to whatever anyone chose to do to them? After all, they are "works of human hands, silver and gold," sticks and stones, matter that is deaf and lacking all sensation. Well may the psalmist sing, therefore, "Everyone would be like them who makes them and trusts in them."[8]

7. Jer 2.27–28.
8. Ps 115.4, 8.

Our property was divided up. Hence there will be no one to cast the line by lot (vv.4–5). He makes clear the force of the words: you lost your inheritance, and your land *was divided up* among others, whereas it was not possible to allot you yours. Now, we shall find the Jews in their arrogance suffering this fate at the time of the Incarnation; by their frenzy against Christ they forfeited their inheritance. Though they were the firstborn and, as Paul in his wisdom says, to them belonged the promises and the ancestors, and of them was Christ in the flesh, yet they lost all hope and claim to this; "the full number of the gentiles entered in" and succeeded to their inheritance. To them in fact belong the promises; theirs is Christ; theirs the ancestors; they are styled children of Abraham, "following the example of the faith he had before circumcision." "Not all Israelites, remember, truly belong to Israel, and not all Abraham's children are his true descendants; only the children of promise are counted as descendants."[9] (630) Accordingly, the divinely inspired John, in order to check their conceit and considerable self-importance, also said, "Bear fruit worthy of repentance, therefore, and do not presume to say to yourselves, We have Abraham as our ancestor; for I tell you, God is able from these stones to raise up children to Abraham."[10] Foolish Israel forfeited its inheritance, therefore, and the mass of the gentiles, as it were, sprang up in its place, and to them Christ allotted the splendid and desirable inheritance of heavenly goods. They have become fellow citizens of the saints, in fact, members of God's household,[11] of one body with Christ and illuminated by oneness with him through the Spirit, and will live a highly desirable life in holiness, sanctity, and incorruption.

In the assembly of the Lord do not shed tears nor let your eyes run with weeping in it: he will not reject reproaches who says, The house of Jacob provoked the Spirit of the Lord. Are these things of his making? (vv.5–7) Surely he is not discouraging Israel from opting for repentance, then? Is God withdrawing his clemency from them, tell me, even if they were to choose to learn what is particularly

---

9. Rom 9.4–5, 11.25, and 9.6–8.   10. Mt 3.8–9.
11. Eph 2.19.

fitting for them, and do what is pleasing to him? This is not what he is saying. Rather, it is customary with some people, if they are perhaps censured by one of the sages for committing sin, to confine the form of repentance to weeping and confessing their sin, (631) and to seek forgiveness in this way alone, instead of putting a stop to the vices of which they are accused. Some of the people of Israel used to do this, sometimes not even sparing their clothing. What was the response of the one who sees the heart and reins? "Turn back to me with all your heart, with fasting, with weeping and with lamenting; rend your hearts and not your garments."[12] So the fact that simply by crying their eyes out and pretending to utter fine words without changing their ways they would not render the judge benevolent and mild towards them he conveys by saying, *In the assembly of the Lord do not shed tears.* Do not make the divine Temple a house of mourning, he is saying, *nor let your eyes run with weeping in it* so as to seem to weep only in the house of God, something that is completely foolish.[13] And let no one say, *The house of Jacob provoked the Spirit of the Lord;* you would not cancel the *reproaches* of which you are guilty even if you chose to employ such fine sentiments. *Are these things of his making?* Which things? "They turned to pondering hardships and devising troubles on their beds, and at break of day they put them into effect because they did not raise their hands to God. They set their heart on properties, robbed orphans, took possession of houses, cheated a man of his house, a man of his inheritance" (vv.1–2). He is therefore saying, *If such things were of his making,* how would you avoid the *reproaches* simply by shedding tears and confessing in these words: *The house of Jacob provoked the Spirit of the Lord?*

It is therefore really necessary for people opting for repentance to rid themselves (632) of the crimes of depravity, on the one hand, and thus, on the other, to weep and confess to God after having given precedence to the practice of good works. After all, God has regard not simply to weeping or fine sentiments,

---

12. Jl 2.12–13.

13. Cyril has not noted Jerome's comment that the LXX has appended the final phrase in v.5, "in the assembly of the Lord," to the beginning of the following verse.

but to actions and behavior. Then is the time it will be useful for some people to weep, he is saying, when patterns of good action are combined with abandonment of depravity; when sin is removed from us, the beginnings of virtue make their entrance.

Are not his words good when they are with him, and do they not turn out right? My people first took a hostile attitude to its peace (vv.7–8). He continues to blame them for being given to fine words while their mind is at variance with their speech. The *words* coming from them are *good* and quite *right*: they confess their crimes, call God good and kind, and adopt many forms of simulation while not ceasing in practice to provoke him. But you would see them at odds with themselves, and rejecting their own peace; *my people* themselves *took a hostile attitude to its peace*, he says. Though it was possible for them, in fact, to enjoy a serene and comfortable life and a stable reputation and to have an abiding sense of satisfaction, provided that God was honored, they deliberately lapsed into apostasy. Consequently, by (633) spurning a life of *peace* by a kind of independence, they brought down war on their own heads.[14]

Now, the fact that uttering fine sentiments to God is not completely valueless for sinners, provided one were willing to be embarrassed by one's sins, we shall demonstrate from the inspired Scripture itself. In the second book of Chronicles, remember, there is a story about Rehoboam: "When the reign of Rehoboam was established and grew strong, he abandoned the commandments of the Lord, and all Israel with him." Then Shishak ruler of Egypt took up arms against Jerusalem, and overran the country with his whole army. After this "the prophet Shemaiah came to Rehoboam and the leaders of Judah, who had gathered at Jerusalem at the approach of Shishak, and said to them, Thus says the Lord: You abandoned me, and I have abandoned you to the hand of Shishak. The leaders of Israel and the king were ashamed and said, The Lord is in the right. When the Lord saw that they humbled themselves, the word of the Lord came to

---

14. The LXX, in departing from the Heb. in this passage, only adds to the obscurity; but Cyril cites a story (of the tenth century B.C.E.) from Chronicles that closes (in the LXX) with a mention of "fine words."

Shemaiah: They humbled themselves; I shall not destroy them."
The text goes on to say, "Because he humbled himself, the
wrath of the Lord turned from him so as not to destroy them
completely; in Judah, in fact, there were good words."[15] Do you
see, then, how having good words on one's tongue is not valueless if one turns to humbling oneself and is ashamed of one's
sins? Therefore, as Paul says, (634) "The kingdom of God depends not on talk but on power," and Christ himself said clearly
somewhere, "Not everyone who says to me, Lord, Lord, will enter the kingdom of heaven, but only the one who does the will
of my Father who is in heaven."[16] It is therefore pointless, as I
just said, to say fine things about God when not confirmed by
what is commendable in action.

They flayed its skin, to remove hope in regard to oppression of war
(v.8). He proceeds to charge those appointed to leadership
with the crime of ruining the masses; they were not capable of
instructing them, providing an upright and secure path, and
adhering inflexibly to a habit of piety towards God so as to reject and abolish as useless and productive of ruin the worship of
images. They personally proved agents of ruin and destruction,
turning the minds of their subjects in the opposite direction,
persuading them to forsake God and instead to take satisfaction in the forms of deception. Consequently, by offending God
they forfeited hope in him, whereas if they had continued to
hold it, there would have been no obstacle to their being able
to prevail over the enemy. As in the case of sheep, therefore, he
says, *They flayed its skin, to remove hope in regard to oppression of war*,
which is like saying, By stripping it of the garments of hope and
(635) peeling off, as it were, care and assistance from me, they
left it exposed and vulnerable; *hope* in God was withdrawn from
them, and for them this meant *oppression of war.* In other words,
just as for brute beasts their *skin* is a secure covering, since their
flesh would be very exposed, so, too, for us hope in God has
the effect of being a secure garment and, as it were, a *skin.* If we
maintain it and in no way offend God, we shall overcome the

---

15. 2 Chr 12.1, 5–7, 12.
16. 1 Cor 4.20; Mt 7.21.

foe, prevailing over every bodily and spiritual enemy, and shall walk on "asp and adder and trample on lion and dragon," as Scripture says. We shall sing in confidence, "Lord God of hosts, blessed is the person who hopes in you."[17]

Hence the leaders of my people will be thrown out of the comfort of their homes; on account of their wicked exploits they were ejected (v.9). Those capable of helping their subjects with instruction and lawgiving, the guides and elders, the shepherds and presidents, "flayed its skin" (v.8) and removed the hope in God through which it was easy for every enemy to be crushed. Consequently, it was right that they should lose the good things of home, be deprived of what was dearest to them, forfeit enjoyment and *comfort*, pass over to the enemy, and pay a bitter penalty for indifference and depravity. That there was no other reason for their fate, and that instead they were personally (636) responsible, he clarifies by saying, *on account of their wicked exploits they were ejected.* "There is no injustice in traps being set for birds," Scripture says, "for they participate in their own slaughter; they store up troubles for themselves."[18]

We shall really do ourselves wrong, therefore, if we choose to commit what is unlawful; we shall even be dismissed from *the comfort of our homes.* Those who offend God, you see, will not see the heavenly mansions on high, remaining instead without a share in the hope of the saints and *comfort* for eternity. Wise and good people, on the other hand, who give their assent to every commendable pursuit, will not be among them. How so? They will have the church as the city in heaven, and will dwell in the mansions on high, enjoying heavenly good things.

Approach everlasting mountains, rise up and walk, because this is no place to rest (v.10). While the verse is still directed at those appointed to leadership, it turns to irony and becomes moral, as it were, presenting as useful what is an offense. In fact, it is as if he were saying, Leaders of the peoples, perhaps the comforts of home, life in your homeland, living in peace, and enjoying an existence befitting free people strike you as tedious and burden-

17. Pss 91.13 and 84.12.
18. Prv 1.17–18.

some. Make your way to the enemy instead, since this seems to appeal to you; betake yourselves to the land of the Persians and Armenians; *approach everlasting mountains*—namely, Ararat—*everlasting* either because they were destined to spend a long time there, (637) or because they were celebrated from the beginning, perhaps for the reason of the ark's resting there.[19]

The verse could, on the other hand, be applied also to the Jews at the time of the Incarnation, who followed the views of the scribes and Pharisees and did not come to the faith. The more eminent of them were, in fact, like *mountains*, elevated to the lofty position of priesthood and arriving at a position of importance. Such distinctions were temporary, however: the shadow has come to an end; the worship in type has, as it were, languished; the priestly class of the time withered. It was then, in fact, that the *eternal mountains* emerged, namely, the heralds and ministers of the New Covenant telling of the mystery of Christ, who were celebrated, conspicuous, and resplendent with the achievements of virtue. God gives them that name, remember, also in another prophet: "The mountains will drip sweetness and all the hills will grow together with them";[20] the message of those speaking of God is very sweet, more tasty than honey itself to those who truly love God, who could properly say to Christ the Savior of us all, "How sweet to the palate are your words, more than honey and honeycomb to my mouth." It is therefore in these spiritual *mountains* surely that those who are not yet believers will find *rest* if they come close—by spiritual attraction, that is; they will immediately unburden themselves of sin, despite having no rest in life according to the Law, if it is true that "the letter kills but the Spirit gives life."[21] Let Jews therefore be among those listening even to us, (638) *Rise up and walk, because this is no place to rest;* that is to say, since you have no rest in the Law, move on and transfer through faith to the teachings of Christ.

Because of uncleanness you are spoiled by corruption (v.10), meaning by *corruption* the infamous defilement of iniquitous and

---

19. Gn 8.4.   20. Am 9.13.
21. Ps 119.103; 2 Cor 3.6.

loathsome idolatry, which is truly vile and ugly. Another form of stain and *uncleanness,* on the other hand, is oppressing brethren, stealing others' property, which is doing wrong to many people in a different way. So he is saying, you perished *because of uncleanness,* miserably *spoiled by corruption* unto death. Now, they, too, perished who fought against faith in Christ for no other reason than *uncleanness.* Christ himself will make this clear in saying to the unbelieving Jews, "In truth I say to you that if you will not believe that I am he, you will die in your sins."[22] Is this not the meaning of *Because of uncleanness you are spoiled by corruption?* After all, they did not expunge their crimes nor partake of salvation from Christ by ridding themselves of the former blame, as did those who accepted the faith.

You fled with no one in pursuit (v.11): you willingly underwent captivity, he means, or flight to foreigners—namely, to the foe; there was no one harassing or pressing them. (639) They thought it worthwhile to commit those crimes, and with great enthusiasm, though it was through them that they were inevitably and unwillingly punished. Accordingly, the columns of the Jews *fled with no one in pursuit;* though they could have lived in prosperity and enjoyed every good if they had honored Christ, they fell headlong into apostasy and offended in manifold ways: disbelieving, guilty of insolence, and saying and doing goodness-knows-what other forms of wrongdoing. Since there is *no one in pursuit,* therefore, we shall pursue ourselves, and when we are responsible for insufferable troubles for our own souls, we shall not continue to blame God, the Giver of all things, but rather ourselves, if we are of sound mind and understanding.

He imparted a false spirit; he distilled wine for you and intoxication (v.11). Some of the people in Samaria occupying the shrines of the idols uttered various kinds of oracles, and with a claim to have a clear grasp of the future they announced to their adherents what was pleasing and acceptable to them in the quest for some slight and loathsome profit and a few obols, or exchanged false words for "a crust of bread," as Scripture says.[23] This it was in particular that corrupted and ruined Israel. So he is saying

22. Jn 8.24.
23. Ezek 13.19.

that *he imparted a false spirit* of evil to Ephraim, and *distilled the wine* of demonic error like a kind of lethal potion, and made it *intoxicated,* as it were, with intemperate payment for every kind of vile behavior. (640)

The evil and apostate dragon also *distilled* for the Pharisees the false opinion and wrongful deceit about Christ, sometimes claiming, If this person were from God, he would not infringe the sabbath, at other times calling him a Samaritan and even a drunkard.[24] If it is true that no one says, "Jesus be cursed," except by Beelzebul,[25] how could one fail to see that it was particularly in their case that *he imparted a false spirit?* He *distilled* into their mind and heart the intoxication of error in which they rightly perish in a frenzy befitting wild animals, employing utter audacity and abuse.

It will be from the dripping of this people; Jacob will gather and assemble along with everyone else. I shall welcome the survivors of Israel, and shall turn their aversion to the same thing (vv.11–12). Bad things are in a short time aggravated; what has a limited beginning develops, constantly takes hold to a further extent, and reaches a stage beyond its original measure. You would see the truth of this in the story of Ephraim if you chose to study it in detail. The first stage, remember, was when Jeroboam and some likeminded people set up the heifers in the shrines, worshiped them, and gave heed to the utterances of false seers and false prophets. The trouble then spread and kept adding others to the initial one (641) until all of Israel was joined and bent on one purpose, a victim of the sin, not divided but totally and wholly united. Hence his saying *from the dripping* that the message of the false seers *distilled* to them; the majority of Ephraim were bent on this. He says that all of *Jacob will gather* with one intention, and the ailment will take hold of everyone. I shall not punish them individually for this, preferring to wait for those who will join the ones already affected (the meaning of *I shall welcome the survivors of Israel*); then it is that I shall bring about a single *aversion* against everyone.

24. Jn 9.16 and 8.48; Mt 11.19.
25. 1 Cor 12.3.

Now, this would be a demonstration of the long-suffering typical of God, who, instead of inflicting punishment immediately, is kind enough to delay it, waiting for the reform and conversion of the deceived. If it does not happen, however, and the ailment seems rather to have increased, he then finally and reluctantly displays *aversion*. It follows that those who experience it necessarily suffer from his *aversion*. Consequently, the divinely inspired David also sings, "Do not avert your face from me or turn away in wrath from your servant."[26] Now, it should be realized that Beelzebul *distilled* to the scribes and Pharisees the false and ill-omened opinion about Christ; the disease took hold of all, as it were, and the rest of the populace betook themselves to the deceit of the leaders. (642) Consequently, they also received the one verdict, namely, condemnation and *aversion*, paying a penalty commensurate with their sins.

Like sheep in distress, like a flock in the middle of its resting place, they will start up in fear of human beings. They cut through before them, passed through the gate, and went out through it, and their king issued forth before them, but the Lord will lead them (vv.12–13). It is frequently the way of the holy prophets, when they see what is foretold as happening in due course, to treat as a present event what will ensue a long time afterwards. The blessed prophet Isaiah, for example, in speaking of events to do with Christ, treats of the saving passion as already realized, "Like a sheep he was led to the slaughter, and like a lamb before his shearer he was silent." He asks a question as though gazing on the marks of the nails, speaking to our Lord Jesus Christ in person, "What are these wounds between your hands? He will reply, I received the wounds in the house of my beloved." The divinely inspired Jeremiah predicts the war that would break out against Jerusalem, and sees, obviously in a prophetic vision, a great mass of the Jews already laid low, and laments in the words, "Woe is me, my soul faints (643) at the sight of the slain."[27] The prophet Micah likewise seems somehow to see the tumult that will break out in the cities of Samaria, many people aghast, others in flight, leap-

26. Ps 27.9.
27. Is 53.7; Zec 8.6; Jer 4.31.

ing walls and ditches, the very columns of the enemy breaking through gates, pouring through them together with the commanders, as if God were protecting them and urging them on against the people of Israel because he was offended.

He therefore says that they will be so astonished as to be like a *sheep in distress,* or a whole *flock* resting in places; then when some people were bent on seizing them, you would see the creatures leaping up and down, and if an opening developed, going through it and fleeing; so would they be when the war of the Babylonians came. *Cutting through gates* in their sight, or *before them,* they would enter and *go out through them;* that is, effortlessly and fearlessly they would pass through to the cities, having the Lord of all as their leader, because dominance over Israel was not the result of their might but rather the decree of God, who surrendered Israel by his will. We claim that this happened also to those who wreaked their frenzy on Emmanuel himself; their cities and towns were plundered by Vespasian and Titus, who were in power at the time and discharged the divine anger on them. (644)

COMMENTARY ON MICAH,
CHAPTER THREE

He will say, Listen to this, leadership of the house of Jacob and remnant of Israel: is it not for you to know judgment? You who hate the good and seek out the bad, robbing people of their skins and the flesh from their bones. As they ate the flesh of my people, flayed the skin off their bones, crushed their bones, chopped them like flesh in a cauldron and like meat in a pot, so will they cry to the Lord and he will not hearken to them. He will turn his face away from them at that time in response to the evil they committed against them in their exploits (vv. 1–4).

 HE ONE WHO OPENED THE GATES to those making war on Israel, who made everything smooth for them and overcame the difficulties so that they might then proceed with great ease and dominate the resistance without effort, is the Lord, who leads them. He it is, too, who *will say* to the *leadership and the remnant* of the people, by *will say* meaning "will address." He charges with indifference those responsible for *leadership*, and with being ruinous and destructive by neglecting those in their care; the subjects who were deceived by the knavery of men in power he lets know that punishment will be inflicted on the wrongdoers for the sins against them. The Creator of all, you see, cares for those who are deceived, having created the human being "for good works, which he prepared beforehand," as (645) the divinely inspired Paul writes, "to be our way of life."[1]

So what is the meaning of *Is it not for you to know judgment?* By *judgment* he means either the holy and unerring verdict delivered against them, or condemnation. Now, by this it would be appropriate to understand experience of the *judgment*, not simply learning of it; after all, what harm would the latter bring to those guilty of the crimes? Or how would the wrongdoers feel distress? Only through actual experience of what is to befall them; when people addicted to sinning pay the penalty to the

1. Eph 2.10.

212

punishers, then it is that they are said to learn the eminence of the authority vested in them and the force of the Lord's judgments. It is therefore necessary, he is saying, for you to learn the *judgment* through what will befall you. You were ever inclined to depravity but uninterested in good; you made savage and heartless attacks on my sheep, falling in no way short of the most cruel beasts, skinning the sheep, tearing their flesh, chopping it unmercifully, and, as it were, cooking it in a pot (referring by this to every form of avarice, greed, and oppression). Though guilty of this, however, they will even *cry out*, he says, and I would not accord them a glance from me, nor would I respond if they cried out in an appeal for mercy. After all, it was they who abused their subjects, and inflicted on them every form of evildoing, harsh and unholy inventions and novelties.

Now, you could very properly apply such crimes to the (646) scribes and Pharisees, who, though leaders of the people and guardians of the flock, cruelly abused the masses who believed in Christ as though a kind of sheep, *flaying, chopping*, and ravaging, as it were, the saints, differing in no way from wild beasts. Accordingly, they also heard God prophesying through Isaiah, "When you stretch out your hands to me, I shall avert my eyes from you; even though you make many prayers, I shall not hearken to you, for your hands are full of blood."[2] (647)

The Lord says this to the prophets who deceive my people, who bite with their teeth and proclaim peace to them, and it was not put in their mouths; they provoked war against them (v.5). He severely blames the people of Israel, on the one hand, for willingly exposing themselves to ruin, involving themselves in troubles of their own making, and being firmly focused on sloth. On the other hand, he proceeds to say that they are gravely wronged by the evil and unclean spirit that misleads and deceives them. He had put it this way: "Approach everlasting mountains, rise up and walk, because this is no place to rest; because of uncleanness you are spoiled by corruption. You fled with no one in pursuit. He imparted a false spirit; he distilled wine for you and intoxication."[3] While for this reason he severely chastised those appointed to

2. Is 1.15. At this point Cyril's first tome on Micah concludes.
3. 2.10–11.

leadership, he now instead helpfully shifts his attention to the false prophets and seers among them, who, as it were, distilled a kind of wine for them, the (648) utterances of the false and unclean spirit—that is, false and misleading prophecy—and then steeped them in a kind of intoxication, depriving them of a sound mind. In fact, on the one hand, they *bit* and severely harmed them by persuading them to heed their words instead of those from God through the holy prophets, while, on the other, they told lies, claiming that they would live in peace and prosperity, and nothing at all could trouble or harm them.

They had not a single message from God, however, to this effect; uttering such fine and acceptable messages would not be entrusted to unclean tongues. Since they persuaded them to give heed, however, *they provoked war against them*: was it that they roused the Assyrians to this end? Rather, they brought on themselves holy wrath; because they gave heed to those people, it was only just that the troubles of war should also be inflicted. It is surely this crime that is particularly applicable to the chief priests and Pharisees; by following them the miserable mass of the Jews perished and were destroyed, being guilty of impiety and of killing the Lord.

Hence night will take the place of vision for you, and darkness the place of prophecy; the sun will set on the prophets and the day will become dark for them (v.6). Since they distilled falsehood like wine and intoxication for the people, he is saying, bit them like wild animals, gave good news of peace by way of false prophecy, and (649) caused them to succumb to the misfortunes of war, consequently it is right that *for you there will be night and darkness*, despite your pretending to see and devoting yourselves to uttering what in your judgment are fine and reliable oracles. In fact, *the sun will set* for you, and even daylight itself *will become dark*. We do not actually claim that the sun really curtailed its shining on them, or that the light of dawn was darkened—only that the enormity of the disaster was like darkness and pitch-black for them, unrelieved sunset and loss of light: which of such things did not happen? After all, dire and insupportable troubles cloud the mind, disturb the heart, and fill it with darkness.

Now, you would be right to claim that the spiritual *sun* did set on the Jewish mob that raged against Christ; God no longer shed light; the spiritual day no longer shone on them—instead, blindness spread over them like night. They have become blind, as Paul says, remember, and "when Moses is read out, a veil lies over their heart"; "claiming to be wise, they were fools, and their senseless heart was darkened." The fact that they will suffer this fate Christ himself has foretold in the words, "As long as you have the light, walk in the light lest darkness overtake you."[4] But since they did not approach the divine light—namely, Christ—they were overcome by darkness, and *night took the place of vision for* them, in the prophet's words.

Now, this same fate will also befall the inventors of heresies, who pretend to see and who claim to (650) be able to understand clearly the mystery of Christ; but the wretches tell lies and, as it were, distill the harmful effects of error into the hearts of simple people, then leading them away from the teachings of truth. So for them *night and darkness will take the place of vision*; they will depart into exterior darkness, "having sinned against their brethren and wounded the feeble conscience of those for whom Christ died."[5]

The diviners of dreams will be ashamed and the seers mocked, and they will all upbraid them because there will be no one to hearken to them (v.7). They for their part prophesied that there would be complete peace, deceived their adherents with mere dreams, and led them to believe that all was going according to plan and would conform to their wishes. When experience, on the other hand, showed that the outcome of events was at variance with their claim and proved to be contrary to their expectations, they were then necessarily condemned as charlatans and quacks. They were reduced to such a degree of infamy that no one was prepared to heed them; how could they, after all, when they made fine predictions, but brought the deceived to a calamity that was unexpected and far removed from what they hoped?

Unless I am filled with strength by the Spirit of the Lord, and with justice and power to declare to Jacob his impiety and to the house of Is-

---

4. 2 Cor 3.15; Rom 1.22, 21; Jn 12.35.
5. 1 Cor 8.12, 11.

rael their sins (v.8). He brings out (651) the fact that those with a distorted notion of prophecy have no option but to speak falsehood; after all, how could the person tell the truth who is not speaking by God, who is truth? Christ said somewhere in reference to Cain, remember, "He was a murderer from the beginning, and does not stand in the truth, because he is a liar" like his father, allowing him as his father the inventor of falsehood, namely, Satan.[6] Now, there is no doubting that those speaking with a spirit that is the devil necessarily tell lies in saying what comes from him. Those who speak from God definitely say what is best and tell the truth, having the truth within them. So how, he asks, could the word of prophecy in some people fail to be false unless *I fill* them through my Spirit with power and righteousness, or *justice*, with the result that they oppose sinners securely and confidently and refute them? In my view, after all, those speaking what comes from God have need of the highest degree and excellence of audacity; they sometimes reprove whole populations, even kings and people of importance, who in particular voice their opposition to anyone wanting to reform them, and do not find the message of their benefactors to their liking. The blessed prophets, in fact, suffered, or rather incurred danger, and in a variety of ways met their deaths by falling foul at times of the unholy wrath of those receiving guidance. The divinely inspired disciples were also chastised; full of power, *justice*, and righteousness, they brought to God through faith in Christ (652) the Jewish populace. But they rejoiced in their ill treatment, and left the assembly rejoicing at the dishonor they received for the name, aware that by suffering with Christ they would also reign with him.[7]

Hear this, you leaders of the house of Jacob and remnant of the house of Israel, who abhor justice and overturn every right verdict, who build Zion with blood and Jerusalem with iniquity (vv.9–10). In his great love and full awareness of the enormity of the troubles about to befall them, he adopts every measure and applies every form of warning and threat in the hope that sinners may be persuaded

6. Jn 8.44. Though the Johannine text makes an implicit reference to Cain's act of homicide, Jesus is speaking of the devil.

7. Acts 5.41; 2 Tm 2.12.

to opt to repent, desist from base behavior, and choose to take the means of easily escaping the effects of wrath. The student and scholar, at any rate, ought to realize that it was the constant theme of the sacred writers in books and writings individually at various times, the result being that, even if they appear sometimes to be saying the same thing, nevertheless it is reasonable to understand that it was not on a single occasion, as I said, or to the same people that they announced such things, but frequently and at long intervals, addressing some at one time and others at another.[8] It was necessary, after all, for everyone to know what would befall them, and for the prediction of the general calamity to be made throughout the land.

It is to you that the word is directed, therefore, he is saying, you who (653) have reached such a degree of stupor as to *abhor justice*, that is, righteousness, and to present the Law, which leads to a knowledge of the good, as distorted; it is to you, who believe in rebuilding Zion by homicide and wrongful *blood*-letting, and in making Jerusalem famous and conspicuous. It would, however, have been better to grasp the fact that they overthrow it instead, although appointed to *rebuild* and restore it in their role as leaders, priests, and guardians of the Law nominated by God.

They truly toppled *Zion* by their *blood*-letting; they slew the prophets and, in addition to them, the Lord of all as well, namely, Christ. Though *builders of Zion*, in fact, they rejected him, despite God's clear statement, "Lo, I am laying a foundation stone of Zion, a chosen cornerstone of great value, and the one believing in him will not be confounded."[9] But, as I said, the *builders of Zion* rejected the chosen stone of great value. Yet he is the head of the corner: Christ has become our king, and king of those from the circumcision, making us "into one new humanity, bringing peace through the cross," and joining us, as it were, in fellow-feeling in the Spirit; Scripture says, remember, that

---

8. This precision serves as a justification for Cyril's opting (perhaps by way of reaction against some of his Alexandrian fellows, Kerrigan suggests) to spend time on the historical background to the "books and writings" of the biblical authors (*prophêtai* in that wider sense here) on which he comments.

9. Is 28.16.

"the body of believers had one heart and soul."[10] Since they are conformed to the cornerstone of great value through holiness and faith, it was right for the divinely inspired Peter in his wisdom to say to them in a letter, "Like living stones you are being built into a spiritual house," "a holy temple, a dwelling place of God in the Spirit," since Christ dwells in the hearts of the believers. Of them (654) he also says somewhere in the statement of a sacred writer, "I shall live in them and walk among them, and I shall be their God, and they will be my people."[11]

Its leaders gave judgment with bribes; its priests responded for a price; its prophets delivered oracles for money, and they claimed support from the Lord in saying, Is not the Lord with us? No harm will befall us. For this reason on your account Zion will be ploughed like a field, Jerusalem will be like a fruit shed, and the mountain of the house like a forest grove (vv.11–12). A loathsome business: unjust judgments and bribery are among the things most hateful to the all-holy God; Scripture says, remember, "The ways of the one who unjustly accepts underhanded bribes will not succeed."[12] Some people, in fact, so far succumb to accursed avarice and base gain as to think nothing of perverting justice and selling the truth. Just as people with dust in their eye lose the faculty of sight, so, too, those whose minds are incapacitated no longer see; Scripture says, "Bribes blind the eyes of the wise, and subvert just causes." Now, people who pervert justice impair the true beauty of the divine dignity; judging is proper to God alone, as blessed Moses was aware in saying, "You shall not be partial in judging, for the judgment is God's."[13] People involved in giving unjust judgments undermine, as it were, the divine throne on high, and (655) should be aware that they are offending the ineffable glory itself, which is given to judging uprightly and justly; judgment is God's, as I said. Furthermore, it is also a terrible thing to make religion the occasion of profit, and to consider what concerns God to be a source of gain; note how he does not allow to go without blame any prophet or priest who is bent on making a

10. Ps 118.22; Eph 2.15–16; Acts 4.32.
11. 1 Pt 2.5; Eph 2.21–22; 2 Cor 6.16; Lv 26.12.
12. Prv 17.23.
13. Ex 23.8; Dt 1.17.

profit from promising to speak to worshipers on condition that they are prepared to bring payment or gifts. Now, it is my view that the passage in this case is referring again to false prophets, and not at all to ministers who act properly according to Law, but to those who are in the habit of setting their sights on such offices and who acquire the position for a price. It would in fact not be a holy prophet or true priest who exposes his own soul to such faults.

Then, in committing such sins, he says, *they claimed support from the Lord in saying, Is not the Lord with us? No harm will befall us.* Admittedly, in fact, the God of all was with Israel, and rescued them from hardship in Egypt, led them into the land of promise, and made them superior and invulnerable to the foe. They needed to have a clear understanding, however, that God could not bear to accompany those guilty of grave sin and condemned for such wrongdoing; holiness is not consistent with profanity, nor purity associated with defilement. So the fact that their thinking was astray when they believed that, even if they were guilty of depravity, even if they chose to commit what surpassed every evil, God would nonetheless continue to be with them, they would acknowledge from the very events due to occur. In fact, *Zion will be ploughed like a field,* the celebrated *Jerusalem will be like a fruit shed,* (656) that is, left desolate and overturned, *and the* very *mountain of the house,* that is, the Temple situated on a high hill, *like a forest grove.* It would be like saying, A haunt of wild beasts and a cave for dragons: just as animals and wild species of reptiles live in the mountains and forests, so, too, in desolate places and where many similar creatures are found.

Now, this befell the mass of the Jews when they vented their spleen even on Emmanuel. Then it was that they perished completely, and no stone remained on a stone, in the phrase of the Savior himself;[14] the once august and admirable Zion then emerged as arable land fit for farming. It should be realized, however, that God is with us as well, not if we have faith alone or on that account rest on him, as it were, but if to faith is added

14. Mt 24.2.

proving ourselves through works; "faith without works is dead," Scripture says.[15] When works are combined with the good things of faith, on the other hand, then it is that God will be with us, will easily invigorate us, consider us friends, gladden us as his familiars, and free us from every evil.

15. Jas 2.26.

COMMENTARY ON MICAH,
CHAPTER FOUR

In the last days the mountain of the Lord will be revealed, established on the crests of the mountains and lifted up above the hills, and peoples will hasten to it. Many nations will come to it and say, Come, let us go up (657) to the mountain of the Lord and to the house of the God of Jacob, and they will show us his way and we shall walk in his paths (vv.1–2).

N THIS IS NOW RECOGNIZED a clear prediction of the church from the nations. When Israel according to the flesh was removed from the scene, sacrifices according to the Law were at an end, the priesthood of the bloodline of Levi deserted, the celebrated Temple itself burnt down, and Jerusalem left desolate, Christ instituted the church from the nations, at the final moment, as it were—that is, at the end of this age, when he became like us. By *mountain*, therefore, he refers to the church, which is the house of the living God.[1] It is on high because there is nothing at all earthly in it; instead, the knowledge of the teachings about God is raised above, and the very life of those justified by Christ and sanctified by the Spirit is transferred on high.

In them cannot be found, in fact, a kind of life that is earthly and trampled underfoot, as of course you could espy even in those of the circumcision; they were in thrall to fleshly delights and base gain, proven to be responsible for unjust killing and guilty of goodness-knows-what other sins. "Those who belong to Christ Jesus," as the divinely inspired Paul says, "have crucified the flesh with its passions and desires." They are so averse to wealth that you would even hear them crying out in forthright

---

1. 1 Tm 3.15. Does the fact that Cyril immediately omits reference to any OT background to the text, and especially his failure to acknowledge the verbatim resemblance of the verses to Is 2.2–3, suggest that by this time he has not written his commentary on Isaiah?

manner, "If we have food and clothing, we shall be content with them, whereas those who want to be rich fall into temptation and (658) are trapped by many senseless and harmful desires that plunge people into ruin and destruction." By contrast, they abstain from killing to such an extent as to turn the other cheek to people striking the right cheek.[2] The *mountain*, on the other hand, could also be understood differently as the church compared with the teachings of the pagans; while they stupidly teach people to adore sticks and stones and the creation itself, the church clearly presents the one who is by nature and in truth God, who designed all of this, ensures its proper existence, and as God is Lord of all.

Now, he says that *the mountain of the Lord is established on the mountains and the hills,* meaning by this that it is situated and exists in a very obvious manner; what is situated on a mountain is conspicuous, very easily visible, and not unknown even to people far removed. The text of the prophecy clearly mentions that the nations were also destined to betake themselves to it with great enthusiasm, and the actual outcome of events has confirmed it and ensured its accuracy; it says, *peoples will hasten to it,* that is, to the house of the Lord—namely, Christ. And what will they say as well? *Come, let us go up to the mountain of the Lord and to the house of our God, and they will show us his way and we shall walk in it.* Do you notice that they call on one another in haste with the proper and prudent direction, *Let us go up?* I would say that it is in their awareness of the earthly and abject nature of the pagan teachings that they say *Let us go up* so as then to exult on high (659) in regard to an understanding of the one who is by nature and in truth God. They long for righteousness and thirst for a knowledge of *the way* of the Lord, and they promise to proceed with great enthusiasm *in his paths.* Who would be the ones to introduce them to it? Clearly the disciples of the Savior, entrusted with the divine message, to whom Christ said, "Go, make disciples of all the nations, baptizing them in the name of the Father and of the Son and of the Holy Spirit, teaching them to observe all I have commanded you."[3]

2. Gal 5.24; 1 Tm 6.8–9; Mt 5.39.
3. Mt 28.19–20.

Because from Zion will issue forth a law, and a word of the Lord from Jerusalem; he will judge between many peoples, and accuse strong nations as far as a distant land (vv.2–3). The countless and innumerable masses of the nations advancing on the mountain of the Lord, that is, the church, yearning to learn the way of the Lord and promising enthusiastically to proceed by it, here state the reason for not wanting to continue, as it were, observing the Law and adhering to Judaism. Before the coming of our Savior, you see, when life according to the Law was still in force, some of the deceived made their approach, claiming to benefit from the evil practices of idolatry, but then were circumcised in the flesh and showed zeal for living by the ways and laws of the Jews. The vast number of these people in their midst was beyond counting; Solomon, for instance, when he gave thought to building the Temple in Jerusalem, enlisted a hundred and fifty thousand stone masons and laborers (660) from the proselytes, as is recorded in Chronicles.[4] Now, what happened was surely a type of the mystery; they were on the point of building for God a temple that was true and conspicuous, that is, the church—not the Jews, however, but people from the nations, Jews inwardly, circumcised not in the flesh but in spirit.[5]

Before the Incarnation, therefore, some idolaters made their approach and lived by the laws of the Jews. When the truly conspicuous mountain of the Lord emerged, however, they made their approach rather to it, rejoicing and saying, *From Zion will issue forth a law, and a word of the Lord from Jerusalem.* They probably meant to suggest, and perhaps also clearly proclaim, that Zion will be bereft even of the Law itself, and Jerusalem stripped of the divine sayings, as if somehow their Law and God's word spoken by angels had departed. In other words, the shadow had disappeared, what was in type was at an end, the sacrifices were done away with, and what came through Moses (as far as text was concerned) was then finished.[6] The fact that it was instead

4. 2 Chr 2.17–18.
5. Rom 2.29.
6. The distinction is interesting, Cyril perhaps implying that while Mosaic teaching retains currency (e.g., the Decalogue), the OT as a document is obsolete. Yet Cyril will (as he is doing here) show the relevance of Psalms and prophets (and of Torah in his *Glaphyra*) to Christian readers.

Christ who was due to *judge* and *accuse* they prophesy, as it were, and foretell. How and in what way *judge* and *accuse* are meant we need to explain. By persuading them to abstain from the forms of error, you see, and demonstrating clearly that they were on their way to ruin unless they chose to live upright lives and expunge the crimes of their former sins (661), he will in a way *judge* and *accuse* not only a single nation but *as far as a distant land*, that is, to the ends of the earth under heaven. The saving message will be recited everywhere, in fact; "this good news will be preached in all the world."[7]

It would seem, however, that the prophetic passage conveys also the vestige of another hidden mystery, outlining, as it were, the way those from the nations would be accepted, abandon their former error, and finally proceed to the mountain of the Lord, that is, the church. It is from the Zion on high, after all, he means, and from the spiritual Jerusalem, that *a law and a word of the Lord will issue forth*. The Word of God came down to us from heaven, in fact, and he also became for us *law* and lawgiver; it is he who will *judge between many peoples and accuse strong nations as far as a distant land*. Now, what *judge* and *accuse* meant to suggest I shall explain as far as I understand it. Satan had exercised an illicit rule over everyone, and together with the evil powers he dominated the land under the sun; by putting the yoke of oppression on everyone he led the race on earth away from God. But "the Lord God appeared to us," as Scripture says;[8] the good shepherd was then seen on earth, rescuing from his oppression those deceived, condemning those who deceived them, and convicting the wrongdoers, namely, "the rulers, the authorities, the cosmic powers of this present darkness, the spiritual forces of evil in the heavenly places." Christ himself also made this clear to us in saying, "Now is the judgment of this world; (662) now the ruler of this world will be driven out; and I, when I am lifted up from the earth, will draw all people to myself."[9] He rendered justice, in fact, to *many peoples* beyond counting—namely, those who had been wronged—and justified them by mercy and

---

7. Mt 24.14.   8. Ps 118.27.
9. Eph 6.12; Jn 12.31–32.

faith. He cast out "the ruler of this world" and canceled his rule over us, convicting him of being unjust, unholy, murderous, an oppressor of the earth under heaven. Convicted along with him were also the other *nations* of the demons, previously terrible and *strong* and enveloping not a single city but pervading *as far as a distant land*, that is, to the ends of the earth under heaven. They divided the land among themselves, in fact, and there was no one at all who was not a victim of their malice.

They will beat their swords into ploughs, and their spears into scythes; no longer will nation lift sword against nation, and no longer will they learn to make war. They will all rest under their own vine and under their own fig tree, and there will be no one to frighten them, for the mouth of the Lord almighty has said this (vv.3–4). Everything became new in Christ, and Paul was right in saying that "in Christ there is a new creation: everything old has passed away."[10] Even the very condition of things has undergone a change for the better, no longer suffering the pangs of wars and fighting that involve intolerable and truly damaging attacks on everyone. The instruments of war, in fact, have been adapted as tools by farmers, and, as the prophet says, *they will all rest under their own fig tree and under their own vine;* the fact that there is no one causing alarm would suggest to us only that there is a profound and unbroken peace and a time of no war. Now, this was in force at the time of the Incarnation; Christ himself said, for example, "My peace I give you, my peace I leave with you."[11]

Now, when and how did peace in the world come to be? When the Romans' rule and famous empire gained control of the earth under heaven, all the nations were gathered together and came under a single yoke. They put an end to war against one another, and were involved instead in the works of peace, namely, in farming, people safely inhabiting their own cities. When Roman government had not yet gained control of them, remember, wars and uprisings occurred in countries and cities everywhere; there was the possibility for those bent on it to plunder anyone they chose, to take and carry off the

10. 2 Cor 5.17.
11. Jn 14.27.

possessions of others they conquered, and it was inevitable that people in every country and city would make full use of the instruments of war and devote themselves to military operations to protect themselves and their children. Once the force of the Roman empire was established, however, such things came to an end; the instruments of war became mattocks, scythes, and even ploughs, and were then adapted to other such purposes.[12] (664)

If, on the other hand, you chose to interpret the passage spiritually, you would understand in turn that it was with Christ dispensing peace to us out of his characteristic clemency, and putting down the rulers and former fighters against those wishing to practice religion, that we ceased to experience terrors and were rid of incursions and fighting, and by turning to cultivation of spiritual things we gather the fruits of righteousness and now rest *under fig tree and vine.* A fig tree will be a symbol of sweetness, and a vine of spiritual gladness; the word of the Savior is sweet, and is in the habit of gladdening the human heart, as Scripture says.[13] Now, furthermore, hope of the future, with which we are endowed by Christ, is sweet and mingled with happiness.

Because all the peoples will travel their own way, but we shall travel in the name of the Lord our God forever and a day (v.5). Those who show zeal for going up to the mountain of the Lord and wish to learn his paths make a promise of compliance, accept the commitments of life in Christ, and thus clearly indicate to us that with all their strength they will devote themselves to practices of piety. While in every country and city, he says, in fact, each is to take the path chosen, and likewise live according to choice or option, our concern is for Christ, and we shall make his utterances our correct path (665) and travel with him, as it were, not only in the present time and the past, but much further. The saying is true: those who suffer with him now will always be

12. Theodoret will also see a reference here to the *pax Romana* as productive of universal peace, whereas, when he comes to comment on the Psalms in the next decade, Roman rule had been impaired by incursions of Huns and Persians in the 430s.

13. Ps 104.15.

with him and share his glory and kingship;[14] they make Christ their concern who prefer nothing to love for him, who withdraw from the idle distractions of the world, and instead seek righteousness, what is pleasing to him and in keeping with virtue. The divinely inspired Paul was a person like that; he writes, for instance, "I have been crucified with Christ; it is no longer I who live, but it is Christ who lives in me," and again, "For I resolved to know nothing among you except Jesus Christ, and him crucified."[15]

On that day, says the Lord, I shall assemble the downtrodden and welcome the rejected and those whom I rejected. I shall make of the downtrodden a remnant, and of the rejected a strong nation. The Lord will reign over them on Mount Zion from now and forever (vv.6–7). He now suggests that Israel would not wholly forfeit hope. Admittedly, it was *downtrodden*, dismissed or cast out on account of its grave impiety, being in opposition to God and idolatrous, loathsome, and profane, and grievously guilty of crimes of homicide, killing the prophets, then finally crucifying the Savior and Redeemer of all. (666) But for the sake of the ancestors the remnant was shown mercy and saved, and even became *a mighty nation.* It is, in fact, true that the holy multitude of those justified in Christ is properly to be understood as the vast *nation.* Its pre-eminence, and the basis of our admiration, is its spiritual goodness, the ornaments of the heart—namely, holiness, hope in Christ, sincerity of faith, the marvel of its virtue, its commendable endurance, and serving under Christ the King himself, being shepherded by him and having him as leader; Scripture says, "We have one leader, Christ." If the dead are to rise, "we, too, who are alive, who are left, will be caught up in the clouds together with them to meet the Lord in the air, and so we shall be with the Lord forever."[16] Now, by *Mount Zion* he means the Jerusalem above, the mother of the firstborn,[17] in whom we shall also be saved with Christ himself.

You, squalid tower of the flock, daughter Zion, to you will come and gain entrance the initial power, the kingdom of Babylon, to daughter

---

14. Cf. 2 Tm 2.11–12.   15. Gal 2.20; 1 Cor 2.2.
16. Mt 23.10; 2 Thes 4.17.   17. Cf. Heb 12.23.

Jerusalem (v.8). He promised the benefits of his clemency to those in difficulties; he said that in due course he would receive the downtrodden, and make them into a mighty nation as well. Meantime, however, he levels an accusation at them, and helpfully reproaches them with being completely wretched, downtrodden, and rejected. Blessed Paul said, remember, "Godly grief produces a repentance that leads to salvation (667) and brings no regret."[18] It is therefore out of love that he punishes them, and out of his concern that they should not willingly descend to a point of experiencing anything that distressed them. Now, he refers to Zion, or Jerusalem itself, as a *squalid tower of the flock*, as if to speak affectionately and, as it were, grieve for it: O Zion, or Jerusalem, wretched daughter, O miserable and nondescript dwelling of my sheep, you will definitely yield to the enemy, albeit unwillingly. *To you will come*, he says, before long there *will come* the most eminent and flourishing of the kingdoms on earth, namely, the Babylonian.[19] Now, he refers to Zion, or Jerusalem, as a *squalid tower* and gloomy dwelling because of the fact that everyone in it will walk in darkness, as it were, as a result of not wanting to make God's Law shine like a lamp, and to admit illumination from it into the mind. This was the only way, in fact, to succeed in traveling by a right road, skirt a ditch, escape sin, and avoid falling into troubles on the way.

Let us also, therefore, sing to God in the words, "Give light to my eyes lest I sleep the sleep of death, and my enemy say, I have prevailed over him."[20] Illumined by the divine light, in fact, and receiving into our mind the beams of heavenly wisdom from on high, we shall be invulnerable to the enemy, and by escaping the effects of divine wrath we shall enjoy the benefit of satisfaction from above, and through Christ we shall live in complete happiness. (668)

Why do you now know troubles? Surely there is no king in you, or your wisdom has failed, because pangs have possessed you like a woman in

18. 2 Cor 7.10.

19. Jerome had pointed out that mention of Babylon occurs neither in the Heb. nor in the alternative versions, whereas the Antiochenes read it in their text. Cyril does not labor the point, though he will continue to cite it as an historical datum.

20. Ps 13.3–4.

labor? Suffer, be brave, and draw near, daughter Zion, like the woman in labor. Hence you will now leave the city; you will dwell in the open country and will come as far as Babylon. From there the Lord your God will rescue you and from there redeem you from the hand of your foe (vv.9–10). While the initial force will come upon you, then, he says, what grounds are there for shattering you with such awful troubles (by *knowing troubles* meaning "falling foul of troubles," or of what normally causes trouble—namely, the misfortunes of war)? *Surely there is no king in you,* or people devoted to forming wise plans or taking good care of you? Again he cleverly chides them, and indirectly reproaches them for being very stupid and not declining to offend God. I shall briefly explain the way he does it.

The God of all had been king of the people of Israel in the beginning, with the all-wise Moses acting as mediator. Then, after him Joshua son of Nun was appointed to the role of general; next, judges emerged at various times, and after them blessed Samuel. When affairs were like this for them and were conducted in the best arrangement, the wretches entertained ideas that bode no good for them; they shook off the yoke, as it were, of God's reign, and approached blessed Samuel in the words, "See, you are old, (669) and your sons do not walk in your ways. Appoint a king for us now to govern us, like the other nations. In Samuel's view it was a wrong idea for them to say, Give us a king to govern us. Samuel prayed to the Lord, and the Lord said to Samuel, Listen to the voice of the people in what they say to you, because instead of rejecting you, they have rejected me from being king over them." Blessed Samuel then outlined to them the rights of kingship, startled them with very grave reservations, and distanced himself from such extremely silly and unholy comments; but they insisted no less, "No, there will be a king over us, and we shall be just like the other nations. Our king will govern us, he will go out before us and will fight our battles."[21]

He therefore reminds them of those earlier faulty decisions, saying it all, as it were, with irony: *How is it that you know troubles? Surely there is no king in you, or your wisdom has failed?* Was it not a king you asked for when you said, "He will go out before us

---

21. 1 Sm 8.5–7, 19–20.

and will fight our battles"? Was it not a good idea you had? See, the outcome of events showed what a fine and necessary plan yours was. You rejected the yoke of God's reign. See, *pangs have possessed you like a woman in labor;* so *suffer, be brave, daughter Zion.* Again the expression is pathetic: O good daughter, (670) he is saying, be patient in your *pangs,* put up with your distress, *draw near* in giving birth; that is, you will not be far from what is expected. Instead, like a woman close to delivery you will cry out in pain, and, leaving cities well furnished with towers, *you will dwell in the open country* and camp in the wilderness, even reaching as far as Babylon itself. But he does not leave it completely without consolation; at once he proceeded to say that it will escape and be brought back through God's compassion.

It is therefore surely an excellent choice to remain subject to God as king and choose him as our strength, protector, and helper, to offer him alone the subjection of our soul, to live by his wishes, and to give priority to his will. If we do not do so, we shall be completely and utterly subject to spiritual Babylon, by which I mean the opposing and unclean powers, and subject to the initial force, namely, Satan, and be cast out, as it were, from the holy city, "of which God is architect and builder,"[22] and dwell in Babylon. We shall in fact be caught up in confusion and panic, potent distractions of the present life (Babylon meaning "confusion").[23]

Many nations were now assembled against you, saying, We shall rejoice, and our eyes will gaze upon Zion. They did not know the thinking of the Lord, and did not understand his plans, (671) *that he had gathered them as sheaves of the threshing floor. Arise and thresh them, daughter Zion, for I shall give you horns of iron, and I shall give you hoofs of bronze. You will pulverize many peoples, and will dedicate their vast numbers to the Lord, and their strength to the Lord of all the land* (vv.11–13). We have already mentioned frequently that when Hezekiah in Jerusalem was ruling the kingdom, Sennacherib plundered Samaria, and along with it he overthrew also many cities of Judea. Then, from Lachish he sent the Rabshakeh, who had poured no little scorn on the divine glory when in a single

22. Heb 11.10.
23. The derivation arises from the word play in Gn 11.9.

night one hundred and eighty-five thousand Assyrians perished at the hand of an angel. This account he refers to again; *many nations were assembled against you*, he says, as if to mock and take satisfaction in your impending fall. But they *did not know* what God had in mind; they were brought *to the threshing floor*, as it were, and trodden under foot *like sheaves.* So *arise and thresh them*, for you will have *horns of iron and hoofs of bronze;* that is, you will be invulnerable and invincible to the foe; this means, you will trample down the adversaries. You see, when he made mention of *threshing floor* and *sheaf*, he was using an expression consistent with the metaphor, like *horns* and *hoofs* in the case of a calf. But since it was not by a human hand that they were wasted and fell, but they were subjected to the effects of divine wrath, do not attribute to yourself the achievements here, he is saying; rather, ascribe (672) to the Lord of all the earth both the vast numbers and the power of the fallen.

While this is the meaning of the account, however, some readers may perhaps be bewildered by the sudden change in the prophet's messages. We just heard him saying, remember, "To you will come and gain entrance the initial power, the kingdom of Babylon" (v.8),[24] and the manner of captivity was described to us; then we straightway see [Jerusalem] saved and trampling on the foe. There is therefore a definite need to discern the difference in periods of time; this is the way that interpretation of what was said will be clear and avoid confusion. While it was when Hezekiah was king, remember, that Sennacherib came up against Jerusalem, there were four other kings later after the death of Hezekiah. Jeconiah was the fifth, and it was then that Nebuchadnezzar took Judea and Jerusalem itself, and deported all of Israel into captivity.[25] The blessed prophet Jeremiah clearly recounts to us the story of this.

24. Cyril observes (Theodore having made a similar comment earlier) the somewhat erratic movement in the text between joy and gloom, which prompts (only) modern commentators to suggest textual interference. Cyril instead solves the problem historically.

25. Cyril, in referring to Jeconiah (Jehoiachin) as the fifth king of Judah after Hezekiah, is omitting Jehoahaz, who reigned for only three months in 608 before Pharaoh Neco replaced him with Jehoiakim (Eliakim)—a mistake he will make also in comment on Zep 1.1–2.

COMMENTARY ON MICAH,
CHAPTER FIVE

Daughter Ephraim will now be hemmed in with an obstacle; he placed a constraint on you; with a rod they will strike the tribes of Judah on the cheek (v.1).

ANY PEOPLES AND MANY NATIONS will be assembled on Zion. Then, when they expected to exult over it and mock it, they were beaten and crushed, since God cast them under the feet of the victors in the manner (673) of a sheaf. The country of the Samaritans was captured and destroyed, wasted by war, and it is of it he says that it will be *hemmed in* and obstructed, obviously when God determines it should be subject to a *constraint* and suffer the effects. Now, by *daughter Ephraim* he refers to Samaria, or the population of Samaria; to its subjects it seemed to act in the role of a father, who was entrusted with kingship, the descendants of Ephraim being kings of Samaria.[1] So he is saying that the country of the Samaritans will, as it were, be constrained and ringed around by the masses of the enemy, who, so to speak, will also *strike it on the cheek*, not slapping it with hands subject to mercy, but beating it with rods and wounding it severely. Now, by this he refers beyond the dishonor to the intolerable hardship of captivity; slapping on the cheek is an unmistakable sign of dishonor. If, on the other hand, it were taken as happening *with a rod*, it would be seen as quite demeaning, appropriate for a servant. So he means that in being ruled by the descendants of the tribe of Ephraim, Samaria will be dishonored and subject to mistreatment and hardship.

The hand of an assailant will be inactive, however, and we

---

1. While Cyril is convinced that Samaria is being referred to, he would have known that mention of Ephraim does not occur in the Heb. text or the Antiochene form of the LXX that, as often, reflects it.

shall be immune to abuse, if with all our strength we avoid drawing upon us the wrath of the Lord of all through doing what is
unlawful and making the object of our efforts what is hateful
to him. By giving preference to good behavior we shall instead
enjoy a high degree of satisfaction, and live a life that is truly
edifying and desirable. (674)

*You, Bethlehem, house of Ephrathah, are too insignificant to be
among Judah's thousands. From you will emerge the one to be a leader
in Israel, and his origin is from the beginning of the world* (v.2). In
this the prophetic statement gives us the good news of the return of our fortunes to their previous state. With great clarity
he refers to the restoration that has occurred in Christ; what
happened through him, as Scripture says, is a new creation; the
old has passed away and has become new through his trans-
forming the human condition and restoring it to a good level of
existence.[2] He has been king, you see, and has made rule over
all once more desirable. Now, he is referring to government of
things in general and in particular; Israel was ruled in the beginning by God, as I said, and in the meantime by holy men.
Not long afterwards it suffered a loss of good sense, scorned life
under God's leadership, preferred human government instead,
and asked for Saul as king. They then sinned greatly; when the
God of all was offended, he said to blessed Samuel, "Instead
of rejecting you, they have rejected me from being king over
them."[3] There is no doubting that actual experience proved
that the development was of no benefit to them, but rather was
troublesome, harmful, and productive of ruin; as a result, they
fell foul of dire and ineluctable troubles. Accordingly, (675) to
bring Israel back to their original state, as it were—I mean serving under God as king—he prophesied aloud that Christ, who
was from *Bethlehem*, would be their Savior and Redeemer.

It would not be at variance with the purpose, however, to
decide to give the passage a general interpretation, as it were.

2. 2 Cor 5.17. The term Cyril uses for "restoration," *anakephalaiôsis*, we as-
sociate with Eph 1.10, shortly to be cited, and Irenaeus and Maximus. He will
employ it more than once later in comment on prophetic statements of Judah's
restoration.
    3. 1 Sm 8.7.

When we people on earth had rejected God's royal rule, adopting a foreign yoke for ourselves and enlisting as lord one who was not Lord by nature, but rather an arrogant apostate—namely, Satan—we incurred every trouble. The God and Father, however, as I just said, resolved "to restore all things in Christ, things in heaven and things on earth," and he "rescued us from the power of darkness, and transferred us to the kingdom of his beloved Son in light."[4]

He addresses *Bethlehem*, then, or *house of Ephrathah*. While the region is called *Ephratha*, *Bethlehem* is a little city or town in the region, whence came Jesse and David, and likewise the holy virgin herself, who bore for us the divine infant, her own son, Jesus, "whose government was on his shoulder, and his name is Angel of Great Counsel." He reigned through the cross, you see, and since he became "subject to death, death on a cross," consequently as the divinely inspired Paul says, "God also highly exalted him, and bestowed on him the name that is above every name, so that at the name of Jesus Christ every knee should bend in heaven and on earth and under the earth, and every tongue confess that (676) Jesus Christ is Lord to the glory of God the Father. Amen."[5] He therefore says, O *Bethlehem, house of Ephrathah*, even if you *are too insignificant to be among Judah's thousands*—that is, all the thousands of splendid and large cities of Judea, full of vast numbers of inhabitants—yet even if your inhabitants and residents are quite few, you will become a nurse and will be called a city of those who reign over Israel, so good a shepherd as even to lay down life itself for the sheep and reign over all Israel.[6] And not just those of the bloodline of Israel, but also those mentioned in the promise of Abraham; God said to him somewhere, "It is through Isaac that offspring will be named for you," by the phrase "through Isaac" meaning "by way of promise."

Accordingly, the promise is clearly applicable not only to those of the bloodline of Israel, "but also to those who follow the example of the faith that our ancestor Abraham had before he was circumcised."[7] So it would be like saying, He will

4. Eph 1.10; Col 1.13, 12.   5. Is 9.6 LXX; Phil 2.8–11.
6. Jn 10.11.   7. Gn 21.12; Rom 4.12.

rule over everyone believing in him and relating themselves to me through him; we are related to the Father through the Son, as he himself confirms by saying, "No one comes to the Father except through me." Christ the good shepherd, therefore, emerged from Bethlehem, he who "pastures us in the garden and among the lilies," provides the sweet odor of the Gospel oracles, and offers what he has to give like fragrant flowers to those willing to pluck them and (677) be spiritually filled with the fragrance coming from them; he said, remember, "I am a flower of the fields, a lily of the valleys."[8]

His origin is from the beginning of the world, the text says, suggesting either the Word's existence before the ages—he is co-eternal with his Father, and is himself the Maker of the ages—or the fact that though he became man at a late point in time, as it were, the mystery concerning him was predetermined, as it were, in the foreknowledge of the Father and before the foundation of the world.[9] So by *origin* he means either the timeless generation by God the Father resulting in the individual existence of the Son, or the emergence that would occur in time when he became flesh, even if *from the beginning of the world* he was predetermined and appointed as Savior and Redeemer by the Father, who was not unaware of what would happen to the human race in the meantime as a result of the transgression by Adam.[10]

For this reason you will give them up until the time of the one in labor; she will give birth, and the rest of their brethren will turn back to the sons of Israel (v.3). The prophet seems to have pondered within himself and given thought to the matter, saying, God will not speak falsely, but will definitely put his promises into effect. If Israel is enjoying such promising expectations, and the leader will be born to them, will rule and deliver them of every

8. Jn 14.6; Song 6.1–2 and 2.1.
9. Eph 1.4.
10. It has been a thorough christological development of a familiar scriptural locus (perhaps enshrined in the liturgy of Cyril's church), its length and profundity (not typical of Jerome's comments) perhaps prompted by Theodore's attempt to bring Zerubbabel into focus as a provisional fulfillment of the prophecy (later disowned by Theodoret). We note also the significance Cyril places on the Fall in the divine *oikonomia*.

trouble, why on earth will he fall into the hands of the enemy? Then, in consideration of the time of the promise, (678) and realizing that it has not yet arrived, he provides himself with a kind of explanation by saying, Since the time of the promise is considerably delayed, and they are caught up in numerous failings without in any way ceasing to sin, consequently *you will give them up;* that is, you will surrender them to the enemy, O Lord, *until the time of the one in labor,* meaning, until that divine infant is delivered from the virginal womb. That will be the time, he is saying, when the final redemption will occur, and they will enjoy secure prosperity, with nothing at all lacking for their satisfaction.

As the prophet meditates on this, and, as it were, whispers it to himself, God makes the response, *She will give birth,* summoning him to firm belief. Similar to this is the word spoken to the prophet Habakkuk, "Yet a little while, and the one who is coming will come and will not delay."[11] In other words, he will definitely be born, and *the rest of their brethren will turn back to the sons of Israel.* An innumerable mass of the Jews did in fact accept faith in Christ, the blessed disciples before the others, whereas those who reveled in their unbelief forfeited hope; yet in the endtime they will be brought to join the others, and will finally hasten at speed, as it were, to what they should have come to rather in the beginning.

He will stand and see, and the Lord will shepherd his flock in strength, and they will live in the glory of the name of the Lord their God, (679) *because now he will be magnified to the ends of the earth. This peace will occur* (v.4), by *stand* meaning "take command": the shepherd will take independent control of his own sheep, entrusting guidance to no one else, as he did of old to blessed Moses. Rather, he will do it himself; it is true that "it was no ambassador, no angel, but the Lord himself who saved us."[12] *He will shepherd* us *in strength,* making us proof against any effort or hardship; he will take a leading role, as it were, and in general will save us, not allowing false shepherds to wrong us by deceit,

11. Hab 2.3.
12. Is 63.9.

or wild animals to ravage the flocks, nor giving leeway to the wicked and hostile powers to be guilty of wanton abuse of the believers or to be oppressive to those who are consecrated. Instead, he will enable us "to walk on asp and basilisk, and tread on lion and dragon."[13] It is from him that our good name comes, in fact, that we are raised to a position of eminence and splendor, and have reached the ends of the earth under heaven; he it is who is our strength and power, he our mediator and reconciler, he our *peace*. After all, he has abolished "the dividing wall, he has canceled the Law with its commandments and created one new humanity in place of the two, thus making peace," as Scripture says,[14] and sealing them in unity with the bonds of peace. *Peace*, therefore, is a term that befits him and is true, even if he is also called Christ. (680)

When the Assyrian attacks your land and when he advances against your country, seven shepherds will rise up against him, and eight bites of human beings. They will shepherd the Assyrian with a sword, and the land of Nimrod in its ditch. He will rescue you from the Assyrian when he attacks your land, and when he advances on your frontiers (vv.5–6). The Hebrew text begins the present text with the clause, *This peace will occur when the Assyrian attacks your land and when he advances against your country*,[15] meaning, This will be the form that *peace* would take if *the Assyrian* intended to invade *your land and country*. In interpreting the verse, we would say that the meaning again departs from material and obvious matters and rises to a higher level, bringing us in detail from the literal image to what was happening spiritually. By *Assyrian* here, you see, he indicates no longer the man from Babylon, but rather the inventor of sin—namely, Satan—or rather, to put it in a nutshell, the implacable and warlike mass of demons which oppose everything holy and fight against the holy city, the spiritual Zion, "which is the church of the living God," a kind of type and similar image of the heavenly Jerusalem above. The divinely inspired psalmist also refers to it similarly in these words: "Glorious things are said

13. Ps 91.13.
14. Eph 2.14–15.
15. Cyril would have noticed the different division of verses in Jerome and also in the Antiochene text used by Theodore.

of you, city of God";[16] Christ dwells in the church, and made it
his own city, as it were, (681) although filling everything by nature of the divinity. This city of God, therefore, is like a *land*
or *country* of people consecrated and enriched with union with
God by the Spirit.

So he says, *When the Assyrian attacks your land*, that is, if the
barbaric and hostile powers were to fight against the saints,
they would not find them lacking leaders; *seven shepherds and
eight bites of human beings* will rise up against them. The reference in the prophecy to the times or to the numbers—namely,
seven and *eight*—is probably to the holy people: those before the
Incarnation, those at the time it occurred, and those coming
after. Before the Incarnation, remember, in the Law of Moses
regard was shown for the sabbath on the seventh day, and the
time still belonged to the shadow; in those days the band of holy
prophets also emerged to act as guides in piety and knowledge
of God. But later, when the Only-begotten came, suffered the
cross for the life of all, and after plundering Hades returned to
life on the eighth day, he then bade the holy apostles to "make
disciples of all the nations and baptize them in the name of the
Father and of the Son and of the Holy Spirit," teaching them
to observe everything commanded them. He therefore refers
to them as *eight bites of human beings*, based on the time of the
Resurrection, indicating those who came at his time and after
him.[17]

Accordingly, when that barbaric foreigner *the Assyrian attacks*,
then it will be that he will come against *seven shepherds and* (682)
eight bites. We shall find, in fact, the holy ones at the time of
the Law, whom he calls *seven shepherds*, and in addition to them
apostles and evangelists and the teachers of the churches at various times, ever fighting and opposing in general the deceits
of the demons and resisting the perversity of the evil one with
their own vigilance, as it were; they save the inhabitants of the
holy country and land, protecting them with advice and secur-

---

16. 1 Tm 3.15; Ps 87.3.
17. Mt 28.19–20. Cyril declines to imitate Jerome and Theodore in a lengthy
exercise in number symbolism here. The puzzling phrase is further complicated
by the LXX reading as "bites" the Heb. for "leaders."

ing them with every kind of excellent guidance. Now, the fact that the band of the holy ones was destined to undermine Satan in some way and to consume him spiritually with *bites* God likewise makes clear also in the statement of a holy one when he says of him, "Alas for the one who heaps up for himself what is not his—and for how long? He locks himself securely in stocks, because suddenly those biting him will rise up and those scheming against you will sober up. You will be booty for them, because you plundered many nations, and all the surviving peoples will plunder you."[18] Do you note that the one who "heaps up for himself what is not his"—namely, Satan—will be bitten and plundered? He then refers to those plundering him as "survivors," or the remnant of the people of Jacob.

If, however, some *Assyrian attacks*—that is, a man led astray to a different attitude, with a faith that does not move in the right direction, limping, as it were, and of unsound mind—they oppose him with the force of truth and reveal the ugliness of the rottenness in him, (683) driving him off like a wolf, snapping at him, as it were, and causing him to keep his distance and move away from the flock of spiritual sheep. These *seven shepherds*, then, understood also as *eight bites, will shepherd the Assyrian with a sword*, meaning by *shepherd* "pursue"; since he mentioned *shepherds*, he retained the verb *shepherd* to suit the metaphorical expression.

The way to understand the *sword* which the holy ones are in the habit of using is clarified by the psalmist when he says of them, "And two-edged swords in their hands, to execute vengeance on the nations and punishment on the peoples"; "for the word of God is living and active, sharper than any two-edged blade." And when Paul equips the person understood to be a soldier in Christ, he gives him "the blade of the Spirit, which is the word of God."[19] Of the fact that the divine and all-powerful sword—that is, the word of God—pursues the *Assyrian* the prophet Isaiah is also no

18. Hab 2.6–8. Cyril illustrates the dependence of interpretation on exegetical skills: if the Heb. text cannot be accessed to check a puzzling term like "bites," one can only look for another occurrence of the term.

19. Ps 149.6–7; Heb 4.12; Eph 6.17. Though we saw Cyril declining to engage in number symbolism as Didymus would relish doing, he can at times resemble the latter's penchant for interpretation-by-association.

less convincing in saying, "On that day God will strike with his holy, mighty, and strong sword the dragon, the twisting snake"; and again, "When the Lord has finished his work on Mount Zion and in Jerusalem, he will punish the arrogant boasting of the ruler of the Assyrians and the haughtiness of the glory of his eyes. He said, in fact, I shall act in strength; by the wisdom of my understanding I shall remove the boundaries of nations; I shall plunder their strength, (684) and shake inhabited cities."[20]

It is by this sword, then, that *they will shepherd the Assyrian with a sword, and* all *the land of Nimrod in its ditch.* In this his meaning is as follows. By *the land of Nimrod* he refers to the country of the Assyrian, or Babylon, around which they say a deep *ditch* was dug. He gives it the name *land of Nimrod* on account of his being ruler of the Babylonians and the origin and father of the race; of him Scripture has this to say: "The descendants of Raamah: Sheba and Dedan. Cush became the father of Nimrod; he was the first on earth to become a mighty warrior. He was a mighty hunter before the Lord. The beginning of his kingdom was Babylon; Erech and Accad and Calneh in the land of Shinar." The divine Scripture says that the tower was built in Calneh, a Persian region.[21] So by *Nimrod* he is referring to Babylon, which is ringed by a *ditch*, as I just said. He is therefore saying that *they will shepherd the Assyrian* to such a degree that they will remain within the *ditch* and no longer expand beyond cities and region, instead staying home, as it were, in fear and dread.

We shall find columns of the demons meeting this fate through Christ, to be sure, no longer oppressing the earth under the sun, as in the past before the Incarnation. (685) Instead, they keep to their own position, driven back by the sobriety and good advice of the saints, and shut out from the land of the saints, who are thus enabled to live a peaceful life untroubled by war, perform what is pleasing to God, and shine with the good order that is dear to him.

The remnant of Jacob among the nations amidst many peoples will be like dew falling from the Lord, and like lambs upon fodder, so that no

---

20. Is 27.1; 10.12–14.
21. Gn 10.7–10. Here Cyril is embellishing the reading by the LXX of a Heb. consonantal text pointed to read "and Calneh" (no such city in the region being known), but generally re-pointed to read "all of them."

one may be gathered or submit to human beings (v.7). I have often said that the remnant of Israel was saved, and it was not the whole of the race descended from Jacob that perished; not a few have come to believe in Christ, and have been enriched with salvation through faith even before the others—I mean those from the nations. Rather, from the remnant that was saved through faith came the divinely inspired disciples themselves as well as those who struggled and suffered with them in the Gospel of Christ. He is therefore saying that they were the ones who were saved *among the nations* like a kind of *dew* coming down on the fields, alleviating the heat of devilish perversity. In other words, just as in gardens or fields the brightness of the sun's beams strikes the grass and flowers, making them lose their beauty and wither and seem even to dry up, so, too, the inventor of sin sometimes inflames people's minds with the love of worldly pleasure, (686) and in a way dries them up and makes them seem very ugly. The Word of God, by contrast, makes them recover, as dew does to flower or grass. This will be the way, he says, also with the descendants of Jacob *among the nations,* bedewing the souls of the converted with words leading to piety like a kind of dew, and lavishly enriching them with Gospel teachings. They will exult like lambs with grass; that is, they will find abundant and ample pasture. The nations, remember, were always more ready to be compliant and disposed to believing in Christ, by which I mean the incomparably better choice of life in the beginning. But just as in the case of abundant and lush fodder set before lambs, who then revel and play,[22] in similar fashion, in my view, the mind of teachers brings enjoyment and satisfaction to those being guided in compliance and those being initiated in obedience.

Our Lord Jesus Christ, for example, turned the obedience of the Samaritan woman into a kind of nourishment suited even to him; he said to the holy apostles, "I have food to eat of which you are unaware." Then to explain it, he went on, "My food is to do the will of the one who sent me and complete his work."[23] So God's work is food and enjoyment to the saints. Accordingly, he says that the descendants of Jacob will exult like animals chew-

22. The PG ed. omits the preceding two clauses.
23. Jn 4.32, 34.

ing *fodder* or lush grass, or, as it were, pasturing those from the nations who believe; they will find the way of preaching so wide that no one (687) *may be gathered or submit* in opposition to them, that is, neither join nor oppose them (the meaning of *submit* in the case where any *human beings* wanted to abuse them).[24] In other words, though many plots and schemes were hatched by a great number against them, they came to no harm, since God repressed the rage of the mighty, enveloped his own in the protection of his goodwill, and against the odds rescued and saved them from every trial.

The remnant of Jacob among the nations and amidst many peoples will be like a lion among the cattle in the forest and like a cub among flocks of sheep in the way that, when it passes through, it separates and snatches, and there is no one who can rescue. Your hand will be lifted up over those afflicting you, and all your foes will be eliminated (vv.8– 9). Stories that are helpful and memorable, even if employing the same words, involve no tedium, but rather are accompanied by deep satisfaction. *The remnant of Jacob*, therefore, he is saying, that is, the descendants of Jacob who have been saved through faith in Christ and have emerged as heralds and ministers of the evangelical oracles, will be like dew among the nations, and will graze like lambs exulting over rich and abundant feed. No less, however, will they also be *like a lion among the cattle in the forest*, uttering a deep and fearsome roar and instilling an unbearable fear even into those at a distance. They will also be like *a cub among flocks*, (688) that is, in the way they leap out boldly and ravage anything they want, with nothing able to resist or to extricate the victim. Our Lord Jesus Christ, remember, said to the holy disciples, "Lo, I send you as sheep in the midst of wolves,"[25] that is, meek and gentle. Even if some people in the world are ready to take life, and do not fall short of the cruelty of wolves, I personally with my characteristic strength will crush the hearts of the warlike, rendering them fearful and timid, and causing them to show you respect.

24. The commentators struggle to get sense from this phrase, where the LXX departs from our Heb.
25. Mt 10.16. The PG ed. abbreviates the following sentence, and turns first person to third.

This is the way they have gained control of the enemy, vanquished adversaries, and proved fearsome to wolves, even if taking the role of sheep; they escaped plots, "dangers from brigands, dangers from my own people, dangers from false brethren," as blessed Paul writes.[26] While the masses from the nations were seized as though by lions, and Satan with his own designs sought to hunt them down and destroy them, he could not achieve it or pluck from the hands of the apostles what was taken for salvation. This is surely the force of what was said to him in Habakkuk, "Woe to the one who multiplies for himself what is not his! How long? Does he firmly load down his collar? Because suddenly they will arise and bite him, your schemers will be on the alert, and you will be their plunder. Because you despoiled many nations, all the surviving peoples will despoil you."[27] It was the *eight* who bit him, and *like cubs snatched* what had been gathered by him; he had gathered for himself "what was not his"; (689) the human being had taken what was God's, or rather everything, nothing at all belonging to him. But he was plundered by the survivors of peoples, that is, those of the remnant, by which you should understand the ministers of the evangelical oracles. Then the Lord, who empowers and protects them, says to them, *Your hand will be lifted up over those afflicting you, and all your foes will be eliminated*; they have conquered through Christ, as I said, proved superior to every scheme, shone brightly in the world, and prevailed over the foe, recovering the lost for God.

On that day, says the Lord, I shall eliminate the horses from your midst, destroy your chariots, ruin the cities of your land, and remove all your fortifications. I shall destroy the potions from your hands, and there will be no one uttering among you. I shall destroy your images and pillars from your midst, and you will no longer adore the works of your hands. I shall cut down the groves from your midst, and wipe out your cities. I shall execute vengeance in wrath and in anger on the nations for not heeding (vv.12–15). Attention shifts back to the problems, and for the time being he comes to an end of the splendid and commendable discourses on Christ. Instead, he resumes, as it

26. 2 Cor 11.26.
27. Hab 2.6–8.

were, what went before, and indicates the future effects of wrath. He had said, "You, squalid tower of the flock, daughter Zion, to you will come and gain (690) entrance the initial power, the kingdom of Babylon."[28] Then it is, he says, therefore, that your cavalry will perish, and with them will be destroyed the pride of chariots; cities will also be laid waste, and you will be divested of the actual fortifications, that is, walls (the cities along with their inhabitants being burnt down by the Babylonians). The objects of your folly, quackery, necromancy, and all the products of deceit will be completely destroyed along with shrines of the idols, and *the groves* will be felled from their very roots.

What will be the upshot of this? The nations nearby would not fail to notice the notorious vengeance and the style of punishment. They will know that they were destined to suffer *for not heeding*, that is, for their crimes of disbelief. Wisdom also said that such a fate will befall those who have an unbridled tendency to unbelief "because I offered you words and you did not heed them; instead, you treated my advice as worthless, and did not heed my words. Consequently, I, too, shall laugh at your downfall, and I shall exult when ruin comes upon you and when panic besets you unawares, and catastrophe comes like a tempest." Now, the fruits of neglect are "wrath and anger, distress and hardship" befalling everyone unwilling to give heed.[29] It is therefore necessary to respond promptly and without any delay to God when he summons us to what is advantageous, and carry out what is pleasing to him; tardiness and indifference in (691) doing what is good will mean a great loss for us and involve us in severe problems. Consider, on the other hand, how, even by calling sinners to account, God works for their benefit; he rids Israel of the loathsome abomination of idolatry, unholy pursuits, potions and false prophecy, altars, shrines, sacrifices, and adoring the works of their hands. It is therefore not without usefulness to be corrected, "provided it happens with justice and not in anger," according to the prophet's statement.[30]

If, on the other hand, you were to say that this happened to the Jewish populace who vented their fury on Christ, you would

28. 4.8.   29. Prv 1.24–27; Rom 2.8–9.
30. Jer 10.24.

not depart from the probable sense of the passage. It is true, in fact, that their cities were left desolate, and all their fighting force was lost to the Romans. Perhaps they paid the penalty of that former idolatry, especially if there were some of them who were still bent on worshiping creation and were attached to quackery; devotees of idolatry are always addicted to it, and in their eyes there is nothing too extreme to deserve a bad opinion.

COMMENTARY ON MICAH,
CHAPTER SIX

Hear what the Lord said: Rise up and come to judgment before the mountains,
and let the hills hear your case. Listen, hills, to the Lord's case, and the valleys,
earth's foundations, because the Lord has a case against his people, and against
Israel a charge will be laid (vv. 1–2).

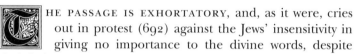HE PASSAGE IS EXHORTATORY, and, as it were, cries
out in protest (692) against the Jews' insensitivity in
giving no importance to the divine words, despite
their being gentle and restrained [words], as though from a father demonstrating sincerity of love for his children and giving
them no grounds for obduracy. Now, it is customary with the
God who loves goodness sometimes to frighten sinners with a
prediction of dire happenings, not to leave them remiss and resistant as though beyond hope, but to lend a note of comfort to
the impending fate, and retain the possibility, as it were, of escaping it, provided they choose to have recourse to repentance.
This is what he likewise does in this case as well from his inherent leniency—hence his saying, *Hear what the Lord said.* Now,
what did he order me? *Rise up and come to judgment before the*
mountains, and let the hills hear your case. It is similar to the statement in Isaiah, "Listen, heaven, and give ear, earth, because the
Lord has spoken."[1] Apparently by the words *mountains* and *hills*
he refers to the spiritual powers that have care of everything by
God's will, repelling the oppression of the demons from people
on earth. Since they are aware before others of the extraordinary degree of God's leniency, come to know the extent of his
care for us from their services to us, and are obedient to laws
from him, he bids the *judgment* be conducted by them.

The prophetic verse, however, is probably implying some-

1. Is 1.2.

thing else as well. You see, since the people of Israel occupied *hills* and *mountains* in offering rites and sacrifices there "under every oak and poplar,"[2] consequently the *judgment* is now delivered on the *hills* where the blatant crimes of the accused were conducted. By *hills* and *earth's foundations* he refers to people of importance who outranked the common herd, and who in particular proved to be a path and a snare for the people subject to them; he had said, remember, "the judgment is directed to you, since you have been a snare on the lookout, and like a net spread on Tabor."[3] So he is saying, O you who outrank the others, O *earth's foundations*, that is, you on whom the fate of the others depends, *listen to the case* against you of the Lord of all. The person of sound attitudes, by contrast, says in song to the Lord of all, "Do not enter into judgment with your servant"; the one who knows everything is utterly pre-eminent, and no one will boast of having a clean heart or would prove to be free of sin.[4] It is therefore a dreadful thing to come to *judgment* with God.

Now, it should be realized that, while the version of the Seventy reads *valleys*, the Hebrew refers to *hills* and *earth's foundations* for us to know by mention of *hills* that the leaders of the people were raised on high, so to speak, exceeding and surpassing the position of the others, and the same ones were *foundations*.[5] In other words, the leaders of regions or cities were conspicuous for their importance, as it were, and raised on high, and thus would be also *earth's foundations*, that is, positioned in a way as basis and foundations of affairs; the affairs of the others fell to them, and, so to speak, rested on them, as I just said. (694)

My people, what have I done to you, what grief have I caused you, what trouble have I brought you? Answer me. Because I brought you from the land of Egypt, I ransomed you from the house of slavery and sent before you Moses, Aaron, and Miriam (vv.3–4). God delivers judgment in the person of the prophet, showing the form of

---

2. Hos 4.13.   3. Hos 5.1.
4. Ps 143.2; Prv 20.9.
5. Jerome had pointed out that where the LXX reads "valleys, earth's foundations," the Heb. has "strong foundations of the earth." Cyril has not adopted this observation.

apostasy on the part of those offending him to be inexcusable and unreasonable. Rather, the crime was the result of complete folly, and its unusual and unprecedented enormity even in people so very ungrateful was due to insensitivity. After all, what excuse could there be, tell me, he asks, for those who offended against me? What was insufferable and completely burdensome in my decrees? What was distressing? Come forward, explain yourself. I infringed the bounds of reason in liberating you from harsh servitude, and in vigorously removing you from mud and bricks and the hardship involved; I exceeded the need for mercy in enlisting the services of nature against the Egyptians in their wrongdoing to rescue my own. Perhaps it is your instructor—Moses, I mean—whom you fault along with me for depriving you of a sense of glory and clearly presenting what is pleasing to God so that you may be able unswervingly to live an (695) edifying life and reach the peak of satisfaction and good repute. Perhaps you will raise no little outcry against priesthood; I anointed Aaron, and bade him mediate between God and you, and appease God with the sacrifices by way of types—are you upset about this as well? What am I to say about Miriam, who mocked the destruction of the Egyptians and was the leader of the dancers? Beating tambourines, she had a vision of horse and rider drowning in the waters[6]—but perhaps to you victory was unacceptable, the things of God of no account, though he allowed you to pass through the midst of the waves while making the sea hostile to the foe.

In a figurative way, therefore, he listed the reproaches to remind them of the favors they had received and to blame them for consigning them to oblivion, when they should have always remembered them and in return gladdened the benefactor by obedience in everything. Now, it was ourselves, too, whom the Savior led out of spiritual Egypt, that is, out of darkness and oppression by demons, and rescued from mud and bricks, that is, fleshly passions and impure hedonism. Ourselves he also enabled to cross the sea of this world's temptations, and, as it were, freed us from the harsh waves that are the perils affecting us, and stamped the divine laws on our mind. He also brought

6. Ex 15.20–21.

forth as our priest (696) Jesus, "the pioneer and perfecter" of our salvation.[7] He also *sent,* as it were, *Miriam*—the church, that is, who will thwart the schemes of the foe by offering glory to the saving God; in churches there are constant hymns of praise and thanksgiving, praising and proclaiming God's glory. Care must therefore be taken by us, too, not to substitute indifference for the Jewish crimes, or consider burdensome what is pleasing to God; as blessed John says, "His commandments are not burdensome," and Christ himself, "My yoke is easy and my burden light."[8] Let us therefore offer what is pleasing to God, because nothing from him is burdensome; instead, everything is easy for those choosing to live a life that is excellent and quite well ordered.

My people, remember what King Balak of Moab had in mind for you, and what Balaam son of Beor answered him from the reeds up to Gilgal so that the Lord's righteousness might be known (v.5). Once more he corrects them for the unholy insolence against his power that is theirs, despite their having nothing to mention as justifiable grounds for being offended and turning to apostasy. I regaled you, in fact, (697) he is saying, with such wonderful mercy and love as never to entertain complaints. The accursed Balak, remember, tyrannical ruler of the Moabites, hired Balaam, soothsayer and augur, and then bade him curse Israel; but the God of all worked the novel and extraordinary miracle of directing the tongue of the false prophet to blessing. When Balak reproved him for it and blamed the augur, he straightway took him to other hills. He then gave orders for erecting altars and sacrificing bulls in the belief that perhaps God's power did not take effect in every place; but he continued blessing everywhere, though moving about from what was called *Reeds,* a place in Moab, to the mountains of *Gilgal.*[9]

Remember, therefore, *what Balak had in mind, and what Balaam answered him.* I for my part, remember, canceled the actual curse

---

7. Heb 12.2.

8. 1 Jn 5.3; Mt 11.30. Cyril betrays no sense that the reproaches in these verses are familiar to him from use in the liturgy of Holy Week in his church.

9. Nm 22–23. Jerome had informed Cyril that the place name in the LXX (for the Heb. Shittim) had resulted from a scribal error.

against you, not allowing the augur even to give offense in words. You, on the other hand, forgot even this, and accorded to lifeless matter the glory due to me, calling out to golden heifers in the words, "These are your gods, Israel, who brought you up from the land of Egypt."[10] When God distributes to us the good things of his love, therefore, enriches us with extreme liberality, disperses the foe, and undermines their efforts against us, what are we ourselves to do in choosing to adopt right attitudes, other than what would lead to ourselves being seen to be (698) godly? Following his will, performing what is pleasing to him, and staying close to him in presence of mind is what is said in the Psalms: "My soul has cleaved to you."[11] (699)

In what way can I gain favor with the Lord, can I secure the attention of my God most high? Shall I gain his favor with burnt offerings, with yearlings? Will the Lord be pleased with thousands of rams or tens of thousands of fat he-goats? Shall I give my firstborn for my impiety, the fruit of my innards for my soul's sin? Has it been told to you, mortal being, what is good and what the Lord requires of you—only to do justice, to love mercy, and to be prepared to walk with the Lord your God? (vv.6–8) To the people of Israel God presented their apostasy as inexcusable, called them to judgment in some way, and clearly established that, while he for his part had showered blessings on them in countless forms, they by contrast had been guilty of immeasurable insensitivity and had seriously offended the one who saved them. They therefore immediately adopted the manner of a penitent, as it were, (700) weeping for all their previous failings and wanting to learn the way to expunge their crimes and become involved in practices most pleasing to God. Hence his saying, *In what way can I gain favor with the Lord?* In other words, what am I to offer, what am I to do after offending so much? Shall I become sinless by sacrificing tender *yearlings?* Would God commend me for *burnt offerings?* I would like to find him—that is, to come near and be accepted into a spiritual relationship: should I offer a vast number of cattle? But aside from that I shall lay hold of *the fruit of my innards?* Surely I shall gain favor by sacrificing to him my special child, namely, the firstborn?

10. Ex 32.4.
11. Ps 63.8. Thus closes Cyril's second tome on Micah.

To someone who, as it were, ponders and says this, the prophet replies in turn, saying in spirit, It is not something hard to discern, not achieved by hard labor. Take completely into account God's goodwill; you have been told what he wills and desires. Are you therefore in any doubt, mortal man? The God of all requires of you nothing else, in fact, than simply *to do justice, to love mercy, and to be prepared to walk with the Lord your God*. *To do justice*, then, is to practice and carry out righteousness, *justice* meaning "righteousness"; *to love mercy* is to possess the virtue of friendly relations and to have a sound reputation for love of the brethren; and *to be prepared to walk with the Lord your God* is to show yourself obedient (701) and compliant in everything. Blessed Paul said that we are also obliged to put on "the breastplate of righteousness, and be shod also with readiness for the Gospel of peace," that is, of Christ; he further bids us to "clothe ourselves with compassion," and the Savior himself said, "Be compassionate as your Father also is compassionate."[12] This is a sacrifice dear and acceptable to God, a fragrance of spiritual offerings surpassing blood, smoke, and incense; while the latter acted as types, the former convey the sweet odor of truth to God, who says also in another prophet, "What I want is mercy, not sacrifice, knowledge of God rather than burnt offerings."[13] Note how the person of the penitent ponders the performance of sacrifices according to the Law, whereas God announces ahead of time that the Law is inefficacious and insufficient for purification of sin, while far better and incomparably superior is the force of life in Christ. Whereas what is done in accord with the Law is unacceptable, he said that what God wants is for us *to do justice, to love mercy, and to be prepared to walk with* him. These are the ornaments of life in Christ.

A voice of the Lord will be invoked in the city, and will save those fearing his name (v.9). In another way as well he makes clear that there is no benefit in blood offerings, whereas the efficacy of

12. Eph 6.14–15; Col 3.12; Lk 6.36.
13. Hos 6.6. As he had in comment on that significant statement of OT morality, so too with these verses of Micah, which Smith calls "one of the great passages of the OT" which "epitomizes the message of the eighth-century prophets," Cyril not only elaborates but also relates to NT development (unlike the Antiochenes).

spiritual worship brings considerable advantage. Now, he used (702) the word *voice* to mean "name" or "invocation." It would perhaps be like saying, If the name of God were to be spoken respectfully in the city, it would without question be saved. In other words, he is saying, do not get the idea, mortal man, that I take satisfaction in blood offerings or consider a city impious and lawless unless it offers calves as a burnt offering. Rather, I would absolutely not rescue it from danger if it chose to sacrifice cattle, even if it stained the altar with blood-letting and opted to offer herds of rams; instead, *invoking the name* of God would suffice for its salvation. The city that honors my power, you see, is mine, doing what is pleasing to me promptly and being of that mind. Then I shall *save those fearing me.*

When we can claim to be God's, therefore, then we also have respect for him and are saved by him, and such would rightly be understood as the force of spiritual worship. The God of all said something similar also in a statement of David: "Hear, my people, and I shall speak to you; Israel, I shall testify against you: I am God, your God. Not for your sacrifices do I rebuke you; your burnt offerings are continually before me." He then went on from this to say that he does not eat meat of bulls or drink the blood of goats; and in similar vein he says, "Offer to God a sacrifice of praise, and pay your vows to the Most High; call on me in the day of distress and I shall rescue you, and you will glorify me."[14]

Listen, tribe: what will adorn the city? Surely not fire and a house of the lawless (703) *storing lawless treasures and iniquities with insolence?* (vv.9–10) The descendants of Israel occupied Judea and also Samaria by tribe and race after the land of promise had been distributed to them by Joshua, who was known also as son of Nun. So it is not one tribe that God addresses, but, as it were, all of them, or one by one, the contents being applicable and proper to one and all. *Listen*, therefore, every *tribe*, a city is saved when it honors the name of God; he never neglects those who fear him; instead, he will be an impregnable wall, the ornament and glory of those willing to do what God loves. If

14. Ps 50.7–8, 13, 14–15.

on the other hand, he is saying, you prefer to witness the opposite, *what will adorn the city? A house of the lawless,* or *iniquities with insolence?* Surely, he says, if on account of grave sin a city is consumed by fire when captured by enemy hands, it will not be presentable and beautiful? Surely *a house of the lawless storing lawless treasures* would not render it resplendent and well thought of, nor *iniquity with insolence* be of benefit to it? Rather, no one in his right mind would doubt that such things make it inglorious; a city would not be captured and consumed by fire unless it had definitely committed grave sin. Why then, he asks, do you neglect the things by which a city is saved and beautified, and instead consider desirable what naturally damages it and prefer the means (704) by which it is rendered vile and ugly, with evil inhabitants who are avaricious and lawless and who *store up lawless treasures?*[15]

Will someone be justified who is unjust in using a balance, with false weights in his bag? They amassed their wealth from their iniquities; their inhabitants told lies, and their tongues were exalted in their mouths (vv.11–12). Surely you do not believe, he says, that *someone will be justified who is unjust in using a balance?* In other words, if I were to evaluate and, as it were, weigh in the balance each one's life, do you believe that despite my love for virtue I could bring myself to award unjust people a verdict of righteousness? Do you think that people *with false weights in their bag*—that is, prepared to enrich themselves from unholy avarice and wrongful profiteering—could escape my wrath? After all, *they amassed their wealth from the iniquity* of such profits, and emerged as lying and arrogant; an addiction to falsehood always accompanies the lovers of inequity, and boasting and haughtiness those already wealthy.

Now, the inventors of unholy teachings keep *false weights in their bags;* they "overturn every right verdict,"[16] beguile the minds of the simple with deception and trickery, and enrich themselves by ensnaring many. In amassing for themselves such wealth that is full of iniquity, however, (705) they admittedly say nothing

15. Cyril is not deterred by the difficulty the LXX finds in an obscure Heb. passage.

16. 3.9.

true, but only what is misleading, false, and discolored, as it were, with every deceitful sophistry. Such people likewise even raise their own voice to "speak unjustly of God," as Scripture says, and "utter bombastic nonsense";[17] to them it is logical to reply, "Listen, tribe: what will adorn the city? Surely not fire and a house of the lawless storing lawless treasures and iniquities with insolence?" (vv.9–10) Far from being an *adornment* to them, in fact, the *fire* of punishment will be a condemnation; and when the houses are used for *storing lawless treasures,* they will bring a curse and condemnation and fall foul of every trouble.

I shall begin to strike you and do away with you in your sins. You will eat and not be filled; I shall expel you by yourself; you will take hold and not be saved; everyone saved will be given over to the sword. You will sow but not reap; you will press oil but not have oil for anointing; you will make wine but not drink it; and my people's rituals will disappear. You kept the statutes of Omri and all the works of the house of Ahab, and you followed their counsels, with the result that I shall make you a desolation and your inhabitants an object of hissing, and you shall bear the scorn of peoples (vv.13–16). Since houses proved to be "storing lawless treasures" (v.10) and amassing wealth from injustice, he now threatens them with retribution, and says that the onset of what was expected to happen (706) was now beginning, the result being that the *disappearance* would be commensurate with their failings. He does well to startle them, and by dread of future events like a kind of bridle he recommends an option for reform and in second place appeasement of God. He compiles a kind of list and sets the punishments before them: they will be punished with famine and lack of necessities; they will be destroyed within themselves and will *take hold* without succeeding in escaping. If, however, some actually did manage to flee the present disasters, they would be taken before long and become victims of others' *swords.*

Now, this is probably what is suggested to us in the passage: a great number of enemies were mobilized against the people of Israel, or against the whole of Judah. But it was not always by foes from outside: they even took up arms against them-

17. Ps 75.5; 2 Pt 2.18.

selves, as was the case at times with Ephraim, or the ten tribes, rebelling against Judah, at other times people in Jerusalem itself campaigning against Ephraim. Cities without number were destroyed, so that they were often driven out *by themselves*; and in being pursued from cities in this way, they *laid hold* of other ones, only to be captured at various times when there was an invasion either by the Syrians and the kings of Damascus, or perhaps by Persians and Medes themselves. In my view this is the meaning of *I shall expel you by yourself; you will take hold and not be saved; everyone saved will be given over to the sword.*[18] (707)

Now, the fact that they would also be deprived of the produce of the fields, would live a miserable life under pressure of the lack of necessities, and pay the penalty of unholy crimes committed by them, he makes clear in what follows. *You will sow but not reap*, he says, in fact (in my view because God destroyed the crops); *you will press oil* (the country of the Samaritans being oil-bearing) but will be in need of oil, so that, even if you wanted, you would perhaps be at a loss to find it for *anointing*. And though your country is very rich in vines and has so much wine that you distribute it to other cities, you yourself would find none to drink. The *rituals* will disappear that you adopted in offering to the idols themselves the produce of the harvest; after all, what offering of first-fruits can then occur if the whole yield is lost to you and the crops of the fields have perished? Or what thanksgiving offerings will you make, and for what proper reason, when you have fallen in your misery and been consumed?

Then, to bring out that no one else would be understood to have been responsible for the misfortunes, and that instead it was he who wronged himself and would be captured for having imitated the ways of those who were particularly guilty, he continues in the same vein: *You kept the statutes of Omri and all the works of the house of Ahab, and you followed their counsels, with the result that I shall make you a desolation.* Omri, king over Israel, was the father of Ahab, but as the sacred text says, "he walked in the ways of Jeroboam son of Nebat," who caused Israel to sin; "he did more

18. Cyril is right to be tentative in offering his interpretation of the passage, of which Jerome remarks, "The LXX departs considerably in this section from the *Hebraica veritas*," without shedding light on many obscure phrases.

evil than all who were before (708) him."[19] Accordingly, he was also consumed by fire, burning his own house over himself, as is written there.[20] By *house of Ahab* he probably refers to Jezebel; murders, robberies, and pursuit of holy people were committed by her. So he says, You observed those practices so that I might justifiably do away with you, and make you a laughing-stock and object of *scorn* to the others.

Now, we shall apply such a passage also to the enemies of truth, who, by trusting in their own eloquence and assembling the refuse of their miserable ideas, grow rich, as it were, from iniquities, amassing for themselves what is not their own, habitually ravaging the masses of the simple in the manner of enemies, and carrying them off into wrongful error. Let them therefore listen to God's words: *I shall begin to strike you and do away with you in your sins. You will eat and not be filled.* In other words, though they dabble in the sacred writings, they then gain no satisfaction from the teachings of truth; though seeming to eat, they die of hunger; though expecting to lay hold of salvation, they would not find it; though sowing the seed, at least in their view, they will meet with no reward for their pains; though crushing the spiritual *olive*, the sacred Scripture, they are in no way enriched with the grace of the Spirit; and though expecting to harvest *wine*, they will be deprived of spiritual good cheer. After all, they *kept the statutes of Omri and all the works of the house of Ahab;* that is, they prostituted themselves, enriched themselves through greed, and involved themselves in persecution of the saints. For them, therefore, there will be (709) *disappearance*, and they will meet with an end that is truly shameful and accursed.

19. 1 Kgs 16.26, 25.
20. Cyril is confusing Omri with his predecessor Zimri; cf. 1 Kgs 16.18.

COMMENTARY ON MICAH,
CHAPTER SEVEN

Woe is me for becoming like someone gathering stubble in the harvest and glean-
ings at the picking, there being no bunches available for eating the first-fruits
(v.1).

UT OF LOVE THE PROPHET MOCKS Israel for being
on the point of going off to destruction, and of reaching such a small number that very few would in the
end be left. They would be like what falls from the sheaves, which
the hands of the harvesters pass by, whereas the few survivors
are quick to collect even *stubble* because of dire need. They no
less resemble also what is called *gleanings*, which the harvesters'
sickles miss. In my view he is suggesting in this also the difficulty
of encountering holy people, for the reason of there being few
of them left at that time, to be found like a single ear of grain
when the crops are harvested, or like rejects of second ranking
among the first fruits of the bunches. When the weather heats
up, you see, the first bunches that grow initially are shaken from
the branches; but as time passes, sometimes a second-rate reject from the bunches succeeds the first. It is difficult for the
pickers to find, doubtless because it easily escapes notice in the
abundant foliage and because of the small number of grapes; it
requires no little effort for them to gather them, following the
pickers and peering into the vines.[1] (710)

The prophetic word in this passage, therefore, seems to lament the dearth of good people. There is no doubting that the
fact was to the disadvantage of the people of Israel—I mean
their suffering a lack of holy people; on occasion the Lord in
his loving-kindness pardoned countries and cities and forgave

---

1. Theodoret will learn from Cyril the lesson of unpacking the author's imagery for the benefit of readers (though in this case even Theodore had gone
to some such trouble).

their very many crimes. If only five holy people had been found among them, the Sodomites' cities would at that time have been saved, since God would have had compassion out of respect for the holy people, few though they were, and checked his wrath.[2]

Woe is me, soul, because the pious have disappeared from the land, and there is no upright person left among human beings; all go to law as bloodsuckers; they each oppress their neighbor with oppression; they set their hands to evil actions. The official makes demands, and the judge speaks soothing words; it is his soul's desire (vv.2–3). In our view the statement is true; the prophet regrets that there is no *pious* person in the whole land, namely, the land of the Jews, despite formerly boasting of a vast number of holy people of high reputation. Consequently, God says also in a statement of Isaiah, "How the faithful city of Zion has become a whore, (711) full of litigation, where righteousness lodged, but now murderers."[3] What was particularly obnoxious, in fact, and brought them to the very extremes of depravity, was their *going to law as bloodsuckers* and committing savage homicide, and rejecting as even quite outdated the performance of good works, the result being that they even considered it an essential practice to *set their hands to evil actions* against other people. To people accustomed to living this way, nothing is left untried, even should it be punishable by law, even if excluded by the norms of freedom.

Surely, then, if the subjects suffered from this ailment, the leaders did not, and the judges were in good health? Not at all, he says: *the official makes demands, and the judge speaks soothing words.* Frequently it happens that many people appointed to public office prove unholy and grasping, readily selling their opinions to those wanting to corrupt them. Even if they are inclined to give the impression of succumbing to bribes and kickbacks, however, they somehow disguise it and strive to put a gloss on their own behavior with a good reputation. How would it not surpass utter indecency for them to proceed to such a degree of wretched and shameful behavior as to stretch out their hand, so to speak, even if not receiving anything, by *going to law* to overturn the verdict of justice and to make shameless threats?

2. In Gn 18.32, in fact, the Lord's compassion peters out at ten good people.
3. Is 1.21.

The statement therefore comes emphatically (712) from someone protesting against oppression, *The official makes demands, and the judge speaks soothing words.* Surely you would not blame the one who brings together in peace those at odds? Further, how would the saying not be true, "Blessed are the peacemakers,"[4] and how great would their reward be? Nevertheless, while the arbiters of peace have achievements of their own, the one who judges uprightly determines what is decreed by the divine law, convicting wrongdoers and completely supporting the wronged. When, on the contrary, we speak *soothing words* to the wrongdoers and do not convict them of committing sin, then we clearly undermine the decree of the Lawgiver, who said, "A priest's mouth will observe justice, and from his mouth they will look for law."[5] Somehow, however, it is always a feature of those given to corruption to fail to deliver upright judgments or forthrightly convict sinners, instead recommending peace, even in the case of people guilty of extreme oppression. The prophet makes clear the cause of this failure: *it is his soul's desire;* that is, he would be quite content with the wrongful action. How will he then punish the wrongdoers? How would blame be apportioned to what he has commended? Avarice and oppression of others is therefore something unholy and truly harmful.

In addition, it is also an accursed crime to succumb to base gain, and to descend to such a degree of misjudgment as to set at naught the patterns of righteous behavior and impartial judgment, (713) and to consider them of no importance, while attaching oneself to people in the habit of wrongdoing, becoming involved with others in impiety, and thus being a part of others' sins. Who in his right mind would doubt that the person who is guilty of such dreadful sins will be completely and utterly liable to wrath and retribution?

I shall do away with their good things like a gnawing moth advancing along a beam on the day of scrutiny (v.4). He threatened to apply a twofold form of retribution. He had said, remember, "I shall begin to strike you and do away with you in your sins. You will eat and not be filled; I shall expel you by yourself; you will

---

4. Mt 5.9.
5. Mal 2.7.

take hold and not be saved." He continued, "You will sow but not reap; you will press oil but not have oil for anointing; you will make wine but not drink it."[6] So the fact that the abundance of a good return from the fields will be lost to them, and they will be lacking necessities and will suffer a shortage of what they need, he conveys by saying that he would consume all these *good things of theirs* like a *moth*, that is, the things that they probably enjoyed greatly and that were the basis of their deep satisfaction. The fact that they were destined to be struck, wiped out, and banished, as it were, by themselves—that is, perishing with one another—and miserably dismissed from their own homes and cities, he makes clear by saying, *Advancing* (714) *along a beam on the day of scrutiny I shall do away with their good things.* Not only *like a gnawing moth*, but *advancing along a beam on the day of scrutiny.* While the phrase is very difficult to understand, I am of the opinion that we could not succeed in grasping it without there being a clear introductory outline of the events relevant to it, which is what I shall try to provide.[7]

Gibeah, then, is a town or little city in Judea situated on a hill; it was assigned by lot to the people of the tribe of Benjamin, and is also called "hill" or *scrutiny.* Now, we recall that a Levite, as is recorded in the book of Judges, when his concubine was violated by the people of the tribe of Benjamin in that very place, Gibeah, cut up the remains into twelve parts and sent them to all the tribes to make clear to everyone the crime of the tribe of Benjamin. It then ensued that by the norms of war the other tribes rose up against the people of the tribe of Benjamin and countless numbers fell; in the beginning the people of the tribe of Benjamin were victorious, but later the other tribes completely wiped them out. The prophet Hosea also recalls the incident, saying, "They planted madness in the house of the Lord; they corrupted themselves on the days of the hill."[8] In other words,

6. 6.13–15.

7. Cyril would have known that while Theodore found the image of the moth an accessible one, Jerome had provided a version of the Heb. bearing no resemblance to the LXX or mention of a moth. Despite that, the word "scrutiny, lookout" must have prompted Cyril to dig into the past for clarification.

8. Hos 9.9, where Cyril gave a lengthy précis of the events of Jgs 19–20, and despite Jerome's information failed to see that the LXX has confused Gibeah with an identical form for "hill, lookout, scrutiny." See FOTC 115, 183–86.

he is saying, since they planted idolatry and false prophecy (what is indicated to us by "madness" here) in the house of the Lord, consequently they also (715) corrupted themselves on the days of the hill, that is Gibeah. That Gibeah means "hill" or *scrutiny* you learn clearly from the text of the first book of Kings; Asa was king of Jerusalem and Baasha king of Samaria at the one time. When they fell out and in their hostility to each other they prepared for war, "Baasha king of Israel went up against Judah and built Ramah to prevent anyone going out or coming in to Asa king of Judah." But when Ben-hadad invaded Samaria, Baasha stopped building Ramah so as to resist the enemy. Leaving Jerusalem, Asa came to Ramah, the text says, "and ordered everyone in Judah to Enakim, and they took the stones and wood from Ramah used by Baasha for building, and King Asa built every hill and scrutiny in Benjamin."[9] So Gibeah means "hill" or *scrutiny;* Gibeah is translated that way on account of being raised on high and situated on a mountain or *scrutiny.*

So "I shall begin to strike you and do away with you in your sins"[10] in no other way than *on the day of scrutiny; I shall advance,* as it were, *along a beam,* I shall not veer to right or left in taking the way of retribution against you. It would seem, however, that the prophetic verse likewise suggests some such meaning to us as the following. Micah, remember, was prophesying in the days of Jotham, (716) Ahaz, and Hezekiah. While Jotham was a pious man, Ahaz by contrast was loathsome, hateful, and guilty of most abominable acts of impiety. In his reign Pekah son of Remaliah, who was reigning over Samaria at the time, made war on Judah along with Rezin king of Damascus as his ally, and killed a vast number on one day. It is recorded of Ahaz, in fact, in the second book of Chronicles, "The Lord his God gave him into the hand of the king of Syria, who struck him and took captive a great number of his people, brought them to Damascus, and gave him into the hands of the king of Israel, who struck him a heavy blow. The king of Israel Pekah son of Remaliah slew a hundred and twenty thousand valiant warriors in Judah because they had abandoned the Lord their God."[11]

9. 1 Kgs 15.17–22.
10. 6.13.

It should therefore be realized that through offending God we shall at once experience the lack of every *good thing*, and we will be struck with a terrible hunger for divine and spiritual goods, consuming one another, as it were, by biting. Christ, after all, does not award his characteristic peace to those who do not love him, as is seen to be the fate of the enemies of truth, who show no sign of spiritual gifts—only cannibalism, as it were, mutual hostility, strife, rivalry, and division; of them God would say, "I have taken away my peace from this people, and they will die of a deadly disease,"[12] lacking strength (717) and fellow-feeling. Why so? He distributes them only to those with a respect for what is his, in whom the good that is peace would abide, who honor the force of truth, who are not distracted by wrongful notions, and who instead are anxious only to admire the beauty of truth.

Alas, alas, vengeance has come upon you! Now they will fall to weeping (v.4). Do you note how he also mimics the sounds of mourners, not expecting future disasters but, as it were, those that have already happened, and weeping in a way befitting women? *Vengeance has come upon you*, he says; the time of retribution has arrived; war is at hand; hardship is at the door. By continuing, *Now they will fall to weeping*, in fact, he clearly brought out that, far from being long delayed, the fulfillment of the prophecy was under their eyes, as it were; after Jotham, remember, the wicked apostate Ahaz immediately succeeded, slaughterer of his own children, whom he offered on the altar of the demons. In his reign a hundred and twenty thousand from the tribe of Judah and Benjamin fell.[13] Now, it should be realized that at that time Israel also paid the penalty; in the reign of Pekah, Tiglathpileser went up against Samaria, destroyed a great number of its cities,[14] took Damascus, and killed Rezin, the result being that at the one time Judah and Benjamin were consumed by the ten tribes in Samaria, and they suffered at the hands of the Babylonians what they themselves had committed. Do you see, therefore, how (718) by traveling along the *beam* of wrath, as it were, at the time of the hill or *scrutiny* he punished the offenders?

11. 2 Chr 28.5–6.   12. Jer 16.5, 4.
13. 2 Chr 28.3, 6.   14. 2 Kgs 15.29.

Those events happened to the ancients "by way of a type, and were written down for our instruction,"[15] so that we should ever avoid being caught up in similar sins and continue to enjoy good fortune by keeping the God of all as a benevolent and loving protector. It would, on the other hand, be very appropriate to apply them to those who distort what is right and undermine the faith of simple people, so that we ourselves should say, *Alas, alas, vengeance has come upon you! Now they will fall to weeping.* "By sinning against members of your family," remember, "and wounding their conscience when it is weak, you sin against Christ." There is no doubt that they will definitely give an account to the judge and "eat the fruit of their own impiety; they will be slain for their wrongs to infants, and examination does away with the impious."[16]

Do not trust in friends or hope in leaders. Be careful not to entrust anything to your partner, because son dishonors father, daughter rebels against her mother, daughter-in-law against her mother-in-law, and a man's foes are all the men in his house (vv.5–6). The people of Israel sinned in manifold ways and provoked the Lord of all to wrath against them. They then learned ahead of time through the holy prophets that they would encounter ineluctable evils unless they chose to appease the Lord with good living, since they were under obligation to adopt right attitudes and to win him over with a change for the better after he was offended. (719) The wretches did not do it. How so? They succumbed to such a degree of folly as to think and believe that they would be proof against the divine wrath and would very easily win any war if they had the neighboring nations as allies and the support and promises of their rulers. That they were relying on idle and vain illusions, however, and displayed a quite groundless confidence the prophet tries to convince them in the words, *Do not trust in friends or hope in leaders;* such expectation was unjustified and quite groundless. Since the Babylonian had come with the intention of devastating Samaria, in fact, by that time the *leaders* of the neighboring nations, although promising them the greatest possible assistance, had no slight problems of their own and

15. 1 Cor 10.11.
16. 1 Cor 8.12; Prv 1.31–32 LXX.

were content to concentrate on their own salvation, not giving thought to helping others. Accordingly, he says, *Do not trust in friends or hope in leaders* because, with God bringing the effect of his wrath to bear on you, not even the law of nature or the force of innate affection will win you benevolence, despite the bonds of blood and relationship according to the flesh; instead, they, too, will resemble enemies. At that time a wife will despise her husband, *sons will rebel against fathers, daughters against mothers;* in fact, he says, the very one who imprints the laws of affection on nature would bring about a change of heart and instead encourage indifference.

We should not form the impression, however, that the kind of indifference referred to here is one and only, but it is twofold and diverse; some people offend against the laws of affection by showing unholy (720) antipathy to their parents, while others do so to bring gladness to God and save their own souls. The Savior said, for instance, "Do you think that I have come to bring peace to the earth? No, I tell you, but rather division. From now on, five in one household will be divided, three against two and two against three; they will be divided: father against son and son against father, mother against daughter and daughter against mother, mother-in-law against her daughter-in-law and daughter-in-law against mother-in-law."[17] We shall therefore crown with an upright verdict such a splendid lack of affection; it commends itself to God, even if separating people from kinship of the flesh, thus enabling them properly to sing the song of David, "My father and my mother abandoned me, but the Lord took me up."[18]

But as for me, I shall look to the Lord; I shall wait upon God my Savior; my God will hearken to me (v.7). This would be very applicable to Zion when repenting and pondering in advance the future end of the hardships of captivity in due course; Cyrus took the city of the Babylonians and eventually released the remnant of Israel, bidding them go home with their sacred vessels and rebuild the Temple in Jerusalem.[19] Then it was, in fact, that they

17. Lk 12.51–53, a text that the Antiochenes do not cite.
18. Ps 27.10.
19. Cyril moves between the eighth and the sixth centuries and speaks interchangeably of Assyria and Babylon, Israel and Judah.

escaped from darkness and unbreakable bonds, as it were, and enjoyed light, thanks to God's compassion, and were restored to the former (721) freedom befitting them, rejoicing to be released. *As for me*, he says, therefore, *I shall look to the Lord* at this late stage and after experience of the trials whose onset I should have obviated. But he says that [Zion] will have hope in God, *wait upon* salvation from him, and be firmly reliant on him, because in his loving-kindness he will hearken to its complaints and accept its prayers.

Now, by the beginning of *salvation* is to be understood, in my view, the eventual direction of the mind away from the former deceit, choosing now to adopt right attitudes instead, and believing that the Lord of all is the very source and governor of salvation, not attributing such a special good to assistance from human beings or having the foolish and ill-advised expectation that the gift will come from the powerless mass of idols. Of old, remember, they went down to Egypt and betook themselves to Assyria to purchase support and assistance from both with countless amounts of money. They also made their approach to lifeless idols, performing sacrifices and furthermore offering prayers for themselves. Now, on the other hand, they claim that they will *look to the Lord and wait upon* him; that is, they will receive salvation and grace from him, and will actually be *hearkened to* by him, continuing to offer supplication, that is, to him and to no other. This, as I said, was true of Zion at its revival, (722) recognizing as it should that the ancient error had been dissipated and that there had been a change of mind for the better and an option to do what is useful.

Do not rejoice over me, my foe, because I have fallen; I shall arise. Because even if I sit in darkness, the Lord will enlighten me. I shall bear the Lord's wrath because I sinned against him, until he declares my cause just; he will give me justice and lead me out to the light, and I shall see his righteousness (vv.8–9). Zion's statement now seems to me to be expressed in a highly festive mood against the harsh, insolent, and arrogant city, namely, Babylon, which is, so to speak, mocking the country of the Jews for being plundered. Do not gloat over me, it is saying, in fact, for having fallen; you have conquered, not by prevailing through your own strength, but by overthrowing me when I was suffering for offending God, and hence being fallen. The time will come, however, when *I shall arise*, even if I was in darkness, "saying to a piece of wood, You are my god, and to a stone, You begot me," and making a statement on the heifers; I said, after all, I said in my derangement, "These are your gods, Israel, who led you out of the land of Egypt."[20] Instead, I shall even be in the light; I shall know the Lord, who saves me, who helps me, the source of my strength. I shall put up with what befalls me; I shall undergo dire happenings; I shall in no way cry out in protest that God is wronging me, but shall rather be convinced that he is delivering me a right verdict, even if sent into captivity. I have sinned, in fact, and bear the effects of wrath, *until he declares my cause just*, that is, until he assigns me (723) punishment commensurate with the sins and then shows compassion, and brings brightness to [Zion], which was plunged into the gloom of error, causing it to enjoy light, as it were, through knowing the one who is in truth and by nature God. He would rightly be admired, it says, for having demonstrated in my case the sincerity of his own righteousness. Just as he did not exceed what is just in punishing it for sin, you see, so he will with equal reasonableness be responsible for according it care and showing compassion to it in its present suffering and repentance, now that it has fallen.

The Lord of all, therefore, is good, and without delay he distributes mercy to those turning back to him, and gladdens them very abundantly with the good things of his clemency, ungrudgingly forgiving former failings.

My foe will see, and shame will cover her, she who says to me, Where is the Lord your God? My eyes shall see her; now she is to be trodden down like mud on the streets. A day for laying bricks, that day your destruction (vv.10–11). Seizure was the fate of the country of the Jews, seizure, and in due course Israel was deported as a captive to the land of the Babylonians and Medes. It was not by the victor's own might that he overcame it; rather, God its Savior turned away from it and, as it were, placed it at the disposal of the foe on account of its opting to adore idols, to undermine

20. Jer 2.27; Ex 32.4.

the law decreed of old through Moses, and in a word to adopt every kind of wrongdoing, leaving no form of depravity untried. (724) The Babylonians next took it, ascribing the conquest to their own powers, arrogating to themselves the divine glory, and thinking they would gain control of Judea, even if the God of all were to choose to save it. They took control of the sinners, treated them with dire and unbearable hardship, and inflicted harsh slavery on them. God said somewhere in Jeremiah, for instance, to the unholy multitude of the Assyrians, or to Babylon, "Lo, I am against you, O arrogant one," and also in reference to the people of Israel themselves, "I gave them into your hand, but you showed them no mercy; on the aged you made your yoke exceedingly heavy, saying, I shall be mistress forever."[21] In other words, with them there is no mercy, no pity for youth, no respect for old age, no sense of compassion.

Consequently, then, they are rightly given into the hands of both Persians and Medes under the command of Cyrus, who took Babylon. It is perhaps of them that the prophet Jeremiah says somewhere, "They will invade you, and you will be caught, Babylon, without knowing it; you will be discovered and captured because you challenged the Lord. The Lord has opened his storehouse and brought out the weapons of his wrath,"[22] by "weapons of his wrath" meaning those plundering it. While it happened that Babylon was taken by Cyrus, then, Israel was released from captivity. Consequently, the ones who have been rescued say, *My foe will see, and shame will cover her;* when she sees her own children lying on the ground and piteously and unexpectedly slain while her former subjects are rejoicing and exulting, will she not then turn tail, and *shame will cover her* completely and utterly, (725) despite at one time asking, *Where is the Lord your God?* In fact, *I shall see her* thrown out and *trodden down like mud on the streets* under the feet of the enemy. The text then says to Babylon herself, *That day your destruction,* meaning the time when you went under the feet of the foe—namely, Cyrus—trampling and crushing you in your pride and arrogance just like *mud.*

21. Jer 50.31; Is 47.6–7.
22. Jer 50.24–25.

To the extent required to understand such matters factually, therefore, our explanation has been given quite sufficiently and clearly. On the other hand, you would apply them no less to the spiritual Zion as well, that is, to the church as she vanquishes the enemy, tramples down persecutors, and mocks the weakness of those bent on warring against her, even if they sometimes seem to prevail and gain control. There are a great number, in fact, who impiously gnash their teeth and vent their spleen at her, and hatch every kind of plot; this is what the pagans are deeply involved in with their own foolish concoctions, and in general they are peddling the deception of the idols. This, too, is what heretics do, especially in deadly attacks on the saints and in a harsh display of savagery against those choosing to adopt right attitudes; or rather, it is what is done even by those who do not belong to the faith. Sometimes, in fact, when God, who can do all things, tries the saints and allows them to encounter temptations, testing, as it were, by fire sincere worshipers, wretched people display their arrogance against them, as if seeing their hardship and (726) stupidly exclaiming, *Where is the Lord your God?* In reply the wise, pure, and holy virgin, bearing no spot or wrinkle,[23] would rightly say, "But as for me, I shall look to the Lord; I shall wait upon God my Savior; my God will hearken to me" (v.7). How could it be doubted that she will *trample down* her adversaries *like mud on the street* without those who usually harass her gloating over her in any way, even if she should somehow be shaken? After all, she is "founded on the rock";[24] her support is Christ, a stable basis and permanent security, Savior and Redeemer.

Now, in my view, this would also be said—that is, *Do not rejoice over me, my foe, for falling,* and what follows—by the soul of a person who had sinned and repented, making the change to repentance and accepting the grace of salvation through Christ. It would say, in fact, to its tyrannical *foe,* sin, *Do not rejoice over me:* admittedly I have *fallen,* ignored the will of God, and given my mind to worldly pleasures. But far from losing hope, I shall also *arise,* even if immersed in darkness and gloom; I myself shall

23. Cf. Eph 5.27.
24. Mt 7.25.

find light in Christ, and the "sun of righteousness will rise" in my mind and make it bright. *I shall bear the Lord's wrath because I sinned against him;* even if I left his presence for a time, and even surrendered myself to an unsound mind, yet I shall be wise, and after rightly suffering I shall bear the penalty and admit its justice: I have not been punished without reason. Since I have paid a fitting penalty, however, *I shall see his* (727) *righteousness.* Now, what else would the righteousness of the God and Father be than Christ? This in fact is the way the God and Father refers to him, saying to us, "My righteousness approaches quickly, and my mercy has been revealed."[25]

Then, after in all likelihood pondering the gift of righteousness in Christ and the disaster that sin is, such a soul will wisely and prudently call out, *My foe will see, and shame will cover her, she who says to me, Where is the Lord your God? My eyes shall see her; now she is to be trodden down like mud on the streets. A day for laying bricks, that day your destruction.* In other words, when Christ came to justify sinners by faith, he shut the mouth of iniquity, on the one hand, and, on the other, its inventor was also, as it were, shamed. The latter was driven off and dismissed from his rule over us, and the former then *trodden down like mud on the streets,* trampled, so to speak, by the feet of the saints. *The day* of Christ also proved to be *destruction* for [iniquity], when he renders all who make their approach to him cleansed of their former sins through holy baptism, seals them in holiness with the Spirit, and enrolls them among God's children.

That day will repudiate your required practices. Your cities will meet with leveling and partition by Assyrians, and your fortified cities with partition from Tyre as far as the river, from sea to sea, and from mountain to mountain. (728) *The land is set for destruction along with its inhabitants from the effects of their exploits* (vv. 12–13). In-between is set the person of Zion, or Jerusalem, already bent on repentance, placing its hope in God, confident that it will be liberated and will see Babylon trampled down despite its arrogant outburst, *Where is your God?* Now, you could apply the force of the text not to what comes in-between, but to what just preceded it;

25. Mal 4.2; Is 51.5 and 56.1.

I shall briefly explain what it was. He had bidden them, remember, not to trust in friends or place hope in leaders, suggesting that a wife would have little regard for her husband, a child would despise its father, and daughters would have little respect for their mothers, since the terrors of war were calling them in that direction. After all, where the fear of suffering appears to beset all alike, in that case concern for one's own life is more important for everyone, and anyone else's is neglected.

At that time, therefore, he is saying, or on *that day* when sons are indifferent about affection for their fathers and daughters likewise for their mothers, *required practices* will be *repudiated*, that is, attention to duty will then lapse. A father will not have the time to blame his son for neglect even of the law of nature, nor will a mother take offense and subject her daughter to appropriate chastisement, since other concerns occupy them—or, rather, destruction and ultimate disaster. The cities will in fact depart for desolation, (729) *partition,* and overthrow; some forces will attack that city; others, the neighboring one; still others, the one nearby, and will invade the whole land *from mountain to mountain,* from east to west, from north to south, so as in brief to plunder the whole land to its limits, *from Tyre as far as the river, and from mountain to mountain.*[26] Now, here by *required practices* he probably means the festivals or sacrifices customarily observed in the shrines of the idols; when the cities were destroyed, and the houses and everything in them plundered, who would be performing what was required and paying homage to the idols' shrines and temples?

Now, the verse could quite reasonably be applied, if you wished, also to people who have different views and trust in their own wisdom, and who overturn the correct teachings of the church. Like *cities,* in fact, they have fallen captive, and met with *partition* by the enemy, that is, the cosmic powers of this age; they have become the portion of foxes, as Scripture says, divided in impiety, the forms of blasphemy, and cursing of truth. Now this happened also to the Jewish masses when they abused

26. Perhaps Jerome's observation that the LXX has misread the Heb. (as Theodore's differing text confirms) is the reason why Cyril does not dwell on the details of these verses.

Emmanuel in an unholy manner, expelled him from the vineyard, as Scripture says, and gave him over to crucifixion, despite
admitting and acknowledging that he was the heir.[27] Consequently, they have been plundered and ingloriously destroyed,
for no other reason than *the effects of their exploits*; though they
should have admired the Creator for loving the world so much
as to "give his only Son so that everyone believing in him would
not (730) perish, and instead would have eternal life," they did
not do it. How so? Puffed up with arrogance, they killed the
Lord, returning him evil for good, as Scripture says, and in an
unholy manner pursuing every form of impiety. Let us heed the
command, then, "Walk in the light of your fire and in the flame
you have enkindled," and as well, "Eat the fruit of your own exploits."[28]

*Shepherd your people, your tribe, with a rod, sheep of your inheri-
tance, living alone in a forest in the midst of Carmel. They will feed
on Bashan and Gilead as in times everlasting. And as in the days of
your departure from Egypt you will see marvels* (vv.14–15). The passage likewise refers to what lies in-between, and adopts a tone of
encouragement, recommending a turn for the better through
hope in the good things understood in Christ, and properly
shifting attention to the option for an upright life. To those taking the easy road to indifference he had caused no little alarm,
you see, by the prophecy of calamities, and in turn he wins them
over by cleverly imparting gladness, the purpose being that
those to whom the piece of advice is given should not despair
and be carried headlong without repentance or restraint; Scripture says, remember, "When a sinner goes to the depths of evil,
he is scornful."[29] Accordingly, either the person of the God and
Father himself is introduced as saying to the Son, *Shepherd your
people, your tribe, with a rod, sheep of your inheritance,* (731) or the
author personally proclaims to Emmanuel himself that he must
shepherd his own *people* or *inheritance with a rod.* Now, Christ's *people*, and indeed *sheep* of his pasture, would be taken to mean
both those from the circumcision who have come to faith and

27. Eph 6.12; Ps 63.10; Mt 21.39.
28. Jn 3.16; Ps 35.12; Is 50.11; Prv 1.31 LXX.
29. Prv 18.3.

those called to holiness from the vast number of the nations; he created one new humanity out of two peoples, making peace and reconciling both in spiritual unity through his body. Christ himself, for instance, said, "I have other sheep as well"—obviously, those from the circumcision—"and them, too, I must bring in, and there will be one flock and one shepherd."[30]

So Christ's *people, tribe, sheep, and inheritance* are not those formed "from works of the Law," but those justified through faith; while the former were "under a curse," in the statement of blessed Paul, the latter would be right to say of themselves, "Blessed by the Lord, who made heaven and earth. The Lord is God, and appeared to us." Now, Christ *shepherds* his own *with a rod*, not by beating them with an iron bar or smashing them like a potter's vessel, in the psalmist's words,[31] but converting them with gentleness and in the manner of a good shepherd, using moderate fear to check the tendencies of the believers to indifference. This in fact is the way the Lord of all speaks somewhere in the person of David when shaping his words about the Son: "If his children forsake my Law and do not walk in my ordinances, if they (732) violate my statutes and do not keep my commandments, I shall punish their transgressions with a rod and their iniquities with a scourge. But I shall not remove from them my mercy."[32] So while he crushes the obdurate, disbelieving, and proud person who does not come to the faith by, as it were, striking them with an iron bar, he kindly guides the believers, pastures them among lilies, and takes them to good grazing and a rich pasture—that is, the inspired Scripture—making clear by the Spirit what is hidden in it to the more prudent. His purpose is for us "to come to maturity, to the measure of the full stature of Christ,"[33] with a mind that is enriched and well nourished, luxuriating in spiritual enjoyment.

Now, we *live alone*, chosen and separated as we are, having parted company with the others, whose concern is only for the things of the earth, who give preference to acquiring what is

30. Eph 2.15–16; Jn 10.16.
31. Gal 2.16 and 3.10; Pss 114.15 and 2.9.
32. Ps 89.31–34.
33. Eph 4.13.

passing, and who through need of the pleasures of the flesh are totally devoted to every form of wrongdoing. With mind at rest, therefore, and ridding it of idle and profane distraction, we are detached, we live an honorable and praiseworthy life, and we are *alone*, like the prophet Jeremiah, of course; he said, "Lord almighty, I did not sit in the company of jesters: I showed respect for the pressure of your hand, sitting alone because filled with bitterness."[34] We *live alone in a forest*, as it were, and on a mountain. By a *forest*, well wooded and leafy, you would understand the twofold instruction, moral (733) and dogmatic, and by a mountain what is elevated, as it were, and on high; there is nothing earthly in what we give our mind to and is the object of our attention in the church. That such pasture is rich and thriving he suggests likewise from rather materialistic comparisons, that those being initiated by Christ *will feed on Bashan and Gilead*, places lush with dense and abundant fodder for the calves and richly endowed with a variety of feed. Let us skillfully leap upwards from the corporeal and, as it were, materialistic level to the spiritual, and study the meaning hidden within, because the mind of the saints takes satisfaction in enjoying the meanings of the divine Scripture[35] and is filled, as it were, with a kind of richness, exercising abundantly, as I said, practical and contemplative virtue, not for some brief and limited time but, as the prophet says, *as in times everlasting*, that is, for a long and unlimited time. After all, whatever is pleasing to the flesh fails and withers along with it, passes like shadows, and shortly diminishes, whereas participation in good things of the Spirit from on high lasts for ages, since the possession of such things is not to be lost.

Now, he said that *you will see marvels as in the days of your departure from Egypt;* that is to say, as the God of all freed Israel from slavery in Egypt and subjected to a range of punishments those

---

34. Jer 15.16–17.
35. The advice is typical of an approach to biblical discourse that Cyril shares with his peers, though we have seen him less ready than Didymus to ignore the "corporeal and materialistic" (and historical) level of meaning and to "leap up" to a higher level. An Antiochene like Chrysostom will make a similar admission (e.g., in regard to anthropomorphisms) of Scripture's use of "materialistic" (παχύτης) comparisons.

bent on oppressing them by (734) wearing them out in making bricks from mud, so the Savior brought us believers out from the hand of the devil and from spiritual slavery, "bound the strong man," as he says, and expelled "the prince of this world."[36] And just as Pharaoh drowned and perished along with his retinue, so in turn Satan, along with the unclean spirits, was, as it were, submerged by being plunged into the noose of darkness. And just as Israel was baptized into Moses, though in the cloud and in the sea,[37] so, too, have we been baptized into Christ; he, in fact, is the spiritual cloud, irrigating the land under the sun with the Gospel teachings like rain of a kind. And just as he sent down to them manna in the wilderness, so, too, he gives us himself for food, being "the living bread that comes down from heaven and gives life to the world." Whereas they were led into the land of the senses, we shall inherit the city on high, the heavenly Jerusalem, the church of the firstborn; the Savior says that this is the land he promised to the meek.[38] You will therefore clearly learn, from the similarity, as it were, to what happened of old in the case of Israel, the force of what has been achieved in us through Christ.

Since, however, it is our duty to contribute to the benefit of the listeners the implications of all details, come now, let us take another path and say what can be taken from the interpretation of the names: (735) *Carmel* means "knowledge of circumcision"; *Bashan,* "shame"; and *Gilead,* "change of covenant." The passage thus has a particularly persuasive message. With Christ shepherding us, then, we shall enjoy a knowledge of circumcision when, of course, it is understood in the Spirit; we have been circumcised by a circumcision not performed by hand, and can claim to be a Jew inwardly, whereas Israel according to the flesh has only the kind that is physical and literal, by no means what is in the heart through the Spirit. Ours, in fact, is the true circumcision, rendering its recipients God's familiars. Consequently, the prophetic word also said to us, "Circumcise yourselves to God; cut away your hardness of heart, men of Judah and inhabitants of Judah."[39]

---

36. Mt 12.29; Jn 12.31. 37. 2 Pt 2.4; 1 Cor 10.2.
38. Jn 6.51, 33; Mt 5.5.
39. Rom 2.28–29; Jer 4.4. Though Cyril finds these etymologies in Jerome,

With Christ shepherding us, therefore, we shall be in *Carmel;* that is, we shall enjoy knowledge of circumcision, and shall be no less in *Bashan*, that is, covered in confusion and shame, not convicted of sin, but, because of having sinned, we are repentant and now bear a sense of sins committed in ignorance, which is the way of salvation. A clear example of extreme insensitivity, in fact, is some people's choosing to live, as it were, with a hard and shameless heart, without in any way being ashamed of their own faults, not to mention perhaps being guilty also of sins committed in ignorance. People who enjoy a knowledge of spiritual and divine circumcision, therefore, are covered in confusion for their own faults, and through having a sense of their natural inclination to offend, they make a complete move to what particularly becomes them. (736) Such people will also be in *Gilead*, that is, in a transfer of legislation or covenant. We shall live a life under Christ, no longer in terms of the Law, but rather according to the Gospel, bypassing the material sense of the letter and performing spiritual worship of God; and by moving to what is incomparably better, we shall exchange the types for the reality.

Nations will see and be ashamed of all their might; they will put their hands on their mouths, and their ears will be deafened; they will lick dust like snakes trailing dirt along; they will be held in their confinement (vv.16–17). By *nations* here he means the loathsome and unclean herds of demons; when they *see* those called in Christ to justification, to sanctification, to redemption, to sonship, to incorruptibility, to glory, to a life that is unconstricted and free, then it is that they will *be ashamed* after being dislodged from their dominance over them and seeing their own strength collapsed and deficient. Our Lord Jesus Christ, in fact, has allowed us "to trample on snakes and scorpions and on all the power of the foe."[40] Those who were previously victorious, therefore, will be prostrate under the feet of the believers, victims of weakness, and unnerved by Christ. *They will put their hands on their mouths*, no longer allowed to accuse sinners; after all, "it is God who justifies: who is to condemn?" as (737) Scripture says, and

---

and proceeds to exploit them, the LXX has made the decision to take the Heb. *carmel*, "garden," as a proper name.

40. Lk 10.19.

somewhere blessed David also said, "All wickedness will stop its mouth."[41] So the wretches will keep silent about their crimes, albeit unwillingly, he says; and, as though thunderstruck with wonderment—at us, obviously—*they will be deafened.* The news about us is extraordinary, a loud and truly supernatural report, especially if it is true that "while we were still sinners, at the right time Christ died for the ungodly," in order that we who were formerly guilty of terrible and insupportable failings should now be sanctified, "not by works of righteousness that we ourselves have performed, but" through mercy and grace, so that we who were formerly distressed and devoid of all hope should now be loved, the cynosure of all eyes, "heirs of God and co-heirs with Christ."[42]

They *will be deafened,* therefore, he says, and as if thunderstruck, to be sure, by God's clemency and the extraordinary degree of his astonishing goodness, *they will lick dust like snakes trailing dirt along;* that is, they will find no nourishment. It is the habit of snakes when in need of food to crush dust with their tongue and treat as food what they come upon. He says the unclean demons will suffer the same need; those who formerly were in the habit of making all the people on earth food to be enjoyed and drink to be quaffed will not continue to find them ready to tolerate this, thanks to everyone's being saved by Christ and achieving such a degree of vigor as to resist those former bites and instead walk on asp and basilisk, as Scripture says.[43] Not only *will they lick the ground,* however; they will also (738) *be held in their confinement,* that is, be gripped by weakness and distress, and when under siege, as it were, from the power of the one who afflicts them—namely, Christ—they will be subject to severe troubles.

Now, he is probably suggesting something else as well to us by *confinement.* In becoming like us, remember, the Only-begotten worked countless marvels, but in my view those not seen were more numerous than those seen. He ordered the unclean spirits to go down into Hades, in fact, and in the future to be held

---

41. Rom 8.33–34; Ps 107.42. 42. Rom 5.8, 6; Ti 3.5; Rom 8.17.
43. Ps 91.13.

in the abyss so that he might rid the earth of the harsher beasts. We see an image of that fact in the ancient texts: when Joshua son of Nun took the countries of the nations, he shut five kings in a cave and sealed its mouth with a stone as a type, as I said, of the inherent force of the Incarnation of the Savior. The demons, for instance, "besought him not to order them to go back into the abyss." So he says that *they will be held in their confinement*, shut, as it were, in Hades from then on and plunged into the noose of darkness so that, as I said, he might then rid the human race of harsh and savage beasts.[44]

They will be astonished at the Lord our God and terrified of you. What God is like you, canceling iniquities and bypassing offenses of the remnant of his inheritance? He did not retain his wrath as a witness, because his wish is for mercy. (739) *He will turn back and have compassion on us; he will submerge our sins, and cast all our sins into the depths of the sea. He will show faithfulness to Jacob, mercy to Abraham, as he swore to our fathers in the days of yore* (vv.17–20). The mystery of Christ, in fact, is truly *astonishing*, and the extraordinary degree of his clemency to us surpasses the bounds of admiration. The divinely inspired Habakkuk, for instance, struck by the manner of the Incarnation, exclaimed with clarity, "Lord, I heard report of you, and was afraid; Lord, I comprehended your works, and was astonished." The Only-begotten, in fact, though having the form of and equality with the God and Father, and though as God "he was rich, became poor for our sakes so that by his poverty we might become rich,"[45] so as to save what was lost, strengthen what was weak, bind up what was crushed, give life to what was corrupt, cleanse what was stained, free what was condemned to punishment, render blessed what was cursed, and dignify with sonship what by nature was in servitude.[46]

Let him therefore hear from everyone, *What God is like you* in your goodness and forgiveness, forgiving crimes *of the remnant of his inheritance?* Now, by *remnant of his inheritance* is to be un-

44. Jos 10.17–18; Lk 8.31; 2 Pt 2.4. In regard to a text about which Jerome is content to say that there is a considerable discrepancy between Heb. and LXX, Cyril strikes out on his own.

45. Hab 3.2; Phil 2.6; 2 Cor 8.9.

46. Cyril waxes lyrical here on the blessings conferred on sinful humanity through the Incarnation.

derstood those who have come to faith from Israel, obviously when the remaining mass has been destroyed for not believing. Christ said somewhere, "The one who believes in the Son is not condemned, whereas the one who does not believe is already condemned for not (740) believing in the name of the Son of God."[47] He therefore *bypasses* sins and leaves to one side *offenses*, and *did not retain his wrath as a witness*, by *as a witness* meaning "forever" or "always." Though we were cast out in Adam, we were welcomed back in Christ; we were cursed in the former, but in turn blessed in the latter. Scripture says, remember, "Just as many died through one man's trespass,"[48] so, too, will people in general have life through one man's being righteous. He forsook *his wrath*, then, *because his wish is for mercy*; at the time of the conversion of all—namely, the Incarnation—he will submerge the sins of all in *the sea*, as it were. Since he promised the holy *fathers*, namely, *Abraham* and *Jacob*, to multiply their offspring like the stars of heaven, he will fulfill his promise; fathers of many nations will be called, the children not being confined only to the descendants of Israel but also given to those of the promise. They are, as it were, a combination of those coming on the basis of faith in the so-called circumcision with those from the Law and circumcision to form a spiritual unity. Scripture says, remember, "Not all Israelites truly belong to Israel—rather, the children of the promise are reckoned as offspring"; all "who believe are blessed with Abraham who believed."[49] It should be understood that the blessing takes the form of grace in Christ, through whom and with whom be glory to the God and Father along with the Spirit, now and forever, for ages of ages. Amen.

47. Jn 3.18.
48. Rom 5.15.
49. Rom 9.6, 8; Gal 3.9. At this point, with the close of comment on Micah, editor Pusey concludes his first volume.

COMMENTARY ON *THE*
PROPHET NAHUM

PREFACE TO THE
COMMENTARY ON NAHUM

ACH OF THE HOLY PROPHETS was employed in some useful and demanding business at times for the purpose of ministering to the divine decrees and transmitting to people the messages from on high. Some foretold to Israel impending misfortunes so as to terrify them in their sins, and openly threatened that unless they decided to do what was pleasing to God, they would fall foul of dire and ineluctable troubles. Others highlighted what had actually happened, and by grieving with the victims skillfully persuaded them to opt for a better life and thus appease the divine wrath from then on. Still others led Israel in its sufferings to enjoy sound hope, and brought them to the conviction that after being reduced to misery for their own sins they would in turn prosper with the return of their affairs to their original state, thanks to the mercy, grace, and power of the God who easily transforms everything (2) to whatever he chooses.[1]

Such we shall find to be the purpose of the material provided us in this case as well.[2] When the country of the Jews was taken, remember, and the people were enslaved and deported to the land of the Persians and Medes after offending by their wrongful apostasy the one who had ever been their protector and champion and had rendered them superior to their adversaries, some who suffered that fate passed an intolerable life of misery caught up in the hardship of captivity. Others, by contrast, who just managed to evade the trap and escape the Babylonians' fe-

---

1. Midway through the entire commentary Cyril summarizes the various roles played by the prophets in history and literature, detailing both prospective and retrospective roles. Page numbers in parentheses refer to Pusey ed., vol. 2.

2. In his systematic and historical manner of proceeding, Cyril identifies the *skopos* of each author and work—within the limits of his perspective, which can confuse kingdoms (north and south), nations, and periods.

rocity, were a prey to unremitting fear and deep suspicion that somehow they might themselves fall foul of equal or even worse troubles if the all-powerful God should hold a grudge against them and fail to allay his anger. They reached such a state of terror as to be scattered in the countries of the neighboring nations and, as it were, to enter the service of others, despite their being foreigners and idolaters. This experience was not without its cost for them: they learned to live by those nations' ways and to pay homage to whatever each of them devised by way of a god. As a result, even Jerusalem itself was in due course burnt down at the hands of Nebuchadnezzar, and the God of all personally bade the survivors not to go down to Egypt, but rather stay at home and keep to their ancestral worship with him as their ally.

Accordingly, in order that the people of Israel might keep hoping to return in due course, and that, instead of living in deep depression, (3) those in captivity might dismiss their despair, keep on praying, and opt for adoration and appeasement of the one able and willing to redeem them, while the residents of Judea might continue to avoid dealing with the countries of the nations, the prophet received the vision directed at Nineveh. It was the chief city of the Assyrians, and he foretold that it would fall when the whole country was overthrown along with it, which happened under Cyrus, son of Cambyses and Mandane, who marshalled Persians, Medes, Elamites, and some other nations along with them against Nineveh. In fact, he took it by force, released Israel from captivity, and bade them return home along with the sacred vessels.

Such, then, is the thrust of the material set before us; what follows we shall expose in detail as far as we can.

COMMENTARY ON NAHUM,
CHAPTER ONE

An oracle for Nineveh. A book of a vision of Nahum of Elkosh (v.1).

E BEGINS BY SPECIFYING the purpose of the prophecy, and helpfully makes precise the focus of his attention. He then makes clear who is speaking and from where he comes, saying it is an *oracle;* that is to say, the prophecy "taken up" and set in our hands has to do with nothing else than *Nineveh*—in other words, let the *oracle* of the prophecy be taken as Nineveh.[1] The book bears the inscription, *an oracle of Nahum of Elkosh,* which is definitely a town somewhere in the country of the Jews; (4) we shall take the phrase *of Elkosh* to refer not to his father but to a place, making this claim on the basis of the tradition of what has been conveyed to us.[2]

A jealous and avenging God is the Lord; the Lord is vengeful in his anger; the Lord takes vengeance on his adversaries and personally disposes of his foes. The Lord is long-suffering; great is his power, and he will certainly not absolve the guilty (vv.2–3). The statement is profound and not easy to grasp except by those willing to give its contents careful study. If, on the one hand, it were taken as directed against the Jews, we would find consolation gently combined with considerable reproof. If, on the other hand, you were to think it was spoken and directed at Nineveh, the sense

---

1. Cyril will meet this term λῆμμα (translated here as "oracle") also at Hab 1.1; Zec 9.1; 12.1; and Mal 1.1, and had read Theodore's unusually lengthy discussion of its suggestion of ecstatic possession (relating the term to λαμβάνειν), which had already appeared in Didymus in opening comment on Zechariah. But like Jerome, who associated such a notion with the Montanists, he skirts such a discussion of modes of prophetic inspiration.

2. Whereas modern scholarship has not located Elkosh, Jerome had been shown such a town in Galilee, but adduced a "Hebrew tradition" that the word is indeed the name of Nahum's father, himself a prophet. Cyril opts for a different tradition.

283

of the interpretation would take a different direction, allowing those in captivity to recover and confirming their hope. As far as possible we shall bring out the drift of the meaning in both cases.

The Jews abandoned the love for God, remember; set no store at all by sincerity of reverence for him; betook themselves to polytheism, outrageous error, and a life in defiance of the Law; erected altars; set up shrines to the works of their own hands; performed rites and sacrifices to Astarte, Chemosh, Baal of Peor, and the golden heifers; and, what was even more irrational than this, they offered to them thanksgiving songs. In their folly, remember, the wretches said, "These are your gods, O Israel, who led you out of the land of Egypt."[3] (5) Yet they were oblivious of the fact that by such terribly unholy actions they were provoking against themselves the God who of old had led and saved them, proving hostile to him and acting the part of enemies, devoting themselves to what were by nature no gods, despite Moses formerly proclaiming of God that he is jealous, like a consuming fire, intolerant of those who choose to offend him. He announced, in fact, "They made me jealous with what is no god, provoking me with their idols; I shall make them jealous with what is no nation, provoking them with a foolish nation."[4] After offending in various ways, therefore, it was right that they also perished.

This is what the prophet says here, too, as if at the same time censuring and consoling the mass of the Jews, who were lamenting what had happened. Yes, he says, in fact, you deplore the desolation that you are unexpectedly suffering and your loss of homes and town and cities and your falling under the feet of the foe, despite having always conquered your adversaries. How then were you not obliged to understand before experiencing it that he is *a jealous and avenging God, the Lord is vengeful in his anger, taking vengeance on his adversaries and personally disposing of his foes*? Even if we were ruined, uprooted, and subject to adversaries, however, he says, we still acted as enemies, waged an unholy war on the all-powerful one, and betook ourselves

3. Ex 32.4.
4. Dt 4.24 and 32.21.

to anything at all that displeased him. But you will reply, *The Lord is long-suffering.* True, I agree: he is like this by nature. But *he will certainly not absolve the guilty;* that is, he will in no way discharge from blame (6) and punishment those who offend him, and this without cessation or restraint. He will, in fact, on the one hand, postpone his wrath out of his inherent clemency, and sometimes bear with people who sin, awaiting their repentance; but when they put it off and delay it at length, he then punishes them and inflicts penalties as on the hard-hearted.

While this is the sense the passage will have for us and while it will be understood if applied to Jews,[5] then, we shall take it differently if referred to Nineveh. Assyrians took the country of the Jews, remember, with God according them victory, doubtless because of the extreme grip of sin on the people of Israel. They were cruel and haughty, with a completely savage mentality, and never ceased doing violence, as it were, to the very glory of God with harsh cries of cursing; they were convinced that they had conquered against his will, and had done violence to the hand assisting the Jews as well as to them. The Rabshakeh, for instance, used ill-omened words in uttering to the people on the wall of Jerusalem only the kind of unholy babbling that belonged to people with no knowledge of the one who is by nature and in truth God;[6] but he immediately paid the price of his arrogance. Still, those in the company of Shalmaneser razed the cities in Samaria and burnt others in addition to them, vented their arrogance on the captives and violated the divine glory.

The prophet therefore comforts the people of the Jews at length in their grief, claiming that (7) the God of all will completely and utterly call to account those making war on them, conveying to them the fact that *God is jealous and the Lord is vengeful in his anger, taking vengeance on his adversaries and personally disposing of his foes. The Lord is long-suffering; great is his power.* After all, with his invincible might he prevails and will overpower those who offend; if he is also *long-suffering* and is seen for a while to hold no grudge, yet eventually *he will not absolve the*

5. Cyril applies the prophecy to Israel after admitting (like his peers) that the text clearly has Nineveh in focus.

6. 2 Kgs 18.28–35.

guilty, being *jealous*. We shall also find the God of all personally moved by what the people of Israel suffered from the cruelty of the Babylonians; he said in the statement of Jeremiah to
the populace or city of the Babylonians, "I gave them into your
hands, whereas you did not show them mercy,"[7] and he also says
in similar terms in the statement of Zechariah, "I am extremely
jealous for Jerusalem and Zion. I am extremely wrathful towards
the nations (296) who have conspired, the reason being that,
while I was slightly wrathful, they conspired with evil intent."[8]

Now, the verse *God is jealous* and the rest would properly apply
also to those not wishing to follow the straight and narrow path
of godliness, but rather to be diverted to a fleshly style of life.
After all, there is no doubt that he *will take vengeance* by inflicting punishment and subjecting to penalties the stubborn and
guilty, especially if it is true that "all of us must appear before the
judgment seat of Christ so that each may receive recompense
for what has been done in the body, whether good or evil."[9] (8)
The passage is no less relevant, however, also to the leaders of
the Jews—I mean the scribes and Pharisees—who rejected faith
in Christ and were guilty of destroying themselves and others.
Their attitude was hostile, in fact, and they took issue with the
Incarnation of the Only-begotten; they "took away the key of
knowledge," as he says himself, not entering themselves or allowing others to enter.[10] If he is also *long-suffering*, therefore, he
still *will certainly not absolve the guilty* who have warred against the
true faith.

*The Lord, his way is in consummation and in earthquake, and
clouds are dust of his feet* (v.3). On the point of predicting the
taking of Nineveh by way of consoling the sufferers and indicating to the wronged that it would be overthrown by God, the
prophet helpfully begins by discoursing on the omnipotence of
the divine nature, and the fact that nothing resists it when it
chooses to achieve anything at all. Rather, everything responds
willingly, and its decisions will prevail, even if to us in our situation some earthly matter may seem difficult to achieve. The Jews

---

7. Not Jeremiah, in fact, but Is 47.6.
8. Zec 1.14–15.   9. 2 Cor 5.10.
10. Lk 11.52.

were convinced, in fact, that the Babylonians would be uncon-
querable and that they enjoyed such invincible power that even
if God willed it, they would not fail before their foes; the cruel
and heartless crimes committed by them throughout their land
encouraged in them, in my view, such a degree of dismay. For
them to realize, therefore, that, when God inflicted his wrath
on them, they would effortlessly fall and be taken (9) without
difficulty, he necessarily says, *The Lord, his way is in consummation
and in earthquake, and clouds are dust of his feet.* In other words,
if that is his plan for some people (the meaning of *way*), it will
definitely take its course like an *earthquake.*[11] Now, a *consummation* and an *earthquake* are something irresistible and quite ineluctable, and in addition to them *clouds* fly up like *dust* and
obscure the sky.

The prophet was probably reminding them of the deluge
that affected the whole human race at the time of Noah; it was
then that God moved also in an *earthquake* against everyone, as it
were, raising *clouds* and, according to the sacred text, releasing
the waterfalls of heaven, and flooding the earth under heaven
with incessant rain.[12] So he is asking, how would the one who
easily prevails over the whole earth and with a single decree destroys everyone in it fail before a single nation, the Babylonian?
In a manner quite befitting God he says, *clouds are dust of his feet:*
just as it is easy for a human being to kick up dust and dirt with a
foot, likewise in my view it is a simple matter for the all-powerful
God to obscure the sky with tempest and clouds.

If, on the other hand, it were necessary to plumb the hidden
meaning of the text, I would think that this should be said: that
in consummation and in earthquake the only-begotten Word of
God took the *way,* or fulfillment, of the Incarnation. When he
became like us, you see, he shook and brought consummation
upon "the rulers, authorities, and (10) cosmic powers of this
present age"[13] by abolishing their oppression of us, canceling
that ancient force, and destroying the very control of death and,
in addition to it, sin. They became *clouds of dust from his feet;* just

---

11. This sentence does not appear in the PG ed.

12. Gn 7.11.

13. Eph 6.12.

as dust is stirred up in front of the walker, so in advance of the Incarnation went the spiritual clouds, that is, the blessed prophets, employing a discourse that was rather obscure and not completely obvious, but bedewing with life-giving pronouncements the mind of those capable of understanding.[14]

Rebuking the sea, drying it up, and exhausting all the rivers (v.4). He develops the expression of the description from what they were familiar with and had experienced, beginning with former events. When God their protector rescued Israel from the Egyptians' unholy behavior and unbearable oppression, remember, he led them through the middle of the sea and bade them walk on dry land, as it were, Scripture saying, "the waters stood up like a wall."[15] So *he rebuked the sea,* and it was a firm track like *dry* land. If, on the other hand, you wanted to connect the previous verses with the meaning of this one, namely, "The Lord, his way is in consummation and in earthquake" (v.3), you would be right to take the following view: the Lord of all, as it were, brought consummation and earthquake upon the land of the Egyptians by the signs worked in it and the death of the firstborn. They perished in a single night, remember, (11) and everything was filled with weeping and wailing, as it said; Israel moved through the middle of the sea, with a cloud from heaven hanging down over them.[16] Blessed David also said something like that, singing in these terms: "God, when you went before your people, when you proceeded through the wilderness, earth shook, and the heavens dripped rain." He says that earth shook—the land of the Egyptians, in my view. Now, the fact that a cloud also hung down and preceded the children of Israel, obvious to everyone, blessed Paul also confirms in saying that all Israel's ancestors were baptized "in the cloud and in the sea."[17]

The prophet continued, *The sea dried up* and *all the rivers were exhausted,* recalling another marvel. When they were brought into the land of promise, remember, under the leadership of Joshua after Moses, then the waters in the area likewise stood

14. Jerome had previously employed the allegory of the clouds as prophets.
15. Ex 15.8.
16. Ex 12.30 and 13.21.
17. Ps 68.8–9; 1 Cor 10.2

still, since the all-powerful God stopped the flow of the streams with unspoken directions and constraints. Blessed David regards this also to be deserving of the highest admiration, speaking in these terms: "Come and see the works of God, how awesome in his plans beyond mortal men. He turned the sea into dry land; they will cross the river on foot," since they crossed the Jordan as well on foot.[18] In case, however, he were also to mean that all rivers dried up when God decreed that what happened in one instance would also happen to all, he bids them stay. (12)

Now, some commentators think that there is also a different sense to be given to the verse. That is to say, if the Lord of all were to decide that an attack should be mounted on Nineveh, it would be done completely by way of *consummation and earthquake;* it would meet its end and easily be shaken. Without delay he would dry it up, extensive though it is, and, as it were, flooding the other nations like a sea; and if the nearby nations burst in like a tempest, he is saying, it would be completely and utterly *exhausted.* On the other hand, our view is that the *sea* and *rivers* that cause floods and inundation are no less the evil and hostile powers, and, before all, Satan. But Christ dried up all their power, once invincible, and put him under the feet of his adherents.

Bashan and Carmel diminished, and all the luxuriance of Lebanon failed. The mountains quaked before him; the hills were shaken; the whole earth heaved in his presence, and all its inhabitants (vv.4–5). The treatment immediately moves by means of other proofs to confirm the strength and invincible power of the divine nature. *Bashan*, you see, is a flourishing and prosperous region, and likewise the mountains of *Carmel* and *Lebanon*, the former in Phoenicia and the latter in Judea, both well wooded and generously endowed with forests. All of it, however—I mean Bashan (13) and the actual district bordering the mountains—was home to terrible and warlike races and "offspring of giants,"[19] according to Scripture; but they were overwhelmed and defeated with God's protection by the people of Israel, who also took possession of their land. So it would be like saying, The

18. Jos 3.16–17; Ps 66.5–6.
19. Dt 1.28 LXX.

countries once teeming with fearsome and warlike men, and luxuriant with warriors like many forests, disappeared and were plundered with the loss of their inhabitants (the sense I think of *diminished*).

How then would the famous Nineveh not be taken? As well as *Bashan* and *Carmel, the luxuriance of Lebanon failed.* While Lebanon, as I said, therefore, is a mountain in Phoenicia, he refers by mention of it to all the country situated beneath it and round about. So he means by *the luxuriance of Lebanon* the rulers of Damascus and Phoenicia at the time, who were also given into the hands of the people of Israel; they were also vanquished at the time, despite having extremely large resources, taking pride in their fearsome and irresistible forces. Now, if you take up the books of Kingdoms,[20] you will find the kingdom of Damascus plundered in due course at the hands of the kings of the tribe of Judah; so *the luxuriance of Lebanon failed*, that is, was done away with and perished many times along with the pick of *Lebanon*, or Phoenicia, that is, the people in charge of things there.

Why mention it, he is saying, when quite easily with God's consent the very *mountains were shaken and the hills* will be moved, and *the whole earth will heave and all its inhabitants*, (14) that is, will pass out of existence and will not be there any more? The one who made it in the beginning, after all, will also do away with it quite easily, and its greatness will come to nothing. Blessed David also seems to have had similar thoughts to this passage in his song, "Why is it, O sea, that you fled, and you, O Jordan, that you turned back? O mountains, that you skipped like rams; O hills, like lambs of the flock? The earth was shaken before the Lord."[21] It is, in fact, what he said before: *his way is in earthquake.* The fact that *the whole earth* is nothing, and what is in it would be accounted of little value by comparison with the ineffable divine glory, the prophet Isaiah will confirm by saying, "Even the nations are like a drop from a bucket, and were accounted as a turn of the scales, and will be accounted as spittle. Lebanon would not be enough for burning and all its animals for a burnt offering; all the nations are like nothing, and were

20. 2 Sm 8.6; 2 Kgs 14.28.
21. Ps 114.5–7.

accounted as nothing. To whom did you liken the Lord, or to what likeness compare him?"[22]

Other people in turn have the view, however, that there are grounds for such sentiments to be taken in indirect reference also to Nineveh itself.[23] They see a comparison to it in *Bashan* as being a fine and celebrated country, and in *Carmel* and *Lebanon* as being conspicuous and prominent mountains. Nineveh was admired and famous, and he says it was so *diminished* as to be well nigh ravaged, along with the *luxuriant* ones in it, that is, its leaders and generals and those more important than the other people. You see, since (15) he had mentioned mountains and wooded regions—namely, *Bashan*—he maintained the figure of speech throughout; by mention of richness and *luxuriance* he referred to those more prominent perhaps through wealth, or more impressive in bodily strength, or in some other way excelling the others.

On the other hand, if you were to focus on the crimes committed by the Jews against Christ, and on the desolation, complete destruction, and ruin inflicted on them after his coming back to life and ascending to heaven, you would be right to apply these things also to them. *Bashan, Carmel,* and indeed *Lebanon* could rightly be taken as Judea—Bashan in being called "a land flowing with milk and honey,"[24] a land of grain and wine and vineyards, Carmel and Lebanon surely on account of being elevated and enjoying a high reputation, being the cynosure of all eyes, and boasting of their inhabitants like innumerable forests. He says it was *diminished*, however, consumed by the Roman might, being felled, as it were, by fearsome and powerful woodchoppers, and toppling like timber. The blessed prophet Isaiah also hints at something similar in saying, as if in reference to Jerusalem, "Open your doors, Lebanon, and let fire consume your cedars. Let the pine lament because the cedar has fallen, because the mighty were in severe difficulties. Lament, oaks of Bashan, because the dense forest has been felled." And else-

---

22. Is 40.15–18.
23. Cyril keeps trying to see the prophet referring to Nineveh (even if often speaking of Assyria as Babylon).
24. Ex 3.8.

where he says more clearly, "The mourning (16) of Jerusalem will be like the mourning for a pomegranate cut down in the open field."[25] You see, since he compares Jerusalem to Lebanon, he speaks of its lofty ones as cedars and pines being toppled, and refers to it as the oak of Bashan, the expression being metaphorical, as I said.

Before his wrath who will stand? And who will resist the wrath of his anger? His anger wastes empires, and rocks are split by him (v.6). He sets the seal of truth on his words with reference to those who have experienced divine *wrath*, saying it is harsh and irresistible. It makes inroads like fire, in fact, in my view, easily *wasting empires* and powers, both earthly and spiritual, and would effortlessly smash even *rocks*, or people as hard as rocks and with a mind resistant to persuasion. We shall find those reigning over the Assyrians to be of this kind, as well indeed as Satan himself, the leader of the unclean spirits, of whom sacred Scripture says, "His heart is fixed like stone, set firm like an untamed thunderbolt."[26] Now, it is obvious to everyone that the leaders of the Jews and those appointed by them to govern—namely, priests and the loathsome bands of unholy scribes and Pharisees—were hard-hearted, unfeeling, and imbued with the deepest insensitivity. They were consumed by the war with the Romans, wasted by unremitting misfortunes like wax, (17) and, though very hard-hearted, they were crushed by the troubles and paid the penalty for their frenzy against Christ.

Now, for our sakes our Lord Jesus Christ in a different way as well crushed "rulers, authorities, cosmic powers of this present darkness, and spiritual forces of evil," so as to rescue and save us. Knowing this, blessed David sings, "You are fearsome, and who will withstand you when once your anger is roused? From heaven you made judgment heard. Earth feared and was still when God arose to judgment, to save all the gentle of the earth." To us he gave "power to walk on snakes and scorpions and on all the power of the foe,"[27] *wasting empires* and crushing like *rocks* the arrogance of the unholy spirits. The wrongdoers

25. Not, in fact, Isaiah, but Zec 11.1–2 and 12.11.
26. Jb 41.15 LXX (in reference rather to Leviathan).
27. Eph 6.12; Ps 76.7–9; Lk 10.19.

had to yield, albeit unwillingly, to the one who was wrathful on our account and for our sake.

The Lord is good to those who submit to him on the day of tribulation, and he knows those who reverence him. In the passage of a flood he will bring about consummation; darkness will pursue the rebellious and his foes (vv.7–8). In a helpful and very skillful way he gives advice, intending neither to undermine the hope of prosperity arising from his promise that *the Lord is good to those who submit to him,* nor to allow them a lax and dissolute life. Rather, his intention is to bring them to orderly behavior and to an option for lawful living through a repetition of the fact that, if he brings the day considered as *consummation* against some people, (18) he will bring it on like a kind of earthquake, and like a rush of mighty and intolerable waters flowing headlong over the country, a terrible and completely ineluctable event. Likewise, if the effect of divine wrath bursts on some people, it will utterly destroy everyone on whom it falls and whom it affects.

He says that his foes will be *pursued* and overwhelmed *by darkness,* not at all that of night, but, in my view, of another kind understood spiritually as a form of suffering. The human mind, of course, is usually plunged into darkness by unremitting misfortune and by severe and unexpected suffering, something that befell the ancients when they were taken off into captivity and their country had been seized. Consequently, God likens such a degree of troubles to wine and intoxication in saying very fittingly to blessed Jeremiah, "Take from my hand this cup of unmixed wine, and make all the nations to whom I send you drink it. They will drink and stagger, and will go out of their minds at the sight of the sword that I am sending among them"; and indeed he says to it in Isaiah, "You have drunk to the dregs the cup of falling, the bowl of anger."[28] So he is saying that those with a hostile attitude to God will be overwhelmed with intoxication and *darkness,* his commendable purpose being to prompt them to consider what is better for them to know and do.

Now, the God of all also moved against the Jews *in the passage of a flood* and *brought about* their *consummation* by calling them

28. Jer 25.15–16; Is 51.17.

to account over Christ. They were also *in darkness*, completely deprived of the divine light, (19) the wretches living as blind dullards. They were not prepared, you see, to follow Christ's call, "While you have the light, walk in the light so that darkness may not overtake you." Instead, since they were unbelieving and obdurate, consequently as the prophet says, "While they were waiting for the light, darkness befell them, and while awaiting brightness they walked in gloom."[29] After all, they were hostile to the divine light, and in an unholy manner they resisted the glory of Christ.

What are you pondering about the Lord? He will cause consummation, and will not take vengeance twice for the same thing through tribulation (v.9). I already said at the very beginning that when Shalmaneser king of the Assyrians plundered Samaria and devastated it along with other cities and towns subject to the rule of Judah, the survivors of the war were reduced to an intolerable plight and took refuge in the countries of the neighboring nations. They probably thought, in fact, that they would fall foul of similar troubles when the Babylonians returned a second time to attack them. So God delivered necessary consolation in the prophet's statement by making this double promise: that he would in due course have mercy on those caught up in the war and experiencing unbearable misfortune and release them from the bonds of captivity, and that he would consign Nineveh to desolation and ruin.

Accordingly, in case they should expect once again to fall foul of similar troubles (20) and find excuse for flight from Judea to the foreigners, he poses the question, so to speak, as to what they were *pondering* and in the habit of thinking about the Lord. Surely, he asks, you do not think that the Lord of all is so harsh and oppressive as to call you to account twice for the same sins? You would seriously fail in what is proper; if you commit nothing further that is at variance with the Law and provokes the Maker of the Law to wrath, he will not deliver chastisement a second time, either. He afflicted you sufficiently for the impiety of which you were guilty. Stop sinning, and he will curtail

29. Jn 12.35; Is 59.9.

his wrath; he has given adequate correction, and will now have mercy on those opting to come to their senses.

The statement is therefore mixed, containing exhortation mingled with it; he thus both encourages them to decide genuinely to perform what is pleasing to God, and to those deciding to do so he gives confidence that he will be kind to them, not releasing unbridled wrath on them, as they themselves supposed. Now, consider how the verse preserves the remnant for Israel: he had proclaimed clearly that God will not bring *consummation* on them, putting the question, *What are you pondering about the Lord? Will he cause consummation?* He will not cause consummation,[30] he says, nor will he deliver Israel to complete destruction after shaking it to its depths. Instead, he will spare it for the sake of the ancestors, and in due course it will be saved, by coming in the wake of the nations (21) through faith in Christ to sanctification and relationship with God through the Son in the Spirit.

They will be demolished from their very foundations, and like a tangled convolvulus it will be eaten, and like a straw quite dried. A plot against the Lord will issue from you, one intending hostile wickedness (vv.10–11). After showing in many ways that the ability to achieve everything comes easily to the God of all, and that nothing at all is beyond him, he shifts attention to Nineveh itself. He says that, even if it reached such a degree of fame as to seem equal to the most wooded of the mountains, namely, Lebanon and Carmel, by being endowed with vast numbers of peoples beyond counting, and even if it was not inferior to Bashan, the time would nevertheless come when it would be left utterly desolate. This, in fact, in my view, is the meaning of *demolished from their very foundations*, the verse preserving the metaphor of mountains and land, trees and wood. Now, he says it will be *eaten* when the Persians and Medes, as it were, graze upon it; they took Nineveh under the generalship of Cyrus. He compares the vast population of the Assyrians to a *convolvulus*, for they inhabited Nineveh. What would be the reasoning behind this, too? The convolvulus is a plant like ivy, constantly crawling upwards

30. The text cited does not correspond to the lemma, and a negative now appears that softens the tone—a liberty the PG text disallows, causing other problems for the sequence of thought.

and releasing tender fronds, and laying hold of plants nearby, with the result that often even the tallest trees are suffocated by it.[31] This is what the Assyrians also did, ever invading countries and cities, suffocating them, as it were, (22) and weighing them down with the entanglements and unbearable oppression of wars. He said it would be set on fire *like a straw quite dried,* straw being something very vulnerable to consumption by fire.

To Nineveh, set on fire, as it were, suffering the effects of wrath, and laid waste, the prophet then explains and clarifies the reason for such sufferings by saying, *A plot against the Lord will issue from you, one intending hostile wickedness.* You will be liable to desolation, he is saying; you will be *demolished,* as it were, and even burnt by fire, for you plotted against God terribly arrogant and *hostile* deeds. The God of all, remember, to punish Israel for sinning, made it vulnerable and brought it under your feet; you will have different ideas, thinking rather of overpowering Judea even against his wishes. We shall find the Rabshakeh guilty of such idle talk in calling God's glory into question in speaking to those seated on the wall: "Do not let Hezekiah deceive you in words that will not be able to deliver you. Do not let Hezekiah tell you that God will deliver Jerusalem from my hand." To such ill-advised and truly unholy babbling God responded in the statement of Isaiah, "Surely the axe will not be given credit apart from the one who chops with it, or the saw extolled apart from one who pulls it?"[32] In other words, just as the axe, even if very sharp and well wrought, would not succeed in cutting down trees unless someone (23) used it on something with his own power, and just as the saw also would be completely ineffectual in its operation with no one to push and pull it, so, too, the might of the Ninevites' kingdom or army would not have gained control of Samaria unless divine wrath had applied it to cities and towns and had used a tool that is worked by someone else and is adopted for useful service, but would be ineffectual by itself. Accordingly, Nineveh is punished assuredly because of *plotting wickedness against God, hostile* to what the nature of things

31. Cyril would have been aware from Jerome that the Heb. "thorns" emerged as *smilax* (convolvulus) in the LXX.

32. Is 36.14–15, 20, and 10.15.

really intends. It was the God of all, in fact, who surrendered Israel for its sin, and it would not have captured them if God had assisted them and still wanted to save them.

The Lord who controls great floods says this: Thus will they be divided, and no report of you will continue to be heard (v.12). While the attention is on haughty Nineveh in its opposition to God, therefore, he says in this verse that the innumerable masses in countries, cities, and nations are *floods* flowing easily like rivers and the sea, as God chooses. He it is, after all, who is their *controller* as Creator, as Lord and God of all, governing by his own decrees what is made by him, and bringing the desires of every heart into accord with his will, (24) dividing and shaping them in the way he wishes. Consequently, he says, O Nineveh, you have now ceased to be fearsome, all-powerful, and celebrated; *no report of you will continue to be heard;* that is, there will now be no lengthy talk of you by everyone. Though formerly you were illustrious, and glowing accounts of you were on everyone's tongue, this is so no longer: they tell a sad tale of you. There is nothing important and worth hearing of you any more.

Now I shall smash his rod, and remove it from you, and break your bonds. The Lord has commanded concerning you (vv.13–14). Again attention is shifted by the prophet to Israel. It is as if to say, Dismissing the memory of those former sins, I shall show pity on you, now that you have paid the penalty; now that you have been sufficiently punished, I shall free you from their oppression, and you will not be subject to the *rod* of the Assyrians, that is, their scepter or kingship, the scepter being a symbol of kingship. I shall also release you from the terrors and bonds of slavery, and restore you again to the prosperity of freedom. The phrase *The Lord has commanded concerning you* you will understand this way: whom has he commanded? Either good spirits and hosts of angels deployed by God for the protection of Israel; or perhaps he *has commanded* the person giving release from captivity in due course, (25) Cyrus son of Cambyses. It was not, however, as though he were addressing a holy man and prophet in *commanding* him, but by imparting to his mind his own wishes and making him a minister of his decrees, despite being profane and idolatrous. Just as he commanded the sea monster to swallow Jonah, remember, and likewise the pumpkin plant to grow up over his head and shade him, and likewise the morning grub to strike the pumpkin plant, so we claim commands were given to Cyrus.

While this has to do with past facts, the God and Father would also proclaim to Jerusalem when it turned to killing the Lord, or to the country of the Jews,[33] "They will be demolished from their very foundations, and like a tangled convolvulus it will be eaten, and like a straw quite dried. A plot against the Lord will issue from you, one intending hostile wickedness" (vv.10–11). It was in fact burnt down and demolished, and consumed like dry straw; they had presumed to plot wickedness against the Lord and to employ unbridled language, at one time calling him a Samaritan, a drunkard, and offspring of prostitution, at another claiming that he misled the crowd.[34] This was in spite of the fact that he had been sent by the God and Father to rid the deceived of deceit, return to God what had taken leave of him, bring back through faith what had in manifold ways slipped into apostasy, enlighten what was in darkness, and bind up the wounded.[35]

Now, since he had not destroyed Israel completely, but, as I have often said, had kept (26) a remnant for him (no small proportion of the Jews having come to faith, and together with the nations confessing Christ), let those of the circumcision of the body give heed to the verse, *I shall smash his rod and remove it from you, and break your bonds. The Lord has commanded concerning you.* Now, there is need to explain what the *rod* is, other than *bonds* of a kind; they were subject to a kind of scepter by being in the grip of the folly and antipathy of the scribes and Pharisees, and were held fast by their commandments as by *bonds* of a kind, and so did not accept the faith. But the *rod* was removed—that is, the control—and the *bonds broken*; they then made their way in freedom of mind to Christ, exultantly crying out, as it were, to one another and saying on the psalmist's lyre, "Let us burst their bonds asunder, and cast their yoke from us."[36]

---

33. Again Cyril reveals his hermeneutical priorities: first a treatment of a passage *historikôs*, then movement to another level—usually to the life of Jesus and/or the church—and even to further spiritual/parenetic development, as later in this case.

34. Jn 8.48, 41; Mt 11.19; Jn 7.12.   35. Ezek 34.16.
36. Ps 2.3.

In addition to them, on the other hand, let those from the nations give no less heed to the verse, *Now I shall smash his rod and remove it from you, and break your bonds. The Lord has commanded concerning you.* Of old, remember, they lay under the yoke of the devil's scepters, were locked in the bonds of worldly pleasures, and worshiped "creation instead of the Creator."[37] They did not know the one who is by nature and in truth God, differing little from brute beasts in their enslavement to pleasures of the flesh, and living a pitiable and most irrational life. But they, too, were liberated when Christ *smashed that rod and broke the bonds*, dragging them away from sin, bringing them from error to knowledge of God, justifying them by faith, and *commanding concerning them*, that is, to the holy angels. (27) Scripture says, remember, "The one who dwells in the help of the Most High will abide in the shelter of the God of heaven"; the holy angels "have been *commanded* to protect us in all our ways and take us in their hands lest we dash our foot against a stone." It is certain that "an angel of the Lord encamps around those who fear him, and will deliver them."[38]

There will be no further dissemination of your name (v.14). It would again be like saying, You will not be scattered to all the nations, either as captive or exile subject to harsh servitude far from your homeland, and in a wretched, pitiable, and miserable condition dispersed among the cities of adversaries. Now, it should be noted that the prophet Nahum lived before the second captivity in Babylon, and after the prophet's preaching Judah was taken and went into captivity, being enslaved to the Assyrians.[39] When Hezekiah was king in Jerusalem, remember, Sennacherib advanced on Samaria, laid waste the cities in it, burnt others, and sent from Lachish the Rabshakeh, who gave vent to abusive words against God; a hundred and eighty-five thousand of the Assyrians were then slain by an angel's hand. After the reign of Heze-

---

37. Rom 1.25.
38. Pss 91.1, 11–12 and 34.7.
39. If Cyril's readers were confused by such a garbled summary of historical events, the following more specific documentation from 2 Kgs 18, 19, and 25 somewhat clarifies it (though perhaps Cyril has in mind the deportation mentioned in 2 Kgs 18.11 of Samaritans by Shalmaneser rather than Sennacherib).

kiah and the lapse of a considerable time, when Zedekiah son of Josiah was king, (28) Nebuchadnezzar besieged Jerusalem, laid waste to the whole of Judea, then took the holy city by force, burnt down even that celebrated Temple, and deported Judah, thus adding to those taken away from Samaria by Sennacherib.

Surely, therefore, the God of all was not false to his promise given through the prophet to the descendants of Israel, *There will be no further dissemination of your name*? How then would it not be foolish, or rather the extremes of every evil, to think that God lies? Perish the thought that the Divinity is dishonest! The truth in fact is as follows: after first mentioning the release that occurred in due course when Cyrus wrested power from the Persians, he then said that Israel would in the future be exile and refugee no longer; they would be restored to their own possessions, would return to Judea, and would dwell in security. Though enemies under Antiochus surnamed Epiphanes advanced against them, they did not go off into captivity, instead dwelling securely in their own land, as I said.

While the verse, therefore, *There will be no further dissemination of your name*, would thus be understood in reference to Israel according to the flesh, the spiritual Israel, on the other hand, that is, those who saw God with the eyes of the mind and were astonished at the glory of the Only-begotten, will very properly be told, *There will be no further dissemination of your name*. Before the faith, in fact, they were under the control of the foe, the neck of their mind subject to the yoke of Satan and the evil spirits with him, and shackled to the evils of fleshly indulgence. (29) But the oppression of those formerly in power was then undone; sin was toppled, and along with them it fell, and the force of the passions was eliminated. Christ undermined it, in fact, and brought them through faith to holiness, despite their being dissipated by effete passions of various kinds and grievous polytheism. They will no longer be scattered abroad, however, but will abide completely in Christ, having one faith, one baptism, one Lord, Savior, and Redeemer, and being linked through him to the God and Father in spiritual oneness.[40]

---

40. Eph 4.5.

From the house of your God I shall eliminate carved figures, and cast images I shall make your tomb (v.14). Israel, for its part, had offended gravely, fallen into apostasy, and sacrilegiously forsaken the God who saved them; consequently, they were taken captive and went off to the enemy, and were thus deported to Nineveh. The survivors in Jerusalem, for their part, were no less indifferent towards love for God, inconsistent in their reverence, neglectful of what was pleasing to God, and uncommitted to the yoke of service to him; they kept sacrificing to Baal, Astarte, and the host of heaven. When threats were delivered by the holy prophets, however, God clearly saying that Jerusalem would be destroyed and its inhabitants would go off completely and utterly as captives along with the others, (30) some of those reigning in it at the time came to their senses and destroyed shrines, overturned altars, and consumed the carved figures by fire.

Of particular prominence in this was Josiah, of whom the man of God spoke to Jeroboam son of Nebat, [Jeroboam] who caused Israel to sin, when he was on one occasion sacrificing; he was standing by the golden heifers offering sacrifice when the man proclaimed against the altar by the word of the Lord, "O altar, altar, thus says the Lord: Lo, a son is born to the house of David, Josiah by name, and he will sacrifice on you the priests of the high places offering sacrifice on you, and human bones will be burnt on you."[41] The sacred text clearly confirms that what was foretold took effect; in the second book of Kings it is written thus about Josiah: "The king commanded the high priest Hilkiah, the priests of the second order, and the guardians of the balance to bring out of the house of the Lord all the vessels made for Baal, the grove, and all the host of heaven. He burnt them outside Jerusalem in Sademoth Kedron, took their ashes to Bethel, and burnt the *chomarim* that the kings of Judah had appointed; they had burnt incense in the high places, in the cities of Judah, and in the environs of Jerusalem, and had burnt incense to Baal and to the grove, to the sun and the moon, to the *mazouroth* and to all the host of heaven. The grove from the house of the Lord he brought outside Jerusalem to the brook

41. 1 Kgs 13.2.

Kedron, and burnt (31) them in the brook Kedron, pulverized them, and threw their dust onto the grave of the common
people."[42] Do you understand, then, how the *cast images* were
placed like a kind of *tomb, and the carved figures were eliminated
from the house of the Lord*?

Another text will also confirm the verse bearing on this; in
the second book of Chronicles it says, "In the eighth year of his
reign"—Josiah's, that is—"while he was still a boy, he began to
seek the God of his ancestor David. In the twelfth year of his
reign he began to purge Judah and Jerusalem of the high places, the groves, and the cast figures; in his presence they overthrew the altars of Baal and the high places dedicated to them,
chopped down the groves and the carved figures, smashed the
cast figures, pulverized them, and scattered the dust on the front
of the tombs of those sacrificing to them. He burned the bones
of priests on the altars, and purged Judah and Jerusalem."[43] So
they perished in the actual shrines, as I said, and on the altars,
and were buried, as it were, with the cast images, in keeping with
the prophet's statement. Now, it should be understood that Nahum prophesied at the time of Hezekiah. Then came Hezekiah's son Manasseh, who ruled for fifty-five years, and Manasseh's
son was Amos, who lived only two years, and after him Josiah, in
whose reign the prophecy was fulfilled, as the text has just been
explained by us.[44] (32)

*Because, lo, swift on the mountains are the feet of the one bringing
good news and announcing peace* (v.15). Though the people of Israel were living in Babylon after being taken captive, they still
nourished the hope of being brought back again one day, and
before long of returning to the noble station received from their
ancestors before, since the holy prophets announced this at
God's direction. Now, the realization of their hope had arrived

42. 2 Kgs 23.4–6.
43. 2 Chr 34.3–5.
44. The Antiochenes, despite their interest in historical fact, provide none
of this textual documentation bearing on the prevalence of idol worship and
Josiah's expulsion of it. This is perhaps because, as Cyril himself states, Nahum's
ministry occurs in the century before Josiah. Undeterred, Cyril provides not
only one version of Josiah's reform; to the one from 2 Kings he couples the
2 Chronicles version.

with the imminence of the wresting of power from Nineveh by Cyrus's reign, and prediction of it to them in turn by Isaiah. He said, in fact, "Thus says the Lord God to my anointed Cyrus, whose right hand I have grasped for nations to be obedient before him: I shall strip kings of power, I shall open doors to him, and cities will not remain locked. I shall go ahead of you, level mountains, smash bronze doors, and shatter iron bars." And a little further on, "He will rebuild the city of Jerusalem and cancel the captivity of my people, not with ransom or with bribes, said the Lord of hosts."[45] So a messenger of *peace* will come to the people of Israel, he is saying in reference to the expedition of Cyrus, when they shook off the yoke of captivity, smashed the rod of those in power, broke the bonds of the slavery to which they were not accustomed, and were saved by arrival home once more.

If, on the other hand, you preferred to apply the drift of the passage to the preaching of the holy Baptist, you would be right to make this application as well. After all, he led his life in the wilderness, and *brought the good news of peace*—Christ, that is—by crying aloud *on the mountains*. Beautiful and *swift*, then, are *the feet* of the one who says, "Prepare the way of the Lord; make straight the paths of our God."[46]

Celebrate the festivals, Judah; pay your vows to your God. Because they will not continue to consign you to oblivion any more (v.15). The Law forbade the offering of sacrifice outside the sacred and divine precincts; instead, it should be "in the place which the Lord your God has chosen to be called by his name."[47] When the people of Israel were in foreign parts, however, and living in the land of the Persians and Medes, they lived without any possibility of discharging what was required of themselves, unable to perform the customary *festivals*, to offer sacrifices, first-fruits, or thanksgiving offerings according to the Law, or to slaughter

---

45. Is 45.1–2, 13. His citation of Second Isaiah's mention of Cyrus's saving role means that Cyril is not only confusing the Babylonian and Assyrian deportations of southern and northern peoples, but also assumes that this biblical text originates from Isaiah of Jerusalem.

46. Is 52.7; 40.3.

47. Dt 12.11.

the lamb on the new moon, and perhaps neglectful even of mere hymns of praise. We would say what the divinely inspired David says in the person of the people in Babylon: "By the river of Babylon we sat and wept when we remembered Zion. On the willows in its midst we hung up our instruments." And further on, "How shall we sing the song of the Lord in a foreign land?"[48] Since they were outside the Holy Land, remember, outside Temple and tabernacle, and had no sacred place, the requirements of the Law were consequently impracticable for them. But when the time for release eventuated, however, (34) someone—the messenger of peace, who had swift feet, or the prophet himself—rightly pointed out that they could celebrate the *festivals*, offer songs of thanksgiving, and properly fulfill the obligations of vows or promises. He also foretold that ruin would soon befall the foe: *they will not continue to consign you to oblivion;* that is, they will not last much longer, nor have extended or unending prosperity, for it would come to an end and on being curtailed would cease.

Now, let the one who is spiritually a Jew most fittingly give heed to these remarks. "For a person is not a Jew who is one outwardly, nor is true circumcision something external and physical. Rather, a person is a Jew who is one inwardly, and real circumcision is a matter of the heart—it is spiritual and not literal. Such a person receives praise not from others but from God."[49] Such a person will *celebrate* with distinction, then, having an unshaken faith—in Christ, that is—sanctified by the Spirit, and distinguished by the grace of adoption. He will offer spiritual sacrifices to God, presenting himself as an odor of sweetness, and devoting himself to every form of virtue—moderation, self-control, fortitude, patience, love, hope, a longing for poverty, goodness, long-suffering—"since God takes pleasure in sacrifices like that."[50] Let the person who is spiritually a Jew know this about every foe and those once in power: that *they will not continue to consign you to oblivion any more;* that is, they will be taken out and dispatched—to punishment, clearly. This is

48. Ps 137.1–2, 4.   49. Rom 2.28–29.
50. Heb 13.16.

also what Christ has effected, bidding the unclean spirits (35) to go off to the abyss, and allowing those who love him to rise up against the foe, do battle with the passions, struggle against sin, and "trample on snakes and scorpions and on all the power of the foe."[51]

51. Lk 8.31–33 and 10.19.

COMMENTARY ON NAHUM,
CHAPTER TWO

It is finished; it is gone. One has come up blowing in your face, rescuing you from tribulation (v.1).

O SUGGEST IN A COMPRESSED FASHION that the necessary destruction of Nineveh would without any doubt happen, he says that *it is finished*, thus indicating the wish for its consummation. He also says *it is gone*, that is, completely felled and utterly done away with.[1] Now, the phrase *one has come up* also applies perfectly to Cyrus, in my view clearly implying something of the kind that the prophet Jeremiah also said of him in foretelling what would in due course befall Nineveh: "A lion has come up from its lair; it has arisen to destroy nations; it has gone out from its place to make your land a waste; your cities will be left desolate with no one inhabiting them"; he sprang on Nineveh like a savage lion and devoured those in it.[2] While he was like a terrible and untamed enemy to them, however, and showed implacable rage, to the people of Israel, on the other hand, he *blew in their face, rescuing them from tribulation*, that is, freeing them from the unaccustomed slavery, releasing them from bonds, and rehabilitating them when they were captives by (36) sending them home and ordering them to rebuild the divine Temple.

Now, the phrase *blowing in the face* he cites on the basis of Jewish tradition and custom. We sometimes find mention of such things occurring also in the inspired Scriptures, like the Jews thinking they had to tear their garments in the case of blasphemy against God; Caiaphas, for instance, tore his clothing when Christ called himself Son of God, crying aloud, "He has

---

1. Cyril passes quickly over these phrases, which are appendages to the final verse of 1.15 (in the Heb. 2.1).
2. Jer 4.7, a passage which Cyril applies to Cyrus.

blasphemed." The divinely inspired disciples Paul and Barnabas both did this, too, when they were in Lycaonia. When they rid one of the sufferers of his ailment to the amazement of the on-lookers, the eyewitnesses of the divine marvel were bent on sac-rificing to them, "saying, The gods have come to us in human form, calling Barnabas Zeus and Paul Hermes because he was the chief speaker."[3] Since their action was a kind of blasphemy, however, they tore their garments, still following Jewish tradi-tions and unwritten customs. But the custom has been repudi-ated, being completely pointless and not according to law. The God of all, for instance, said to the Jews when they behaved that way and departed grievously from the true religion, "Turn back to me with all your heart, with fasting, with weeping, and with lamenting; rend your hearts and not your garments."[4] So just as it was the custom for some people to rend their (37) clothing, so too was *blowing in the face* of people who were in some way ail-ing. This was the quite wrongful practice of those in particular who were given to taking oaths even with idle incantations, pre-tending to rid sufferers of spirits and ailments. Hence the ex-ample is cited from what was customary with them in the words, *One has come up blowing in your face*—namely, Cyrus—*rescuing you from tribulation*; some people pretend to be able to effect this, as I said, by blowing on others.

Now, it is a wise and truthful statement that the power of the devil and of sin's tyranny over us has been checked; death has, as it were, been taken captive, and corruption completely done away with. Christ, in fact, has *come up* from Hades and returned to life, *blowing in the face* of the holy apostles and saying, "Receive the Holy Spirit."[5] We have thus become free of every trouble, sharers in the Holy Spirit, restored to nature's former beauty, and spiritually stamped with the original image,[6] for our Lord Jesus Christ has taken shape in us through the Spirit.

Keep watch on the road, gird your loins, summon your strength to the utmost, because the Lord has turned aside the abuse of Jacob, like the abuse of Israel (vv.1–2). As though speaking to people on their way to Judea and due to reach home, he necessarily states the

3. Mt 26.65; Acts 14.11–12.   4. Jl 2.12–13.
5. Jn 20.22.   6. Gn 1.26.

need now to have an eye to *the road* and *gird their loins*, that is, (38) to be equipped and ready for the hardship of traveling, to overcome all lethargy, and to prove superior to long delays by applying irrepressible enthusiasm. Having one's *loins girt* and, so to speak, decent is a sign of readiness; our Lord Jesus Christ, for instance, says to the holy apostles, or rather also to all who believe in him, "Take your place with loins girt."[7] It is in fact the right and proper way to travel for those preaching the divine Gospel and being ready to proceed in that direction. He therefore says, *gird your loins*, meaning, "be ready and equipped for departure," for *the Lord has turned aside the abuse of Jacob, like the abuse of Israel.*

Note once again the distinction necessarily drawn here: by *Jacob* he refers to the inhabitants of Samaria, that is, the ten tribes ruled over by kings from the tribe of Ephraim and Manasseh, descendants of Joseph, who was son of Jacob, whereas by *Israel* he refers to those in Jerusalem, namely, Judah and Benjamin. Since at the devastation of Samaria by Sennacherib Jerusalem was not captured, thanks to God's protecting them and destroying the Assyrian by the hand of an angel, and since Cyrus released not only the captives from Samaria deported to Nineveh but also those from Jerusalem as a result of Nebuchadnezzar's capture of the country, the prophet consequently says, *because* (39) *the Lord has turned aside the abuse of Jacob, like the abuse of Israel*, meaning by *abuse* enslavement or service.[8] Now, the fact that God will release everyone, not protecting some and leaving others to be consumed by hardship, he conveys by saying, *he has turned aside the abuse of Jacob* as that of *Israel* will be turned aside; all returned to Judea, as we said, escaping from the toll taken by captivity.

Now, in my view there is also a very urgent need for those redeemed by Christ to be wanting no longer to live a heedless life; rather, they should be attentive to following the straight and

---

7. Lk 12.35.
8. Cyril's insecure grasp of distinctions between northern and southern kingdoms and between Assyria and Babylon (not true of Jerome or the Antiochenes) has the consequent effect of an insecure notion of Nahum's prophetic ministry in the north in the eighth century bearing on the fate of Nineveh.

narrow path of a way of life pleasing to God, and *gird their loins*, that is, rise above bodily indulgence and pleasure and "make no provision for the flesh to gratify its desires,"[9] and prevail over passions and all lethargy. This is the way, in fact, they will come to the holy city, the heavenly Jerusalem, and there offer God spiritual sacrifices, having shaken off the yoke of the former servitude, and they will live a glorious and free life that is rid of all depravity.

Because they shook them and their branches violently. They destroyed weapons of their power from human beings, strong men disporting themselves in fire. The reins of their chariots on the day of his preparation, and the horses will be alarmed in the roads; the chariots will be confused and will collide in the streets; their appearance is like fiery torches, and they flash by like lightning (vv.2–4). Since it was the omniscient God (40) who made future events resound in the holy prophets, they necessarily foretold them as he wished. Often it came to them in actual visions of the events. Consequently, they were startled to see them occurring before their own eyes, as it were, and they delivered a prophecy of them. Something of this kind the prophet now seems to have experienced in the case of the inhabitants of Nineveh and the comrades of Cyrus: that they even *shook them and their branches violently*, and the prophecy was delivered as though by accident to the vines: the bunch is *shaken* and drops its grapes, either because a wild gale blows, or burning heat flares up, or some other damage so befalls it that even the *branch* itself along with its fruit proves to be divested even of its foliage. This was the way they *shook* them like vines. But their *weapons* were also *destroyed*, that is, their *power*, "weapons" sometimes meaning "power."[10] He says that the cavalry, fearsome though they are and skilled in fighting in *chariots*, were affected by such terrors as to be put to flight, colliding with one another, shattered and broken, and convinced that the enemy columns were advancing at such a rate as to be comparable to *torches*, and in their rapid and unbridled course burning them *like lightning*.

9. Rom 13.14.
10. Cyril does not comment on the phrase in his text "from human beings," which the LXX has mistakenly seen in the Heb. "is red" (a solecism not noted by Jerome).

Their champions will remember, will flee days (41), *and will faint in the way; they will hasten to the walls and prepare their lookouts* (v.5). With the war pressing on their strongest men along with the others, they will take thought, he says, of what they did in seizing Judea, or what they wrongfully said in giving vent to blasphemous remarks when the wretches, as it were, assailed the glory of God with their own babbling. Then, when they are brought to a recollection of these events, they will know at that time that God is ill-disposed to them and brings them down under the feet of the enemy, fearsome though they once were and very difficult to repel for those they were bent on attacking. Once they are put to flight, however, they would find escape beyond them, and, *fainting in the way,* they would have recourse to other plans; they would concentrate on the *walls* and set *lookouts* on them. Now, in this he shows them completely at a loss, with no knowledge of what to do, doubtless because of a clouding of their judgment as if under the influence of unmitigated misfortunes like a kind of wine, quite distraught and bewailing the loss of security, easily swinging from one extreme to the other, and wasting their efforts on both. His statement *They will flee days* has this meaning in my view: though fearsome, as I said, invincible, and fierce, they will then be reduced to such depths of fear as to make a clear decision to flee, and to do so without disguising it, despite once (42) avoiding the slightest suspicion of being charged with this.

Now, the evil powers have also been vanquished by the majesty of Christ; incapable of resisting his divine decrees—the ones clearly having to do with us, I mean—they were shattered by fear and really took to flight, finding salvation in no source of security. After all, if God were to inflict penalties, who could escape? Or what recourse would be of benefit to the offenders?

Gates of the cities were opened, the palace fell, and its contents were revealed. She went up, and her maidservants were led away like doves muttering in their hearts (vv.6–7). While the mighty ones, he is saying, then, will find flight impractical and *will hasten to the walls and prepare their* watchmen, their keeping guard will be useless for them, since it is God who *opens the gates of the cities* to the adversaries, surrenders *the palace*—that is, the residence of the kings—*reveals* what is hidden in it, and exposes its *contents* for robbery (by *contents* referring obviously to wealth amassed by robbery and oppression of other people). He next sees, as though likewise occurring in a vision of what would happen, taken off into captivity the queen city (Nineveh, that is) and those under her and around her, which he calls *maidservants,* doubtless because they are yoked and subjected to her service. He says that they were *like doves muttering in their hearts*, not openly, that is, but furtively; the bird normally bemoans anything sad and depressing in its heart. It is not improbable that something like this happens to those who fall into the hands of the enemy and are then dragged off into captivity; they bewail their misfortune, stifling their laments, as it were, within themselves, since sometimes they are not allowed even to weep.

Regarding Nineveh, her waters are like waters of a pool, and the fugitives did not stop, and there was no one to look on. They plundered the silver, they plundered the gold, and there was no end to her finery; they were weighed down with all her desirable possessions (vv.8–9). He compares Nineveh to a *pool* full to overflowing, doubtless because of the vast number of her inhabitants and the innumerable races flooding to her assistance. He is, as it were, astonished at the *fugitives,* or rather he mocks them, for being reduced to fear despite being numerous beyond counting, and though formerly confident of winning any war by reason of their copious forces, and taking great pride in themselves. It was the God of all, however, who depressed their minds with fear, made them faint-hearted, and undermined (44) their prowess in battle. The saying is true, "A king is not saved by his large force, nor will a giant be saved by the immensity of his strength";[11] rather, the Lord of all quite easily saves those he wishes. What does the prophet say next? *They plundered the silver, they plundered the gold*—the meaning of "contents" (v.6)—*and there was no end to her finery*. By this he probably refers to the precious stones of the Indies with which he says she was *weighed down*, although she was depressed also by other *possessions;* the Assyrians, or Ninevites, in fact, were in the habit of earnestly making a vast col-

11. Ps 33.16.

lection of precious stones and being so lavishly adorned as to
strive even in battle to appear conspicuous for their splendor
of ornamentation. Now, in this the prophet proceeds concisely
and systematically, mentioning at one time those being felled,
at another their colliding with one another, being at a loss to
flee, mounting watchmen to no purpose, while at another time
he depicts in word those being plundered, underplaying the
grieving of those in captivity, skillfully beguiling them with the
prophecy of such events, and bringing them to a sense of satisfaction through the attractive descriptions.

Now, Satan was also *plundered*, first by Christ the Savior, then
after him by the holy apostles, of whom the prophet Jeremiah
somewhere said, "Because suddenly they will arise and bite him,
and your schemers will be on the alert, and you will be their
plunder."[12] In his Gospel teachings Christ also introduced the
account in the form of a parable, as it were: "Or how can one
enter a strong man's house and plunder his possessions (45)
without first tying up the strong man and then plundering his
possessions?"[13] Those worshiping Satan, in fact, are his chosen
possessions, and precious to him, and they make their approach
to the faith when Christ the Savior of us all leads them instead to
reverence for God, and the holy apostles also persuade them to
move in that direction.

Shaking, reshaking, quaking, panic at heart, looseness of knees,
pains in all the loins, and everyone's faces like a hot pan (v.10). He
says it will be crushed with every kind of crushing. After all,
what else does *shaking, reshaking,* and also *quaking* imply to us
than that? What is shaken and reshaken is in fact completely
torn apart. The consequence will be, he says, *panic at heart,* obviously when God instills the panic leading to fear, and *looseness*
of knees, that is, bodily weakness and lethargy, and as well *pains,*
namely, those that arise from nausea. I mean, how were they
not destined to feel such awful troubles after being embroiled
in everything likely to offend God? He insists that, in addition,
everyone's faces will be *like a hot pan;* the faces of depressed people

---

12. Not Jeremiah, but Hab 2.7.
13. Mt 12.29.

generally darken, and the onset of dread has the dreadful effect of robbing the eyes of brightness.

Now, we are right to claim that such things happened also to Satan himself, who was (46) guilty of oppressive rule over us, and to the evil powers with him. After all, since they had forfeited their former eminence and glory, how would it not be fair that they should completely and utterly suffer such a fate?

Where is the lions' den, and the pasture meant for the cubs? The place where the lion went to gain entry, a lion's cub, with no one to inspire fear. A lion caught enough for his cubs, and throttled his catch for his lions. He filled his lair with prey, and his den with his catch (vv.11–12). By *lions' den* he refers to Nineveh; those who dwelt there and constructed a splendid and marvelous residence and a secure palace included its rulers at various times—Pul, Shalmaneser, Sennacherib, and also Nebuchadnezzar—the ones who made war on Judea. In my view the word *Where* does not suggest a questioner—I think we should avoid such a fatuous idea—but rather someone mocking and by this means highlighting the fact that it was so completely destroyed that no trace of it remained; "it is finished; it is gone," as he himself says.[14] So he asks, *Where is the lions' den*, namely, Nineveh? And where *the pasture meant for the cubs?* While by *cubs*, in my view, he means those acting in submission to the mighty king and owing their position to him, namely, satraps and generals, he uses the word *pasture* of those in their power and control (47) who contribute taxes and make a collection of money; as Scripture says, "The poor are the pasture of the rich."[15] With Nineveh completely *gone*, then, as well as the whole surrounding country, he asks, *Where is the lions' lair, and where the pasture meant for the cubs?* The fact that Nineveh was once, as it were, a secure base of the former kings he brings out by saying, *The place where the lion went to gain entry, a lion's cub, with no one to inspire fear;* the city wall, strongly constructed with a magnificence beyond telling, was impregnable. But after Nebuchadnezzar laid waste to Samaria, and even Judea and the holy city—namely, Jerusalem—and deported the children of Israel

14. 2.1.
15. Sir 13.19.

to his own city, he disposed of the captives under his authority in such a way as to keep some in bonds under his control and bestow others upon other people and sell them, thus keeping his own country and city full of prisoners. Consequently, he says, *A lion caught enough for his cubs, and throttled his catch for his lions. He filled his lair with prey, and his den with his catch.*

Once again the description is developed in keeping with what normally happens: when wild animals catch what simply comes their way, they consume what they need and nourish their cubs with the remainder, making their effort worthwhile. Once again, too, such events could be applied as well to Satan in person when Christ exterminates him and his, and removes his prey from the earth. He smashed the lions' (48) teeth, remember, as the psalmist puts it, "The Lord broke the tooth of the lions."[16]

See, I am against you, says the Lord almighty, and I shall burn your hordes in smoke, consume your lions with a sword, and exterminate your prey from the land, and your works will not be heard of again (v.13). God sets himself in opposition and in his own right takes the role of adversary, impelling them to despair of salvation; after all, when God is bent on bringing trouble, who will save us from it, or who will divert the Lord of hosts from his decision to cause destruction? As Scripture says, "Who will divert his uplifted hand?"[17] He says that he will *burn her hordes in smoke*, for us to understand again what such an event is like. When beekeepers want to extricate the honeycombs from the hives, they kindle a fire and drive out the bees with smoke lest they offer opposition and sting them when flying about in droves. Something similar happened also to those summoned to aid Nineveh in its crisis; they took to flight and sped off as though the smoke of battle were propelling them, frightening them into faintheartedness and instilling unbearable terror into them. By *lions* he refers to the strong and bold warriors, who had confidence to resist; but they fell to the sword of Cyrus. Since the expression made mention to us of *lions*, he consequently says that he would *exterminate their prey*, the result being that in the future there would be

16. Ps 58.6, the PG ed. omitting the final clause.
17. Is 14.27.

nothing (49) worth hearing of them. It was customary for them, you see, to fall upon cities and countries and, like wild beasts, to savage anyone they wished and to commit so many countless crimes that the misfortune of the victims was the stuff of songs and laments for many people. So he says that they *exterminated their prey*; what likelihood was there, in fact, of their continuing to prey on people when the herds had been startled and taken to flight, as it were, because of *smoke*, and the warriors who used to fall on their adversaries like *lions* had been cut down?

COMMENTARY ON NAHUM,
CHAPTER THREE

O city of blood, completely false, full of iniquity (v.1).

E GAVE IT THE NAME *city of blood*; those who reigned over Nineveh were bloodthirsty and disposed to murder, while on a different note its inhabitants were warlike, ever on the alert to conduct wild sorties against whomever they met. He says it was *false* because awash with idols, whose utter falsity could not be gainsaid; its handmade gods, falsely named, stole glory from the Divinity, (50) being only "silver and gold, works of human hands," as Scripture says. Jeremiah in his wisdom somewhere calls it "a land of statues."[1] In another way as well, it could be understood to be *false*, the falsity being taken to refer to knavery, scheming, and deceit that is hated by God, obviously because accompanying *iniquity*. After all, where there are deceit and scheming, there follows without question iniquitous behavior as well.

Now, Jerusalem, killer of the Lord, was also *city of blood, completely false, full of iniquity*; we recall Christ's words, "Jerusalem, Jerusalem, who kills the prophets and stones those sent to her." He also said somewhere in the statement of the prophets, "Woe to them, because they have strayed from me. They are in a wretched state for their impious behavior to me. I redeemed them, but they told lies against me."[2] They impugned the glory of Christ, in fact, once by saying that it was through Beelzebul that he expelled the demons, at another time by calling him a drunkard as well as a Samaritan, and other vile things.[3] In fact,

1. Ps 115.4; Jer 50.38. The fact that Jeremiah is speaking of Babylon would not register with Cyril.
2. Mt 23.37; Hos 7.13.
3. Mt 12.24 and 11.19; Jn 8.48.

only their slanderous speech would be capable of the things they presumed to say.

Prey will not be taken in advance. Sound of whips, sound of rumbling wheels, pursuing horses, hurtling chariots, charging horsemen, flashing swords, gleaming weapons, numbers of wounded, heavy casualties. There was no respite for its nations; they will be weak in their bodies from the great degree of prostitution (vv.2–3). Again the treatment (51) is developed on the basis of what normally happens. Bird catchers, you see, envelop the densely compact bushes with nets, and in many cases catch those hidden under them by laying hold of them—no mean feat. He says that *prey will not be taken in advance* by them; in other words, some would not hunt as in the past, seizing others' possessions for themselves, nor would there be a snare and trap for the weaker ones, since a different concern occupied them and a struggle for the ultimate hung over them with the *sound of whips* being heard there.

I have the impression that once again the prophet describes clearly the tumult arising from war, as though before his eyes. He observes, for example, how the city rings to the sound of horses and is struck with the wheels of chariots, men in gleaming battle armor plundering it, the wreckers beyond counting, and its houses shaken down (he mentions *heavy casualties*, note). He is aghast at the fact that a vast number of nations are assembled in it, many faint-hearted, stricken with culpable weakness and a prey to deep fear. Immediately he supplies the reason, that *they will be weak in their bodies from the great degree of prostitution*; depraved and vicious in their habits, idolaters to boot, and wrongfully disposed to error, consequently they will duly be weak and timid, unable even to give a thought to resistance. (52)

Prostitute charming and graceful, leader of sorceries, she who sells the nations with her prostitution, and tribes with her sorceries (v.4). Commendation of vile acts highlights their criminality, as if to say, for example, a skillful thief, a brave brigand, a clever sorcerer. If, therefore, you were to say of Nineveh *charming and graceful*, it would not so much be a compliment—far from it; instead, you would render the satire more damning. Courtesans, after all, seem to be giving attention to charm especially when they have the appearance of being talkative and garrulous. Nineveh was also like that, expert in evildoing, not lacking resources for taking cities and countries, and seeming to be fond of convincing them to adopt her own way of thinking, namely, quackery, false prophecy, profane rites, and idols' ruses. It descended to such depths of frivolity, in fact, as to want to be *leader of sorceries* and to consider it a mark of distinction, and to boast of such vile and reprehensible deeds.

Now, it was the custom of some of its inhabitants to *sell nations* and countries for their *sorceries;* how so, we shall explain as far as possible. When the Assyrians wanted to go to war and take up arms against others, they were customarily anxious to learn the future in advance by means of the arts of soothsayers; to gain the good graces of the king, these men bade him embark on any war, and falsely promised him that he would prevail over the opposition by his own efforts. That was the kind of thing (53) that Balak king of the Moabites wanted to do; he hired the wretched Balaam and took him up a mountain with the instructions, "Come now, curse Israel for me."[4] They were convinced, in fact, that the events would correspond to the soothsayers' curses. By *prostitution,* therefore, he refers here to the quackery and the art of soothsayers by means of which the experts in these matters *sold nations and tribes* by consistently promising power to those who paid them.

Lo, I am against you, says the Lord God almighty. I shall uncover your rear to your face, and show nations your shame and kingdoms your dishonor. I shall cast loathing upon you in your uncleanness, and make an example of you (vv.5–6). Again he indicates that neither the complaint nor the war was with human beings; rather, the Lord of hosts was angry with her, and roused Persians and Medes against her. Now, who can resist the all-powerful God, who has control of everything, if he chooses to make war on someone? He next says, *I shall uncover your rear to your face.* The remark once again was made as though in reference to a courtesan, who to onlookers seems to be attractive as far as face and external charm goes, but if she undergoes disrobing and removal of adornments, she is quite ugly in her nakedness, displaying the

4. Nm 23.7.

ugliness of her limbs quite openly. He therefore says, (54) *I shall uncover your rear;* that is to say, everything about you is unsightly, and I shall make an example of you in front of everyone. After all, what else would *to your face* suggest to us other than that? Now, he promised to *uncover her dishonor* no less openly than *to nations and to kingdoms.* On the one hand, Nineveh seemed somewhat charming and desirable when puffed up with the artistry of the soothsayers, very strong, invincible, and overwhelming compared with anyone else. When captured and fallen, on the other hand, she was shown to be ugly and vile to those who knew her, who now considered her abominable and completely condemned her for groundless boasting and idle trust in the support of soothsayers—or, rather, their quackery and deceit. He confirmed that he would *make an example of* her, as if some people were to say, if a city or country were destroyed, plundered, and fallen, "like poor Nineveh."

Now, the God of all, as I said, has made war at times also on the synagogue of the Jews, and exacted penalties for its impiety against Christ, showing her naked, unattractive, and completely divested of clothing from above. He foretold this also in the saying of Hosea, "Hence I shall have a change of heart and take away my grain in its time and my wine in its season, and I shall take away my garments and my linen from concealing her shame. I shall now uncover her uncleanness in the sight of her lovers, and no one will rescue her from my hand." In other words, while the church of the nations will give praise in the words, (55) "Let my soul rejoice in the Lord, for he clothed me with the garment of salvation and the tunic of happiness,"[5] she by contrast is now found to be naked, unattractive, and ugly, as I said, not having the clothing of the divine graces, instead being *an example* and loathsome figure, suffering every form of worldly *uncleanness.*

All who see you will shrink from you and say, Poor Nineveh, who will groan over her? Where shall I seek consolation for her? (v.7) If anyone with previous knowledge of her influence were to see her fallen and desolate, he is saying, this one would grieve deeply

5. Hos 2.9–10; Is 61.10.

and shrink back in horror, saying, *Who will groan over her?* He says this as though there were no one, or no survivor, capable even of contemplating it. In his great wisdom he adds to this the question, *Where shall I seek consolation for her?* The meaning of the statements is something like this: when warfare and fighting combine to affect cities and regions, sometimes part of them suffers harm while part is spared and escapes the victors, which is *consolation* for the inhabitants. Not all is burnt; part remains unplundered, or the majority are saved when some have fallen. But in the case of Nineveh, *where* could anyone find *consolation?* Or what form of comfort will she enjoy? She has in fact been totally captured and totally plundered, and everyone in her has been lost. The clause *Who will groan over her?* could, on the other hand, be taken differently, as if to say, Is there any artist so skilled at dirges and funereal songs as to say something appropriate to the events and shed tears to match the sufferings?

Prepare a part, fit a cord, prepare a part of Ammon, who (56) *is positioned on rivers, with water all about her, the sea her rule and water her walls. Ethiopia was her strength, Egypt too, with no limit to your flight, and the Libyans were her helpers. She will be deported as a captive, and they will dash her infants to the ground at the head of all her streets; they will cast lots for all her prize possessions, and all her mighty ones will be bound in fetters* (v.10). While the meaning of the passage is very obscure, it could be grasped in no other way than by an outline of the facts referred to in it, which are as follows. After Israel had lapsed into apostasy, worshiped idols, and provoked the God of all by countless acts of impiety against him, Nebuchadnezzar took up arms against Judea and against Jerusalem, divine wrath having prompted him to do so. Then, though there was need for the people of Israel to put an end to their practice of impiety, cease wanting to adore other gods, overturn altars, burn down shrines, smash cast images, appease God with recourse to repentance and good living, and call on his aid, the wretches did not do so. Instead, they were convinced that by relying on assistance from human beings they would prove superior to the Babylonians and dominate the foe, even if God chose not to save them. Consequently, they paid many of the neighboring nations, and even sent legates to the Egyptians to what is called Ôn, or *Ammon*, which is now (57) Alexandria. They promised to join forces with them and easily succeed in driving off the Babylonians, and they provided the people of Israel with grounds for thinking that even if God did not save them, they themselves would be up to it, with no one else needed.

After Nebuchadnezzar took Judea, however, with the help of God, who prostrated his adversaries under him, he later advanced also on Egypt under the impulse of divine wrath, and took it all, including Ôn, or *Ammon*, called in due course Alexandria, as I said. It was much more splendid than the other cities of Egypt, a safe and secure base, doubtless on account of its being surrounded on all sides by water, with the sea to the north and another kind of sea to the south, broad and long— namely, the marsh Mariotis—and fortified also by other rivers and swamps. The neighboring inhabitants of *Libya*, which extended as far as *Ethiopia* to the west and south, also rendered assistance to it; they were the Garamantes, situated beyond the land of Afron. Some of the Ethiopians to the east and south, who occupy the city of Meroe in the interior and graze a wild and black land, also joined forces with them.[6]

So much for an account of the factual background. Let us move on to clarification of the meaning of the passage. By *Prepare a part* he means, It is like saying, O wretched Nineveh, choose a portion for yourself; since you are conceited, take the view that you will be completely impregnable on account of your being (58) encircled with high walls and having countless numbers wanting to join forces with you. Advance on any country you choose that had been plundered by you, despite its presenting great preparedness, he is saying, in being proof against defeat and capture. *Fit a cord*, that is, become the subject of song and story for cities and countries for having suffered such a fate at the hands of Persians and Medes as you yourself had meted

***

6. Modern commentators take this verse as a clear indication that Nahum, who had predicted the fall of Nineveh in 612 B.C.E., knew also of the fall of Thebes to Ashurbanipal in 663, with implications for dating his ministry. Cyril, however, is at a relative disadvantage by the LXX's failure to see in the Heb. *No-Amon* a reference to Thebes; Jerome had not helped him by accepting the advice of his Hebrew teacher that Alexandria is meant.

out to others. By *Prepare a part for Ammon* he means, Let Ammon be your *part* and portion; you must suffer what you did to her. *Ammon, who is positioned on rivers*, that is, well fortified by sea and rivers, boasting of the help of the *Egyptians* and the archers of *Ethiopians*, enjoying the strong hordes of the *Libyans*. Yet despite having such support, strength, and assistance from outside, *she has been deported* and become *a captive, her infants dashed to the ground*, her prominent citizens taken by lot, her important people the portions of the victors and *bound in fetters*. So just as you took Ammon despite its being impregnable from the viewpoint of assistance and support, since it was God who surrendered it, so you yourself will be given over completely into the foes' hands, even if you have great confidence in the number of warriors and your walls. "I am against you" (v.5), remember, and no one will divert my hand.

You will be drunk, and will be overlooked, and you will seek a position for yourself from your foes (v.11). Just as Ammon (59) was reduced to the hardship of enduring the shafts of your ferocity and the calamity resulting from your attack, he is saying, so, too, you yourself will be plunged into darkness and will be, as it were, intoxicated, lacking a secure *position*, that is, shaken and toppled by the foe and deprived of supervision from on high. After all, to those whom God supervises he shows complete mercy, causing them to achieve their wishes with stability. In its hostility to God, Jerusalem, too, was, as it were, *drunk*, lacking sobriety, doubtless on account of its not being illumined by a divine light, and refusing to heed Christ's words, "I am the light of the world," and again, "While you have the light, walk in the light so that darkness may not overtake you."[7] Ignorance of what is proper could be understood as drunkenness, darkness of mind, and night in the heart, as could the complete inability to recognize the way of salvation. No one could doubt that unsteadiness is involved, and lack of commitment to the works of righteousness; it lost hold of the basis of everything and has no secure foundation, namely, Christ. It was *overlooked* and surrendered to the enemy, or perhaps the Romans, or those who

---

7. Jn 8.12 and 12.35.

introduce it to every kind of passion, that is, the unclean spirits.

Christ and faith in him, therefore, will free us from all trouble, render us proof against the malice of the foe, and set us in the sight of God, who will never neglect those who love him.

All your fortifications are like fig trees holding watchmen: if they are shaken, they will fall into the mouth of the eater (v.12). Ripe figs easily fall off if the tree is shaken, jumping, as it were, into the hand of the shaker, and of their own accord going to those who need something to eat. So when Cyrus was attacking and besieging Nineveh, and he applied the destructive machines, or rams, to its walls, the allies manned the battlements; but the archers attacked and easily felled them. He uses a comparison from what normally happens with ripe figs, and consequently says, *All your fortifications*—that is, the walls—*are like fig trees holding watchmen*, which very easily fall into the hand of the person wanting to eat them if you merely shake the tree.[8]

Now, this is also the way it will be with every soul that slips from divine assistance and is deprived of it, exposed and vulnerable and effortlessly taken by *the eater*, Satan. Scripture says, remember, "His food is specially chosen."[9]

Lo, your people like women in your midst. The gates of your land will be opened wide to your foes; fire will consume your barricades (v.13). He shows their hope to be vain; they were convinced that they would never be captured, having assembled an immeasurable horde of fellow defenders, and dwelling in a city with unbreachable walls. But he openly prophesies that even this will be of no use at all to them, saying that the defenders will lapse into such timidity as to be no different from weak *women*. He says *the gates will be opened*, (61) obviously under pressure from the enemy. It is true, after all, that "unless the Lord guards the city, in vain did the guard keep vigil."[10]

There is need to have security from on high, therefore, and to trust not in ourselves but in God who saves us, and not to

8. The text of Cyril and the Antiochenes makes mention of "watchmen" instead of "fruit," the reading of other forms of the LXX, with which Jerome is familiar.

9. Hab 1.16.

10. Ps 127.1.

boast of assistance from men or think it possible to avoid divine wrath if God has been provoked. In fact, no one will deliver from alarm and trouble any person with whom the Lord of all is angry. The divinely inspired David was very wise to say in his song, "Not in my bow shall I trust, and my arm will not save me." "With God I shall do valiantly," in another of his sayings.[11]

Draw water for yourself for the siege (v.14). They say that when Cyrus and his company were ravaging the nearby territories of Nineveh, and cutting off all their support, the Ninevites were then in fear of the destruction.[12] So they dug very long channels in the land surrounding the city that made it difficult of access for the enemy, diverting the rivers in them, filling them with water, and covering the land with marshes. But the fighters were superior to such stratagems; or rather, it was the will of God betraying them. So the fact that this project would be of no benefit to them he brings out in the words, *Draw water for yourself for the siege.* Some commentators think that here by *water drawn* should be understood the gathering or multitude of the nations summoned to assistance. (62) Such an interpretation, in fact, will not be wide of the mark, since the multitude of the nations is often referred to as "waters."

Occupy the fortifications, trample clay, tread in the straw, take hold of the brick (v.14). Such recommendations would not be from God; since he had complete foreknowledge of the future, he mocks the precautions, and in this passage he shows, as I just said, that all their efforts would be in vain. Since the walls happened to lack battlements or some other provision, you see, they were making *bricks*—obviously from *clay*—but strong ones; bricks require firing to work if they are not to be fragile. So he says, *tread in the straw*, and make the brick. Be as bold and merciless in fighting as, of course, this brick itself; you will thus be vulnerable and in no way unbroken, offering no resistance to those who know how to shake you and make a charge stronger than your toughness.

There fire will consume you, a sword will destroy you and consume

---

11. Pss 44.6 and 108.13.
12. As also in comment on v.15, Cyril cites an unnamed authority ("they say").

you like a locust, and you will be weighed down like a young locust (v.15). By *there* he means "then," since we take the word to have a chronological and not a local sense. That is to say, even if this happened and you made the bricks, you would be consumed as if (63) by fire, and the enemy would feed on you and your country in the manner of a locust. You will also be impeded by lethargy, and as slow to flee as *a young locust weighed down.* They say, in fact, that when there is a hailstorm and rain falls, the young locust is slow to fly away, his wings being saturated. He is therefore suggesting as well the Ninevites' ineptitude in fleeing, using the example of what happens to young locusts.

You increased your commerce beyond the stars of heaven. A young locust made its advance and flew away. Your mercenary wandered off like a wingless locust, like a locust mounted on a rampart on a frosty day; the sun rose, and it flew away, and its location was unknown (vv.16–17). By *commerce* here he probably refers not to that involving money, bribes, and oppression, but rather to what was entered into in the assembling or gathering of the nations. They paid the surrounding nations, as I said, remember, as though importing people to die, and assembling for fighting those who would soon perish, in numbers beyond counting. Consequently they are compared to the vast number of the *stars.* But even if they assembled and have come together, he says, they will be aghast at the fighting, and will take flight like a *young locust* and like *a wingless locust.* This is a species of small locust; when it hits the *ramparts* or walls of gardens in a frost and teeming rain, as I said, it stays quiet and still, avoiding flight under pressure of the dampness; but when the sun comes out and (64) sheds warm rays on them, they make a quick departure and normally fly away. This is the way, he says, *your mercenaries* will be: they will fly away and head for home, frustrating your expectations. "It is therefore good and reliable to trust in the Lord, rather than to trust in man," as the inspired writer says.[13]

Woe to them! Your shepherds have fallen asleep; the Assyrian king put your warriors to sleep; your people went off to the mountains, with no one to welcome them (vv.17–18). He laments the fact that the

13. Ps 118.9.

crowds are reduced to such a degree of timidity and fear as to faint at the mere advent of war, to scamper up the crests of the *mountains,* and to turn the trackless countryside into a kind of protection from danger. He then supplies the reason for their fright by giving a skillful account of the destruction of those appointed leaders; adopting a moral tone, instead of saying that they were overrun and destroyed, having proved untrained in warlike skills, he used the term *they have fallen asleep,* and said that the people with power and authority and the crowd leaders who were invested with important positions and honors were *put to sleep.* They experienced the *falling asleep* at the hands of the *Assyrian king,* that is, one of their own number; Cyrus was native-born, and of Persian blood. Now, the prophetic statement, as it were, offers us the pretense of mourning, or at least ridicules the ease of their becoming terrified, the text saying, *your people went off to the mountains, with no one to welcome them,* (65) that is, without anyone prepared for a show of bravery, anyone restraining the terror of the fugitives, capable of holding in check the timid mob of retreatants bent on surrender. People of that inclination perished first, in fact, along with the experts in military skills.

Now, the verse could rightly be understood of the mass of Jews: *Woe to them! Your shepherds have fallen asleep; the Assyrian king put your warriors to sleep.* In fact, *woe* really applies to those who killed the Savior and Redeemer of all, and to those who sacrilegiously added the Lord's blood to that of the saints. That was their fate because of the *falling asleep* of the leadership in this folly and of those appointed in the role of *shepherds,* namely, scribes and Pharisees and those invested with the rank of priesthood, who were *put to sleep by the Assyrian king* in a spiritual sense, namely, Satan. (The Babylonian power is often taken to represent him.) Now, there is no doubting that the shepherds and the warriors among them were put to sleep when, in this passage and that, the divinely inspired Scripture attributes to them the destruction of the people. The text says, "Woe to the shepherds who destroy and scatter the sheep of the pasture," and again, "The priests did not say, Where is the Lord? Those who handle the Law did not know me, the shepherds offended me, and the prophets prophesied by Baal." Isaiah in turn says, "How has city Zion, full of justice, become a whore? Righteousness lodged in her, but now (66) murderers. Your silver has become dross; your innkeepers mix water with the wine; your princes are unfaithful, companions of thieves, loving bribes, chasing gifts, not judging in favor of orphans and not attending to the widow's cause."[14]

There is no healing for your wound; your scar was inflamed (v.19). When some unwished-for suffering befalls us, provided it is within limits and does not exceed reason, the sufferers entertain sound hope that they will succeed in recovering, as it were, from the illness and will manage to return to healthy life and enjoy well-being, once there is a change for the better in their situation. When, on the other hand, their situation reaches a pitch of misery, then the misfortune becomes completely unbearable or, rather, quite ineluctable. To Nineveh in this condition he says that it has been crushed and destroyed, the hope of cure despaired of, and the ailment seriously inflamed and begging for the ultimate intervention.

Now, it would be true to say that this happened also to Jerusalem for killing the Lord; it was often wounded by the assaults of the foe, but cure followed when God showed compassion and, as it were, assuaged the *wound* affecting them. When they provoked the Lord of all, however, it was crushed and brought down, and *there was no healing*, as the prophet says; instead, the *inflammation* of their fate remained unassuaged. Consequently, (67) the blessed prophets also said in comparing it to Babylon, "We tried to heal Babylon, but she was not healed; we are all forsaking her and going to our own country, for her judgment is reaching up to heaven, and has been lifted up even to the stars."[15] The sin and the judgment reached even to heaven because, as I said, they provoked not simply one of the saints but the Lord of the saints.

All who hear the news of you will rejoice and clap their hands at you, because who at any time escaped your malice? (v.19) No one's lamenting her in any way is clear proof of the justice of the verdict

14. Jer 23.1 and 2.8; Is 1.21–23.
15. Jer 51.9.

from God in the overthrow of Babylonian rule. Rather [than lamentation], there was *hand-clapping*, exultation, and mockery of her fall, doubtless because of her oppression and infliction of unbearable calamities, and her causing people to experience things most calculated to arouse grief. She was, in fact, burdensome and intolerable to everyone, responsible for bringing even to people far away a sense of her inherent malice.

Now, I would claim that the inventor of sin—namely, Satan—who spreads everywhere the net of his malice, snares the land under heaven in error, and binds it in the toils of ruin, would rightly hear these words when overthrown by Christ and driven from his despotic rule over us: *All who hear the news of you will rejoice and clap their hands at you, because who at any time escaped your malice?* (68)

COMMENTARY ON THE
PROPHET HABAKKUK

PREFACE TO THE
COMMENTARY ON HABAKKUK

HILE THE PRESENT PROPHECY has also been developed for us with great wisdom and skill, we shall find it concentrating on God's management of things in a way becoming the saints. It becomes even the saints, in fact, to make the open admission, "It is not you who are speaking, but the Spirit of your Father speaking in you." Now, for those wanting to have an understanding there is need of no little sagacity, since you would notice the drift of the prophecy giving birth in you to a twofold level of meaning, both spiritual and factual.[1] For your benefit I shall, while keeping it brief, detail in advance the parts of the prophecy, and mention what their reference is; in this way readers would come to the meaning easily and meet with no difficulty.

Israel, then, was considerably irked (69) by the predictions of the prophets; they were aware, in fact, they were aware that they would in due course become captive, fall into the hands of the foe, and be subjected to an unfamiliar slavery. The blessed Habakkuk actually tries to convey the fact that by a just decree of the God who controls all things, such a fate will in due course befall them, and with good reason. After all, they had personally preferred a wrongful life at variance with the Law, had adopted every form of dishonesty, and had not ceased developing in themselves a contaminated mind before the miserable fate befell them. He makes this clear by directing his criticism at those opting for an unholy life, making it, as it were, the focus and theme of his whole prophecy, and then introducing God to threaten those contemptuous of him with the assault

---

1. Mt 10.20. As usual, an Alexandrian commentator assumes that there are at least two levels of meaning in a text. In the case of Habakkuk, Cyril notes a preoccupation with divine providence or *oikonomia*, as will Theodoret.

of the Babylonians. Since it was his duty, however, not only to take the role of prophet of harsh realities calculated to cause the utmost distress, and not only to take a public stance and predict that the worst of all possible disasters would befall them in due course, but also to provide a helpful description in advance of what would serve as a cure and to foretell the way the sufferers would be likely to gain respite, he deplores also the Babylonians' cruelty itself and calls those people contemptuous who burnt down the divine Temple itself, ransacked the holy city, and made no exception of the sacred vessels. "Why do you gaze on the contemptuous," he says, "[and] keep silence when the godless swallow the righteous?"[2]

With great wisdom he then proceeds (70) to mention also the capture of Babylon and the eventual redemption by Cyrus of the victims of unaccustomed servitude. From the individual redemption the treatment moves naturally to overall and generic redemption, namely, that achieved through Christ for all those redeemed by faith, who have set aside the yoke of sin and escaped a harsh and inflexible master in Satan. You thus have a brief synopsis of the drift of the whole prophecy; we shall expound it by dealing with each part as far as we can.[3]

2. 1.13.
3. Theodoret will follow Cyril in identifying Habakkuk's "theme" (*hypothesis*) and "drift, purpose" (*skopos*), whereas Theodore initially notes the different genres in the work.

COMMENTARY ON HABAKKUK,
CHAPTER ONE

The oracle that the prophet Habakkuk saw (v.1).

Y 'ORACLE' HERE HE REFERS TO reception of the vision, or premonition, that he had when God gave it. It is he, after all, who, according to Scripture, multiplied visions, and he who spoke to prophets, foretelling the future to them through the Holy Spirit and, as it were, setting it before their sight as though already happening.[1] Now, of the fact that they were not in the habit of uttering sentiments of their own heart,[2] but rather communicated to us the words from God, he clearly convinces us, calling himself a prophet and showing himself to be filled with grace for that purpose.

How long, O Lord, shall I cry aloud and you will not hearken? Shall I call to you when wronged and you will not save? (v.2) The prophet adopts the point of view of the oppressed person, (71) subject to the insufferable insolence and provocation of people addicted to wrongdoing, and he very skillfully testifies to God's lovingkindness surpassing all bounds, presenting him as very ready to forgive, although committed to hating evildoers. The fact that he does not immediately call the fallen to account he clearly demonstrates by saying that he reaches such a degree of silence and long-suffering that there is now need even to *cry aloud* in complaint that some people commit against others an oppression no longer bearable, and, as it were, direct unrestrained insolence at the weak. The protests at this which he levels at God's tolerance, in fact, testify to God's unbounded loving-kindness:

---

1. Hos 12.10. When this term "oracle" occurred at Na 1.1, we saw that Cyril took Jerome's advice to avoid any suggestion of ecstatic possession, unlike Theodore; and he may be following that advice given again here. See p. 283, n. 1. He does not, however, follow Jerome in debating the time of the prophet's ministry.
2. Jer 23.16, an oft-cited basic criterion for an authentic prophet.

How long, O Lord, shall I cry aloud and you will not hearken? Shall I call to you when wronged and you will not save, despite your threats of justice against those bent on extreme and harsh acts of lawlessness?

Why did you make me see hardships and gaze upon troubles, wretchedness, and impiety? (v.3) From this you would also learn the holy ones' hatred of wickedness, referring to others' *troubles* as their own. Consequently, Paul in his great wisdom also says, "Who is weak, and I am not weak? Who is made to stumble, and I am not indignant?" He also bade us in our own case to "weep with those who weep,"[3] showing that sympathy and love for one another are particularly appropriate for the saints. Now, he says that God had made him see *hardships and troubles,* namely, on the part of the transgressors, and *impiety* on the part of those given to injustice—not that it was he who caused him to suffer, but that he was (72) long-suffering to the guilty ones even for such a long time, or that he was capable of releasing him from life to prevent his being a spectator of such wrongful behavior. Now, it was customary with the holy ones, when suffering such severe depression, to seek to be dissolved, as for example blessed Jonah: "Now Lord, take my life from me, because it is better for me to die than to live." Paul in his great wisdom also writes that "it would be better for me to be dissolved and be with Christ."[4] For people anxious to live a holy life, you see, relief from troubles is riddance here and now of the affairs of this world, and respite, as it were, from burdensome cares here below.

Judgment has gone against me, and the judge accepts bribes. Hence the Law is undermined, and justice does not take effect, because impious people have control of justice; for this reason a perverted judgment will be delivered (v.4). He brings out clearly that, far from its being some personal matter that induces discouragement in him, it is rather the recognition by him, as a holy man concerned for justice, of people setting the divine commandment at naught—not ordinary people but those elevated to the highest office, leaders of the people appointed to the rank of judges. He claims that right verdicts have been set aside, despite the clear direction of

3. 2 Cor 11.29; Rom 12.15.
4. Jon 4.3; Phil 1.23.

the Law, "You shall not be partial in judgment, for the judgment is God's."[5] Delivering judgment is therefore important, and the incorruptible judge would be wise to imitate divine transcendence and glory, (73) unwilling to have a righteous verdict set aside. The venal judge is extremely injurious, and offends against the divine appointments themselves by giving a lie to the beauty of truth and being intent on perverting the course of justice by calling "evil good and good evil," and sacrilegiously declaring "darkness light and light darkness."[6] So the prophet shows that the whole Law is in one fell swoop trampled underfoot in this single excellent and pre-eminent commandment: how would the person who fails in his primary duty be secure in what is weightier? The prophet presented himself as witness and observer of oppression. Since, he says, right judgment is bypassed, consequently *the Law* is weakened, and, instead of the correctness of judgments *taking effect* in keeping with God's will, *impious people have control of justice.*

Now, this was the crime of the assembly of the Jews, and it was the charge leveled by God in the statement of other prophets. He said, in fact, "Its leaders gave judgment with bribes," and against it likewise in the statement of Isaiah, "Your silver has become dross; your innkeepers mix water with the wine; your rulers are disobedient, companions of thieves, lovers of bribes, in search of rewards, not judging in favor of orphans, nor giving attention to the cause of the widow." Here the prophet Habakkuk wanted also to fulfill that statement in the book of Proverbs, "Call it as you see it."[7] He proceeds to show that he had also made a reasonable complaint about the gentleness characteristic of God; while it becomes him to be so tolerant, (74) since God is good, yet to the human mind his tolerance surpasses the bounds of reason.

Now, also in the case of Christ there was fulfillment of the verse, *a perverted judgment is delivered, and the Law is undermined.* The one whom it would have been better to venerate as God and hence a wonderworker, in fact, the leaders of the Jews did not cease maligning, leaving no excessive descriptions untried

5. Dt 1.17.   6. Is 5.20.
7. Mi 3.11; Is 1.22–23; Prv 25.7.

in presuming to accuse him of every form of wrongdoing, such that at one time they thought he cast out the demons by Beelzebul, and at another they called him a drunkard and possessed by a demon.[8] Next, while the wretches should have referred to him as Savior and Redeemer of all, they sacrilegiously killed him, *delivering a perverted judgment* against him, despite the Law's clear direction, "You shall not kill the innocent and those in the right."[9] In other ways, too, Christ accused them of being unwilling to have right and proper attitudes; instead, on the one hand, they kept silent and, as it were, closed the eye of their mind to what Moses says, although failing to observe the Law regarding the sabbath; on the other hand, they assailed him very severely for his actions in keeping with God on the sabbath, and he spoke in these terms: "I performed one work, and all of you are astonished. Moses gave you circumcision (it is, of course, not from Moses but from the ancestors), and you circumcise a man on the sabbath. If a man receives circumcision on the sabbath in order that the Law of Moses may not be broken, are you angry with me because I healed a man's whole body on the sabbath? Do not judge by appearances, but judge with right judgment."[10] (75)

See, you contemptuous ones, and take note; marvel at marvelous deeds, and disappear, because I am performing a work in your days that you would not believe if someone recounted it (v.5). The prophet had deplored the oppression by lawless people, and had, as it were, criticized the extended tolerance of them, since a righteous soul loves virtue and hates evil. So the God of all now makes a pronouncement to those given to contempt to *see and take note* and consider *marvelous* everything it is proper to marvel at. This referred to what was, as it were, hanging over them and soon to befall them, including an assault best avoided and an abhorrent attack, which he had bidden them consider in advance for their benefit. It was quite capable of making those on whom it proved to fall *disappear*, being *marvelous*, unexpected, against the odds, intolerable, capable of astonishing them owing to its

8. Lk 11.18 and 7.34.   9. Ex 23.7.
10. Jn 7.21–24.

extraordinary horror, and perhaps even beyond belief. After all, the proximity of an enormity of troubles is generally likely to force people to disbelieve, especially if they are perceived to befall them when they do not expect to suffer them from any quarter. In fact, who would ever have thought that the beloved Israel, the firstborn of children, on whose account Egypt perished and countless nations fell—Canaanites, Amorites, Hivites, Perizzites, and Jebusites—would have descended to such a degree of wretchedness that the whole of their country would be overturned, and they would suffer such ignominious and unbearable servitude, wandering in foreign lands after the assaults of war, (76) which beggared description even if you wanted to recount them all? What happened, in fact, were burnings, slaughter of menfolk, rape of womenfolk, smashing of infants to the ground, and, as the prophet Jeremiah says, "Hands of compassionate women boiled their own children."[11] The actual holy things themselves were plundered, and none of extreme misfortunes went without experience by the captives.

It therefore beggared belief and description on account of the enormity of the cruelty of those responsible. Consequently, he says, a deed was being done *in* their *days that they would not believe if someone recounted it* to them. Now, by saying *in your days* he gave them to understand that it would not be long in coming; instead, the war was at the very doors, close by and immediate, and justice was not far off.

Because, lo, I am stirring up the Chaldeans, warriors, the nation that is harsh and fleet of foot, traveling across the breadth of the earth to take possession of dwellings not its own (v.6). He immediately brought out what would be beyond belief if an account were given of it: he threatened to dispatch against them the Babylonians, a warlike and most fierce race, yielding in no way to the wildest of animals in cruelty, always condemned for unmitigated rage. He called them *fleet of foot,* all of them being mounted, and *harsh* because they were severe, unyielding, clever tacti-

11. Lam 4.10. Cyril seems implicitly to be heeding Jerome's information that in "you contemptuous ones" the LXX had misread "the nations" of the Heb., and so sees the nations (e.g., of Jos 24.1) wreaking havoc on Israel. Paul cites the verse in Acts 13.41 in the LXX form.

cians, and thoroughly practiced. Strength combined with sagacity in (77) the requirements of war would, in my view, very easily achieve the purposes of the combatants, and easily prevail over the confidence of adversaries. Now, since it was proverbial that the Babylonians never stayed at home, nor did they repel hostile attacks on them by offering the enemy assistance, but instead, as it were, spread over the whole earth, ravaged others' territory, and consistently made an inheritance of what in no way belonged to them, he consequently says, *the nation that travels across the breadth of the earth to take possession of dwellings not its own.* In other words, as I said, it was in the habit of furiously attacking others' lands and consistently extending its own empire.[12]

Now, the Jews had some such experience after killing the Lord; although able to occupy their own land without effort, with no one to trouble them, they were surrendered to the powers that be, became subject to tribute and taxes, and fell under the control of those who spread everywhere and conquered the whole land under heaven. Having rejected the reign of Christ, in fact, they openly declared, "We have no king but Caesar."[13] Now, it should be realized that if a human soul sets no store by the divine laws, it will be subject to harsh tyrants, the unclean demons, and will be enslaved to evil powers, which forever thirst *to take possession of dwellings not* their *own.* The human being, you see, belongs to God, who dwells in the saints, and lodges in the souls of the holy ones.

Fearsome it is and notorious; its judgment will come from itself, and its oracle will proceed from it (v.7). The treatment moves on to the leader of the nation, namely, (78) the ruler of the Babylonians, perhaps Nebuchadnezzar, who took Judea, burnt down the divine Temple itself, and took off Judah as a captive to his own land. So he calls him *fearsome* on account of his cruelty, uncontrollable anger, immovable attitude, and implacable vengeance, and likewise *notorious* for his ambition, boasting, and insatiable thirst for glory. The kings of Babylon, in fact, were very arro-

12. Though Cyril acknowledges the reference in the text to Babylonians, he does not proceed to use this as a clue to the time of the prophet's ministry, whether bearing on the fall of Assyria or of Judah.

13. Jn 19.15.

gant and vainglorious. Since they had control over their plans for every enterprise, however, giving orders for the implementation of their wishes by those under them, hence he says, *its judgment will come from itself;* that is, of their own volition there was a movement to implementation, and on the basis of their conceitedness there was no brooking opposition, even if they were to order the impossible, the Persians' decisions being unreasonable.

Since, on the other hand, their custom was to seek divination of their battles, and to try to determine in advance by the skills of soothsayers how their plans would succeed, he likewise says, *its oracle will proceed from it.* By *oracle* he refers to the divination; it was not from other nations or places that he would summon practitioners of the art of divining, but instead they had local practitioners, who consistently lied and knew nothing of the truth, always assuring them and in the habit of foretelling that they would win. The Babylonian rulership also greatly prided themselves on this. Balak king of the Moabites, for instance, (79) when he resolved to have the people of Israel cursed, and sought knowledge of the future, had Balaam summoned from Mesopotamia,[14] thinking that the Babylonian augurs were fearsome and accurate, expert in being able to achieve anything at all by their augury.

If you do not mind, however, we shall proceed to the meaning of the passage in a different way. Having identified the ruler of the Babylonians and having said that he is *fearsome and notorious,* he immediately proceeded to add that *his judgment will come from himself, and his oracle will proceed from him.* We can take him to be of that kind; God the Lord of all had determined to punish Israel for choosing to live a vile and depraved life. So this is the *judgment* that will come upon it from him, namely, the Babylonian. It would be like saying, He will be an instrument of my wrath, through him I shall punish you, and the *oracle* which is to do with you—that is, whatever plan and purpose I adopt—likewise *will proceed from him,* that is, will be enacted; the effects of my purpose and plan will take effect.

14. Nm 22.4.

Its horses will leap forth more rapidly than leopards and more swiftly than the wolves of Arabia; its horsemen will ride out and attack from afar, and they will fly like an eagle eager to eat (v.8). He likewise terrifies them with the enormity of the horror, and tries to convey the fact that the vast number of the enemy is fearsome and irresistible. He drives them to repentance and to (80) the need to learn what it would be better for them to be found performing. Accordingly, he likewise convinces them that the Babylonians are nimble in flight, audacious and bold, no different from wild beasts and given wings like those in danger of being taken. He compares the horses to *leopards*, the leopard being very lithe, very ready to spring upon what is being pursued, and to the *wolves of Arabia*, which they say are more wild than the others and charge in rapid flight against whichever prey they choose.[15] He says they are not only like wolves, but also like *eagles* in flying down and attacking dead bodies, as I said.

Now, the mind of the Jews was also very vulnerable, and their heart whinnying and easily set in motion under the influence of the passions of the flesh, the unclean spirits themselves, and in addition the forceful attacks of the Romans. For they have offended the one who said, "For them I shall be, says the Lord, a wall of fire round about, and I shall be as glory in its midst."[16] Now, in my view, every mind is vulnerable and easily overcome when deprived of strength from on high, since our strength and security is from God; it is through him that "we shall do valiantly, and it is he who will set at naught those oppressing us," as Scripture says.[17]

An end will come upon the godless, resisting with faces against them (v.9). This is the fulfillment (81) of the promises and culmination of the troubles: the Chaldeans will come; they will be of that kind; they will do those things and proceed to other things as well as what accompanies them, the complete and utter destruction of the godless along with their cities and towns. God will in no way show compassion, but will allow desolation to overtake those who sacrilegiously resist his decrees, oppose him, as

15. The LXX reads "Arabia" for the Heb. "evening."
16. Zec 2.5.
17. Ps 60.12.

it were, *face* to face, and are openly hostile and blatantly set up their own will in opposition to what God wishes.

An end will come similarly for the synagogue of the Jews also for taking a position opposed to Christ, resisting the Lord's teachings, blatantly and shamelessly confronting him *face* to face, doing and speaking the worst of all evils, so to speak, even nailing him to the cross and decrying the resurrection. In fact, they not only killed the Savior and Redeemer of all, but also paid money to Pilate's soldiers at Christ's resurrection to say that, far from his coming to life, his disciples secretly stole him away.[18]

And it will gather captives like sand. It will delight in kings, and tyrants will be its playthings; it will make fun of every fortification, heap up a mound and gain control of it (vv.9–10). Despite the holy prophets' predictions hither and yon to the Jewish populace of what would befall them, and, as it were, their recitations of such troubles to them, (82) they descended to such depths of ignorance and unholy speculation as to be inflamed with audacity and rage, inflated with a sense of their own importance, and at times to think that they would easily prevail over the foe by their vast numbers, while at times they were confident that they would gather the neighboring kingdoms in support and that the invaders would yield the victory to them without a fight. Having grown indifferent about ancestral practices, they no longer sought help from God on high, but, as I said, they enlisted the help of the nearby nations, at one time the Egyptians, at another the Syrians, and even the Tyrians, the result being that they rested their hope in unshakable prosperity, and continued to live lives of luxury and satisfaction.

Accordingly, the fact that such was their intention in all probability, whereas the actual outcome for them was not as planned, he goes on to explain. On arriving, he says, even if the Babylonian were to find the race of Israel equal in number to the sand of the seashore, he would return home with the inhabitants of Judah as his captives; and even if they were to have countless strong allies, he would easily prevail over them. *It will delight in kings, and tyrants will be its playthings*; he took off Jeco-

---

18. Mt 28.12–14.

niah in chains to Babylon and not a few other princelings, who were the object of mockery to their captors. He will take control of the cities, even well fortified ones, in such a way that the capture of each will be reckoned a joke by him. He will also build and raise *mounds*. (83) He likewise took Tyre, despite its reaching far from the mainland into the sea like an island.

Now, Satan also took Israel captive when it failed to believe in Christ, and all its leaders became a *delight* to him, boasting of the glory of the priesthood, whom I think it not indelicate to refer to as *tyrants* on account of their leadership of the people and enjoying much importance and influence over them. They would not have become *playthings* of the devil's malice, however, if they had followed the commands of the Savior and observed faith and holiness in the Spirit. To them, in fact, the Savior of all, who put every foe under his feet, would have said, "Lo, I have given you the power to walk on snakes and scorpions and on all the power of the foe."[19]

Then he will change his spirit; he will pass on and be appeased (v.11). The fact that, instead of the whole of the race of Israel perishing or being overlooked forever, there will be for it a time of prosperity and relief from the intolerable misfortune for the returned exiles with the fracture of the yoke of slavery, he allows them to understand by mention of a *change of spirit*. In other words, he means that the Lord of all will adopt a change of plan and a different purpose. Not that he will condemn the decision previously passed against them as though it did not represent a proper decision at the time; rather, having called them sufficiently to account and inflicted punishment commensurate with the transgressions, he will move instead to mercy and *pass on* from wrath, and will be propitious to those suffering hardship—the sense, in my view, of *he will be appeased*. (84)

This power belongs to my God. Are you not from the beginning, Lord God, my holy one? May we not die (v.12). Since God had promised to show them compassion, and announced a change of a difficult situation for the better, the prophet, as it were, leaps for joy and says that it would become no one else to bring Israel

19. Lk 10.19.

back, to free it from bonds and slavery, and to have mercy on the broken, than God alone, who is easily able to achieve everything, who alleviates difficulties, and, as it were, levels what is steep and high, and of whom it would be said by every holy one, "You can do all things, and nothing is impossible for you."[20] The prophet then says, *Are you not from the beginning, Lord God, my holy one? May we not die.* That is to say, even if Israel has been led astray and seduced into error and worship of the false gods of foreigners, still you are the God of all, the holy one who of old showed compassion for transgressors, kept them from destruction, and did not let Israel as a whole perish. It is therefore not beyond hope that it will be saved and its difficulties disappear, because you are compassionate and your achievements beggar description. The holy ones also rejoiced on learning of the salvation of Israel at the end-time, recited prayers, and offered sentiments and songs of thanksgiving. The blessed David, for example, knowing in advance through the Spirit the clemency that would be shown them, and, as it were, seeing them released from the bonds of captivity, (85) sings in the words, "Lord, you were favorable to your land; you reversed the captivity of Jacob. You forgave the iniquities of your people, closing your eyes to their sins."[21]

Lord, you brought him to judgment, and formed me to give proof of his correction. Your eye is too pure to see wickedness, and you are unable to gaze upon efforts (vv.12–13.). While the words are those of the prophet once again, it is very obscure who it is he says is *brought to judgment.* So come now, let us, by peering closely of necessity into the sense of the passage, plumb its meaning. You see, if, on the one hand, it were said of the king of the Babylonians that he was *brought to judgment* by God, we would say that he was *brought* to fulfill the *judgment* passed originally against the people of Israel, namely, despoliation, captivity, burning of cities, and, in a word, ravaging of Judea. If, on the other hand, this is not the case, we shall direct the force of the meaning to the person of Israel, and claim in turn that it was *brought to judgment* by God,

20. Jb 42.2.
21. Ps 85.1–2.

judgment meaning "condemnation." Our Lord Jesus Christ, for
instance, said of the Jews, "I came into this world for judgment
so that those who do not see may see, and those who do see
may become blind,"[22] where "judgment" means "condemnation." So Israel is condemned for its wrongdoing, for being indifferent about the Law, for egregiously offending the Lord of
all. It is *me*—that is, the prophet—he (86) *formed*, or made and
prepared for the duty of *giving proof of correction*, which he determined against him. War was inflicted on Israel as *correction*
and scourge, and what happened was a form of punishment,
not simply the Babylonians' initiative.

If, however, you were to ask the following question, he says,
Why has the Babylonian been appointed to punish, or Israel to
be condemned and to suffer? the reply would be, Because the
Lord's *eye is pure*, and he could not ever bring himself to be a
witness of *wicked* and unholy actions. Nor would he *gaze upon
efforts* of evildoers and oppression conducted against the weak;
he always averts his eye from those in the habit of committing
such crimes. When it happens, a dire fate will completely and
utterly ensue, and the victim of the aversion will find himself
in extreme trouble. Aware of this, the divinely inspired David
prays, "Do not avert your face from me, nor turn away in wrath
from your servant";[23] the effects of wrath will definitely follow
upon the divine aversion.

*Why do you gaze upon the contemptuous, keep silence when the god-
less devour the righteous? Will you make people like fish in the sea and
like reptiles that have no leader?* (vv.13–14) Having foretold that
the eye of the Divinity is pure, and would never glance at evildoers or gaze benevolently at people opting to practice oppression
or (87) inflict pain on the weak, the prophet is somehow caught
up immediately in thoughts of this kind. The cruel hordes of
the Babylonians, in fact, committed countless acts of extreme
severity and hardship on the Jewish populace, and aggravated
the enormity of their savagery to such an excess of ferocity as
to spare not even the divine places, to set fire to Jerusalem and

22. Jn 9.39.
23. Ps 27.9.

the celebrated Temple, to lay hold of the ministers of the divine altars along with the masses, and to profane the holy places, as Scripture tells. When they were at home, they lived in a state of satisfaction, enjoying wealth from looting, not called to give an account of their unholy exploits, fearing no foe, no dread of war. Rather, it was they who took the contest to everyone, easily gaining control of anyone they chose, prospering greatly, exulting over the misfortunes of the lost, and boasting of their unrestrained wrath, unbridled oppression, and superiority over everyone.

The prophet is therefore aghast to see them developing their prosperity, and he questions divine justice. He endeavors to pry into what was puzzling to everyone and inscrutable to every mind, and he prays to learn what reason there would be for such extreme tolerance on the part of God, who is able to do everything, that a gentle and kindly eye falls even on those normally *contemptuous* and given to an unholy life, and he *keeps silence* and puts up with an impious man who, as it were, devours the simple and *righteous*. For this reason, (88) he says: that inevitable punishment does not follow immediately on sinners, and instead anger is delayed. Consequently, people on earth are thus drawn into scheming and plotting in the manner of *fish* to take advantage of weaker ones and, as it were, to swallow one another down with a wide and insatiable mouth. They also live such an unfeeling, isolated, and severe life as to be little different from *reptiles* in mountains and holes, which for their extreme ferocity and excessive savagery cannot be tamed and do not resemble the nature of the other animals, which are gregarious and do their grazing under the guidance of a single leader set over the flock, and give the impression of following a leader. Now, the Babylonians were also isolated, unapproachable by the others, harsh, venomous, dealers in destruction, greedily swallowing weaker people.

Now, it is not implausible that the prophet's statement would seem to be directed against the devil and the evil powers along with him. They are really *contemptuous*, in fact, resisting in every way the fear of God, and reaching every extreme of complete depravity and likewise knavery, despite God's extraordinary

tolerance. Once we became subject to them, we wretches fed
off one another; we had no *leader* to act as arbiter of peace—
namely, Christ, Lord of earth and heaven and all things. Consequently, we became like *fish*, completely without reason and
speech; (89) we lacked the reason of piety and the speech in
praise of God, and instead we slew one another and had a life
without reason, living like fish in the world. Each one's mind
was so harsh as to seem completely transformed into a wild animal, and then to rival venomous creatures in anger and severity,
or even to succeed in surpassing them.

*He drew him to his end with a hook, pulled him in with a net, and
gathered him with his haul. Hence his heart will rejoice and be glad;
hence he will sacrifice to his haul, and make offerings to his net, because
through it his portion increased and his choice foodstuff. Hence he will
cast his net, and never spare the nations from slaughter* (vv.15–17).
After referring to them as *fish*, he persists with the metaphor
and conducts his treatment as do fishermen or anglers, who
have many ways of pursuing their business of catching fish.
They land fish either with *hooks*, drawing them in with fishing
lines from the waves as they dart along, or with *nets*, encircling
them in bulk and *pulling* them in, or trapping them with some
other devices. When their work is successful and a great number are amassed, they *rejoice* in their skill, *sacrificing*, as it were,
to their tools of trade so as to (90) devote a very rich *portion* to
them. The prophet says that this was the kind of thing done
by Nebuchadnezzar, who, as it were, with his *hook, haul, and net*
encircled Israel itself and took it off along with other nations to
his own country, setting them as a banquet, as it were, for his
own comrades, bidding them enjoy and making the captives an
allotment and rich *portion* of the captors. Consequently, he says
he will also *sacrifice to his haul, and make offerings to his net*, that
is, to his own forces by whom he snared the nations, and offer
Israel in thanksgiving. Since his exploit turned out as he wished,
he says, would he not refrain from *slaughtering nations*, seizing
tribes, appropriating countries, and according no mercy?

Now, Satan also did this to the whole human race, and Israel
in particular, encircling everyone, as it were, with a single *net*
and a single *snare*—namely, by sin, and, in the case of Israel, by

its impious behavior towards Christ. *His foodstuff* was *choice*, the text says, the Jews being chosen before others in respect of their lifestyle. Scripture says, remember, "When the Most High apportioned the nations, when he scattered the children of Adam, he fixed boundaries of nations according to the number of the angels of God; the Lord's portion was his people Jacob, Israel the cord of his inheritance."[24] So Israel was surely chosen before the others as firstborn of the children, as springing from a holy root—namely, that of the ancestors—as (91) possessor of the Law as a guide, and called to a knowledge of the only one who is God by nature and in truth. Yet despite enjoying such fame as well as grace, it, too, was taken along with the others. While some of them, by being deceived, became the devil's *portion*, others, although knowing the one who is God, sacrilegiously killed the one born of him, the one who is Son by nature and who took human form and appearance like ours, and [these] were taken in his *haul*, his purpose being to destroy absolutely all those on earth and to *spare* no one.

24. Dt 32.8–9.

COMMENTARY ON HABAKKUK,
CHAPTER TWO

I shall stand at my watchpost, climb upon a rock, and keep watch to see what he will say to me and what response I should make to my correction (v.1).

N THIS HE EXPLAINS to us a prophetic mystery. It was customary with the holy ones, you see, if they wanted to learn what was from God and to gain knowledge of the future when he was inspiring their mind and heart, to remove their mind far from distractions, concerns, and every care of this life, and by keeping it at leisure and rest, to leap up, as it were, to some peak or eminence or *rock* with a view to gaining an insight into what the Lord of all knowledge would choose to reveal to them. He looks, you see, for earthly and lowly elements of the mind to be put away from him, and for hearts that are capable of flying on high, relieved of earthly concerns and evanescent desires. Scripture says, remember, "The mighty ones of God (92) are raised to great heights over the earth," and again, "A vulture's chicks fly high"; in other words, the mind of the holy ones is far removed from earthly habits and lowly practices. He therefore says, *I shall stand at my watchpost;* that is, I shall make alertness my regular custom, I shall purify my mind, I shall clear it of worldly concerns, I shall, as it were, fly up *on a rock,* that is, to some secure place firmly set on high, as it were. Once there, I shall survey the scene in a spiritual sense from an eminence, so to speak, to find whatever words from God may be coming to me, and what I would be likely to say on my own account if God were to decide to *correct* me for being wrong in saying, "Why do you gaze upon the contemptuous, keep silence when the godless devour the righteous?"[1]

---

1. Ps 47.9; Jb 5.7; Hab 1.13.

The Lord replied to me in these words: Write down the vision clearly on a wooden tablet for the reader to pursue it. Because the vision has still a time to reach its fulfillment, and it will not be in vain (vv.2–3). He bids him commit to writing the *vision*, or revelation of the future; it is something worth hearing and particularly remarkable. Now, what is given particular mention in writing is generally held in honor in lengthy recollection that never ends. So he says, O prophet, *Write down the vision* so that people later may know the predictions, and in perusing your words may follow them through, that is, may desire to understand their force, and thus come to believe that what is predicted will be completely true. In fact, *the vision has still a time* to go, that is, a delay and postponement, and a short period will intervene. It will take effect before long, *and it will not be in vain*; truth never tells lies, and what is told by it would not be idle and vain.

If he is delayed, wait for him, because the one who is coming will come and will not delay. If he shrinks back, my soul is not pleased with him, whereas the righteous one will live from faith (vv.3–4). After giving no specific mention of anyone, he says *wait for him*, that is, look forward to him even if delayed, and, far from letting your hope in him waver, keep it firm and unshaken, even if some lapse of time should occur. So the God of all is probably inspiring the prophet's mind and conveying the spiritual revelation that the one foretold will definitely come, and bidding him *wait for him*, doubtless in the intervening time, as I just said. Should any *shrinking* or tedium occur on the part of the believer, in fact, *I would not be pleased with him*, (94) he says, to see him succumb to faults of the soul, nor would I forgive such a one; rather, I would class him as unbelieving and execrable. To the one confirming the truth with my words, on the other hand, there will definitely be granted a share in life, a privilege accorded those who honor God and a fine reward of benevolence.

As far as the historical account goes, then, it was Cyrus son of Cambyses to whom reference is made in the phrase, *If he is delayed, wait for him;* it was he who took Babylon, plundering other cities along with it. But as for a mystical treatment and spiritual account, I would say that the force of the expression would rightly be applied to Christ the Savior of all; he is the one "who is and who was and who is to come,"[2] and the word of the holy prophets foretold that he is to come in due time. Now, the fact that in coming he intended to overthrow the power of the devil and expel the unholy and profane multitude of the demons from their oppression of us the sacred text clearly predicted in an oracle, as the actual outcome of events will then independently confirm. But the prophecy *has still a time* to go; the Onlybegotten shone forth in the final days of the present age, and *the one who shrinks back* and foolishly rejected faith in him offended God, remained without a taste of heavenly goods, and was expelled from the sacred multitude of the saints, according to the prophetic statement, "like a wild shrub in the desert, which will not see (95) when good things come."[3] The one who overcomes lethargy and *delay*, on the other hand, and introduces into their mind and heart love and faith in him, enjoys a reward for such an attitude, namely, the special privilege of an uncurtailed life, rejection of sin, and sanctification through the Spirit. We have, in fact, been justified "not by the works of the Law," as Scripture says, but by faith in Christ; while "the Law brings wrath,"[4] summoning transgressors to retribution, grace offsets wrath, undoing the offenses.

But the conceited and the contemptuous, an arrogant man, will bring nothing to completion (v.5). Having previously mentioned that the person foretold will come in due time, undoing troubles and relieving the oppressed from all hardship, he now recalls the ravager, who invested them all with every kind of inhumanity and cruelty typical of a wild animal. While in this there is reference in a factual sense to the profane and warlike Nebuchadnezzar, likewise [there is a reference] in a spiritual sense to Satan. He is referred to as *conceited, contemptuous, and arrogant*, and rightly so; he is like this by nature, whether the force of the expression is directed at Satan, or you would refer to the Babylonian as the *man*. By *conceited* he means he is ruthless or stupid, and

2. Rv 1.8, which Cyril sees determining the sense of Habakkuk, not vice versa. The familiar Alexandrian hermeneutical terminology is called into use: after reference is made to the factual situation (*historia*), a spiritual (*mystikos, pneumatikos*—or, as elsewhere, *noêtos*) meaning may be sought.

3. Jer 17.6.

4. Gal 2.16; Rom 4.15.

likewise speaks of him as *contemptuous and arrogant* for his extreme haughtiness and vanity in being unwilling to admit the
incomparable superiority of the God who can do all things.
(96) Such a person *will bring nothing to completion*; nothing he
intends will take effect: his enjoyment will not be complete, nor
his extension of power, nor his high reputation. There is truth
in what the blessed David also said in the psalm: "I have seen
the wicked oppressing, and towering like the cedars of Lebanon. I passed by and, lo, he was no more, I looked for him and
his place could not be found." Pride always leads to a fall, in
fact, whereas a temperate attitude is crowned with honors from
on high. The Savior's disciple confirms this for us in writing in
these terms: "Let the believer who is lowly boast in being raised
up, and the rich in being brought low because he will disappear
like a flower in the field."[5]

*He opened wide his soul like Hades, and like death he is unsatis-
fied; he will gather all nations to himself, and bring all peoples within
his grasp* (v.5). God is in accord with the prophet, and demonstrates his truthfulness in producing as factual the crimes both
of the devil and of Nebuchadnezzar in the words from himself.
The prophet said, remember, "He drew him to his end with
a hook, pulled him in with a net, and gathered him with his
haul,"[6] whereas the God of all attributes responsibility to what
is still greater and more accurate, now drawing a comparison
with *Hades* and *death,* death and Hades being insatiable. Now, in
the Babylonian's plans *all peoples were brought within his grasp;* and
such troubles would rightly be understood as the criminal effects of Persian ambition; for them the earth under heaven was
puny, and they would not be content with subjecting to themselves the whole of humankind.

On the other hand, the inventor of sin—namely, Satan—
would himself also be found striving to subject to himself the
whole earth, so to speak, and, like Hades, to devour those destroyed by malice on his part. He personally said somewhere, "I
shall gather in my hand the whole world like a nest, and remove
them like eggs left behind, and there is no one who will elude

5. Ps 37.35–36; Jas 1.9–10.
6. 1.15.

me or oppose me."[7] The beast is insatiable and indomitable, full of arrogance, truly detestable, hating humankind.

Will they not cite all this as a proverb against him and a rebuttal in describing him? They will say, Woe to the one who multiplies for himself what is not his! How long? Does he firmly load down his collar? (v.6) He clearly states that neither his control nor his satisfaction with the vast numbers assembled together is unshakable, and instead he will be completely dislodged from both rule and reputation, and become a byword for many people. He said that they *will take him as a proverb* (98) and, as it were, *a rebuttal* and popular saying on the tongues of many people. What kind of saying? *Woe to the one who multiplies what is not his and firmly loads down his collar,* that is, renders himself more liable for his offenses, namely, destroying nations, amassing whole countries, consistently laying hands on what does not belong to him, and subjecting by force to his own rule and keeping under control numberless peoples. In the middle he inserted the phrase *How long?* to bring out his insatiable appetite for oppression, unbridled lust for cruelty, and regret at an end to injustice. The Babylonians, then, were insatiable tyrants, fearsome in their cruelty, and given to committing the vilest crimes.

On the other hand, Satan is also like that, ever amassing what is not his and bringing upon himself heavier punishment. To him the statement is made somewhere, "Just as a garment stained with blood will not be clean, so neither will you be clean, because you have ruined my land and slain my people; you will not abide forever."[8] Which peoples, in fact, have you not destroyed? Which nations have you spared? What utterly intolerable crime are you not guilty of committing? *Woe* will therefore justly be directed at him, and he will become a *proverb* for being removed from his rule and expelled from his oppression of everyone. Likewise, Jeremiah in his wisdom also hints at this in saying of him, "A partridge crowed; it gathered what it did not give birth to, making its wealth unjustly; in midlife they will abandon it, and at its end it will be demented."[9]

---

7. Is 10.14, in the mouth of the king of Assyria.
8. Is 14.19–20 LXX, in a taunt directed at the king of Babylon.
9. Jer 17.11, in an oracle against Judah.

Now, this happened in actual fact; the Babylonian took Judea, and (99) Samaria as well, and, after ravaging other countries along with them, he took them off to his own country. But when Cyrus attacked the land of the Babylonians along with the Persians and Medes, the people who had been gathered together took their leave, and those held in the bondage of captivity became airborne, as it were, and went home. The people from the nations also abandoned the service of the devil, forsook the one who formerly had cried out to call them to him, and made their way to Christ; the former had assembled *what was not his*, whereas Christ welcomed what was his, being Lord of all as God.

Because suddenly they will arise and bite him, your schemers will be on the alert, and you will be their plunder (v.7). He says that unexpectedly those who were, as it were, *biting* and devouring will rebel against him, consuming the forces subject to him with military attacks. These were definitely Cyrus and those in his company—Persians, Medes, and Elamites—who, so to speak, rubbed sleep from their eyes, and, as though becoming *alert* after drunkenness, they will finally prevail over the former terrors, take up arms against him, and in general mount a charge. Then, by manifold *scheming*, they will easily gain the upper hand, driving off and carrying away the Chaldeans' possessions and making the Babylonians their *prey*.

We shall also find the wretched Satan suffering this fate; (100) he carried off as a whole all the nations for himself, setting the snare of the error of polytheism and spreading the nets of sin. But those *biting* him *rose up*—that is, the preachers of the Gospel oracles—with their teeth, as it were, rending his body, namely, those choosing to adopt his attitudes; just as "the person clinging to the Lord is one spirit with him," so the one clinging to the devil is one body with him. So his *schemers will be on the alert;* aware that [the devil] has now been put under the feet of the saints, since Christ said openly, "Lo, I have let you walk on snakes and scorpions and all the power of the foe,"[10] they will snatch those adopting his attitudes and easily bring them to the knowledge of the truth, teaching them who it is who is God by

---

10. 1 Cor 6.17; Lk 10.19.

nature and in truth, and explaining the mystery of Christ, who also proved to be the first to *plunder* [the devil]. It is therefore possible to hear him saying, "Or how can one enter a strong man's house and plunder his property without first tying up the strong man? Then it is possible to plunder his property." Immediately upon being born of the holy virgin, he began to plunder his property; the magi arrived from the east inquiring, "Where is the one born King of the Jews? We have seen his star in the east, and have come to adore him."[11] They did in fact adore him and honor him with gifts, and became the first-fruits of the church of the nations; though they were the devil's property, and the most precious of all his members, (101) they betook themselves to Christ. Now, the fact that he was destined to plunder the property of the strong man the prophet Isaiah also foretold obscurely, referring to him this way: "Because before the child knows how to speak of father or mother, he will take the power of Damascus and the spoils of Samaria before the king of Assyria."[12] On the one hand, therefore, the force of the expression seems to involve a hint of what happened in actual fact: Samaria was plundered by the king of Damascus and the ruler of the Assyrians. But there is a suggestion of the spiritual mystery, the prophetic word suggesting to us that the Savior's power will easily despoil those ravaging his people.

Because you despoiled many nations, all the surviving peoples will despoil you because of human bloodshed and crimes against land and city and all its inhabitants (v.8). The statement is accurate, even if it is to be taken in reference to both; while it was the Babylonian who plundered *many nations*, Satan also was guilty of this. Consequently they suffered the same fate: the Chaldeans' fortunes were plundered by Cyrus, and Satan by the saints. The crimes of both were the same and their sins related, just as there was a kinship between their ferocity and cruelty to everyone; they destroyed countries and cities, in a physical sense in one case and in a spiritual sense in the other, employing sin as a sharp javelin.

11. Mt 12.29 and 2.2.
12. Is 8.4. After previously seeing Habakkuk referring to Nebuchadnezzar and the Babylonians as the villain (or Satan at a spiritual level), now it is the king of the Assyrians who represents Satan.

Now, he does well to say that *all the surviving peoples will despoil him*; he means that when (102) the Babylonian did away with everyone, those who succeeded in escaping were very hostile to him, and though few in number they easily took control, since God accorded them the victory and allowed them to manage to set everything to rights. On the other hand, it would be true to understand it as applying to the enemy of everyone himself, namely, Satan; he took and plundered everyone on earth, and subjected them to the yoke of sin. But he himself was also seized by *the surviving peoples*, that is, those justified by faith through Christ and sanctified by the Spirit. The remnant of Israel in fact has been saved; from their number came the divinely inspired disciples, who were the first-fruits of those who plundered the destructive wretch. Next after them the leaders of peoples in addition now plunder him by correctly crafting the message of truth and bringing into the paths of piety those in submission.[13]

O the one who has insatiable and wicked greed for his house so as to place his nest on high with a view to being delivered from the hand of troublemakers. You devised shame for your house by eliminating many peoples, and your soul sinned (vv.9–10). The passage is directed against the Babylonian again for wishing to develop his control out of greed to the detriment of everyone, raising his house on high, intending to gild his house to an excessive degree and to fortify it strongly so as to be readily able *to be delivered from the hand of troublemakers*, that is, always to avert impending troubles. (103) The Babylonians' purpose, in fact, was always to be surrounded by great numbers of allies and have innumerable tactical experts skilled in the conduct of war so as to be able easily to ward off harm from those attacking them. The fact that it will turn to their shame and disgrace, however, when their expectations are thwarted, he brought out by saying, *You devised shame for your house, eliminating* or exterminating *many peoples* when you suffered complete ruin. Since *your soul sinned*, you will pay the penalty; though formerly famous and *placing his nest on high*, he will prove to be piteous in being unexpectedly thrust under the feet of his foes.

13. 2 Tm 2.15.

On the other hand, the passage would also apply very closely to Satan himself and the originators of heresies, who, unable to resist ambition and the appearance of being leaders of many, *eliminated many peoples* and introduced to their own houses a really evil greed. They placed their nests on high, "speaking bombastic nonsense" and giving vent against the divine glory to what befits only their tongues and minds. So their *souls sinned* in raging against Christ himself, the Savior of all, "sinning against the brethren and wounding their conscience when it is weak," as Scripture says.[14]

Hence a stone will cry out from a wall, and a beetle will utter the same things from a beam (v.11). The divine Scripture often attributes statements even to inanimate and (104) insensate things, not as if they were capable of speech, but as though the situation were actually crying aloud. Blessed Isaiah, for instance, says, "Be ashamed, O Sidon; the sea has spoken," and David also, "The heavens are telling the glory of God, and the firmament proclaims his handiwork."[15] That is to say, creation itself proclaims the glory of the Maker through the very things for which it is admired for being well made; so statements are made in what happens, even if words are not uttered. This kind of thing you will understand in this case, too: *a stone from a wall and a beetle from a beam* cried out against the Babylonian; how so, I shall explain. In assaulting the cities of Judea and the others, the Babylonian set fire to all the houses in them; inevitably *stones* were then smashed and *walls* toppled, and *timbers* fell down from them as well as roofs because of their great age, since they contained small *beetles* or worms. Consequently, he says, what was leveled *will cry out* against the savagery, including stones brought down and lying in the middle of the streets, and half-burnt timbers testifying to the antiquity of the cities by their rotted condition. Burning of such old and antique cities by the Babylonian, destruction of the houses, and doubtless slaughter of those in them were therefore a crime.

Now, it should be realized that, instead of saying *beetle*, some of the translators put "wooden joint." From this you could adopt

14. 2 Pt 2.18; 1 Cor 8.12.
15. Is 23.4; Ps 19.1.

the view that the girding of the houses and the (105) binding or linkage of the timbers they called *beetle* at that time because of the positioning of the roof on many feet, as it were.[16]

Woe to the one who builds a city by bloodshed, and establishes a city by injustice! This is not from the Lord almighty. Enough peoples have perished by fire, and nations that were numerous have diminished (vv.12–13). He once more deplores the Babylonian's elevating his own glory and the splendor of his rule in his anxiety to do so, on the basis not of need but of what was least necessary. He should not, in fact, have been celebrated for annihilating many peoples; instead, he should have gloried in a distinction of a different kind, and been found to gain luster from the ornaments of righteousness. Setting this aside as useless, however, *he built on bloodshed and injustice;* the fact that Chaldean rule was very cruel, and, in a word, abused all cities and countries in the manner of a wild beast, inflicting troubles that beggar description, would be obvious to all readers of the divine Scripture. *This is not from the Lord almighty*, however; such troubles cannot in any way be said to have come from on high, nor should his glorying in them be thought to be God-given. They will therefore not prove stable—rather, they will not escape justice; what the divine and incorruptible mind is not in the habit of praising it definitely punishes as being improper. After all, how could it fail to be hateful and completely unholy that *enough peoples have perished by fire, and nations that were numerous have diminished*, that is, (106) that famous cities have been burnt along with their inhabitants, and whole nations and tribes have succumbed to troubles?

Now, you would be entitled to declare this also to the leaders of the Jews, who slew all the holy prophets in the conviction that they would considerably benefit Jerusalem and *build it in bloodshed* and oppression of everyone. They abused them; in fact,

16. Theodore had admitted that the "beetle" of the LXX was not the version of the other translators, or of the Syriac (which as elsewhere he belittles). Jerome cites the Hebrew term (a *hapax legomenon*, its meaning disputed by modern commentators), and agrees the LXX had misread it. Thus alerted to this background of the term in his text, Cyril creatively claims that people of the time used the word "beetle" with good reason, having already cited scriptural documentation for vocal expression by animate and inanimate creation.

they killed them, they stoned them, and they finally included the Son among them,[17] the pretext for their madness being the Law; they feigned the impression of being grieved by Christ's flouting the commandment given through Moses. But the fact that their zeal was displeasing to God and "not enlightened," as the divinely inspired Paul writes, the prophet would clearly suggest in saying, *This is not from the Lord almighty.* Accordingly, they *perished by fire and have diminished,* consumed by war and wasted by famine; such things befell the Jewish masses for their frenzy against the Son and, as I said, for killing the prophets before him.[18]

Because all the earth was filled with the knowledge of the glory of the Lord so that much water covered seas (v.14). The divine Scripture is often not interested in times, and cites future events as though already enacted. So we shall find this happening here, too; *was filled* in the text should be taken to mean "will be filled." When the divine wrath is inflicted on Babylon, then, and when, by means of (107) Cyrus and his allies, everything in it that was once fearsome and audacious, ever exposing the others to its unbearable cruelty, now appears piteous and weak, totally desolate, and under the feet of the foe, then it is that all the earth under heaven will realize the extent of the divine *glory,* and will be *filled* with *knowledge* of this. The rule of the Chaldeans used to prevail, and was the cynosure of all eyes, fearsome and invincible, because God was tolerant and allowed it to have power even over Judea and to overthrow countless cities. But when he decided to invest it with the troubles due to it, it was toppled and fell and was consigned to desolation. The prophet Jeremiah also said something like this in reference to it: "How has the hammer of the whole earth been broken and shattered? How has Babylon become destruction for nations? They will attack you, and you will be taken, Babylon, without knowing it; you were discovered and seized, because you challenged the Lord. The Lord has opened his storehouse and brought out the in-

---

17. Mt 21.35–39.
18. Rom 10.2. What was a "hateful and unholy" fate meted out to Nebuchadnezzar's victims becomes appropriate for the Jewish leaders of NT times in Cyril's polemic.

struments of his wrath, because there is a task for the Lord God in the land of the Chaldeans, because its time is up."[19]

Now, it should be realized that after the plundering of Jerusalem, Christ turned to the nations, and all the earth under heaven came to know the *glory* of the God and Father; that is, they knew him as though a torrent flooding the land. In other words, Christ turned to them like a river, having said of old through a prophet, "Lo, I shall turn to them like a river of peace and like a torrent, flooding nations with glory."[20] When Israel at one time in the wilderness made a calf, remember, (108) and consequently offended God, he promised the revelation of the Savior and an abundance of grace through him, saying, "As I live and my name lives, the glory of God will fill the whole earth." Everything, in fact, is suffused with Christ, who is the glory of the Father. Consequently, he also said, "I glorified you on earth; I completed the work you gave me to do."[21]

O for the one who makes his neighbor drink deadly overthrow and intoxicates him so that he gazes on their caves. Drink the satiety of dishonor from glory (vv.15–16). Once more he utters *O* at the unholy crimes of Nebuchadnezzar,[22] foretelling what he will suffer, and thus indicating that the punishment will involve severe pangs. By *deadly overthrow* he probably refers to the unmitigated distress or outrage that he, as it were, *makes* the captives *drink* in making them seem little different from those in wine and drunkenness. What ensues from that? As though opening a kind of *cave*, he makes clear each one's thinking to all the others;[23] by inflicting severe outrage on the more prominent of the captives, or perhaps even on the kings themselves, he also then unmasks their sometimes hidden cowardice or terror under insupportable pressure. He was so fearsome and ruthless that,

---

19. Jer 50.23–25.   20. Is 66.12.
21. Nm 14.21; Jn 17.4.
22. The five woes in the Heb. beginning vv.6, 9, 12, 15, and 18 the LXX does not clearly recognize.
23. Jerome had indicated that the LXX had missed the sense of some Heb. terms in the passage; the former term, for which he cites a variety of versions, suggests "wrath," and by offering "cave" the LXX had misread the *hapax legomenon* for "nakedness." Cyril does not acknowledge the former, but will eventually admit the latter after getting value from the LXX reading.

while he should have shown pity and compassion for them, he took delight in their grief and considered it an ornament of his own dominance. This, in my view, is the meaning of *makes his neighbor* (109) *drink deadly overthrow and intoxicates him so that he gazes on their caves,* that is, their hidden secrets. Since he gave vent to unmitigated anger, therefore, with no trace of any pity, and invested small and great, significant and insignificant, with unbearable calamities, consequently the Lord of all says, *Drink the satiety of dishonor from glory;* that is to say, Though you were celebrated, famous, the cynosure of all eyes, and notorious for cruelty, you will now be dishonored and suffer a penalty commensurate with the height of your fame.

Now, it would be appropriate, if you like, to claim that this is true also of the unholy Pharisees themselves; they *made their neighbor drink deadly overthrow,* which we say means their teaching, human commandments,[24] and in addition the frenzy against Christ and the crimes of blasphemy. While he offered an invitation to life, in fact, they were caught up in such madness as even to say to the listeners, "He has a demon and is mad: why listen to him?"[25] Now, they did this so as to reject the message of salvation, which enlightens the mind, and to *gaze into their cave,* that is, their dark, unlit, and dead teachings. Consequently, they *drank the satiety of dishonor,* despite once being conspicuous and acquiring no little *glory* in being leaders of flocks, priests, and judges.

Such a passage would apply also to the inventors of the unholy teachings, which in truth *make the neighbor drink deadly overthrow,* pouring the venom of deceit into the souls of the simple (110) so that they may also *gaze into their cave.* Their mind is dark, you see, full of deceit, truly immersed in the devil's gloom, in my view no different from caves, which are full of bones and every stench and uncleanness.

With a view to greater clarification of the passage, however, I think there is need to say the following. The Hebrews tell a story, which comes by way of tradition,[26] that when Nebuchadnezzar plundered Judea and all the other countries and took

24. Mt 15.9; Is 29.13.
25. Jn 10.20.
26. Jerome attributes the story to a certain Jew.

the leaders of the nations to his own country, in due course he prepared potions. He then brought in the captives, plied them with the specially prepared concoctions, and made them dance. When they were whirling about, falling down, and lying naked, they sometimes also exposed their private parts, which gave cause for mockery and an occasion for enjoyment; they say that this was naturally called *caves.* The story is somewhat plausible; for *caves* the other translators put "nakedness," so that the text would read, *O for the one who makes his neighbor drink deadly overthrow and intoxicates him so that he gazes on their nakedness.*

And you, heart, shake and tremble; the cup in the Lord's right hand has come round to you, and dishonor has gathered upon your glory. Because Lebanon's impiety will cover you, the mistreatment of wild beasts (111) *will terrify you on account of people's bloodshed and the impious behavior of country, city, and all its inhabitants* (vv.16–17). In the souls of arrogant people there are unfortunately found natural signs of extreme insensitivity of mind, and in addition the conviction that they will enjoy an unalloyed experience of prosperity, while, on the other hand, they reject in general terms the expectation that there will ever be a turn for the worse in their affairs. Resembling this is the statement of David spoken on the part of those enjoying satisfaction and enjoyment: "I said in my prosperity, I shall never be moved."[27] It is therefore to the Babylonian in his obdurate condition of extreme pride that he now, as it were, directs his attack as though to someone ruthless in the words, *And you, heart, tremble;* that is, in case you think that you are firmly established in unshakable prosperity, admit the thought of distressing circumstances, get a sense of what is to come, and give way to experience, even though beforehand you have given not the slightest thought to the fact that you, too, will sometime be in difficulties, and your *heart* will be beset with what naturally causes considerable distress.

What, then, is there to make it *shake* and strike it with grief? *The cup in the Lord's right hand has come round to you, and dishonor has gathered upon your glory.* In other words, just as you yourself *made the neighbor drink deadly overthrow,* in the same way you have

27. Ps 30.6.

become the victim of the effects of divine wrath, and you will be loathsome and dishonored by all, piteous and outcast, and completely deprived of that former reputation. (112) Now, in saying that it is *the cup in the Lord's right hand,* the blessed prophet urges him to take the view that he could not refuse to drink it, since it is God who proffers it; he was definitely obliged to suffer the effects of wrath, as Scripture says, "If you close the door on someone, who will open it?" and as the prophet says, "Who will avert the uplifted hand?"[28]

Why such things will befall him, then, he makes clear by saying, *Because Lebanon's impiety will cover you, the mistreatment of wild beasts will terrify you.* Lebanon is one of the most conspicuous mountains in Phoenicia, covered in trees and sweet-smelling because of producing incense. Sacred Scripture sometimes compares Jerusalem to it, doubtless because of the pride it takes in its many holy heads, raised up and meditating on things in heaven, and enveloped in the beauty of piety. Blessed David also mentions these things in saying to God, "The cedars of Lebanon, which you planted, there sparrows will nest";[29] each of the holy ones, like a cedar, as I just said, is raised on high, by refusing to meditate on what is abject—that is, things of earth—and is a kind of shelter for the others, welcoming like sparrows those willing to be his disciples. Since the Chaldean sacked Jerusalem, therefore, offended God by setting fire to the divine Temple in addition to the city, and seized and abused the holy things themselves, consequently, he says, (113) *Lebanon's impiety* committed against him *will cover* him.[30] Now, by *Lebanon* he refers either to Judea or Jerusalem; you would think that the Temple itself would perhaps be very sweet-smelling, bedecked also with the heads of the priests like cedars of a kind. How the *impiety* committed against Lebanon was destined to *cover him* he demonstrated by proceeding, *Because the mistreatment of wild beasts will terrify you.* By *wild beasts* he probably refers to the Persians and

28. Jb 12.14; Is 14.27.
29. Ps 104.16–17.
30. In a passage where Cyril is taking "Lebanon" to mean Jerusalem, this clause appears in the PG ed. as follows: "consequently, he says, the impiety committed against Lebanon will cover him."

Medes, allies of Cyrus, for being quite indomitable and prone to cruelty. The fact that, far from punishing idly, God inflicts punishment that is commensurate with whatever one does, he brought out by adding, *on account of people's bloodshed and the impious behavior of the city and all its inhabitants.*

Now, each of the Pharisees, who were promoters and accomplices in the frenzy against Christ, will hear the words, *And you, heart, shake and tremble.* In fact, *the cup in the Lord's right hand has come round to* them, *and dishonor has gathered upon* their *glory.* Like a cup of destruction they drained the wrath befalling them, and were dishonored and removed far from every distinction, having offended against *Lebanon.* Now, by *Lebanon* you will understand the church, which is truly sweet-smelling, the conspicuous mountain, familiar to people everywhere; but they persecuted the church after the crucifixion of Christ. Consequently, they were also terrified by the wild beasts ravaging them, and, having been guilty of the slaughter of many of the holy prophets, they added to that the slaughter of those who believed in our Lord Jesus Christ, of whom (114) the first-fruits was blessed Stephen, who emerged as the initial trophy, as it were, and first-fruits of the holy martyrs.

What good is a carved image because they carved it? They made a cast figure of it, a figment of their imagination, because the craftsman had faith in his craft of making dumb idols (v.18). The drift of the verse is to this effect, then: *What good is a carved image because they carved it?* And what good is *the craftsman because he had faith in the craft?* The prophet's purpose, on the other hand, we shall explain as far as possible. When Cyrus and the Medes attacked the Babylonians, and word of the war was bruited abroad, the soothsayers followed their usual custom in calling on the false gods for aid to the city at risk, and offered sacrifices and libations to the insensate objects, placing all their hope of survival in them. It was idle talk and quackery, however, deceit and persiflage, and nothing more; [the city] was taken and plundered, though never expecting to suffer this fate. Accordingly, the God of all mocks those who had failed in their purpose and their hope in inanimate things: *What good is a carved image*, which is nothing more than *a figment of the imagination* that lacks any reality? How or where would divine power be believed to exist in what is made by human hand? Trusting in them, therefore, is vain and truly ridiculous in the estimation of people of sound mind and alert mentality.

On the other hand, you could judge that the force of the passage could be explained in a different way. Having taken the cities and devastated all the countries, so to speak, the Babylonian had no hesitation in setting his sights on high in his arrogance, and in his wretched state he decked his own head with the glory due to God, carving a golden image, as the divinely inspired prophet Daniel recorded.[31] He then bade people of all tribes and languages to adore it; the penalty for refusing to do so was death. So what good, tell me, he says, came from that? In the belief that he was a god, he was then driven to an excess of every evil, and was caught up in misfortunes beyond description.

Woe to the one who says to the wood, Awake, get up, and to the stone, Arise. It is imaginary, it is a product of gold and silver, and there is no breath in it. The Lord, on the other hand, is in his holy Temple; let all the earth pay obeisance before him (vv.19–20). The force of the passage proceeds directly, as I just said; he rightly castigates those who are deceived for abandoning the one who is by nature and in truth God, and who by forsaking the way of piety towards him go to their ruin, crying out *to the wood, Awake, get up, and to the stone, Arise.* People who are deceived, in fact, (116) if some fear alarms them, normally cling to altars, open up shrines, and cry aloud to the lifeless idols, Have mercy, save us, and you, *stone, get up,* as a god protect those venerating your power and opting to adore you. It is right, therefore, to say *Woe* to such people because it is to *products of gold and silver,* with *no breath* in them, that their devotees make such statements as would better be said to God, who dwells in heaven and has as his own temple the city above; the holy one dwells among holy people, and stays with those venerating him.

It is therefore a useful and necessary utterance the prophet makes to us, *Let all the earth pay obeisance before him.* After all, for people of sound thinking the one who is by nature and in truth

31. Dn 3.

God must be worshiped, and to him every wise person will pay homage, offer prayers to him, look to him for salvation, and confess him to be Creator, Lord of all, Savior and Redeemer, omnipotent, all-holy, changing the nature of things to whatever he chooses at the time, and governing everything by his own decrees.

COMMENTARY ON HABAKKUK,
CHAPTER THREE

A prayer of Habakkuk the prophet in song (v.1).

AVING THOROUGHLY PRESENTED the message to the Babylonian, and adequately foretold that those who sacked the holy city and deported Israel in captivity would pay a heavy penalty, he appositely moves to the mystery of Christ. And as though the redemption had already occurred in the case of a single nation individually, he shifts his attention to it in the case of all in general, whereby not only the remnant of Israel was saved but the whole earth was to no lesser degree saved. Cyrus son of Cambyses, remember, released Israel from captivity, destroying the haughty kingdom that was hateful to God, namely, the Chaldeans'. Now, what happened was an image and type of the things achieved by Christ; finding all humanity in captivity, as it were, and subjected to tyrannical rule, since Satan ruled over us through sin, as it were, (118) he freed us from bondage and hardship, released us from the very servitude of wrongdoing, and brought us, as it were, into the holy city, the heavenly Jerusalem. We became, in fact, "citizens with the saints and members of the household of God," as Scripture says, and thus enrolled in the heavenly homeland. Struck by the force of the mystery, therefore, and admiring the ineffable Incarnation of the Only-begotten, which befitted God, he offers the prayer as though in the form of a song, in keeping with that uttered by David, "My tongue will meditate on your righteousness, on your praise all day long."[1]

---

1. Eph 2.19; Ps 35.28. Cyril ignores Jerome's information that the LXX is wide of the mark in coming up with "song" in 3.1; he generally does not discuss genres, though alert to the comparisons made in figurative language. He is also not inclined to find grounds in the mention of "song" for thinking of Habakkuk as a cultic prophet, as do some modern commentators.

Lord, I heard report of you, and was afraid; Lord, I comprehended your works, and was astonished (v.2). The verse could be taken also, if you wished, as directed to the Father and God of all in person as revealing the Son, and the *report* giving clarification about him from the Spirit, or also properly directed to the Incarnate Word. If you were to say it was perhaps addressed to the Father, we would understand it in these terms: O Lord of all, I am astounded by the revelation or *report* that has been given about your Son; the account is startling and beggars description, and the Incarnation would surpass all understanding. If I were to scrutinize the force of your works in detail with the eye of my heart, it would be a matter of *astonishment*, and nothing less.

On the other hand, if the verse bears on the Son, we shall propose nothing less in the following manner: O Lord and Ruler of all, (119) even if you were actually made flesh, I am struck with fear on hearing the *report* of you, or news and revelation. I am astounded, and rightly so, at the magnitude of the event, knowing that, though you share form and equality in everything with the one who begot you, you would willingly empty yourself, become a human being like us from a woman, endure the form of slavery, entitle your own Father as God with us, and become obedient, even to death, death on a cross.[2] Accordingly, *I heard report of you, and was afraid; I comprehended your works, and was astonished*; you brought the good news of sight for the blind; you proclaimed release to captives; you healed the broken-hearted; you brought back the wayward; you bound up the wounded; you became light to those in darkness, a door and way to life and sanctification; you became peace, by faith binding into a single people both those from circumcision and also those from nations; you became "a cornerstone, chosen, precious";[3] you restored the world to the God and Father; you freed from sin those entrapped because of weakness; you delivered them from the devil's grasp; what was enslaved was enlightened by the grace of adoption; man moved from earth to become a citizen of heaven. And furthermore, this, too, is worth hearing, in my

---

2. Phil 2.6–8.
3. 1 Pt 2.6; Is 28.16.

view: the one who gives life to everything has endured with us death in the flesh; but you became "firstborn from the dead," "first-fruits of those who have fallen asleep,"[4] and spoils of a humanity that has been restored to incorruption. By returning to life as God, in fact, you have trampled on the harsh and ill-omened beast, namely, death, canceling (120) the force of that ancient curse; an end has been put in you and through you to the sentence delivered against us: "Earth you are, and to earth you shall return."[5]

You will be known in between two living beings (v.2). People interpret this in different ways. While one commentator claimed that *two living beings* refers to the Spirit and the Son, *in between* whom the God and Father is known, I think this interpretation is uninformed; after all, who would dare to claim that life—namely, the Son or the Holy Spirit—is a living being?[6] Rather, in fact it is what gives life that is life, and the *living being* gains a share in life from someone else. On the other hand, for a different reason it would be wrong also to understand the Father as being *between* both, since he is the one who is named first in the sequence of the confession of the holy and consubstantial Trinity. We do not in any way claim that by taking precedence to the Son and the Spirit in the listing he is superior to them, which would be an idle and rash statement; rather, our position and belief is that from eternity he has the Son originating from him, and what exists did not have existence without his Spirit; instead, as soon as the Father is understood to be God, immediately the existence of the one whose Father he is came into play, as likewise his divine and holy Spirit. Since, however, he is like a fountainhead of the one begotten by him, he is appropriately named first. I cannot understand how he is *between* Son and Spirit. Perhaps they will reply in all likelihood, however, that *between* should be understood locally. (121) But that is also improper: the Divinity is not confined to a place, being neither bodily nor measurable.

---

4. Col 1.18; 1 Cor 15.20.
5. Gn 3.19. Thus concludes a remarkable paean by Cyril in praise of Christ.
6. The LXX has prompted the lengthy debate by rendering the "years" of the Heb. as "two (living beings)."

Other people have claimed that the *two living beings* are the New and the Old Testaments, *in between* which Christ is known. In interpretations of this kind let each person follow the path of individual choice; but for our part, when once we direct discussion to the person of Christ, we shall conduct the explanation of ideas in terms of the Law. Our Lord Jesus Christ therefore became the mercy seat by faith; the divinely inspired Paul chose to think and talk in that fashion. It is through him, in fact, that we were rid of every fault, and found the Father propitious and ready of access. The divine John confirms it in these words: "Children, I am writing these things to you so that you may not sin. If anyone does sin, we have an advocate with the Father, Jesus Christ the righteous, and he is the atoning sacrifice for our sins, and not for ours only, but also for the whole world."[7] Since the things that were expressed of old in riddles were types of the reality in the future, however, come now, let us present the Son as the mercy seat from the Father by mentioning what happened in the holy tent.[8] The God of all, then, bade an ark and a lampstand be set up in the holy tent as well as a table; then in addition a mercy seat made of gold, purple, twisted linen, and spun scarlet, and it was raised and suspended from the holy ark by four poles. Then two cherubim made of gold were placed to the right and left of (122) the mercy seat directing their faces to it.

Now, this was an obscure reference to the mystery of Christ; the Word became flesh, though God and Lord of all, proceeding from the God and Father by nature. But even if he became flesh, and was appointed as mercy seat by the Father, he did not forfeit what he was, namely, being God; instead, that is what he is as regards authority and glory befitting God, and the powers on high likewise attend on him in performing the rituals assigned them. Consequently, the cherubim are placed at the ends of the mercy seat and constantly face it; it is customary

7. 1 Jn 2.1–2.

8. The details are drawn from Ex 25. While Jerome had alerted Cyril to the divergence between the LXX and the Heb. (see n. 1, above), and had also noted a similarity to the cherubim of Ex 25, it is Cyril who develops the beautiful notion of Christ as mercy seat, a notion Theodoret will find fruitful in his commentary on Rom 3.25.

with the powers on high, holy and all-pure as they are, ever to contemplate the things of God, to gaze at him, and always to support what pleases and is dear to him. *You will be known,* therefore, O Lord, he is saying, for who you are on becoming like us; that you are the mercy seat, on the model of the one in the holy tent, will be clearly known. You have taken your place, in fact, *in between two living beings,* that is, the cherubim, and your name is "mercy seat." It is a true statement, as Christ himself says, "The Father sent the Son into the world, not to condemn the world, but that the world might be saved through him."[9]

In the approach of the years you will be acknowledged; when the time arrives, you will be brought to light (v.2). While the Law gave a premonition of the mystery of Christ, and as well the band of the holy prophets gave voice to it in advance, (123) it was the spiritual guides who in a variety of ways firmly established us in faith in him by helpfully comparing what occurred and was achieved at the time of his coming with the ancient Scriptures about him, and we shall often find them confirming their own position from that source. What it is can be seen from the statement of the evangelists; our Lord Jesus Christ drove out of the Temple the sheep and cattle merchants, and overturned the tables of the money-changers by "making a whip of cords and driving them all out in the words, Stop making my Father's house a marketplace." What ensued from that? "His disciples remembered that it was written, Zeal for your house will consume me."[10] When at one time Joseph thought that the virgin betrothed to him had been defiled, and wanted to dismiss her privately, "an angel of the Lord appeared to him in a dream, saying, Joseph son of David, do not be afraid to take Mary as your wife, for the child conceived in her is from the Holy Spirit. She will bear a son, and you are to name him Jesus, for he will save his people from their sins." He then cited a sacred text in confirmation, going on to say, "All this took place to fulfill what had been spoken through the prophet, Lo, the virgin will conceive and bear a son, and they will name him Emmanuel."[11]

9. Jn 3.17.   10. Jn 2.15–17.
11. Mt 1.20–23; Is 7.14.

We shall also find Emmanuel personally confirming faith in himself from the predictions of the prophets, requiring people to acknowledge him on the basis of previous events themselves, (124) and, by comparing the outcome of his achievements with the earlier prophecies, to have no doubts that he is the one who was proclaimed in advance in Law and Prophets. Some of John's disciples, remember, came to him with the question, "John the Baptist sent us with the question, Are you the one who is to come, or are we to wait for another?" Now, although he could have said, I and no other, he urged them to refer to the ancient prophecy in the words, "Go and tell John what you have heard and seen: blind people see, lame people walk, lepers are cleansed and deaf people hear, dead people are raised, poor people have the good news brought to them, and blessed is anyone who takes no offense at me."[12]

It is therefore true, as the prophet says, *In the approach of the years you will be acknowledged*, and that at the time determined of old, by the will and decree of the God and Father, Christ was *brought to light.* In the last times of the age, in fact, he was made manifest to us, was *acknowledged,* and has been confessed, as of course even before the others Nathanael proclaimed in the words, "Rabbi, you are the Son of God, you are the King of Israel."[13] So *in the approach of the years* he was *acknowledged*, that is, at the time of the Incarnation. *He was acknowledged* both by the holy ones and now by all the earth under heaven; we have come to know the one *in between two living beings*, the mercy seat as foreshadowed in the Law's riddles—namely, Christ.

In the disturbance of my soul you will remember mercy in wrath (v.2). (125) Humankind offended the Creator as a result of the transgression by Adam, who showed extremely little regard for the commandment given him. Accordingly, we were both *disturbed* and destroyed; in our wretched state we fell foul of curse and retribution, and were under the power of death for having provoked God. Our forefather Adam heard the words, remember, as root of the race, "Earth you are, and to earth you

---

12. Lk 7.20–23; Is 29.18–19, 35.5–6, and 61.1.
13. Jn 1.50.

will return." But instead of ignoring us forever, the Creator had mercy on us as God; even if "death in its power swallowed us," as the prophet says, still "God wiped away the tear from every face, removed the people's disgrace from all the earth." By Christ, in fact, the power of death was abolished, and sin was done away with, the source of our disgrace; for "the Lord remembered us and had mercy on us," as the divinely inspired David sings.[14] He restored us to incorruption and life, in fact, despite our being *disturbed*, as I just said, by divine wrath so as to suffer a lack of the Spirit, that is, depression and dejection of soul, this being the way death is exercised in us.

Now, the fact that we have been condemned to death for offending God, and in turn saved by being shown mercy, blessed David confirms by saying to the Creator of all things, "When you avert your face, they will be disturbed and return to their dust; when you send forth your Spirit, they will be created, and you will renew the face of the earth."[15] In other words, we suffered the aversion on account of the transgression by Adam, and returned to the dust from which we were made; but when in turn we were enriched with the divine Spirit in Christ and through Christ, (126) we became sharers in his nature, according to the Scriptures,[16] and we were restored to our original condition, and have been renewed and saved. What the divine Paul himself writes is in fact true: that everything "in Christ is a new creation; old things have passed away; lo, everything has become new."[17] So although we were *disturbed* from the beginning in suffering the effects of divine wrath, *in the approach of the years* when Christ was *acknowledged* and *brought to light* at the time determined of old, then he *remembered mercy*. We have been justified, in fact, not "by the works of the Law," as Scripture says, nor "because of any works of righteousness that we have done, but according to his great mercy."[18]

God will come from Teman, and the holy one from densely shady Mount Paran (v.3). The sense of the passage is twofold, and we shall explain it as far as possible, *Teman* meaning "south." Now,

---

14. Gn 3.10; Is 25.7–8; Ps 115.12.   15. Ps 104.29–30.
16. 2 Pt 1.4.   17. 2 Cor 5.17.
18. Rom 3.20; Ti 3.5.

Paran is situated to the far south, where Horeb is also said to be, the place where Moses represented the people of Israel to God when he determined the norms of behavior. So in taking the passage in one sense we would say this: *God will come from Teman, and the holy one from Mount Paran,* or Horeb; that is, the one who in olden times in the southernmost wilderness on Mount Horeb appeared to the ancestors in the form of fire, the same one who in olden times uttered the Law, *will come* and will be seen in the flesh like us in the role of prophet and mediator, (127) as of course the divinely inspired Moses also did, to whom it was said by God, "I shall raise up a prophet like you for them from their brethren, and put my words in his mouth, and he will tell them all I command him."[19]

If, on the other hand, you wanted to offer a different interpretation for the text, it would go this way: *Teman,* as I said, was the name they gave to the southernmost wilderness. Accordingly, they say that Bethlehem, where Christ was born, is situated in the farthermost southern regions of Judea; it is said in regard to it in a prophet's statement, "You, Bethlehem, house of Ephrathah, are too insignificant to be among Judah's thousands. From you will emerge the one to be a leader who will shepherd my people Israel."[20] So *God will come from Teman,* that is, from Bethlehem in the south; the one who is by nature and in truth God, the only-begotten Word of the Father, in becoming like us was born of a woman in Bethlehem. Since it is the custom of the divine Scripture, however, to compare the assembly of the Jews sometimes to the most conspicuous of the mountains, doubtless because it is seen to be thickly populated with innumerable famous men, consequently here, too, he likens it to *Mount Paran* in the words, *He will come from a densely shady mountain,* calling the mountain *shady* and *dense* because of the ancestors from whom Christ is descended. You can, for instance, clearly hear blessed Luke's genealogy leading from Joseph to Adam, and Matthew's in turn moving systematically from David

---

19. Dt 18.18. Jerome mentions both possible interpretations, the second (the reference in Teman to Bethlehem) deriving from a Jew.

20. Mi 5.2, in a somewhat different phrasing from the text commented on earlier.

and Abraham, as I said, to Joseph.[21] (128) The assembly, therefore, is *shady* and *dense*, producing at various times many people
from whom Christ sprang. After all, there is no doubting he
comes from Jews; he descended from Abraham and David—in
the flesh, I mean—and he says of himself, "Salvation is from the
Jews."[22]

His virtue covered the heavens, and the earth was full of his praise
(v.3). While the only-begotten Word of God became a mercy
seat through faith to people on earth when he appeared like us
even in the form of a slave, that is, a human being, he somehow
seemed for this reason to be inferior to the holy angels themselves and to rank after them in importance, though as God he
was Most High. Paul in his wisdom confirms this in the words,
"We see Jesus, who for a little while was made lower than the angels, crowned with glory and honor because of the suffering of
death," since he had become "obedient unto death, death on a
cross." Consequently, as the same writer says, "God highly exalted him and gave him the name that is above every name, so that
at the name of Jesus every knee should bend, in heaven and
on earth and under the earth, and every tongue should confess
that Jesus Christ is Lord to the glory of God the Father."[23]

The prophet is therefore right in saying, *His virtue covered the
heavens, and the earth was full of his praise.* In other words, the
inhabitants of the holy city, who live in the mansions on high,
"are all spirits in the divine service, sent to serve for the sake of
those who are to inherit salvation," whereas he is established on
the throne of Divinity. To none of the former was it said by the
God and Father, "You are my Son," whereas he confesses him to
be Son and calls him Beloved, having him on the throne with
him to be praised and adored with him; the divinely inspired
Paul likewise said of him, "Again, when he brings the firstborn
into the world, he says, Let all God's angels adore him."[24] So
even if he became a mercy seat by descending to human nature
on account of us and for us, he is no less God and above all creation—visible and invisible, I mean. In fact, *his virtue covers the
heavens,* and *the earth* will be *full of his praise.* The holy seraphim

21. Lk 3.23–38; Mt 1.1–11.   22. Jn 4.22.
23. Phil 2.7; Heb 2.9; Phil 2.8–11.   24. Heb 1.14, 5, 6.

have also openly proclaimed this while attending on his divine throne and in praise properly paying homage to him as Lord of hosts and God of all, saying that heaven and earth are full of his glory.[25] If, on the other hand, you preferred to say that *the glory* of Christ is so great and eminent as also to *cover the heavens* themselves, you would take a plausible view, provided that the greatness is within measure. Blessed David also said somewhere, remember, "Lord, your mercy is in the heavens, and your truth extends to the clouds,"[26] signifying the eminence of goodness and the extraordinary degree of truth in terms of body and place.

His brightness will be like light (v.4). The fact that (130) the mercy seat of faith—that is, Christ—will come to illumine those in darkness would be clear also from the statement of the holy prophets. One said, "Land of Zebulun and land of Naphtali, and the other nations who dwell on the coast of Galilee, the people seated in darkness have seen a great light"; and another, "Shine, shine, Jerusalem, for your light has come, and the glory of the Lord has risen upon you." The God and Father has himself confirmed this in the words, "For Zion's sake I shall not keep silent, and for Jerusalem's sake I shall not rest, until my righteousness emerges like a light, and my salvation burns like a torch," by "righteousness" and "salvation" meaning Christ, "who became for us wisdom from God, and righteousness and sanctification and redemption," as Scripture says.[27] So like a torch for people walking in darkness, Christ emerged for us, by Gospel instruction ridding us of that ancient gloom which the enemy of all imparted to our minds, not allowing us to contemplate the one who is by nature and in truth God, nor to consider the path of piety and life. The *brightness*, therefore, which Christ showed us, *will be like light*, that is, not faint and weak like, of course, that coming through Moses, since the Law involves riddles and shadows; instead, *like light* pure and unaffected by gloom, entering into mind and heart, flashing spiritual brilliance on us, and shedding the beam of genuine knowledge.

Horns are in his hands (v.4). The word *horn* is used consistently

25. Is 6.3.   26. Ps 36.5.
27. Is 9.1–2, 60.1, and 62.1; 1 Cor 1.30.

by the inspired writings (131) either for kingship and power, or for arrogance. Blessed David also conveys this in the words, "I said to the transgressors, Do not transgress, and to the sinners, Do not lift up your horn, do not raise your horn on high, and do not speak injustice against God." "In uttering bombastic nonsense," in fact, some people speak injustice against God, as Scripture says,[28] undermining the correctness of the teachings about him, or even insulting him in some other way.

Now, *horn* suggests power when it refers to the God and Father revealing the Son to us: "He raised up for us a horn of salvation," and again, "His horn will be uplifted in glory."[29] Now, all that Christ achieved against the odds was done with distinction. The Only-begotten comes in a form like ours, then, putting up with the appearance of our limitations in respect of flesh and humanity;[30] but as God he has all the *horns in his hands*, that is, all kingdoms, in terms of all the force of the opposing activities. When we say *in his hands*, we mean "in his power"; we are taught to say to God in prayer, "My lot is in your hands."[31] Now, there is no doubting that every diabolical power has been subjected to Christ along with the so-called *horns*, that is, all those throughout cities and tyrannical places of the unclean spirits. They had divided up the whole earth, in fact: (132) some he drove out of people authoritatively; others approached him and "begged him not to order them to go back into the abyss," as is written by the holy evangelists. The fact that he also dislodged from his tyrannical rule over us the very leader of the unclean spirits—namely, Satan—we shall easily perceive from the words of Christ himself, "Now is the judgment of this world, now the ruler of this world will be driven out. And I, when I am lifted up from the earth, will draw all people to myself."[32] Even though he became man, therefore, he still has *in his hands*—that is, in his power—the tyrannical rule, or kingdoms, or powers, of the opposing forces. If, on the other hand, you wanted to be more particular in taking the view that Christ has *horns in his hands*, that is, invincible and irresistible strength, and that he easily and effortlessly uses a horn to

28. Ps 75.4–5; 2 Pt 2.8.
30. "Appearance": Greek, *dokêsis*.
32. Lk 8.31; Jn 12.31–32.

29. Lk 1.69; Ps 112.9.
31. Ps 31.14–15.

strike and cleave any of the enemy he chooses, and launches on them an unbearable assault like that of a young bull, you would likewise be correct in your interpretation.

And he placed a powerful love of his strength (v.4). Christ came to achieve two things: on the one hand, to destroy adversaries who led astray the whole earth under heaven, robbing God the Creator by purloining the glory due to him alone and be-decking their own heads with it; and, on the other, to rescue those who were deceived and subjected to a truly unbearable oppression. (133) The fact that the power of the former was lost and completely disappeared he conveys by saying, *Horns are in his hands,* namely, those that overturn their control and strike down their arrogance with a horn, as it were. And the fact that he was destined to rescue us he demonstrates in advance by say-ing, *He placed a powerful love of his strength;* in other words, we have been saved, "not by works of righteousness that we our-selves performed," not by achievements of the Law, since "the Law made nothing perfect," but from the clemency of the God and Father, who for our sake *placed a powerful*—that is, strong and mighty—*love* of the Son. The God and Father, remember, "so loved the world as to give his only Son so that everyone believing in him might not perish but have eternal life."[33] It is therefore out of the love of the God and Father that we have been saved, as well as by the Son's enduring death for us, even if he came to life again, canceling the control of corruption and removing sin from us; accordingly, he said, "No one has greater love than this: to lay down one's life for one's friends."[34] *The love of the strength* of the God and Father is *strong,* therefore, since through it we have been delivered from death, sin, and the op-pression of the devil.

Before his face will go a word (v.5). A pronouncement will pre-cede him, he is saying, and rumors will fly up in advance, and there will be many words about him. In other words, as soon as Christ was born of the holy virgin, immediately there came also from (134) the east the magi, as if the star that unexpect-

33. Ti 3.5; Heb 7.19; Jn 3.16.
34. Jn 15.13.

edly appeared in the sky reported to us the birth occurring in
the divine plan. Since with the arrival of the due time he also
began to be a worker of astonishing signs, then "word of him
went out to the whole of Syria," as the evangelist said.[35] In fact,
he really became celebrated even throughout the whole earth
under heaven: who was ignorant of the glory of Christ? Which
nation or country remained unacquainted or unaware of the
force abiding in him? As he himself likewise said, in fact, the
Gospel has been preached to all the nations,[36] and like the
sun the splendor of what was done by him has enlightened the
whole earth.

And his feet will go forth into the countryside (v.5). It would be
like saying again, Nothing is difficult or impossible for him. He
proceeds in every circumstance as though by a level and flat
path; accessible and level parts of the *countryside* are easily nego-
tiated. So everything was simple for Christ, and whatever way he
wished to traverse—meaning everything that was being accom-
plished—would be completely free of every difficulty. After all,
what would he not achieve without the slightest problem, being
by nature God and Lord of the powers? He therefore clarifies
the interpretation by a practical comparison with people going
into the countryside. If, on the other hand, you wanted to understand the *countryside* as the humble (135) of heart, who are also
styled "a chosen land" and "God's field" in the sense of receiving seed from above and from heaven, and yielding a crop,
some a hundredfold, some sixty, some thirty, you would likewise
be right.[37] The Son, in fact, emerges into such a *countryside*, as
it were, to cultivate it, according to the statement made by him
in the form of a parable, "The sower went out to sow his seed."
David also somewhere sings, "Your countryside will be filled
with richness," and goes on to say, "The valleys will abound with
grain." The fact that he allowed the valleys to be understood
spiritually he proceeded at once to imply, saying, "They will

35. Mt 2.2 and 4.24. In the lemma the LXX has read Heb. *dabar*, "word," for
deber, "pestilence"—an understandable error, Jerome explains, when the Heb.
offers only the three consonants.
36. Mk 13.10.
37. Mal 3.12; 1 Cor 3.9; Mt 13.23.

cry out and sing praise";[38] real valleys cannot sing praise or cry out—only spiritual ones, and on these the divine word would alight from above like dew.

He took his place, and the earth shook (v.6). The phrase *took a place* would frequently be understood in the inspired Scripture to mean something reaching fulfillment, as if you were to say, The event, or word of this, took place; that is, it was over and done with. Thus, after circumcising her child with Moses' flint, Zipporah said to the destroying angel, "There had taken place blood-letting in the circumcision of my son";[39] she meant to convey, not that blood-letting had ceased, but that the rite of circumcision has been performed, and what was wanted had been done, since the one who is circumcised by the spiritual flint cheats death. (136) Now, the spirit of Christ is such a flint, as of course Joshua is, too, who after the time of Moses had brought the people of Israel across the Jordan, and bade them be circumcised with blades of stone as a type of circumcision in spirit;[40] just as Christ is called a stone, so too his Spirit is called a flint, or stone blade.

Took place therefore, often means also fulfillment of something. Christ, then, *took his place;* that is, events concerning him reached fulfillment, and he appeared to people on earth, *and the earth shook.* By *earth* he means the inhabitants of earth, who also *shook.* In what way—come now, let us explain as far as we can. People of old, you see, who were of set purpose in wanting to do evil, were fixed in impiety, committed to fleshly pleasures, and devoted to error, were *shaken* and moved, and were brought to the knowledge of God and a desire for virtue. Similarly moved in respect of worship according to the Law were also the descendants of Israel who embraced faith in him; they changed to an option for life by the Gospels and to living by the laws of the Savior. Now, the fact that being *shaken* sometimes suggests change from one thing to another would be clear from blessed David's singing in these words: "He sits enthroned upon the cherubim; let the earth shake"[41]—not that we claim he urg-

38. Lk 8.5; Ps 65.11, 13.   39. Ex 4.25.
40. Jos 5.3.   41. Ps 99.1.

es the earth to move; rather, he seeks a change from worse to better. (137)

While this is one sense of the passage, you could take it also in a different sense. *The earth took his place, and shook:* the earth experienced two things, taking its place and shaking. There is need to give a clear explanation in both cases. It *took its place*, then; intoxicated, as it were, easily moved to any kind of wrongdoing, and tossed about, as it were, by every breeze, it then gains a firm and stable position, with Christ steadying it, in accord with that statement in Isaiah made to the assembly of the Jews, "Take your place, Zion."[42] But it has been *shaken* again, as I foretold previously, by forsaking its former deception and respecting the change to everything that is pleasing to God. For the earth at the one time to *take its place* and also *be shaken* is paradoxical; Christ is the one who both makes it committed to every good work and is involved in encouraging the adjustment from worse behavior to better.

He looked down, and nations withered, mountains were violently shattered (v.6). God's *looking down* suggests an inspection, on the one hand, as though made sometimes with gentleness and love, and at other times in anger and threatening. Scripture says, for example, "On whom shall I look down, if not the one who is gentle and peaceable and who trembles at my words?" The divinely inspired David also prays somewhere in these words: "Look down on me and have pity on me." In a (138) statement in Ezekiel he said of someone, "I shall set my face against that person; I shall leave him desolate and do away with him, and shall remove him from the midst of my people, and you will know that I am the Lord."[43] Now, this came from him when threatening wrath, destruction, and the retribution due to offenders. At the same time Christ *looked down*, that is, directed his eye on some people in wrath, and immediately they *withered* like wax, and like a flaming fire *mountains were violently shattered*. Now, by *nations* and *mountains* he means the unclean spirits and people proud of themselves, conceited, and, like mountains, overbearing others; their haughtiness comes completely from depravity and their

42. Not Isaiah, in fact, but Jer 31.21 LXX.
43. Is 66.2; Pss 86.16 and 119.132; Ezek 14.8.

oppression from arrogance. Or perhaps it suggests the extent of the ferocity innate in them; in their arrogance the demons oppose God and strive to apply to themselves the glory due to him. But they *were violently shattered*; they are shattered by the power of Christ, depart into impotence, and are made subject to the believers. Satan likewise in some other place is called a *mountain*, God saying somewhere in the statement of the prophet to him in the person of Nebuchadnezzar, "I am against you, O destroying mountain, that destroys the whole earth."[44]

Eternal hills melted (v.6). By making an obscure reference to the wicked and hostile (139) powers, which oppose also the glory of Christ and divert people on earth towards sin, he inevitably introduced also the leaders of the Jewish synagogue, whom he calls *hills*, doubtless on account of the impression of being raised on high and dominating others from their rank of priesthood and the dignity accruing to it. He calls them *eternal* because of the permanence of the situation, service of God being incessant; he is praised at every moment and time. After all, even if the force of worship in shadows and types has come to an end, yet the nature of the practice has changed for the better; the presidents of the holy churches worship God no less, and celebrate the bloodless sacrifice to him. So the *hills* are *eternal* because of the permanence and continuity of the worship. Nevertheless, they are crushed together with the spiritual mountains, and *melted* along with the nations; since they formed attitudes pleasing to the demons and carried out the will of the devil, consigning the Author of life to the cross and raging against him in many ways, consequently it was right for them to suffer retribution and collapse with them, and, as the prophet says, "The house of Israel collapsed, and there is no one to raise it up."[45]

At his eternal passage for hardships I saw (v.6). It is customary with the sacred writings to refer by *passage*, ways, and paths to the divine commandments, as in the case of the statement in (140) Jeremiah: "Stand in the ways, ask the ancient paths, and

44. Jer 51.25.
45. Am 5.1–2.

see which is the good way; travel by it, and you will find purification for your souls." As well, in the statement of blessed David:
"I walked in the way of your commandments when you enlarged
my heart."[46] So *hills melted*, he says, that is, those appointed to
the position of leadership among the Jews and possessing the
ornaments of priesthood according to the Law. The *passage* or
commandments of Emmanuel, in fact, that is, the Gospel oracles and teaching, *for hardship I saw* to be incomparably better
and clearer than the ancient utterances; that is, they considered
it burdensome and full of labor, despite the clear statement of
Christ the Savior of all, "Come to me, all you who labor and
are heavily burdened, and I shall give you rest. Take my yoke
upon you, and learn from me, because I am gentle and humble in heart, and you will find rest for your souls. For my yoke
is easy and my burden light."[47] Some, on the other hand, in a
different fashion considered his *passage* intolerable, though by
means of it one could easily reach eternal life; our Lord Jesus
Christ clarifies the force of the spiritual blessing in the words,
"Amen, amen, I say to you, unless you eat the flesh of the Son
of Man and drink his blood, you will not have life in you." Some
of those listening to such august words, however, foolishly said,
"This saying is hard: (141) who can accept it? How can he give
us his flesh to eat?" The evangelist testified that "as a result of
this, many of his disciples went away, and no longer walked with
him." And when Christ pressed the disciples themselves as to
whether they also wanted to leave, "Surely you do not also wish
to depart?" the divinely inspired Peter cried out in reply, "Lord,
to whom shall we go? You have the words of eternal life."[48] That
is to say, instead of their taking his *passage for hardship*, to them
the statement was pleasing and truly acceptable.

He says that the *passage* is *eternal*, never ceasing, but bringing the one who begins it to *eternity*, and making the saving
preaching of the Gospel last forever, despite the former commandment of the Law being obsolete and not above reproach,

46. Jer 6.16; Ps 119.32.
47. Mt 11.28–30. The verb "saw" in the lemma can be read as first person
singular or third person plural, and Cyril reads either where it suits him.
48. Jn 6.52–68.

as Paul says in his wisdom, and hence the introduction of the second covenant, which is said to "have been enacted through better promises." The divinely inspired David, for example, cried out in spirit to our Lord Jesus Christ, "Your righteousness is an everlasting righteousness, and your Law is truth."[49] What was in shadows did not abide, as I said; instead, the types came to an end, whereas what is from Christ has lasted and is forever unchanging.

Tents of Ethiopians will be terror-stricken, and tabernacles of Midian (v.7). More useful stories always contain something worth hearing (142) and an unrestrained denunciation, even if the same words are employed. Having previously announced the lapse into weakness by the opposing forces, then, and shown them to have *withered* in a manner similar to the nations and to have been crushed like mountains, he proceeds to compare them to the foreigners who campaigned against the land of the Jews. These were the *Ethiopians*, located close to the Indian sea to the east and south, and also the *Midianites*, who occupy the neighboring wilderness. They *will be terror-stricken*, then, he says, in fighting against the holy city, which we are to understand as the spiritual Zion, or the church of Christ, occupied by the saints, the chosen race, like the Israel of old as a type, Israel meaning "Mind that sees God." Nathanael also was admired for being "truly an Israelite, in whom there is no deceit."[50] We shall therefore understand the *Ethiopians* and *Midianites*, who were ever bent on harming the chosen race—that is, Israel—by way of image and type as the columns of the demons, who are hostile to the saints.

On the other hand, you might also claim that in a different sense the *Ethiopians* refer to the idolaters, whose life is of the flesh and the earth and is involved in unclean things. Ethiopians are like that; instead of having the divine light in their minds, they are, as it were, black at heart and dark in their thinking, and they are said to have a dragon for food; David somewhere sings in speaking to the God of all, "You crushed

49. Heb 8.13, 7, 6; Ps 119.142.
50. Jn 1.47.

the head of the dragon; you gave him as food to the Ethiopian peoples."[51] In other words, just as we have the life-giving Word of God for spiritual and holy food, so, too, those who love sin (143) and have no knowledge of the one who is God by nature feed, as it were, off Satan, having him for their mind, and thinking and saying what is his. The *Midianites* in turn would be, as I said, those hostile to the saints. If, on the other hand, you chose to examine further the force of the name, Midian means "sentenced" or "condemned." Such a title would fit Satan and the wicked powers with him, "for whom the deepest darkness is reserved forever."[52]

Surely you were not angry with rivers, Lord, nor was your wrath against rivers, nor your fury against the sea? Because you will ride on your horses, and your riding is salvation. You will draw your bow against scepters, says the Lord (vv.8–9). The prophet's purpose was to present the second as better than the former arrangement, clearer and involving incomparably greater goods. In the former case Israel was through Moses delivered from the slavery of the flesh, with the transformation of the Egyptians' rivers into blood and the performance of signs and wonders; then the Red Sea was parted, the redeemed brought across, and the Egyptian warriors drowned in the waters. When the only-begotten Word of God became man, on the other hand, he rescued the whole earth under heaven from its subjection to the devil's oppression, not by turning rivers into blood, (144) not by venting his own wrath by waters, not by parting waves of a sea, not by inflicting destruction on people, but by slaying the murderous dragon himself, by destroying the sin devised by him and as a result of him, by undoing the daunting power of death, and by calling everyone to knowledge of God through the holy apostles, who traversed the whole earth under heaven, bruiting abroad the name of Christ, and were quite rightly admired.

Accordingly, he is saying, O Lord, what you yourself have done independently is thoroughly worthy of note, containing much that is better than what was achieved by you as well through Mo-

---

51. Ps 74.14, cited also by Jerome.
52. 2 Pt 2.17; Jude 13. The derivation is Jerome's. The PG ed. reads *katakekrummenos* instead of *katakekrimenos.*

ses; you will not inflict wrath on *rivers;* you will not rage against a *sea;* it will not be by these means. By what? The marvel will be resplendent by your power, which befits God: *you will ride on your horses, and your riding is salvation.* Now, what would the *horses* be? The blessed disciples, apostles, and evangelists, who were completely subject to the divine wishes, who were compliant, obedient, and ready to do anything at all pleasing to him, with Christ as their rider and driver. One of them is blessed Paul, of whom he personally says, "He is an instrument whom I have chosen to bring my name before the nations." Now, the *horses* are very swift, traversing the whole earth under heaven. Likewise, "God's chariotry is said to be ten thousandfold, with thousands of stalwarts," innumerable at the time, (145) and after them came leaders of peoples subjecting their rebellious minds to the Savior's yoke, spreading abroad his glory everywhere, correctly expressing the message of truth,[53] and by their mounts, as it were, subduing the whole earth. *Your riding is salvation*; far from traveling without purpose, they meant to save cities, countries, and nations, with Christ overthrowing the rule of the demons, who had tamed the whole earth, so to speak, subjecting its inhabitants to their wishes. Since the former rule of the demons was destined to collapse, however, he is consequently right to say, *You will draw your bow against scepters.* As I just said, he will not vent his *fury against the river or sea;* instead, he will overturn *the scepters* of the demons.

   The land of rivers will be split. Peoples will see you and suffer pangs. Scattering waters of his passage (v.10). He mentions again the Savior's achievements, and to the other nations, against whom the bow is drawn or will be drawn, he says will be added also *the land of rivers*, implying perhaps the land of the Babylonians, since at that time the land between the rivers belonged to it. His purpose is that by mention of this, using the figure of bodily enemies, there may be reference also to the vast number of spiritual and unseen enemies with whom the saints struggle.[54] The prophets' discourse is generally obscure; hence (146) by mention of a part of the land between the *rivers* there is a reference to the land of

53. Acts 9.15; Ps 68.17; 2 Tm 2.15.
54. Eph 6.12.

the Babylonians, and through it in an obscure manner to the herd of the demons.

Or perhaps the prophetic verse suggests to us something else as well: by *rivers* he probably refers to Judea, doubtless because of the great number of prophets in it, watering the nation like rivers and, as it were, inundating it with divine floods. I think that it is in reference to them that blessed David also says, "Rivers will clap their hands as one," and as well God says in Isaiah, "The beasts of the field will bless me, sirens and daughters of sparrows, because I gave water for drinking in the desert and rivers in the dry land to my chosen race, my people to whom I made it my business to outline my doughty deeds." It is our Lord Jesus Christ, in fact, who is referred to as a "torrent of delight,"[55] and he truly is, and a river as well; it was in reference to him that he said in the statement of the holy ones, "Lo, I shall direct peace on them like a river, and inundate them with the glory of nations like a torrent." It is also said in the statement of David, "The force of the river gladdens the city of God."[56]

Now, no harm is done in comparing it to him and in referring to the holy prophets themselves as *rivers*, for the reason that they are similar to him in a spiritual sense. Just as he is the true light, you see, but said somewhere to the holy apostles, "You are the light of the world," so, too, while he it is who is a river and also living water, he grants to the saints the right to glory in the same role. Accordingly, the *land* of the spiritual (147) *rivers*—namely, Judea—could not bring itself to drink the living water, nor accept the message of the holy prophets or that of Moses; if they had believed Moses, they would have believed Christ, since he wrote of him.[57] It *will be split*, that is, will thirst; thirsty terrain splits.

The prophet marvels, therefore, making, as it were, the moral remark, The land that formerly had many *rivers* and an abundant supply of the divine streams will be thirsty and lack water. But when *peoples* in a spiritual sense witnessed your coming, O Lord—that is, those of the nations who understood the mystery

---

55. Ps 98.8; Is 43.20–21; Ps 36.8.   56. Is 66.12; Ps 46.4.
57. Jn 5.46.

in your case—they immediately accepted the good amidst the birth pangs, and proved fruitful. You could apply to them as well the statement, "For fear of you, Lord, we conceived, suffered birth pangs, and gave birth; we produced a spirit of your salvation on earth."[58] In other words, by choosing Emmanuel as Savior and Redeemer, they felt the pangs of divine fear; every issue of their mind will be a fruit of virtue, and their efforts will result in a spirit of salvation. Therefore, *peoples will see you and suffer pangs* by drinking of your streams and being inebriated with the evangelical streams. They eagerly made the approach to the one who says, "If anyone thirsts, let them come to me and drink," for you were so munificent and kind as even to *scatter waters in his very passage*, that is, the life-giving message of the Gospel teaching. As Matthew says, in fact, "Jesus went around all the cities and towns teaching in their synagogues, preaching the good news of the kingdom, and healing every disease and every ailment of the people"[59]—the meaning, in my view, of *scattering waters of his passage*. There is no doubting that the message of inspired teaching is referred to as "water" in the sacred texts.

The deep gave forth its voice, the height of its imagining. The sun was lifted up, and the moon stood in its place for light (vv.10–11). By *deep* he refers to the peoples suffering birth pangs and proving fruitful, presenting them as numerous beyond counting, like *the deep*. The vast number of the holy angels are also given this name in the statement of Ezekiel; God said somewhere, for example, about Satan in the person of the ruler of Tyre, "When they dispatched him to Hades, the deep mourned for him"; after all, since it was the descent and fall of the one surpassing all others in splendor, who was also "ranked with the very cherubim," in the words of the prophet himself,[60] it was not unlikely for him to be deeply mourned by the spiritual *deep*, that is, the masses of the spirits on high, and, as it were, lamented for his fate and his offense to the God of all. It is *the deep*, therefore, he says—that is, the immeasurable and incomprehensible multitude of believers—and as well *the height of its imagining*—that is, everything in it

58. Is 26.18.
59. Jn 7.37; Mt 9.35.
60. Ezek 31.15 (in reference rather to the Pharaoh) and 28.14.

that is splendid and elevated, gleaming with the finery or empty glories of this world—that *gave forth its voice.* Christ is praised, in fact, by every nation of human beings, and you could see small and great enthusiastically doing so, (149) important and insignificant, those more famous than the others, enjoying a preeminence of glory or of wealth and splendor in this life—what he rightly called *imagining* or *height of imagining,* being nothing more for them than appearance, because "all flesh is grass, and all human glory is the flower of grass."[61] The fact that *the deep gave forth its voice,* and small and great venerate our Lord Jesus Christ, blessed David also clarifies by saying, "Praise the Lord from the earth, you dragons and all deeps." To them he adds "mountains and hills, fruit trees and all cedars, wild animals and all cattle, creeping things and flying birds," and proceeds, "Let rulers and all judges of the earth, young men and maidens, elders with youngsters, praise the name of the Lord." The mighty Isaiah also said somewhere to us in reference to him, "Kings will see him and be afraid, and rulers will bow down before him."[62]

He supplies the reason, as it were, why *the deep* and also *the height of its imagining gave forth its voice,* proceeding at once, *The sun was lifted up, and the moon stood in its place for light.* Now, just as we interpreted the *deep,* not in physical terms, which would be very materialistic, but spiritually and intellectually, so, too, in this case we shall not direct the eye of our mind to the heavenly bodies, namely, *sun and moon;* instead, moving by way of comparison from them to a better level, we shall perceive the force of the ideas. By *sun,* therefore, we claim that there is a reference to the lightsome and shining spiritual guidance of the Gospel oracles, and likewise by *moon* to the lesser (150) and more indistinct light of the Law, which shone at the time before the coming as though at night and in darkness. Day is the name given, in fact, to the time when Christ shone forth, the sun of righteousness, the spiritual morning star, rising in the hearts of the believers. The divinely inspired David says, for instance,

61. Is 40.6. Cyril is unaware that "imagining" in the LXX replaces the Heb. form for "hands," thus rendering "it lifts its hands on high," as "the height of its imagining was lifted up"—though Cyril's text divides this verse and the next differently.

62. Ps 148.6–13; Is 49.7.

"This is the day the Lord has made; we shall be glad and rejoice in it."[63] Just as the material sun, when it is still near the ground and hardly risen from the earth, not yet full and brilliant, keeps its light to itself, suppressed, as it were, whereas when it leaps up it casts the blinding bolt of its beams to people everywhere, so, too, the teaching of Christ, while suppressed in the beginning and unknown to many, rose like the sun, as it were, in a short time climbed on high, and by releasing the beam of the knowledge of God strikes the *deep*, that is, the whole human race, and consequently *gave forth its voice*. It gives praise, in fact, as I said, calls on God, and confesses Emmanuel to be Lord and Redeemer of all.

The sun was lifted up, then, and no less *the moon*—that is, the Law—*stood in its place for light*; the instruction from Moses gave way to the Gospel teaching, that being *its place*, since it is shadow and type. But since Christ is the fullness of Law and Prophets, the Law also gained brilliance; comparing the outcome with what was formerly promised in it, we also marveled at the light of the Law itself (151) nicely prefiguring to us in many ways the mystery of Christ. So it *stood for light*. Christ also personally blesses those who combine in themselves the teaching of Law and Gospels, saying, "Hence I tell you, that every scribe"—that is, the person who knows the Law—"trained in the kingdom of heaven is like a rich man who brings out of his treasure new things and old."[64]

Now, we shall accept also another sense different from this, which is not implausible in my view—rather, it is quite probable. We say, remember, that Emmanuel is *sun*, and quite properly; this is his name, and it is true. The reference in *moon*, on the other hand, should be taken, on the basis of comparison with the heavenly body, to be the church of God, made visible to people in darkness, and, as it were, shining in the night. So when *the sun was lifted up*, in terms of the prophet's statement—in other words, when Christ ascended the precious cross for our sake—then it was that the church from the nations also shone forth and *stood in its place for light*, that is, like a full moon, and

63. Mal 4.2; 2 Pt 1.19; Ps 118.24.
64. Mt 13.52.

by adhering to its peculiar cycle it became light to those in darkness, as I just said. Now, the fact that it was when Christ was lifted up and endured the cross for the life of all that the church came into existence, he himself likewise teaches: "Very truly I tell you, unless a grain of wheat falls and dies, it remains by itself, but if it dies, it bears much fruit." And again, "And I, when I am lifted up from the earth, will draw all people to myself."[65] (152) So the *lifting up of the sun* suggests either the passion on the cross or the ascension into heaven, for this is the way we say he was lifted up.

Your shafts will proceed into the light of the flash of your weapons (v.11). Here by *shafts* that travel throughout the earth, dispatched, as it were, from a bow or strong hand, he means the holy apostles and evangelists, of whom blessed David also said somewhere, "Like javelins in a warrior's hand are the sons of the shaken."[66] While the nation of the Jews was in fact shaken and rejected, doubtless because of their frenzy against Christ when he invited them to life, their offspring, though of the bloodline of Israel, became *shafts* and javelins as the chosen disciples, flying, as it were, from a strong hand, and easily penetrating every victim mortally. *Shafts* of this kind, in fact, when dispatched, as it were, from the hand of Christ, become embedded in the devil's entrails and do away with the dragon. Blessed David, for example, sings a hymn to our Lord Jesus Christ in the words, "Your arrows are sharp, mighty one; peoples will fall under you in the heart of the king's foes." The columns of the demons are therefore destroyed by such *shafts*, and prove the ruin of the foe, while, on the other hand, for those that acknowledge and respect his coming through faith, they fulfill a different purpose, (153) making them wounded with love, as the bride says in the Song of Songs, "I am wounded with love."[67]

It is in a different fashion as well, however, that they emerge as *light of the flash of* his *weapons*. Understood as his *weapons* would be what blessed Paul bids us apply in our own case, "Put

65. Jn 12.24, 32.
66. Ps 127.4.
67. Ps 45.5 (where Chrysostom and Theodoret note the unusual sequence of thought); Song 5.8.

on the armor of God," namely, the breastplate of righteousness, the helmet of salvation, the shield of faith, with our feet shod in the readiness for the gospel of peace, the sword of the Spirit.[68] Such, then, are the *weapons* of Christ, not worn by him but given by him to those who are worthy. They are shining weapons, as it were, *flashing*, virtue being a splendid thing; so the *shafts* will produce *light of the flash of your weapons*. Because the weapons are flashing, in fact, those who teach the ignorant enlighten them; while to those addicted to sin, virtue is, as it were, ugly and not yet splendid, it is nonetheless *flashing* to those familiar with it, splendid and bright, making a person conspicuous to everyone everywhere. First, then, the inspired disciples, who emit the flashing of their weapons, will provide its *light* also to others. You see, just as those with medical skills, when they come across people with eye problems shunning the light of the sun's rays, rid them of the complaint by persuading them to put up with the effect of light, and would thus prove to be a kind of light to them, so, too, (154) the inspired disciples, by admiring and commending the virtues, which have been assigned as weapons by Christ, prove to be for other people a kind of *light of the flashing* or splendor within them.

With threats you will diminish the earth, and in anger you will bring down nations (v.12). After implying to us the devastation of the land of the Jews and the ruin of the nations inhabiting it, the prophet here gives us a glimpse of it. Since they had in fact not professed faith in Christ, but had rebelled against him and "killed the Author of life," consequently they were also given over to desolation, as Isaiah had prophesied to them in the words, "Alas for the lawless: an evil fate will befall him in keeping with his behavior."[69]

You issued forth to the salvation of your people, to save your anointed; you sent death on the heads of the lawless; you raised up bonds as far as the neck forever (v.13). Once more he outlines, as it were, the whole plan of the Incarnation of the Only-begotten. While he saved those who have been justified by faith, anointed with the Holy Spirit, and made sharers in his divine nature, he allowed

68. Eph 6.11–17.
69. Acts 3.15; Is 3.11.

those opting for unbelief to be wasted by their sins, (155) saying to them, "I say to you truly that unless you believe that I am he, you will die in your sins."[70] Accordingly, *you issued forth*, the text says, like some king advancing on the columns of the adversaries and armed in warlike fashion. The purpose of his issuing forth was *to save your anointed*, namely, those anointed by the Holy Spirit, of whom he gave instructions of old through prophets: "Lay no hand on my anointed ones, and do my prophets no harm";[71] to *the lawless* deliver *death*, which they would be guilty of bringing on their own heads for not accepting the faith that justifies. Consequently, they have been surrendered also to unbreakable bonds, and are held in the chains of their own sins,[72] not partially, but, as it were, on their whole body *as far as the neck*.

If, on the other hand, the reference were to the *bonds* of Christ, let no one be alarmed; what happens by God's permission is generally attributed to him, as with the statement, "There is no evil in the city for which the Lord was not responsible"[73]— not that he causes evil, only allowing it to happen to cities' evildoers. If, on the other hand, the *bonds* referred to here were taken to mean complimentary things, again we claim that, though *death was sent on the heads of the lawless*, the God of all embraces, as it were, with *bonds* of love those approaching him, justified by faith and sanctified by the Spirit, in accord with the statement made in the prophet about the descendants of Israel, "And I bound (156) Ephraim; I took him up in my arms; I drew them in the bonds of my love."[74] Now, the *bond as far as the neck* here is understood as the compliance of those submitting their will to him and submitting to the truly loving yoke of our Savior.

You cut down heads of warriors in a stupor; they will be shaken by it (v.14). The term *stupor* is taken in various ways in the inspired Scripture. Sometimes, in fact, it suggests amazement, as if you were perhaps to say of those sinning against the people of Israel, "Heaven was astonished at this," and again, "Astonishment

---

70. Jn 8.24.   71. Ps 105.15.
72. Prv 5.22.
73. Am 3.6, the saying that Chrysostom also cites as a popularly misquoted text used to justify moral irresponsibility.
74. Hos 11.3–4.

and terror fell on the earth." Sometimes, on the other hand, it suggests a change from an earthly attitude to some divine and spiritual condition of behavior and living; the divinely inspired Paul, for instance, writes to some people in the words, "If we are beside ourselves, it is for God; if we are in our right mind, it is for you."[75] In other words, just as we say that the movement from base to better things is a *stupor* acceptable to God, so, too, we affirm that the change from good things to base is a vile and loathsome *stupor*.

Accordingly, he says, *You cut down heads of warriors* when they were *in a stupor* of that kind, referring to those of the leaders of Israel, definitely scribes and Pharisees and the priests who ministered by Law. They really moved *in a stupor* from an upright attitude, sound outlook, and love for God, by not accepting the Son but rather killing him, (157) even though consciously admitting that "this is the heir." Now, the manner in which the *cutting down* should be understood is properly clarified by the statement of the divinely inspired David to God, the Savior of all, "Allot them their fate in their life," since Israel was God's "lot" and "cord of his inheritance."[76] Since they were guilty of sacrilegious frenzy against the Son, however, the beloved was rejected and divided, and forfeited the hope of those who believed, was disinherited and discarded, excluded from his presence, in second place behind the nations, who make this claim of themselves: "Blessed are we by the Lord, who made heaven and earth," and "the Lord is our God, and has appeared to us."[77] Accordingly, Israel was *cut down*, and in losing the blessing it was no longer God's lot, but rather the devil's, dishonored and loathsome.

He next says in reference to the *stupor* that *they will be shaken by it;* that is, they will fall; what suffers trembling and shaking is close to falling. The prophet, as it were, laments their manifold destruction in saying, "The house of Israel fell, there is no one to raise it up."[78]

They will relax their reins like a poor man eating furtively (v.14).

---

75. Jer 2.12 and 5.30; 2 Cor 5.13.   76. Mt 21.38; Ps 17.14; Dt 32.9.
77. Pss 115.15 and 118.27.   78. Am 5.1–2.

Though there is extreme difficulty in both context and text, we shall comment on it to the extent possible by clearly distinguishing the force of the ideas. After outlining the condition in which the heads of the important people should definitely have been—namely, those of the synagogue of the Jews appointed to leadership—he immediately moves to the holy apostles, who in the beginning had deep fear of the persecutors. (158) After all, they had been scourged in the council and ordered to speak to no one in the name of Christ. But they met in secret and offered supplication to God in these words: "For in this city, in fact, both Herod and Pontius Pilate, with the gentiles and the people of Israel, gathered together against your holy servant Jesus, whom you anointed. And now, Lord, look at their threats"—namely, those of the Jews—"and grant to your servants to speak your word with boldness."[79] So those who were, so to speak, restrained by fear as by some *reins* and forced to keep silence, having been scourged and abused, only speaking to some people *furtively*, and resembling, as it were, *a poor man eating, will relax their reins*, as if you were to say, they will definitely develop such forthrightness as is most appealing and fitting for them. Far from caring about the synagogue of the Jews, they will scorn their threats, and, as it were, by snapping the *rein* imposed on them, like dashing and bucking horses they will now whinny, deterred by no one, and fill the earth under heaven with their own cry. The divinely inspired Isaiah also said something like that to those ministering the Gospel message: "Get you up to a high mountain, O Zion, herald of good tidings; lift up your voice with strength, O Jerusalem, herald of good tidings; lift it up, have no fear. Lo, our God, lo, the Lord comes with might and his arm with lordship."[80]

So those who formerly, he is saying, were *like a poor man eating furtively*, that is, lacking forthrightness, only secretly nourished by the faith of the believers, (159) *will relax their reins* in satisfaction, in the sense already explained. The fact that the faith of those saved is a kind of nourishment both for God and the saints Christ himself confirms in the words about the conver-

79. Acts 5.40 and 4.27, 29.
80. Is 40.9–10.

sion of the Samaritans: "I have food to eat of which you are unaware"; and again, "My food is to do the will of the one who sent me, and to complete his work."[81]

You rode your horses into the sea, churning up many waters (v.15). The verse continues to maintain the tenor of the comparison; after mentioning *reins* he used the word *horses* in reference to the holy apostles, on whom Christ himself was also riding, mounted, as it were, on their mind and heart. So he endeavors to convey the fact that they were due to guide towards faith not only the people of Israel but also the vast and immeasurable multitude of the other nations. On the one hand, in fact, he compares the world to a *sea*, in keeping with the statement of praise in the Psalms, "This sea is great and wide; creeping things innumerable are there."[82] On the other hand, he compares to *many waters* the hordes of the nations throughout the earth, and to horses, as I said, the holy apostles, who traversed the whole earth under heaven and helpfully *churned up* the idolaters who were snorting, as it were, and resting in error; they frightened them by calling them to fear because they were heading for punishment and destined to undergo retribution by fire (160) unless they opted to repent and acknowledge the one who is by nature and in truth God. The divinely inspired Paul, for example, addressing the Athenians, and then claiming they were more religious than all other people, caused them considerable alarm by proceeding, "While God has overlooked the times of ignorance, therefore, he now gives the command to people for everyone everywhere to repent, because he has fixed a day on which he is due to judge the whole world in righteousness by a man whom he has appointed, providing assurance to everyone by raising him from the dead."[83] So the *water churned up* is the multitude throughout the world, which is frequently compared to waters, and rightly so, especially since human life resembles a sea, because there is a great turmoil of affairs in it, confusion and change this way and that in every respect. Now, the *water was churned up* as far as Israel was concerned: while some were a single nation, others defied counting.

81. Jn 4.32, 34. 82. Ps 104.25.
83. Acts 17.22, 30–31.

I kept watch, and my heart was struck with the sound of a prayer of my lips; trembling penetrated my bones, and my being was undermined. I shall rest on the day of my calamity from going up to a people of my sojourn (v.16). It is customary with the holy prophets to use the term *watch* or "listening" to refer to the observation of heart and mind that they would make when the Holy Spirit is conveying to them the knowledge of the future. Accordingly, Habakkuk himself says, (161) "I shall stand at my watchpost, climb upon a rock, and keep watch to see what he will say to me and what response I should make to my correction." Another one likewise: "I heard a report from the Lord, and he dispatched a confinement to the nations"; and furthermore the divinely inspired David also says, "I shall listen to what the Lord God will say in me."[84] It is something like this that the prophet now suggests by saying, *I kept watch, and my heart was struck*—meaning, I have observed the force of the words—and then I was deeply *struck with the sound of a prayer of my lips.* In other words, he made supplication to God in song, and singing was the form his prophecy took;[85] but his purpose and intention were not directed at rhythmical utterance—rather, his anguish gave expression in grief, and he was very afraid as the Spirit put into words in him the fate of the people of Israel in times to come. Now, what particularly alarmed him and convinced him to be afraid, in all probability, was this alone: that somehow he would be left in the troubles, would contemplate the people's collapse, and would witness death falling upon the heads of the lawless and their being *cut down in a stupor* and shaken in it, in the sense already explained.

Next, on learning that the vision still had a time to go,[86] and what was promised would be long delayed, he is, as it were, uplifted from unmitigated depression and now says, *I shall rest on the day of my calamity from going up to a people of my sojourn.* In other words, I shall not be caught up in such troubles, nor would I survive in this life when that time arrives when (162) such troubles will definitely befall the people of Israel; I shall depart from here, and transfer to a *people* that is *sojourning* in this life, as of course I myself also am, since all the saints are sojourners and pilgrims

84. 2.1; Ob 1; Ps 85.8.   85. See n. 1, above.
86. 2.3.

in this world. Consequently, they say, "We have not here a lasting city, but seek the one that is to come," and somewhere blessed David also sings to the God of all, "Grant me relief, because I am a sojourner on earth and a pilgrim, like all my ancestors."[87] Accordingly, the saints' intentions were commendable, unwilling as they were to witness anything that would offend God; they preferred departure from this world to life itself if what contributed to the glory of God could not be preserved. The divinely inspired Paul, for instance, said that it would be better to be dissolved and be with Christ for those who had achieved such a desire as to consider life in the body a *sojourn*.[88]

Because a fig tree will not bear, and there will be no fruit on the vines; produce of an olive will be deceptive, and the fields will not yield food. Sheep lacked feed, and there will be no oxen in the stalls from their healing (v.17). There is a similarity here: when someone asks and wants to learn why it is important to depart this life, or rather *go up to a people of his sojourn*, he clouds in deep obscurity the fruitlessness of the synagogue of the Jews, (163) and, as it were, seems to lament the barrenness befalling it—something he conveys to us in many figures, saying it will be like a *fig tree* which would produce no *fruit*. Similarly the Savior himself gave it this name, saying in figurative terms, "A man had a fig tree planted in his vineyard," and since it bore no fruit, he then said it should be cut down lest it waste the soil. And somewhere on the outskirts of Jerusalem he also declared the fig tree cursed; on finding no fruit on it he said, "May no fruit ever come from you again."[89]

He compares it also to a *vine* bare of grapes; likewise, as the prophet Isaiah says, "The vineyard of the Lord of hosts is the person of Judah, something newly planted, beloved," but "though he cultivated it, built a wall, erected a tower in it, hewed out a wine vat, and waited for it to produce grapes, it brought forth thorns." Consequently, as David says, "a boar from the forest ravaged it, and a solitary animal fed off it"; he destroyed "its wall, and all who pass along the way have plucked its fruit."[90]

As well, *produce of an olive will be deceptive*, that is again, of the

87. Heb 13.14; Ps 39.13, 12.   88. Phil 1.23.
89. Lk 13.6–7; Mt 21.19.   90. Is 5.7, 2; Ps 80.13, 12.

synagogue of the Jews. The prophet Jeremiah, in fact, also points to it in saying, "The Lord called you a fair olive tree, shady in appearance at the sound of its circumcision; fire was enkindled against it; great was the distress befalling you; its branches were rendered useless; and the Lord of hosts who (164) planted you has had evil things to say against you."[91] Since, however, as the prophet says, its *produce will be deceptive* in that, though guided by Law and Prophets towards Christ, they did not embrace the faith; consequently it was cut down, its branches felled, and then grafted on were those from the wild olive—namely, those from the nations, who became "sharers in the rich root of the cultivated olive."[92]

He next says that *the fields will not yield food*, again comparing Israel, in my view, to spoiled crops from which the farmer could not harvest enough for *food*—a clear demonstration of utter fruitlessness. He makes clear the fact that by suffering the famine of divine teachings they were destined to succumb to the worst of all troubles, saying, *Sheep lacked feed*—that is, they had nothing to eat—*and there are no oxen in the stalls*. The suggestion from this is the complete failure of the sacred and chosen class among them, namely, those of the tribe of Levi, who like oxen grind the grain on the spiritual threshing floor and remove the layers of obscurity from the message conveyed through the all-wise Moses, providing, as it were, the kernel of the ear to the others for understanding and for a kind of spiritual *feed*. These men were in *stalls*, feeding off the offerings from the people, tithes, first-fruits, thanksgiving offerings; hence, though *sheep lacked feed*, no longer *are there oxen in the stalls*, that is, the leaders and teachers of the people. Accordingly, (165) the divinely inspired Paul also directs at the heads of the teachers the requirement, "You must not muzzle an ox while it is treading out the grain," clearly interpreting for us what is in the Law.[93]

The oxen are deprived, he says, of *their healing*. While this is unclear, it suggests the following, in my view: since they ill-

---

91. Jer 11.16–17, where the LXX has confused a rare Heb. term (probably meaning "din") with the word for "circumcision."

92. Rom 11.17.

93. 1 Cor 9.9; Dt 25.4.

advisedly showed no interest in being healed by Christ, despite his strengthening the weak and justifying the impious, consequently they went *lacking;* that is, they were completely weak and dissolved into nothingness. Offending God, therefore, is surely a fearful thing, and will be productive of utter fruitlessness; we shall also be deprived of spiritual nourishment, and suffer extreme trouble as a result of it.

I shall rejoice in the Lord, be glad in God my Savior. The Lord my God is my strength, and he will set my feet towards the end. He makes me mount the heights for me to be victorious in his song (vv.18–19). In this case, either the actual person of the prophet is clearly introduced in making this statement, or you could claim that the words come from those justified by faith, who find contentment in Christ, are glad in him, acknowledge him as the source of the strength abiding in them, and claim to be capable of everything through him, as of course the divinely inspired Paul also says, "I can do all things through Christ, who strengthens me." Blessed David also sings somewhere, (166) "You are the boast of their strength."[94] From him alone comes their expectation of being generously enriched with constancy in reverence; the phrase *He will set my feet towards the end* suggests to us nothing else than that. The Hebrew text, at any rate, put "security" for *towards the end;*[95] what else would be suggested to us by "feet set towards security" than constancy in reverence, as I said, perseverance in virtue, and firmness in faith and love for Christ? The fact that the life of those justified by Christ is not earthly and abject, but is elevated and superior to every worldly and fleshly affair, he declares by saying, *He makes me mount the heights,* the ornaments of the evangelical lifestyle being *the heights* in God's eyes.

Now, the fact that we shall prevail over the adversaries and prove superior to the foes by singing his praises he affirms in the words, *for me to be victorious in his song.*[96] (167)

94. Phil 4.13; Ps 89.17.
95. This not a variant known to our Heb., Jerome, or the Antiochenes, who all put "like the feet of a deer."
96. Jerome and Theodore do not help Cyril see in this clause rather a rubric for the benefit of the choirmaster.

INDICES

INDEX OF PROPER NAMES,
VOLUMES ONE AND TWO

INDEX OF HOLY SCRIPTURE

This index combines the Scripture
references in volumes 1 and 2.